Huck

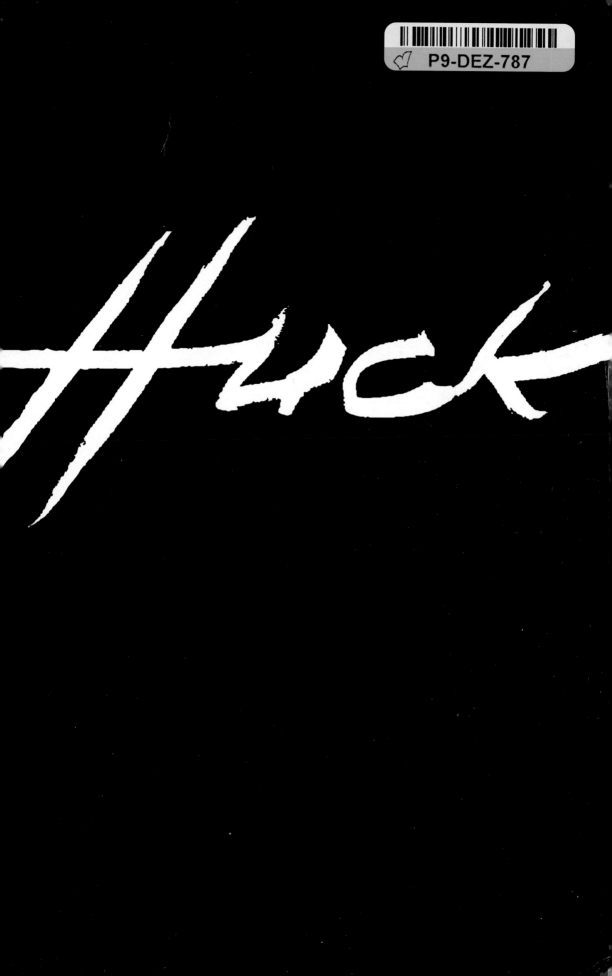

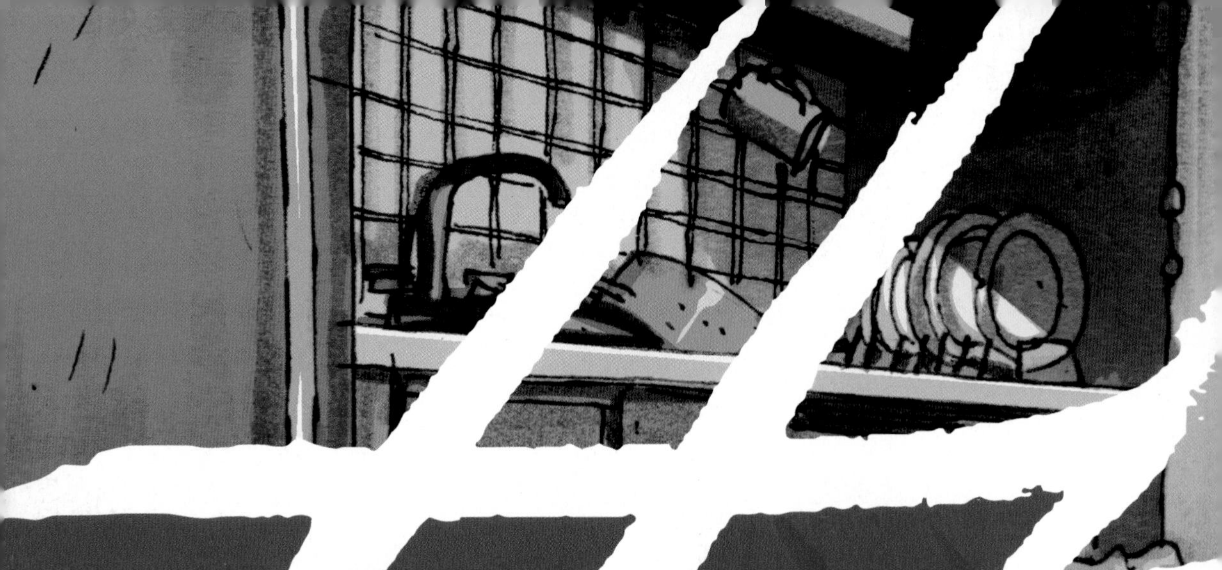

Mark Millar
writer

Rafael Albuquerque
artist

Dave McCaig
colorist

Nate Piekos of Blambot®
lettering & design

Nicole Boose
editor

Rachael Fulton
associate editor

Huck

created by
MARK MILLAR and
RAFAEL ALBUQUERQUE

IMAGE COMICS, INC.

Robert Kirkman – Chief Operating Officer
Erik Larsen – Chief Financial Officer
Todd McFarlane – President
Marc Silvestri – Chief Executive Officer
Jim Valentino – Vice-President
Eric Stephenson – Publisher
Corey Murphy – Director of Sales
Jeff Boison – Director of Publishing Planning
and Book Trade Sales
Jeremy Sullivan – Director of Digital Sales
Kat Salazar – Director of PR & Marketing
Emily Miller – Director of Operations
Branwyn Bigglestone – Senior Accounts Manager
Sarah Mello – Accounts Manager
Drew Gill – Art Director

IMAGECOMICS.COM

Jonathan Chan – Production Manager
Meredith Wallace – Print Manager
Briah Skelly – Publicist
Sasha Head – Sales & Marketing Production Designer
Randy Okamura – Digital Production Designer
David Brothers – Branding Manager
Addison Duke – Production Artist
Vincent Kukua – Production Artist
Tricia Ramos – Production Artist
Jeff Stang – Direct Market Sales Representative
Emilio Bautista – Digital Sales Associate
Leanna Caunter – Accounting Assistant
Chloe Ramos-Peterson – Administrative Assistant

HUCK Book 1: All-American, July 2016. First Printing. Published by Image Comics Inc. Office of publication: 2001 Center St, Sixth Fl, Berkeley, CA 94704. Copyright © 2016 Millarworld Limited and Rafael Albuquerque. All rights reserved. Originally published in single magazine form as Huck #1-6. "Huck," the Huck logo, and all characters and institutions herein and the likenesses and/or logos thereof are trademarks of Millarworld Limited and Rafael Albuquerque, unless expressly indicated. "Image" and the Image Comics logos are registered trademarks of Image Comics, Inc. No part of this publication may be reproduced or transmitted in any form or by any means (except for short excerpts for journalistic or review purposes) without the express written permission of Millarworld Limited, Rafael Albuquerque, or Image Comics, Inc. All names, characters, events, religions, institutions, and locales herein are entirely fictional. Any resemblance to actual persons (living or dead), events, religions, institutions, or locales, without satiric intent, is coincidental. Printed in the USA. For information regarding the CPSIA on this printed material call: 203-595-3636 and provide reference # RICH – 690204. Representation: Law Offices of Harris M. Miller II, P.C. (rights.inquiries@gmail.com)

STANDARD COVER, ISBN: 978-1-63215-729-4
BOOKS-A-MILLION VARIANT COVER, ISBN: 978-1-63215-918-2
FORBIDDEN PLANET VARIANT COVER, ISBN: 978-1-5343-0000-2
NEWBURY COMICS VARIANT COVER, ISBN: 978-1-63215-968-7

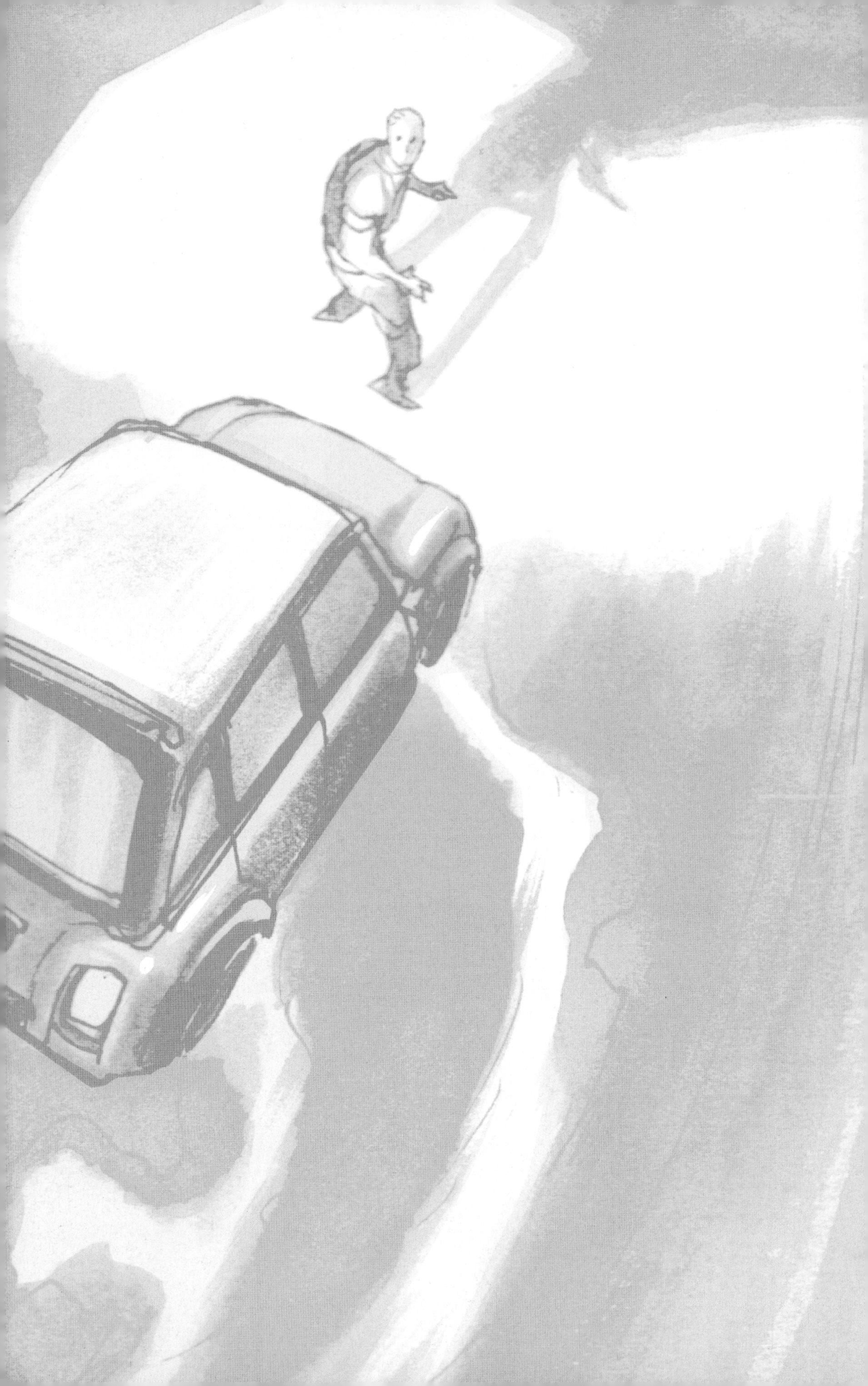

ONE

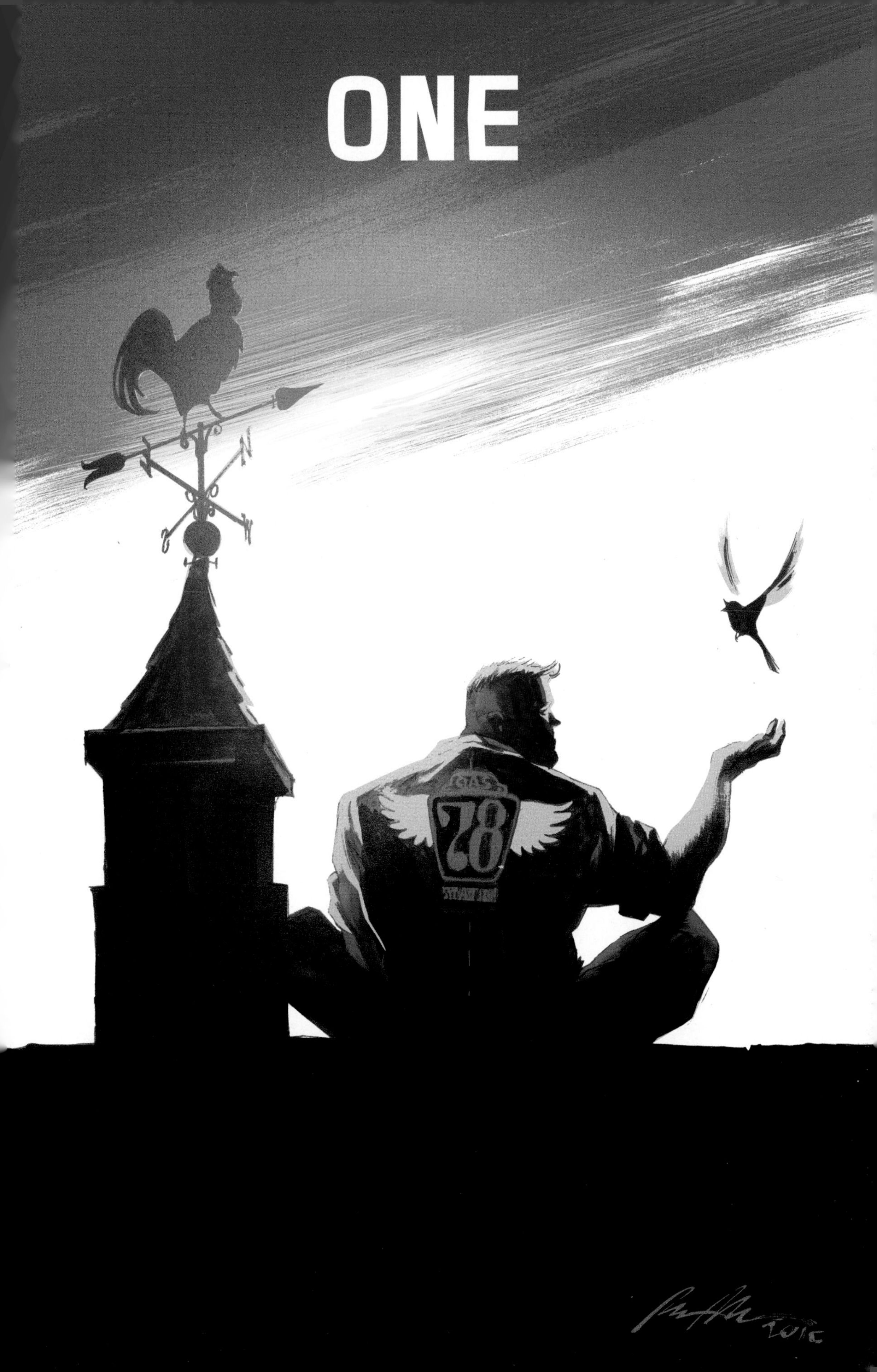
28

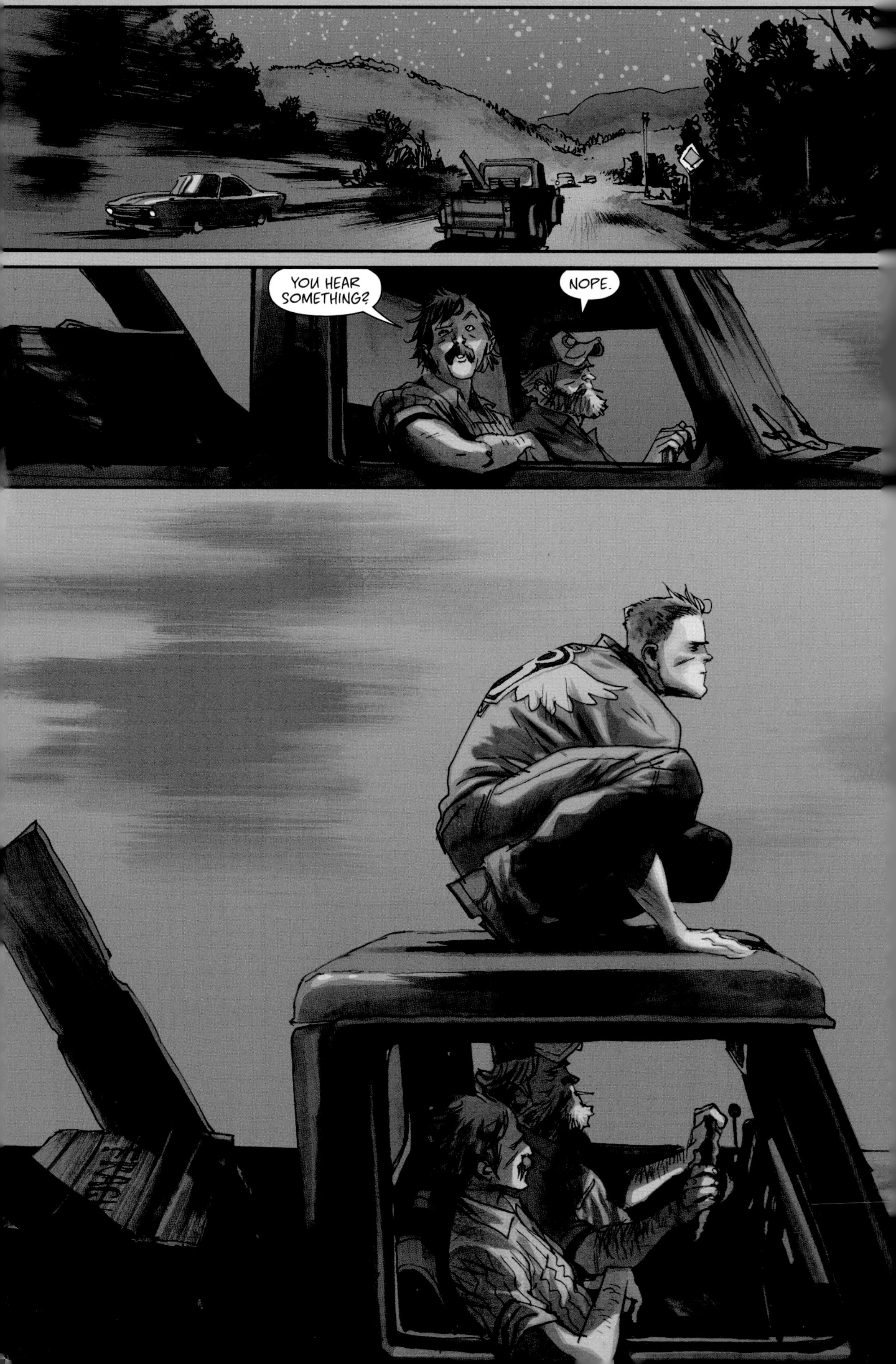
YOU HEAR SOMETHING?
NOPE.

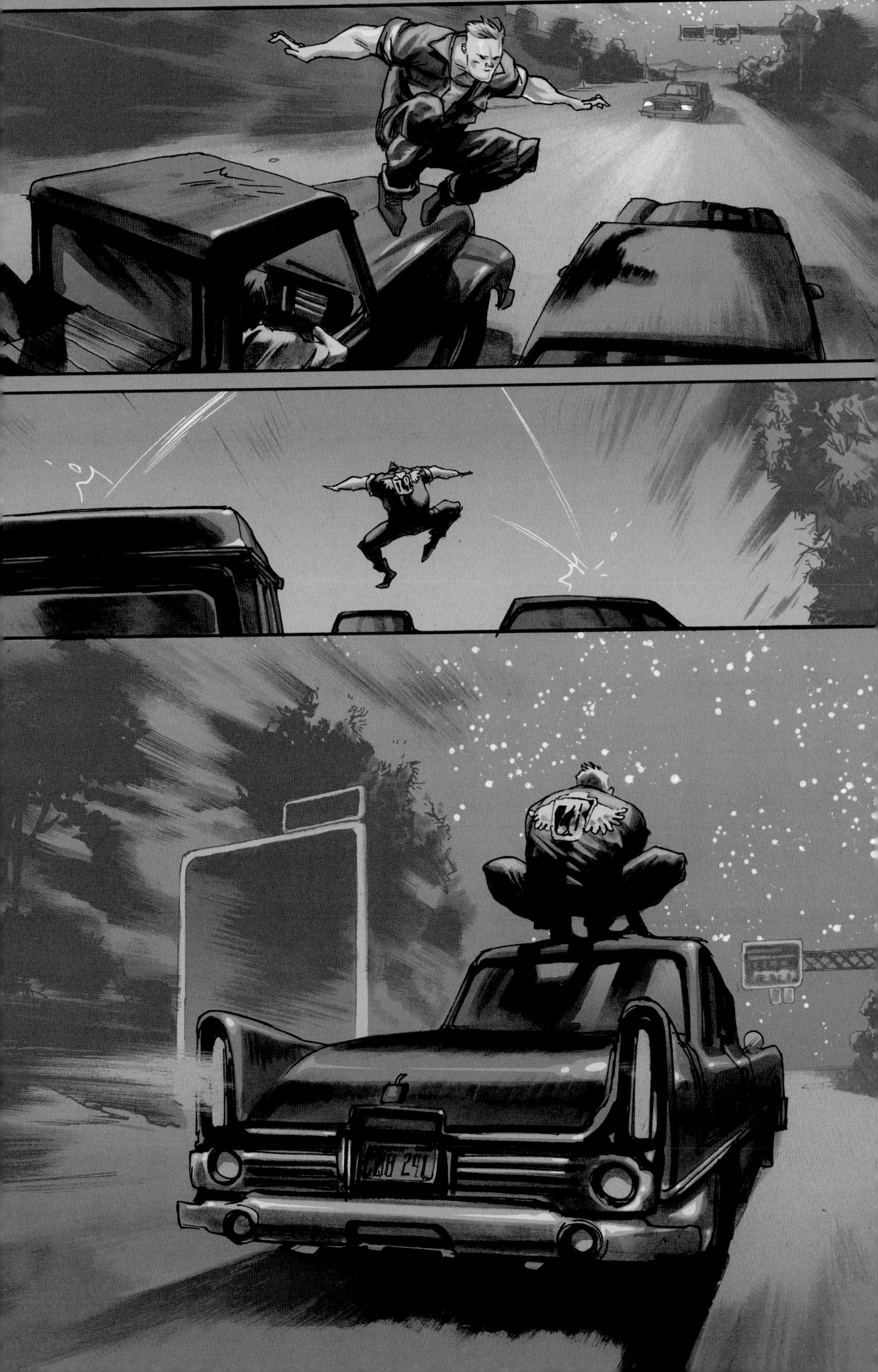

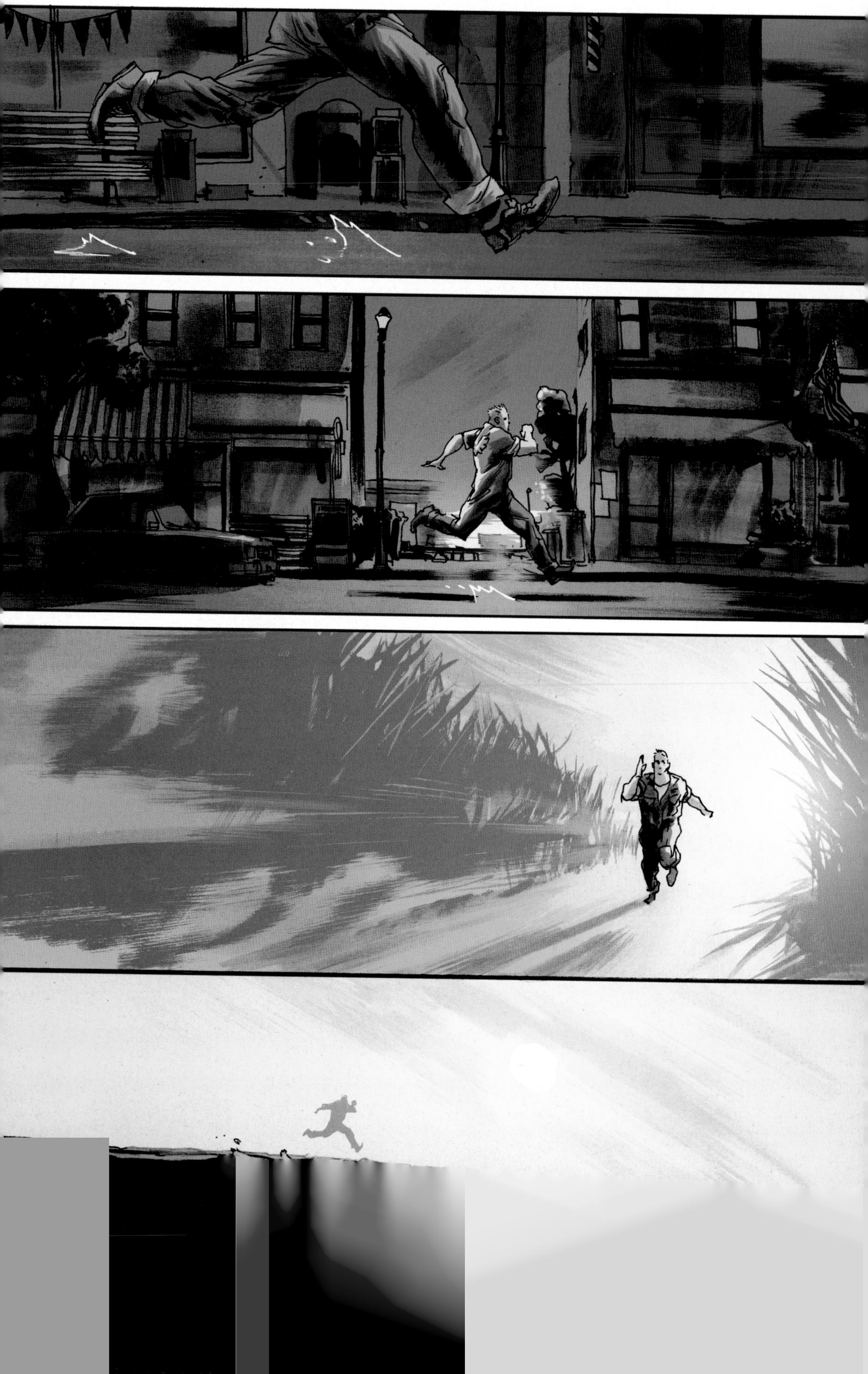

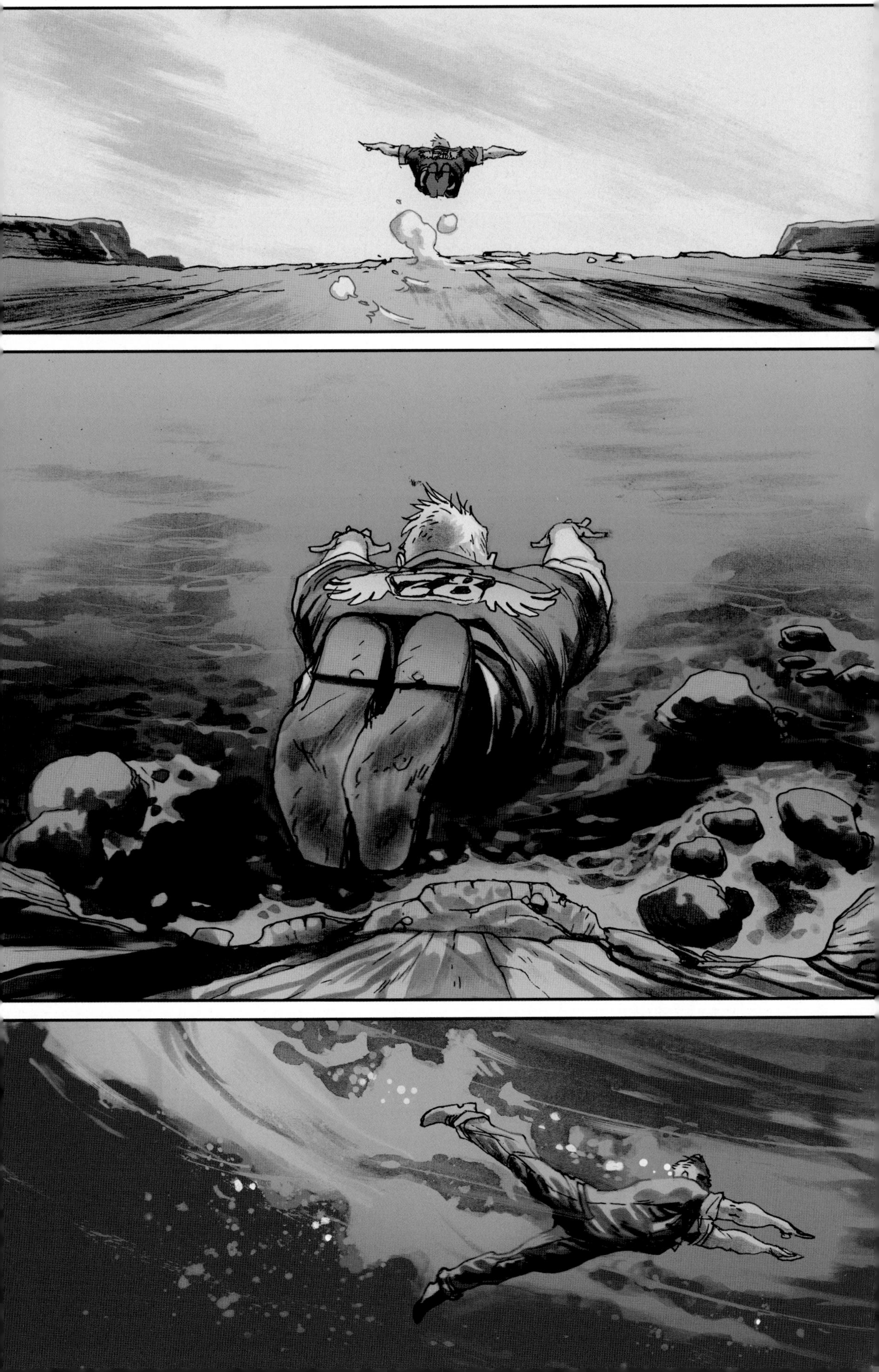

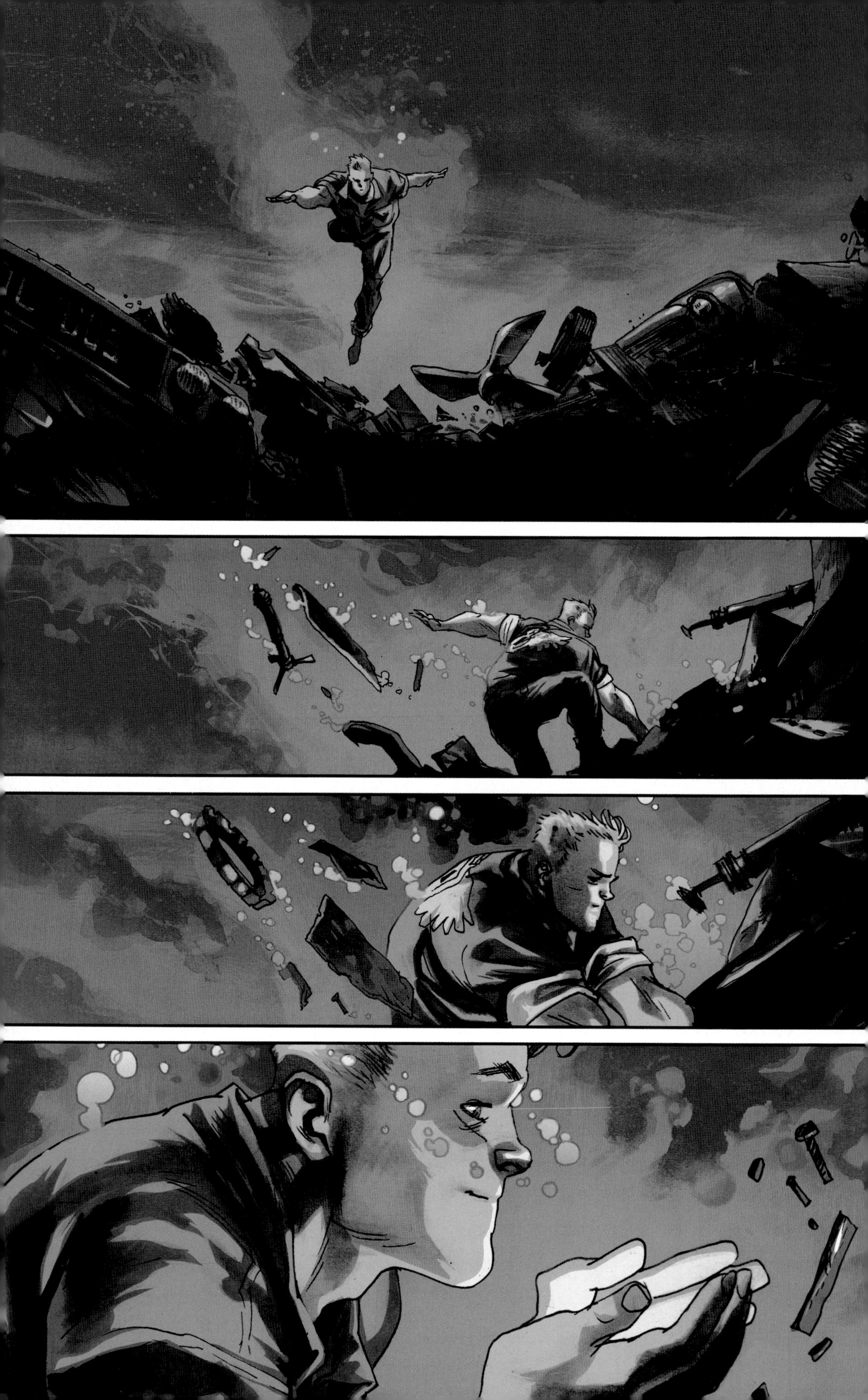

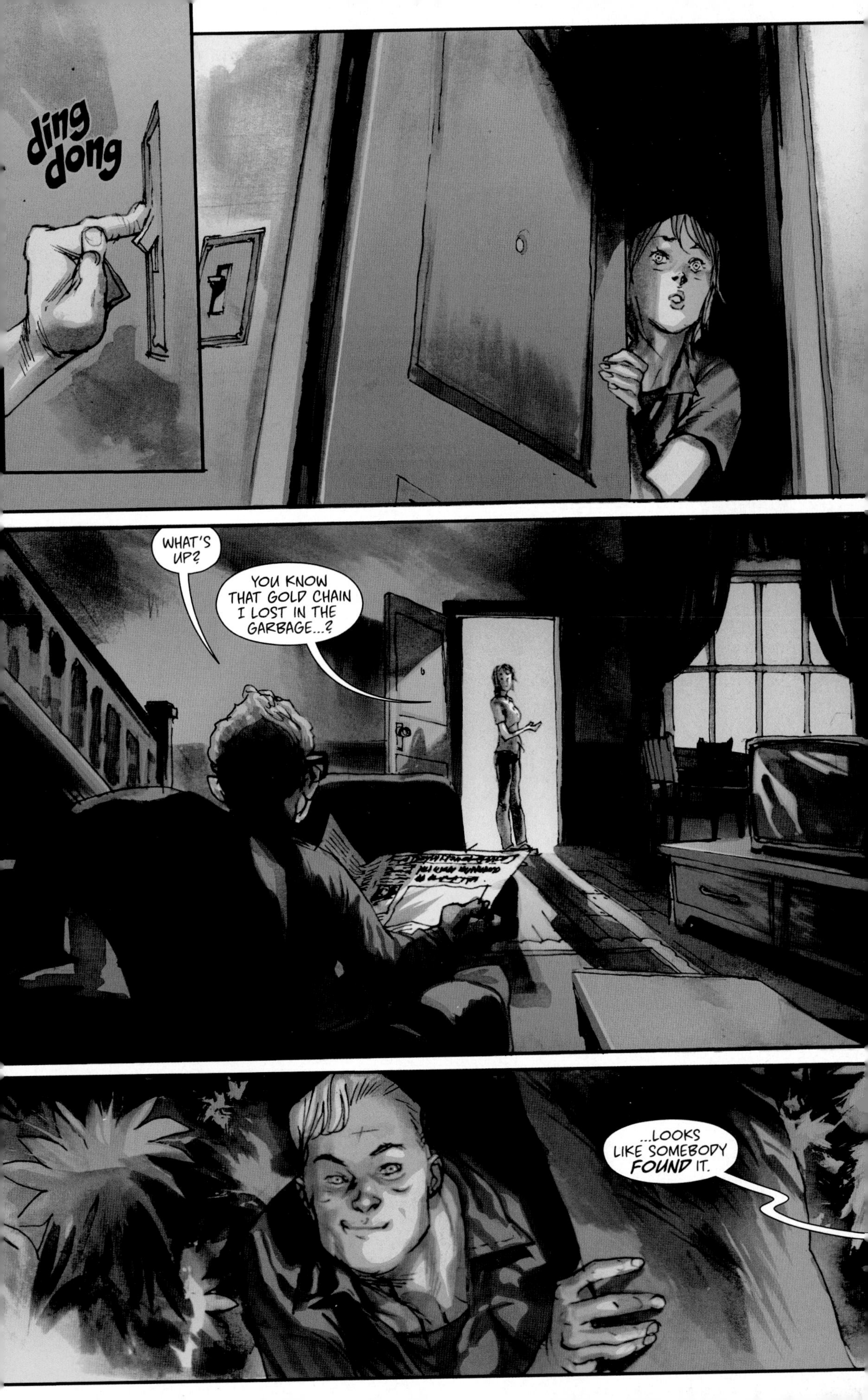
ding dong
WHAT'S UP?
YOU KNOW THAT GOLD CHAIN I LOST IN THE GARBAGE...?
...LOOKS LIKE SOMEBODY FOUND IT.

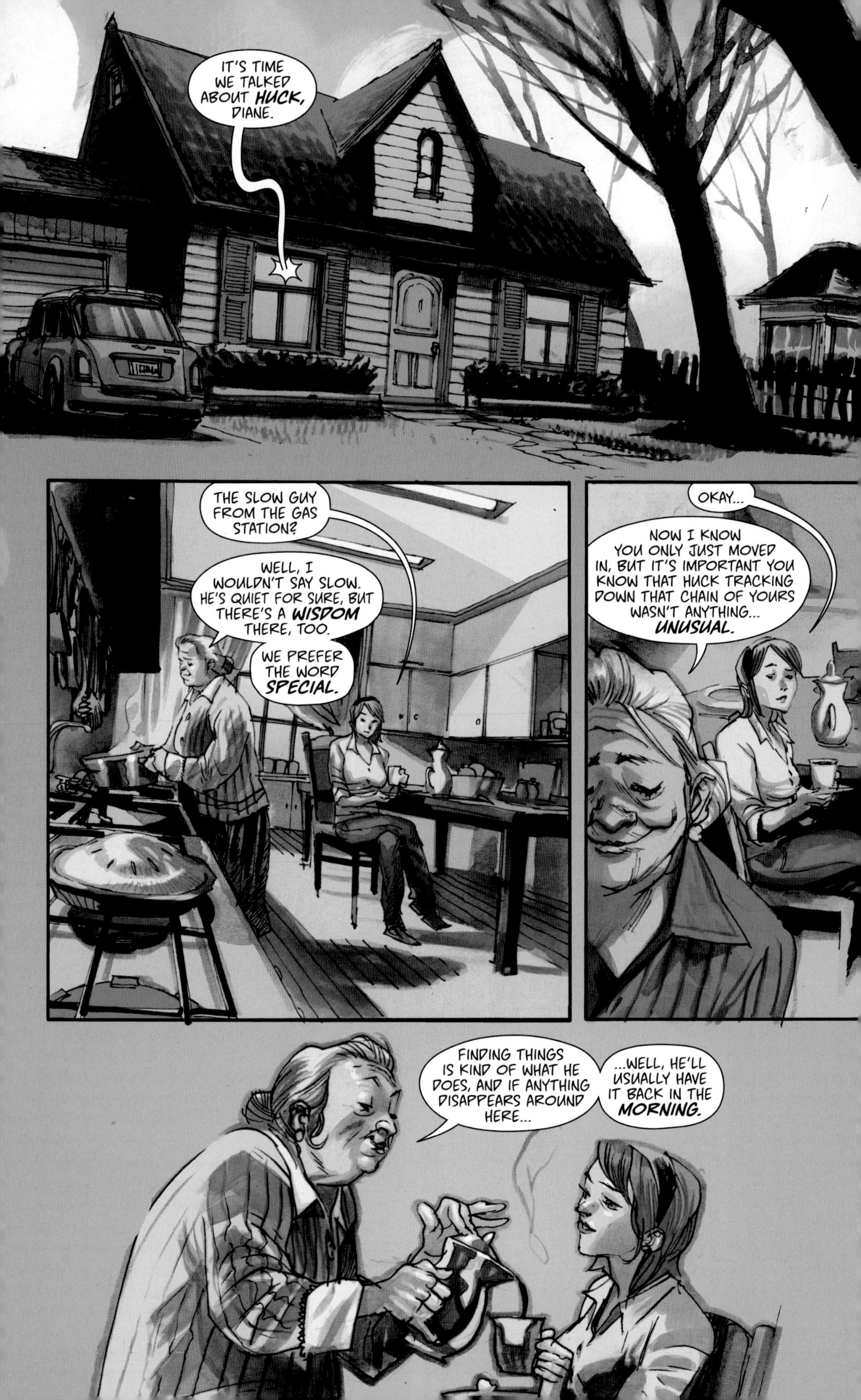
IT'S TIME WE TALKED ABOUT HUCK, DIANE.
THE SLOW GUY FROM THE GAS STATION?
WELL, I WOULDN'T SAY SLOW. HE'S QUIET FOR SURE, BUT THERE'S A WISDOM THERE, TOO.
WE PREFER THE WORD SPECIAL.
OKAY...
NOW I KNOW YOU ONLY JUST MOVED IN, BUT IT'S IMPORTANT YOU KNOW THAT HUCK TRACKING DOWN THAT CHAIN OF YOURS WASN'T ANYTHING... UNUSUAL.
FINDING THINGS IS KIND OF WHAT HE DOES, AND IF ANYTHING DISAPPEARS AROUND HERE...
...WELL, HE'LL USUALLY HAVE IT BACK IN THE MORNING.

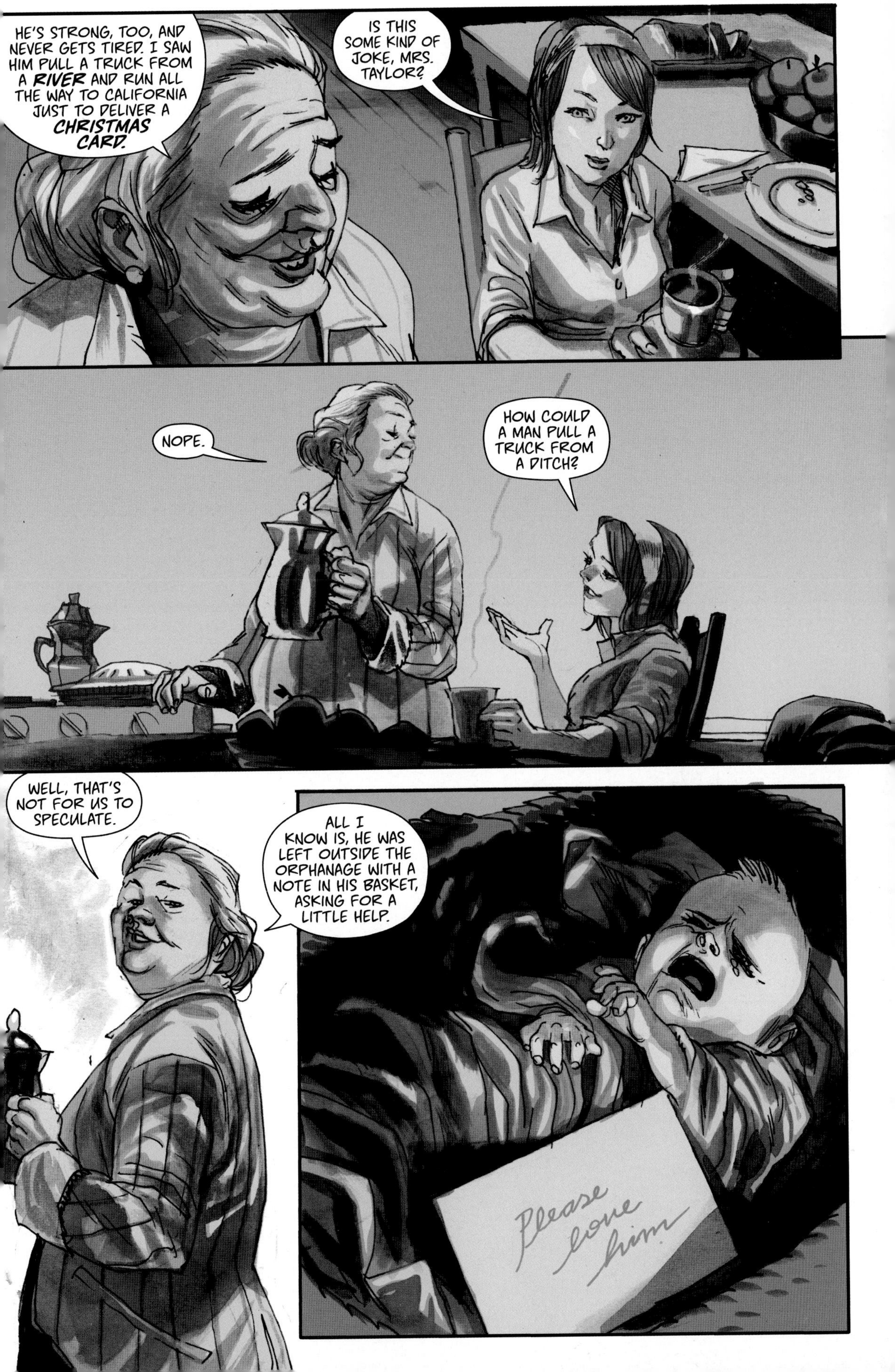
HE'S STRONG, TOO, AND NEVER GETS TIRED. I SAW HIM PULL A TRUCK FROM A RIVER AND RUN ALL THE WAY TO CALIFORNIA JUST TO DELIVER A CHRISTMAS CARD.
IS THIS SOME KIND OF JOKE, MRS. TAYLOR?
NOPE.
HOW COULD A MAN PULL A TRUCK FROM A DITCH?
WELL, THAT'S NOT FOR US TO SPECULATE.
ALL I KNOW IS, HE WAS LEFT OUTSIDE THE ORPHANAGE WITH A NOTE IN HIS BASKET, ASKING FOR A LITTLE HELP.
Please love him

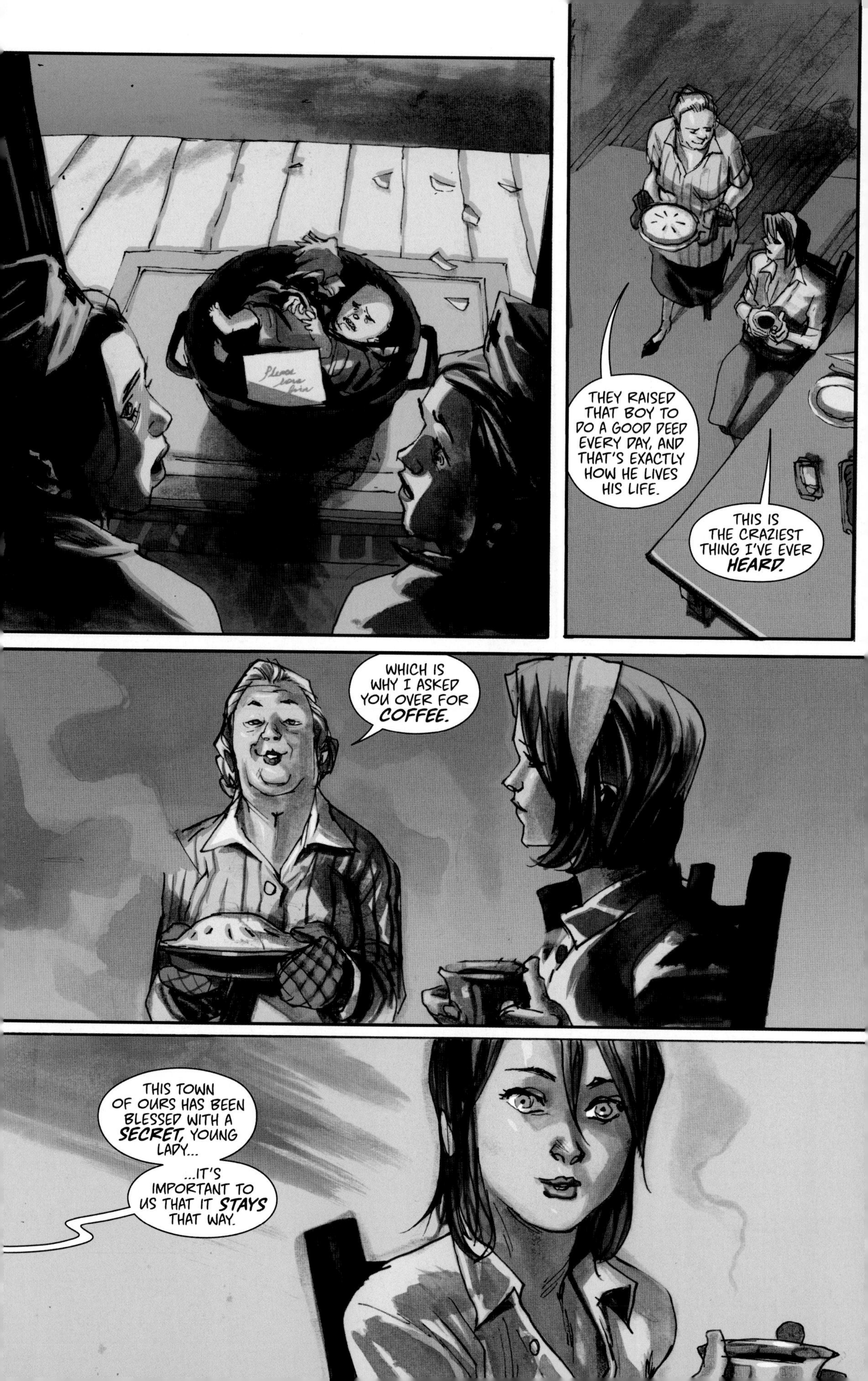
THEY RAISED THAT BOY TO DO A GOOD DEED EVERY DAY, AND THAT'S EXACTLY HOW HE LIVES HIS LIFE.
THIS IS THE CRAZIEST THING I'VE EVER HEARD.
WHICH IS WHY I ASKED YOU OVER FOR COFFEE.
THIS TOWN OF OURS HAS BEEN BLESSED WITH A SECRET, YOUNG LADY...
...IT'S IMPORTANT TO US THAT IT STAYS THAT WAY.

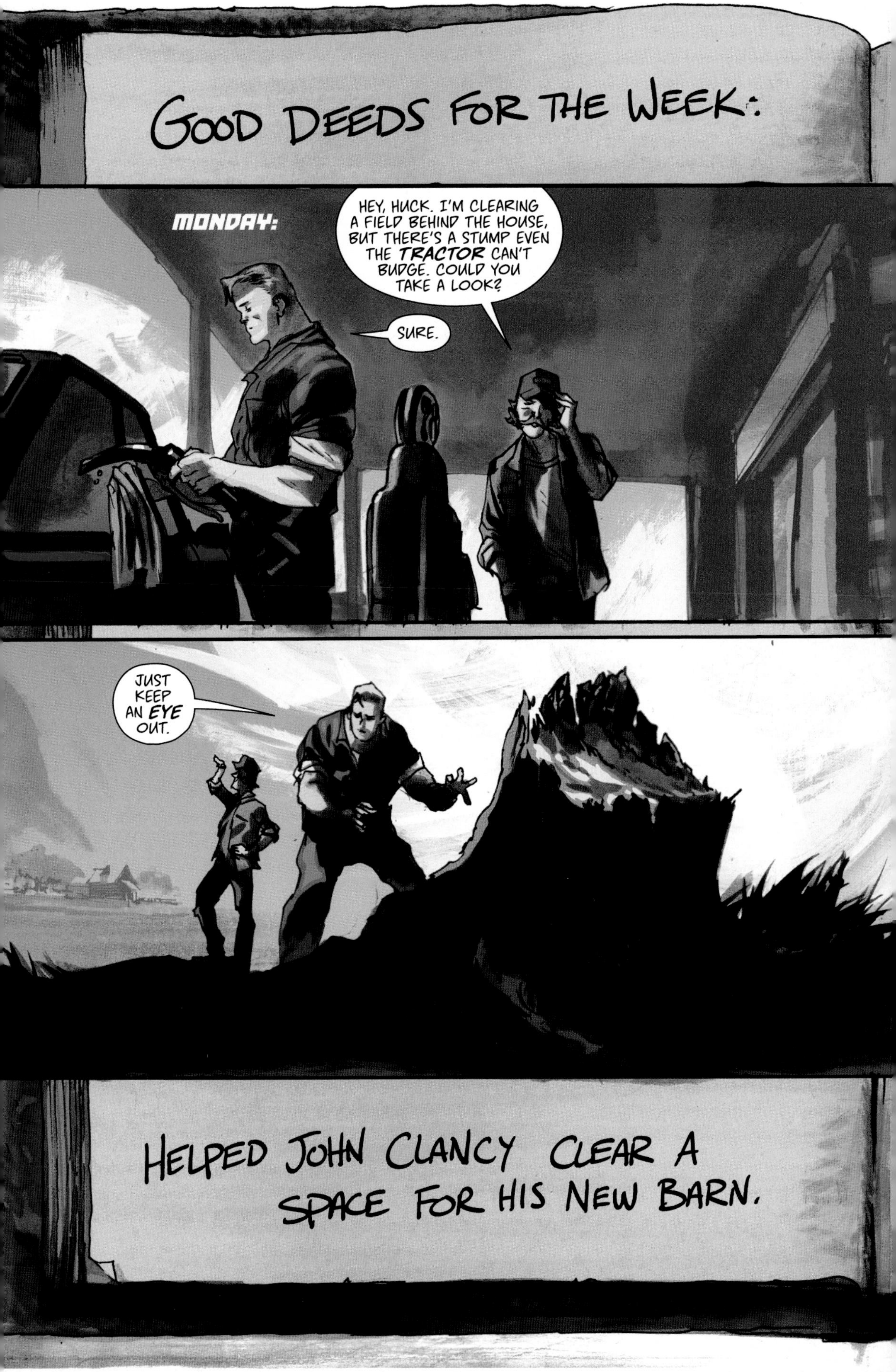
GOOD DEEDS FOR THE WEEK:
MONDAY:
HEY, HUCK. I'M CLEARING A FIELD BEHIND THE HOUSE, BUT THERE'S A STUMP EVEN THE TRACTOR CAN'T BUDGE. COULD YOU TAKE A LOOK?
SURE.
JUST KEEP AN EYE OUT.
HELPED JOHN CLANCY CLEAR A SPACE FOR HIS NEW BARN.

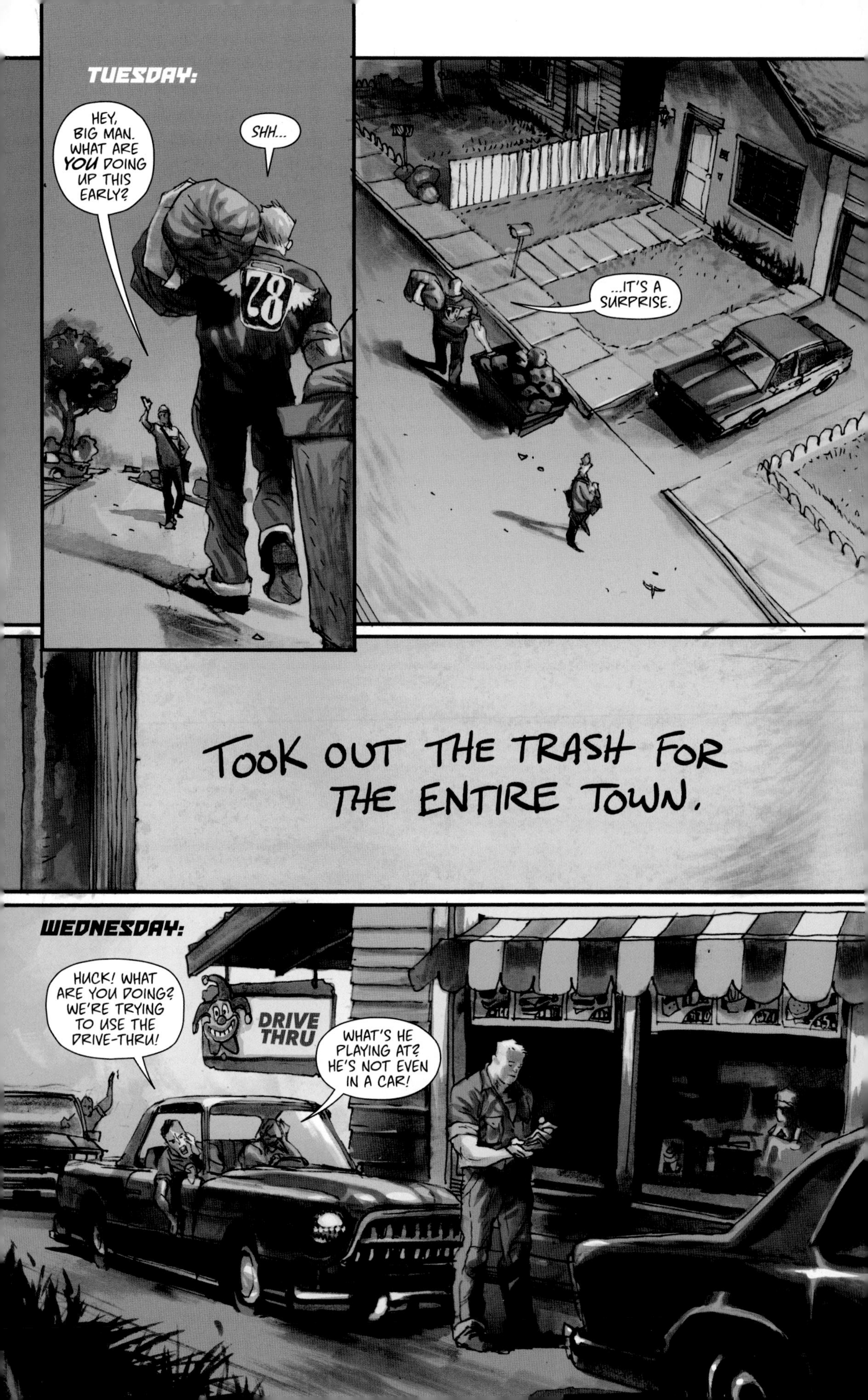
TUESDAY:
HEY, BIG MAN. WHAT ARE YOU DOING UP THIS EARLY?
SHH...
...IT'S A SURPRISE.
TOOK OUT THE TRASH FOR THE ENTIRE TOWN.
WEDNESDAY:
HUCK! WHAT ARE YOU DOING? WE'RE TRYING TO USE THE DRIVE-THRU!
DRIVE THRU
WHAT'S HE PLAYING AT? HE'S NOT EVEN IN A CAR!

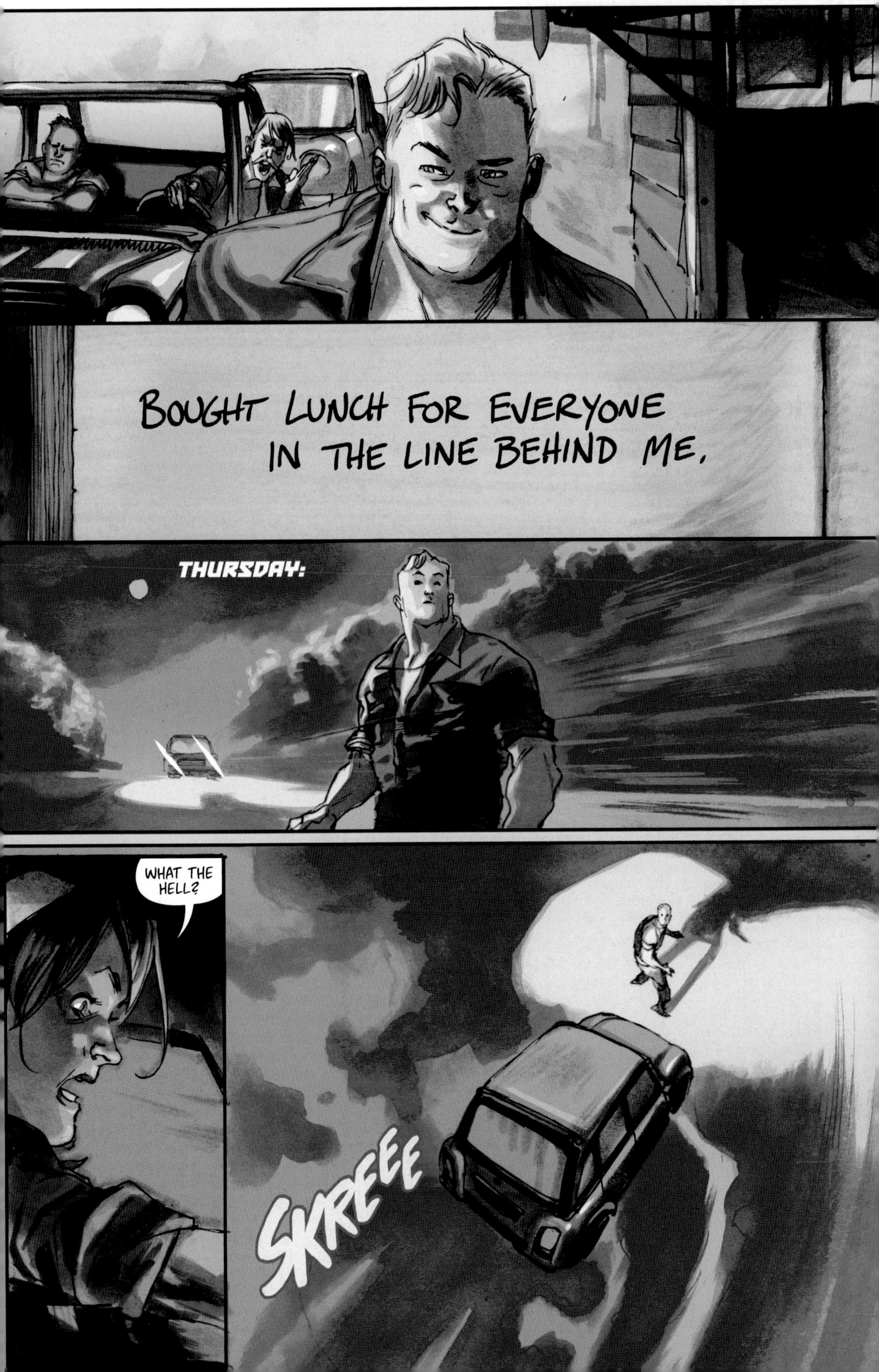
BOUGHT LUNCH FOR EVERYONE IN THE LINE BEHIND ME.
THURSDAY:
WHAT THE HELL?
SKREEE

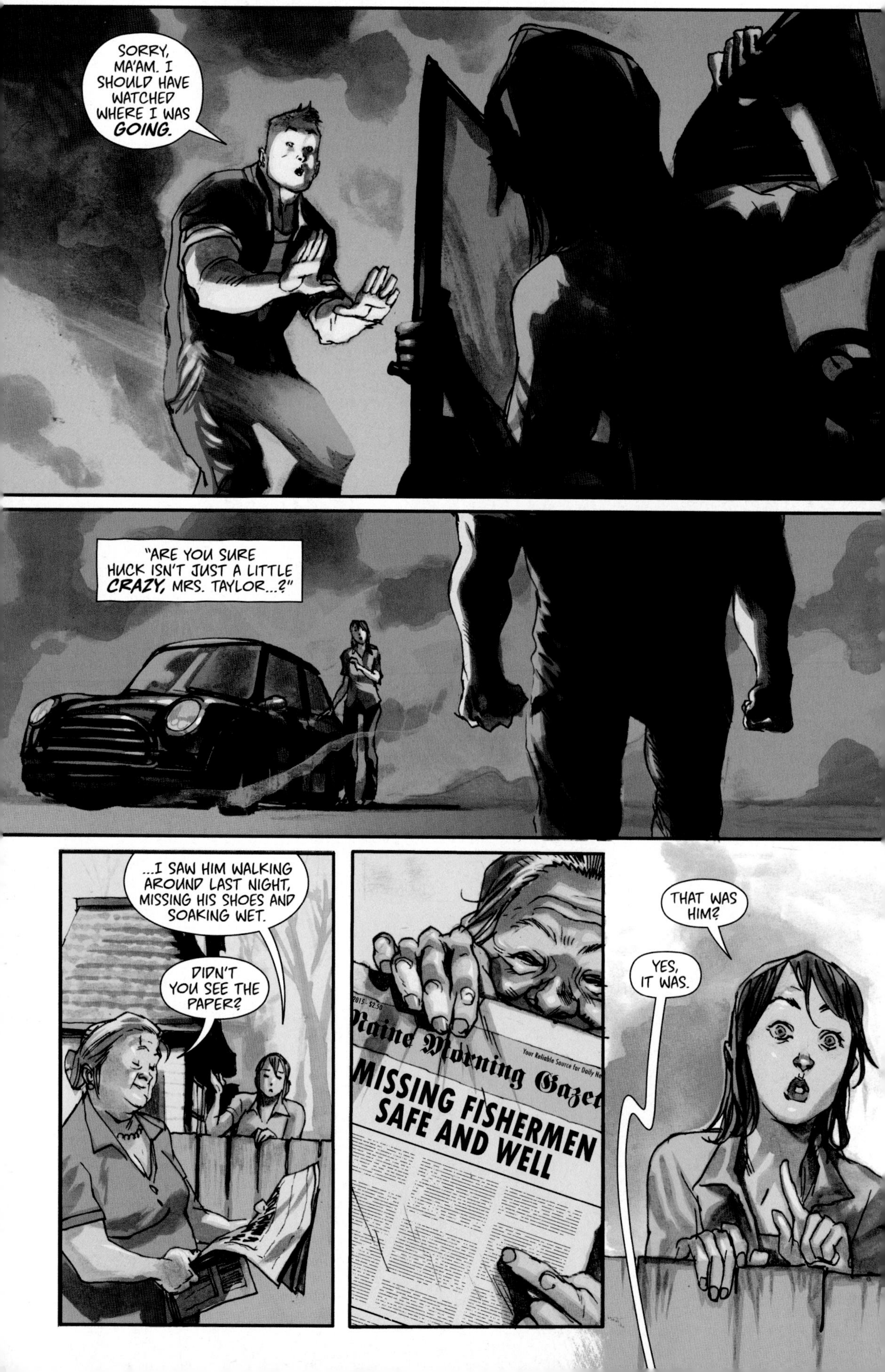
SORRY, MA'AM. I SHOULD HAVE WATCHED WHERE I WAS GOING.
"ARE YOU SURE HUCK ISN'T JUST A LITTLE CRAZY, MRS. TAYLOR...?"
...I SAW HIM WALKING AROUND LAST NIGHT, MISSING HIS SHOES AND SOAKING WET.
DIDN'T YOU SEE THE PAPER?
MISSING FISHERMEN SAFE AND WELL
THAT WAS HIM?
YES, IT WAS.

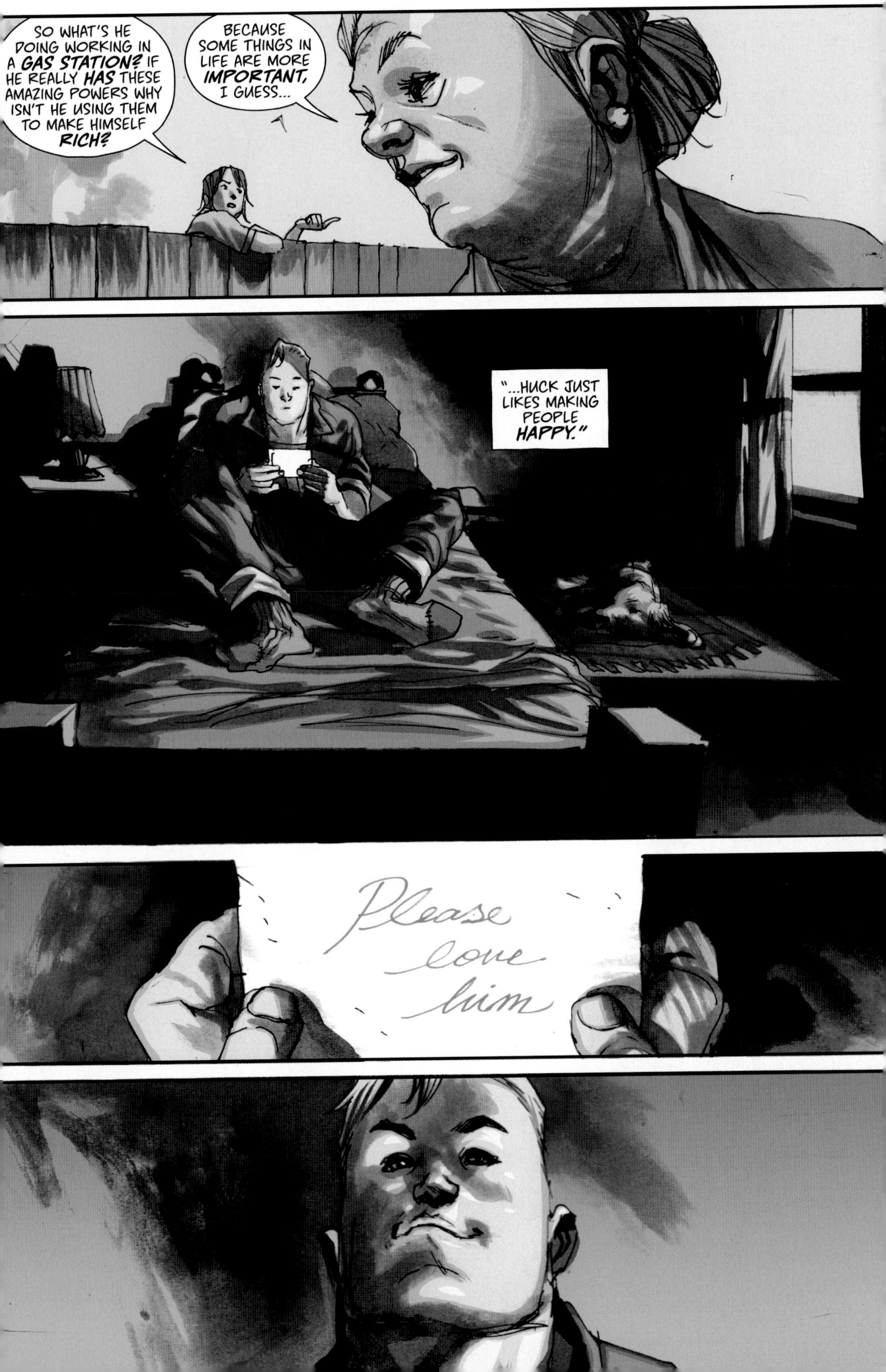
SO WHAT'S HE DOING WORKING IN A GAS STATION? IF HE REALLY HAS THESE AMAZING POWERS WHY ISN'T HE USING THEM TO MAKE HIMSELF RICH?
BECAUSE SOME THINGS IN LIFE ARE MORE IMPORTANT, I GUESS...
"...HUCK JUST LIKES MAKING PEOPLE HAPPY."
Please love him

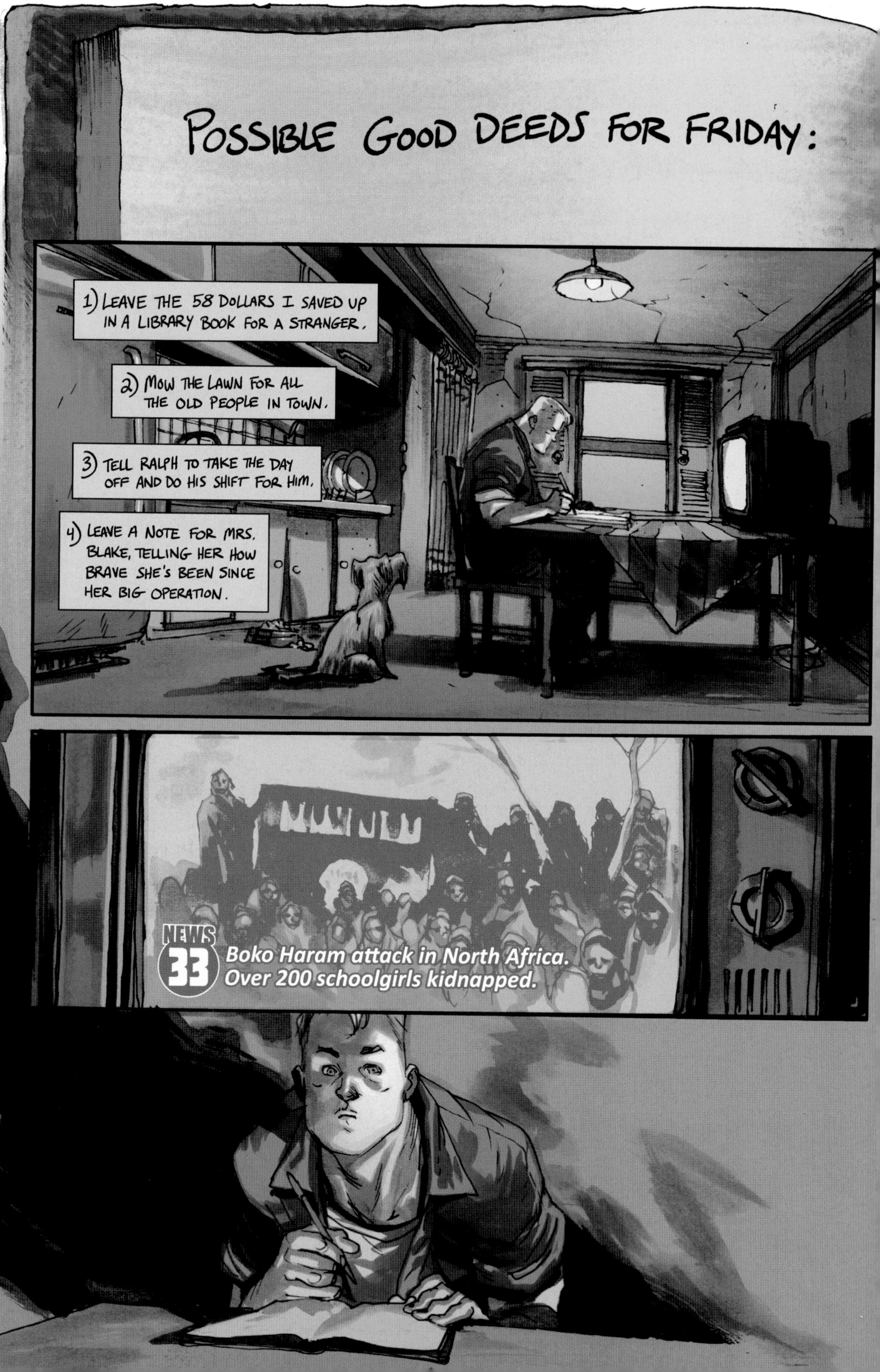
POSSIBLE GOOD DEEDS FOR FRIDAY:
1) LEAVE THE 58 DOLLARS I SAVED UP IN A LIBRARY BOOK FOR A STRANGER.
2) MOW THE LAWN FOR ALL THE OLD PEOPLE IN TOWN.
3) TELL RALPH TO TAKE THE DAY OFF AND DO HIS SHIFT FOR HIM.
4) LEAVE A NOTE FOR MRS. BLAKE, TELLING HER HOW BRAVE SHE'S BEEN SINCE HER BIG OPERATION.
NEWS 33
Boko Haram attack in North Africa.
Over 200 schoolgirls kidnapped.

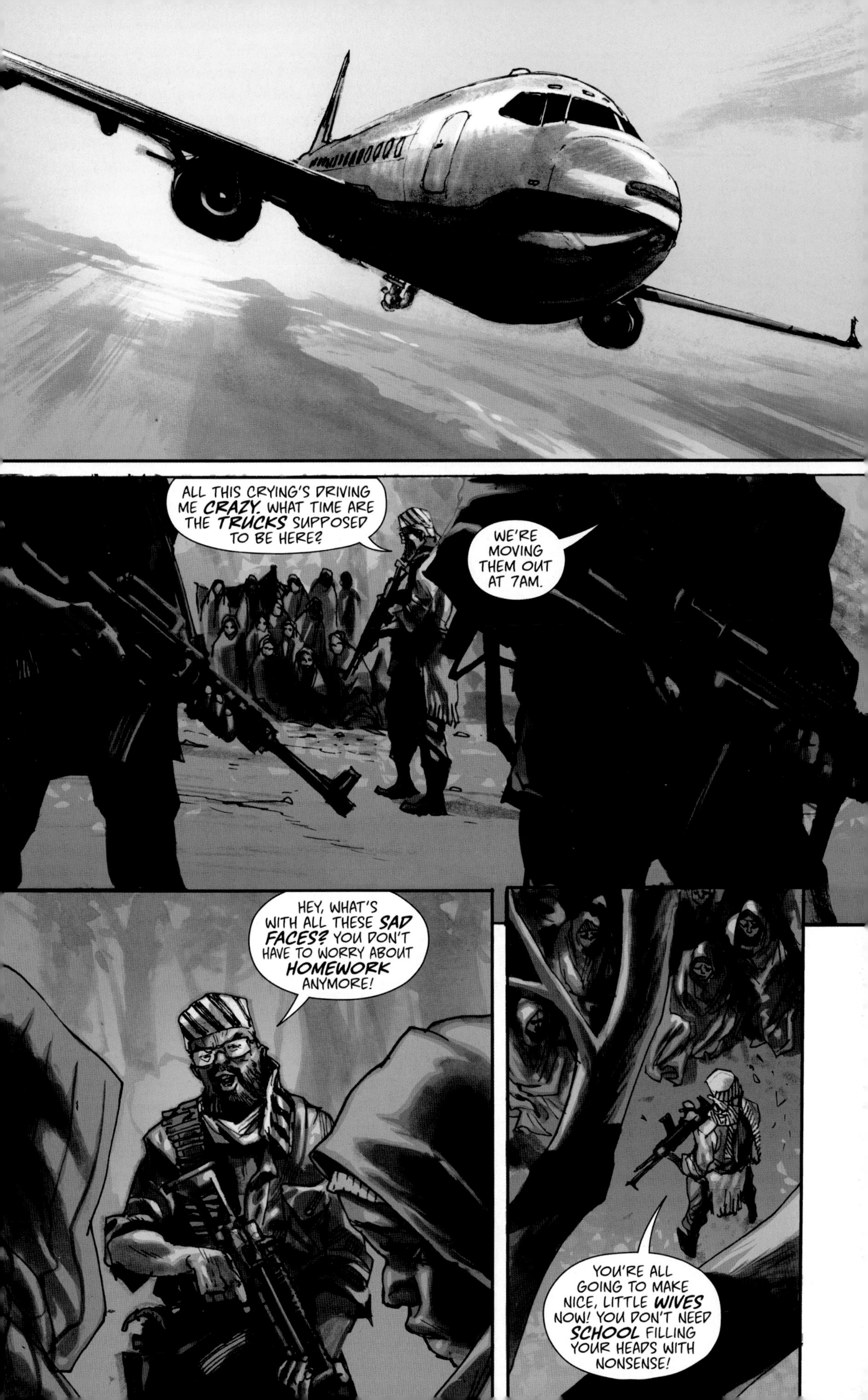
ALL THIS CRYING'S DRIVING ME CRAZY. WHAT TIME ARE THE TRUCKS SUPPOSED TO BE HERE?
WE'RE MOVING THEM OUT AT 7AM.
HEY, WHAT'S WITH ALL THESE SAD FACES? YOU DON'T HAVE TO WORRY ABOUT HOMEWORK ANYMORE!
YOU'RE ALL GOING TO MAKE NICE, LITTLE WIVES NOW! YOU DON'T NEED SCHOOL FILLING YOUR HEADS WITH NONSENSE!

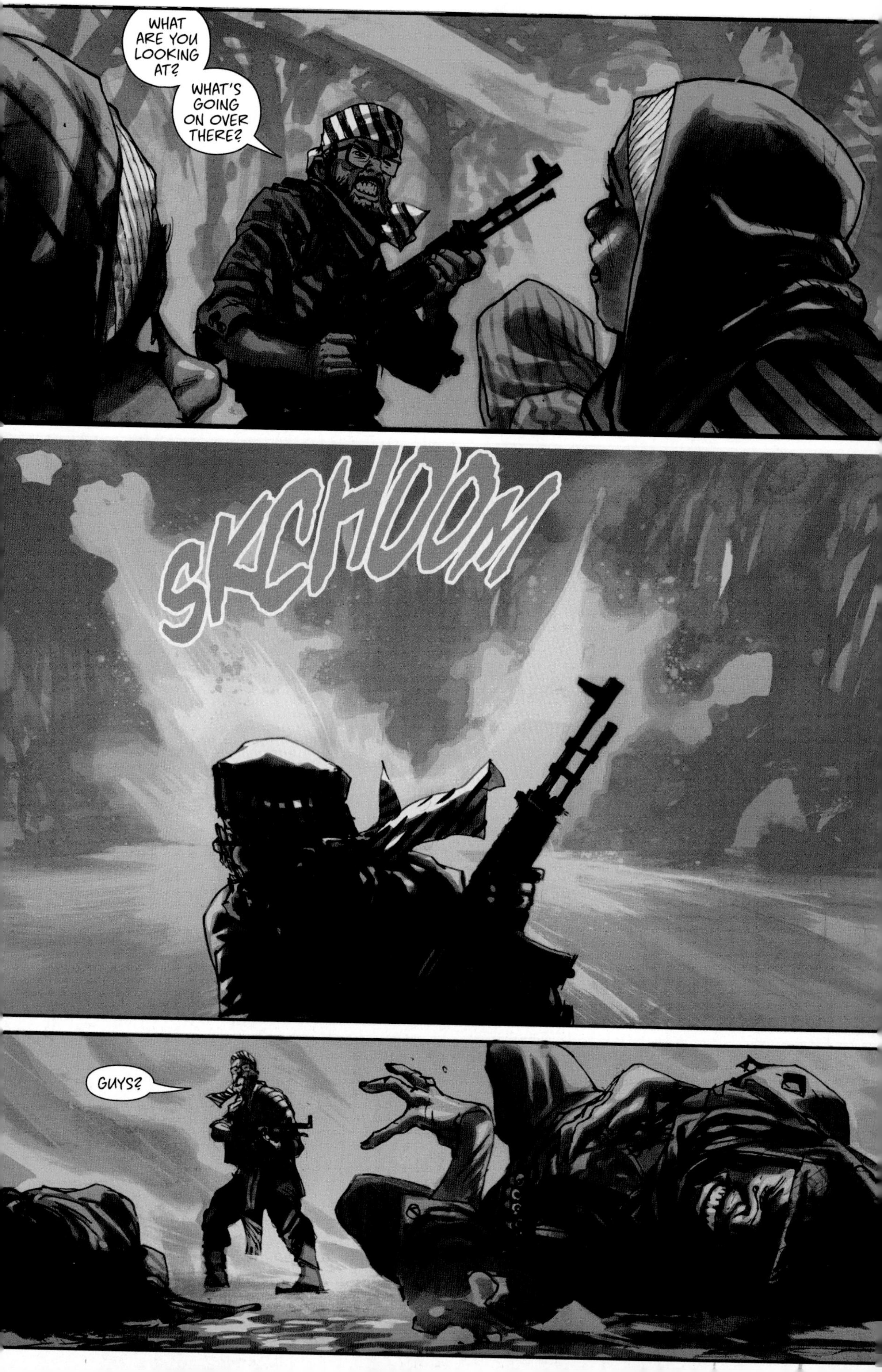
WHAT ARE YOU LOOKING AT?
WHAT'S GOING ON OVER THERE?
SKCHOOM
GUYS?

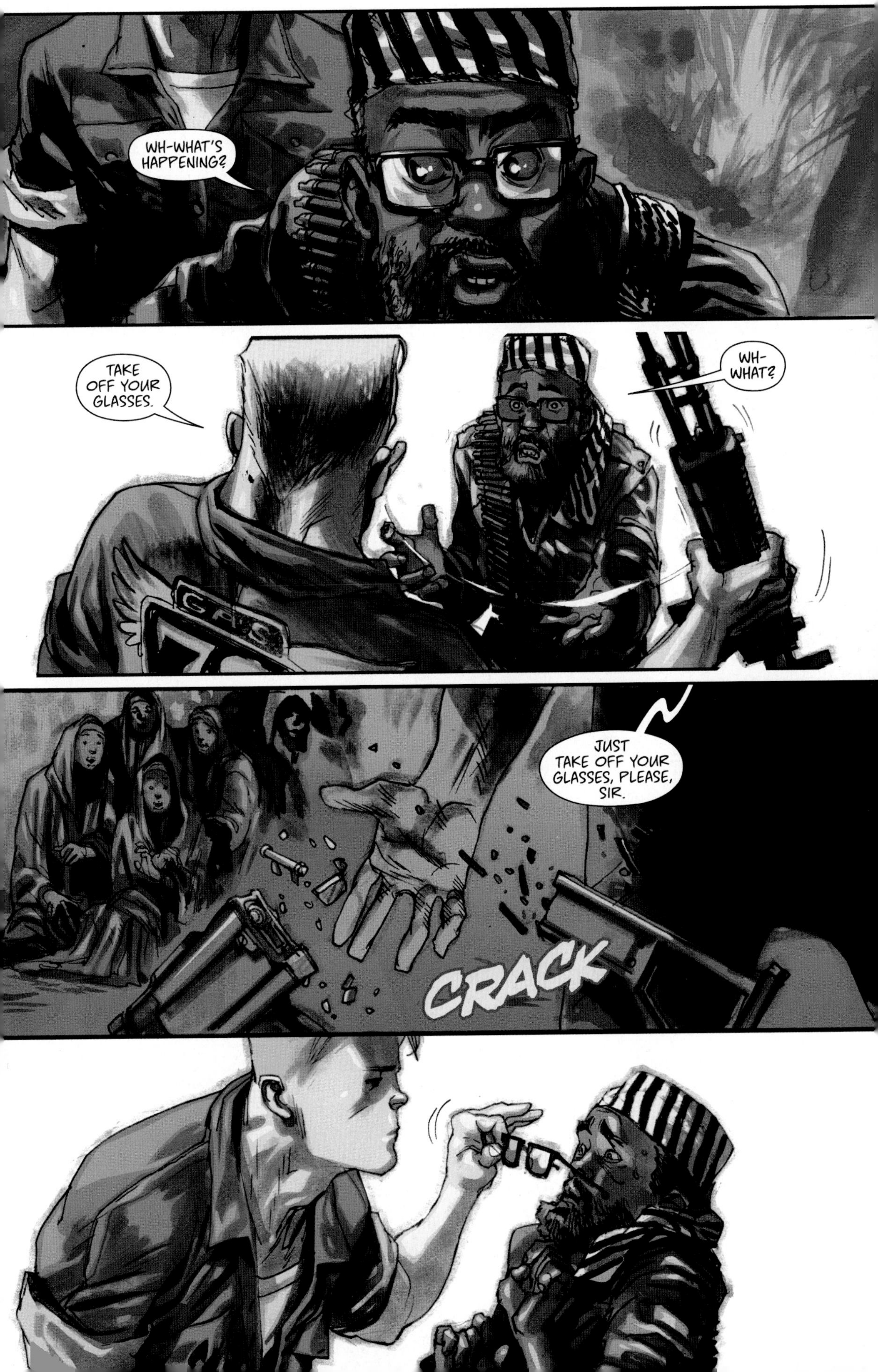
WH-WHAT'S HAPPENING?
TAKE OFF YOUR GLASSES.
WH-WHAT?
JUST TAKE OFF YOUR GLASSES, PLEASE, SIR.
CRACK

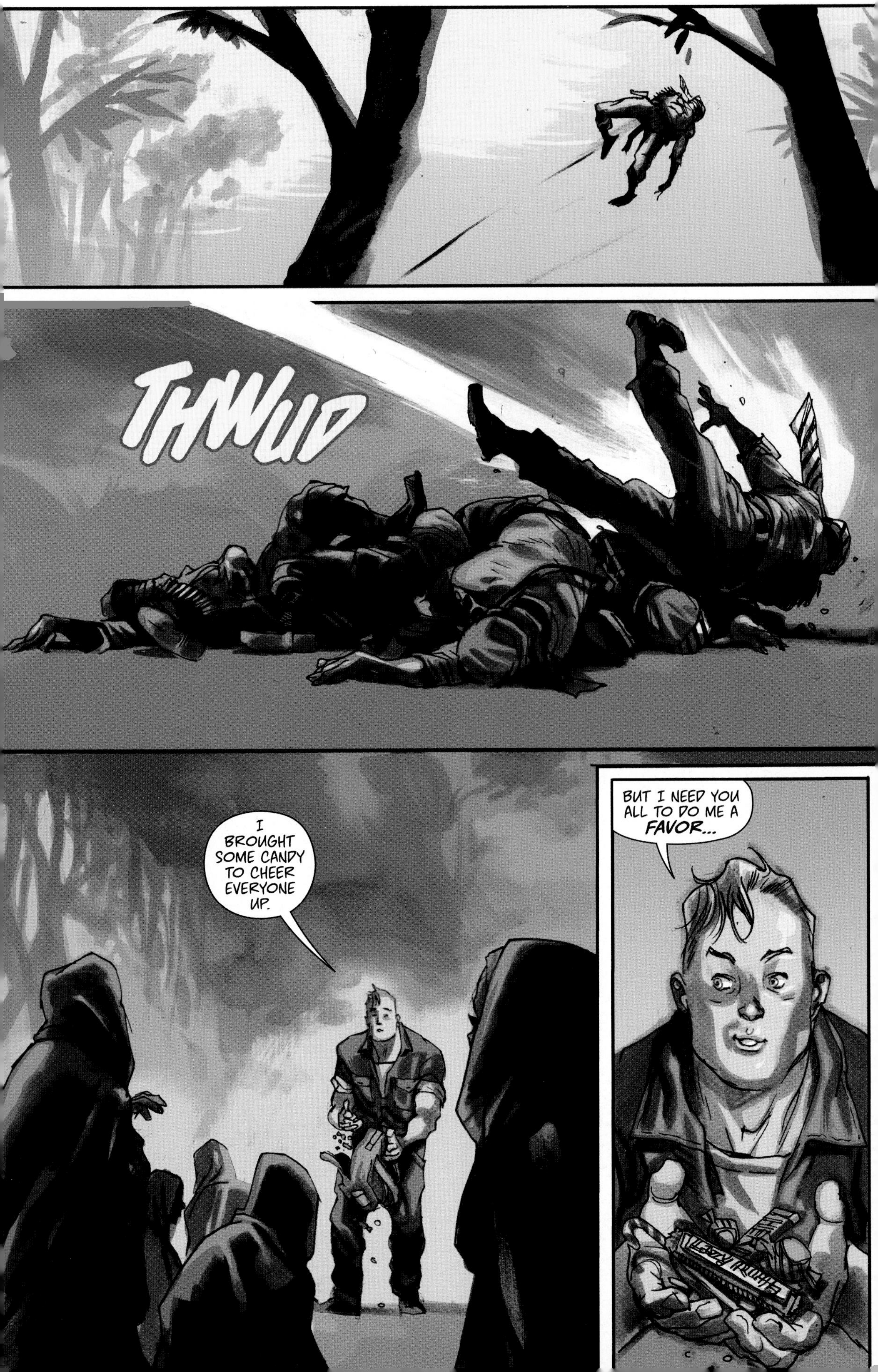
THWUD
I BROUGHT SOME CANDY TO CHEER EVERYONE UP.
BUT I NEED YOU ALL TO DO ME A FAVOR...

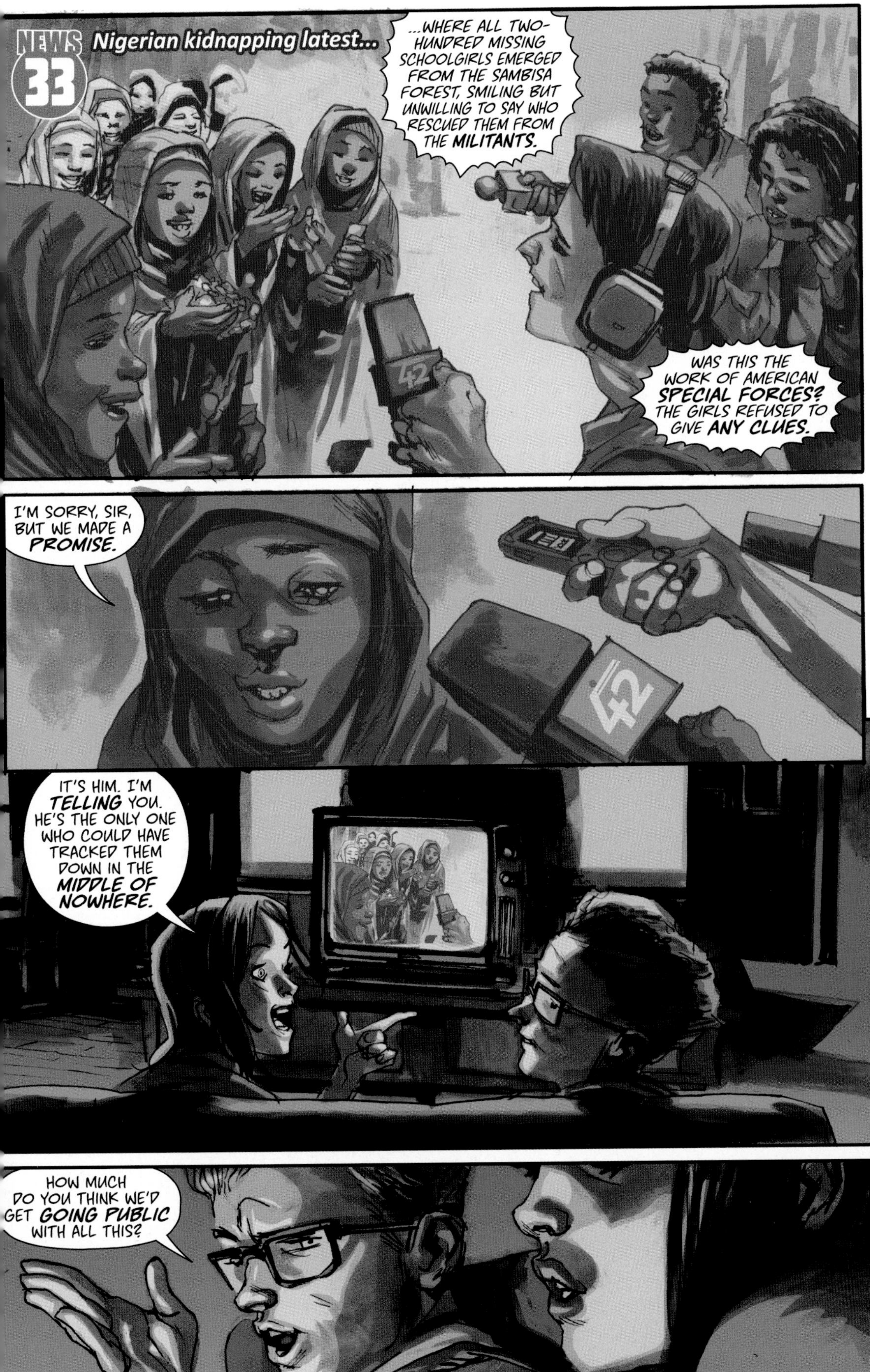
NEWS 33 Nigerian kidnapping latest...
...WHERE ALL TWO-HUNDRED MISSING SCHOOLGIRLS EMERGED FROM THE SAMBISA FOREST, SMILING BUT UNWILLING TO SAY WHO RESCUED THEM FROM THE MILITANTS.
WAS THIS THE WORK OF AMERICAN SPECIAL FORCES? THE GIRLS REFUSED TO GIVE ANY CLUES.
I'M SORRY, SIR, BUT WE MADE A PROMISE.
IT'S HIM. I'M TELLING YOU. HE'S THE ONLY ONE WHO COULD HAVE TRACKED THEM DOWN IN THE MIDDLE OF NOWHERE.
HOW MUCH DO YOU THINK WE'D GET GOING PUBLIC WITH ALL THIS?

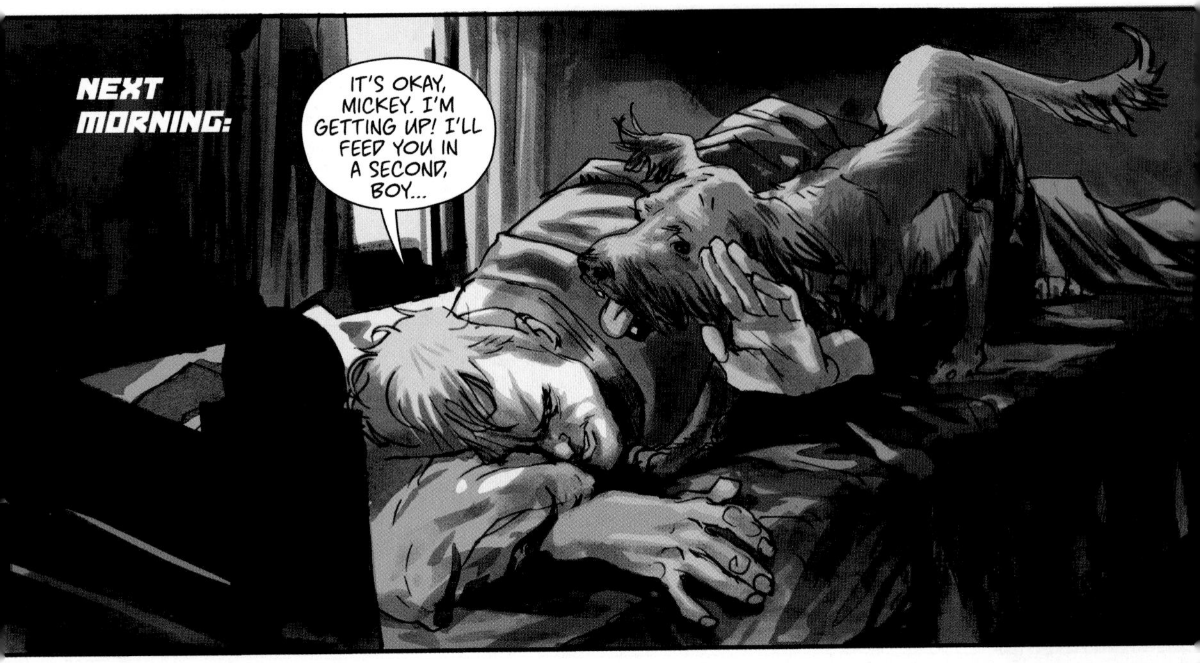
NEXT MORNING:
IT'S OKAY, MICKEY. I'M GETTING UP! I'LL FEED YOU IN A SECOND, BOY...

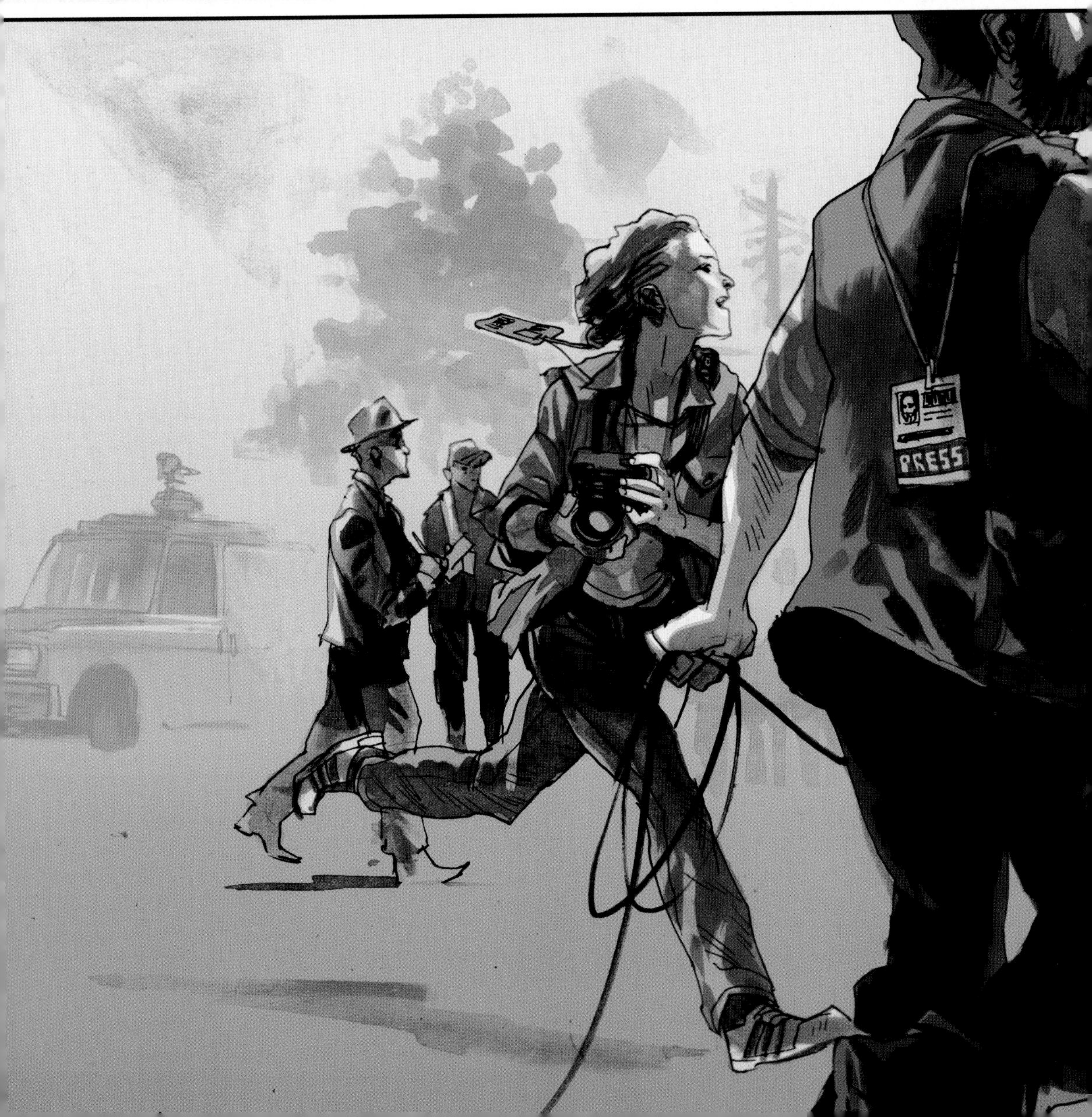
PRESS

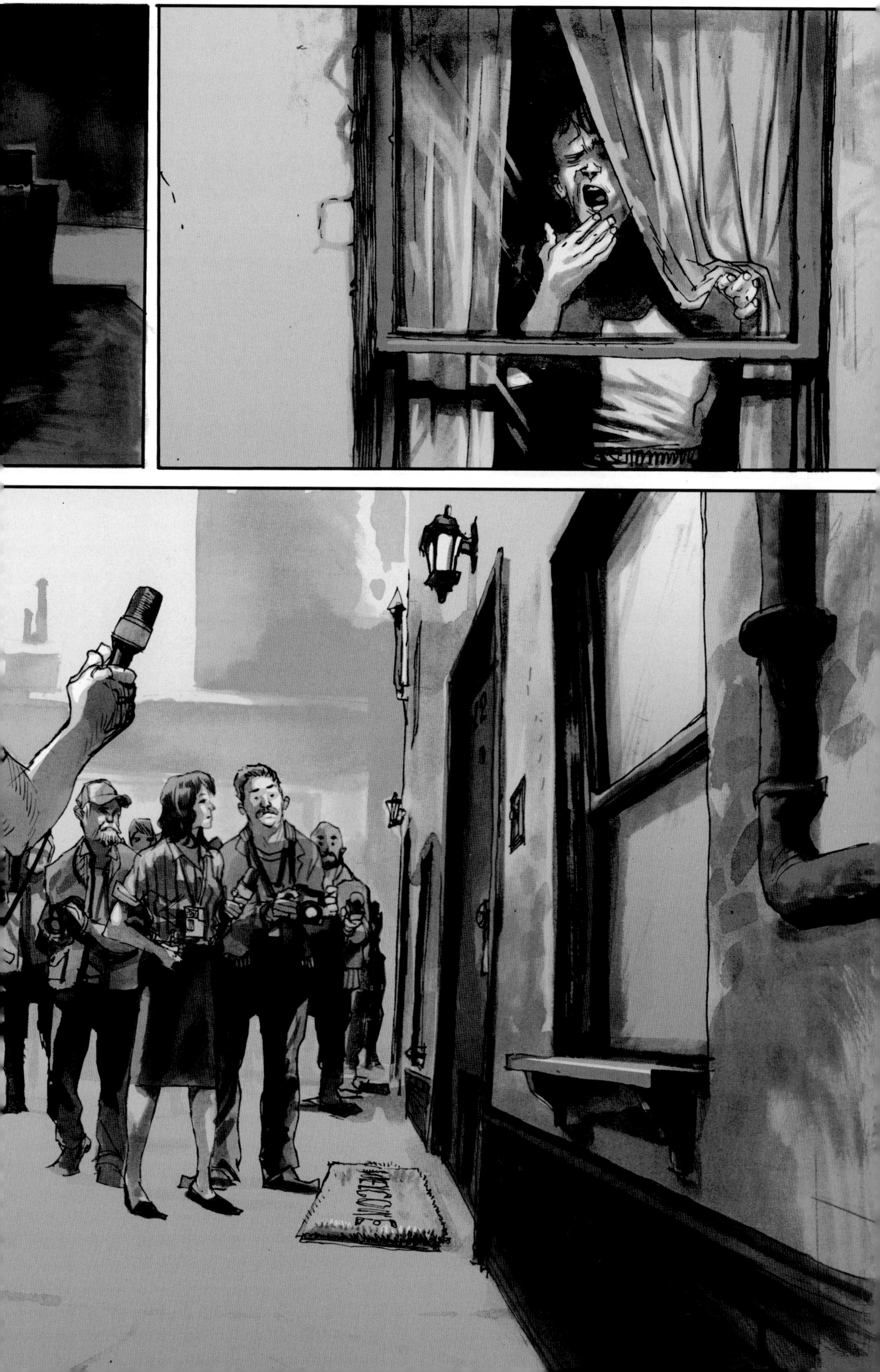
WELCOME

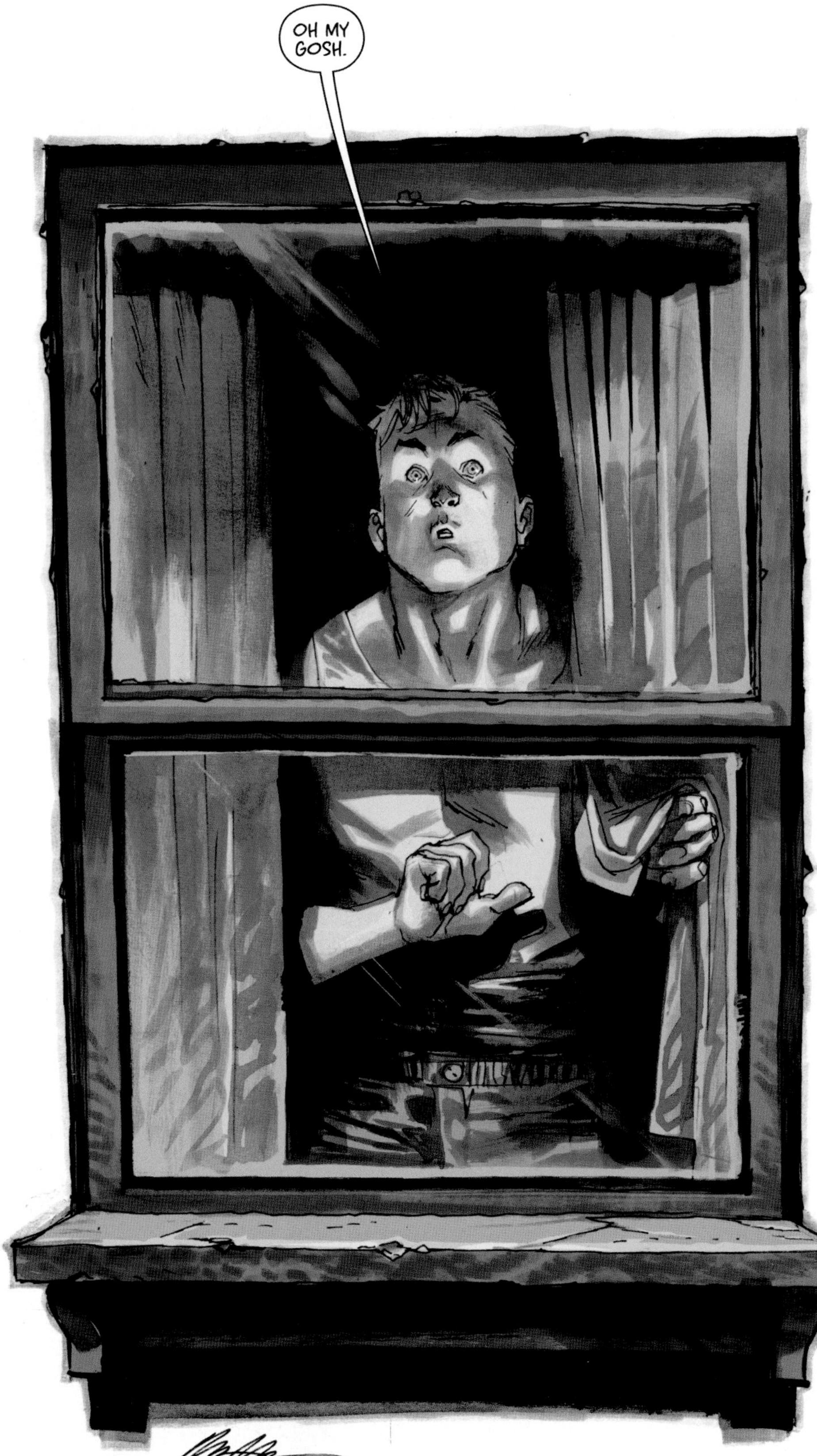
OH MY GOSH.
-2015-

FIND MISSING DOG
- FIND MARY'S KEYS
- PAY LUNCH FOR EV
- BUILD A BARN
- FIND JA
- TAKE TH OF
- COLLECT ONE'S
- FIX THEODORE'S CA
- BUILD A HOUSE F
- BRING THE G
- FIND JOH
- FIND MIS
- FIND MA
- PAY

TWO

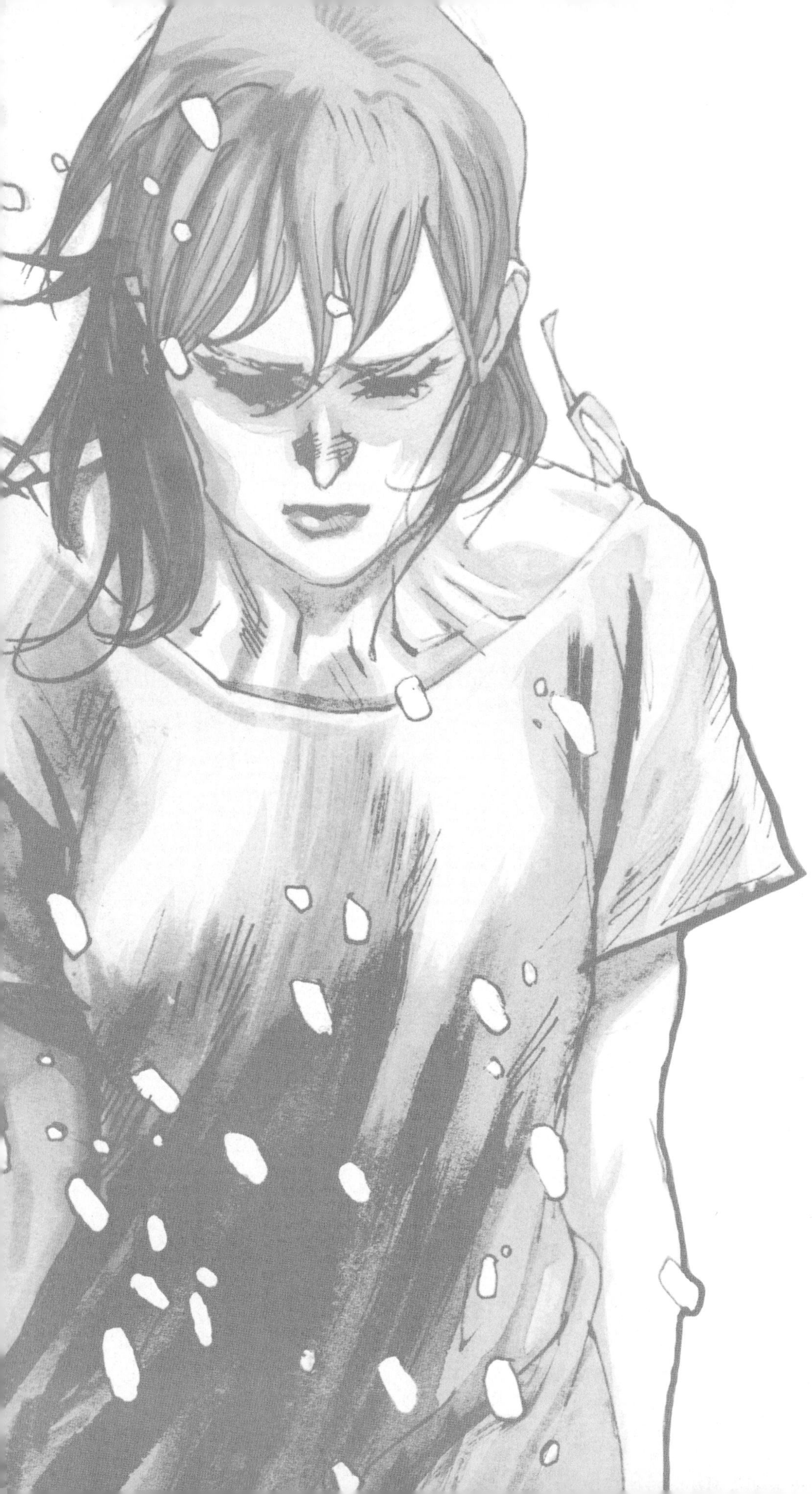

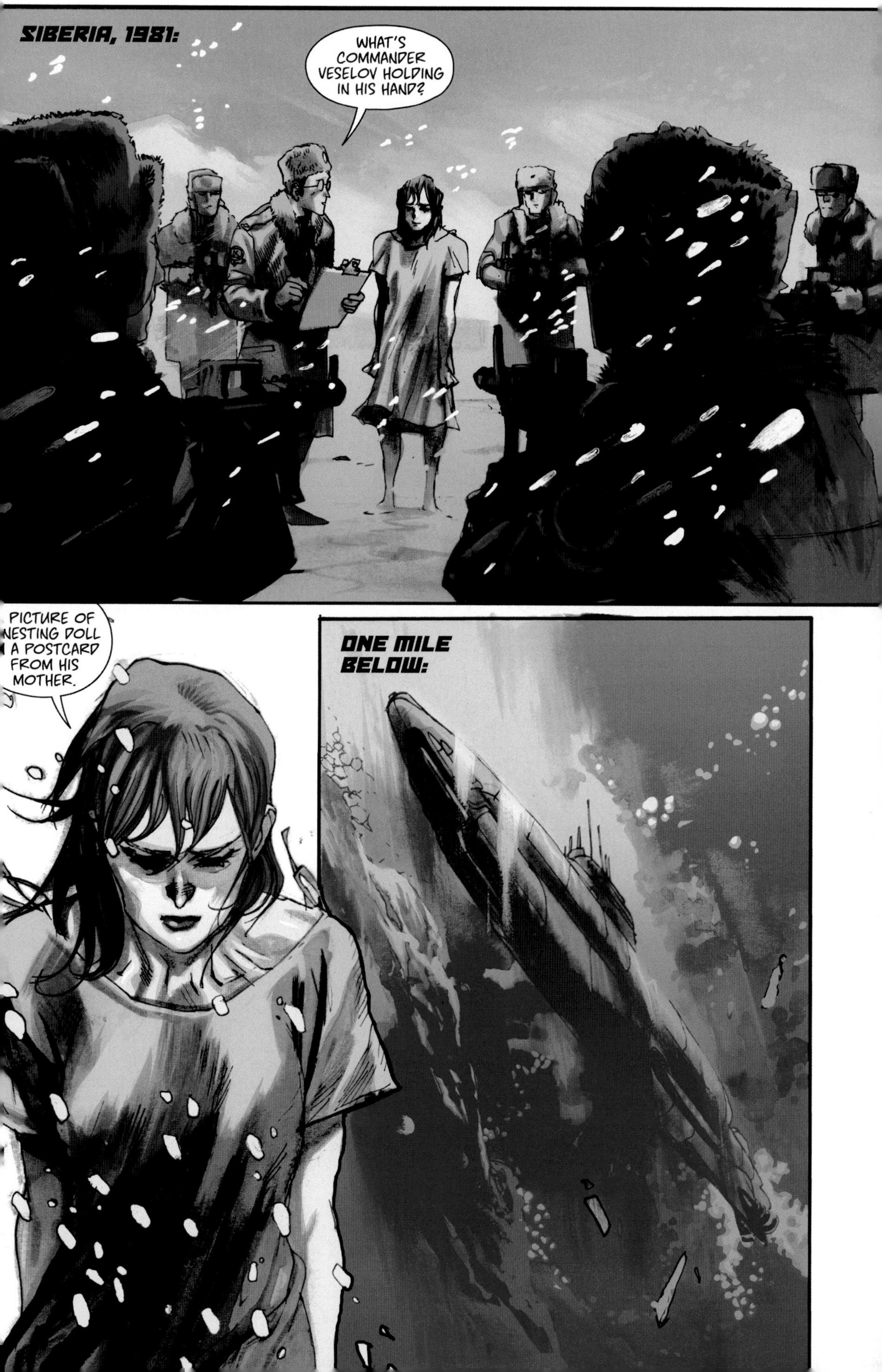
SIBERIA, 1981:
WHAT'S COMMANDER VESELOV HOLDING IN HIS HAND?
PICTURE OF NESTING DOLL A POSTCARD FROM HIS MOTHER.
ONE MILE BELOW:

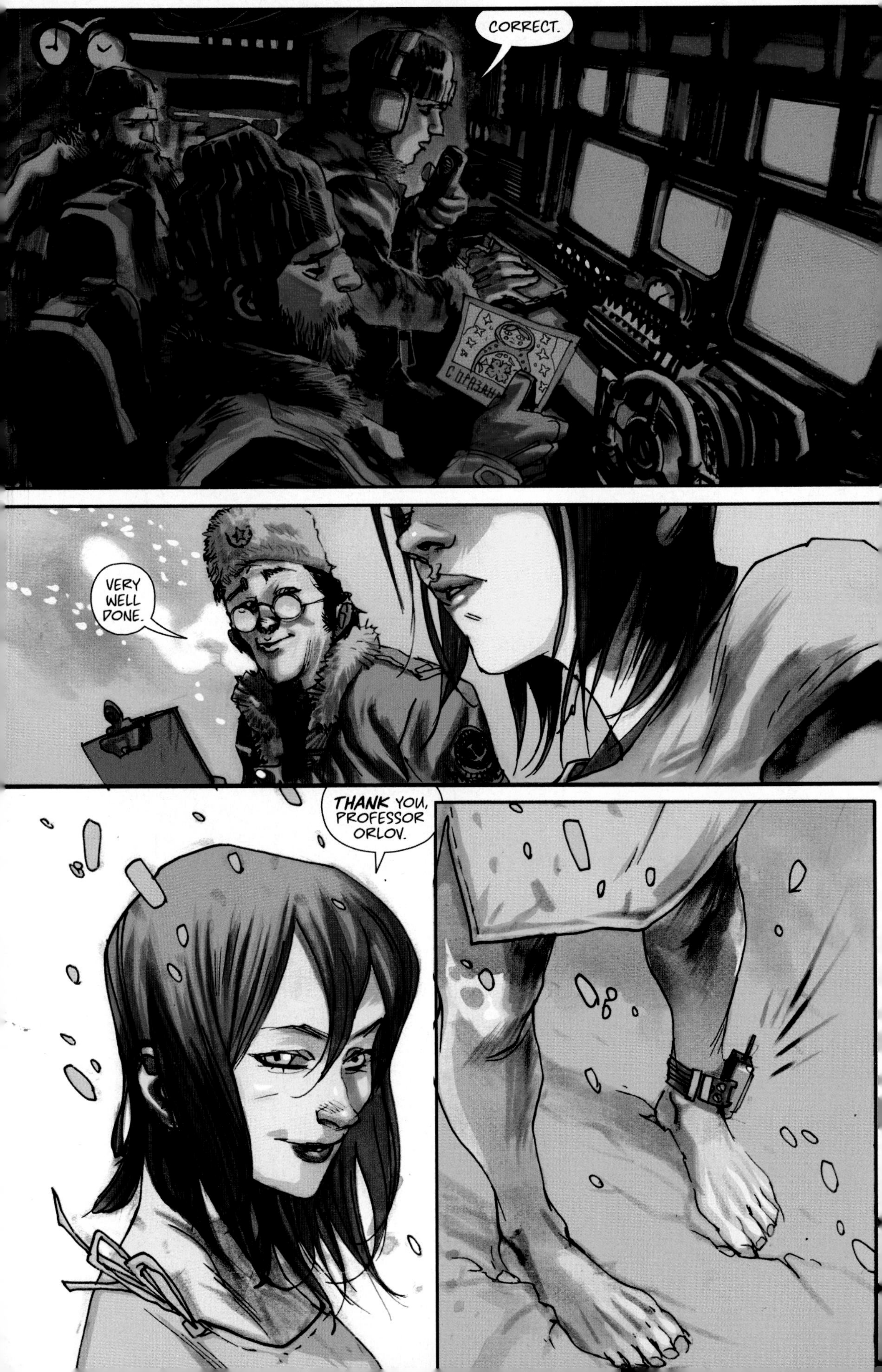
CORRECT.
VERY WELL DONE.
THANK YOU, PROFESSOR ORLOV.

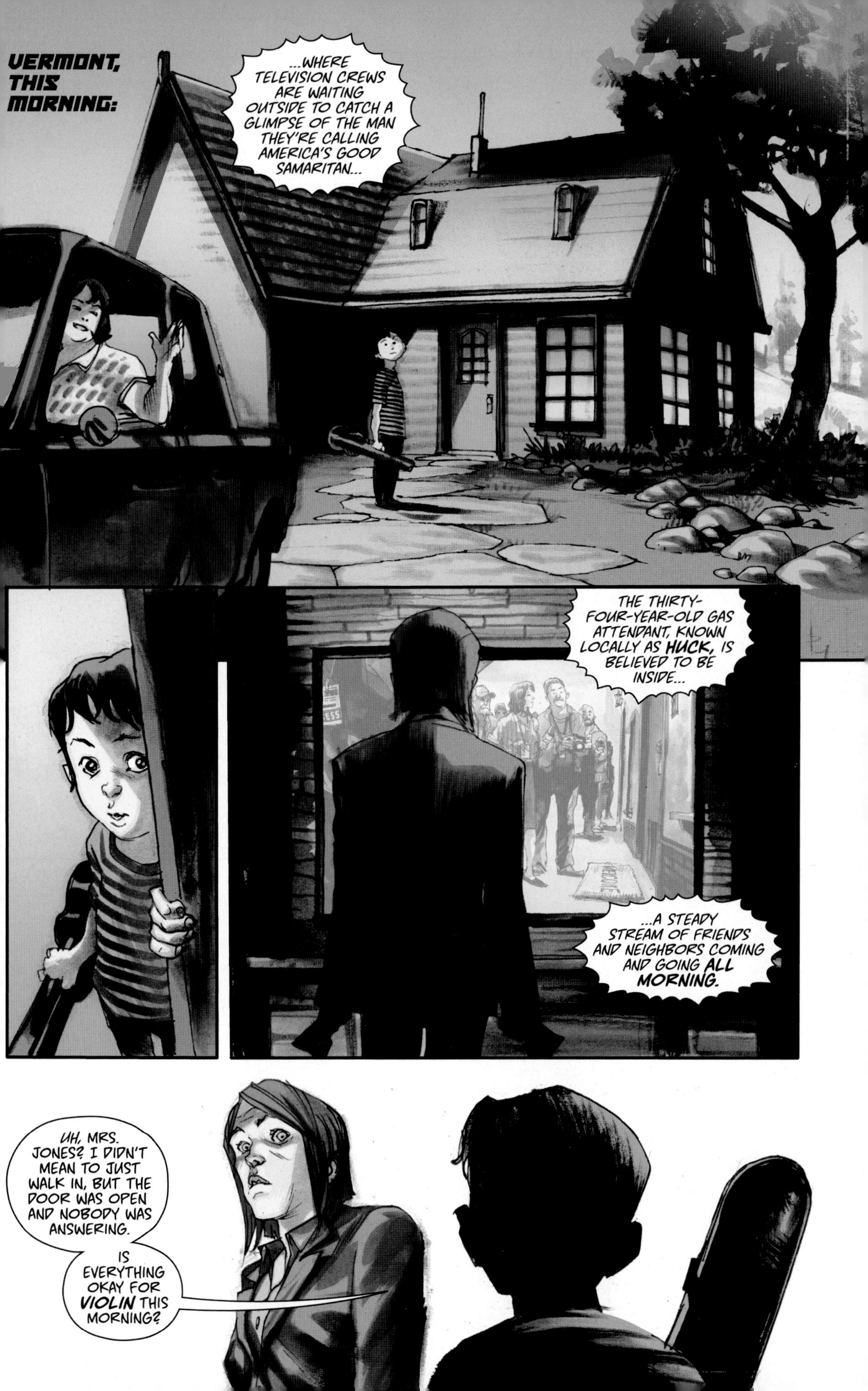
VERMONT, THIS MORNING:
...WHERE TELEVISION CREWS ARE WAITING OUTSIDE TO CATCH A GLIMPSE OF THE MAN THEY'RE CALLING AMERICA'S GOOD SAMARITAN...
THE THIRTY-FOUR-YEAR-OLD GAS ATTENDANT, KNOWN LOCALLY AS HUCK, IS BELIEVED TO BE INSIDE...
...A STEADY STREAM OF FRIENDS AND NEIGHBORS COMING AND GOING ALL MORNING.
UH, MRS. JONES? I DIDN'T MEAN TO JUST WALK IN, BUT THE DOOR WAS OPEN AND NOBODY WAS ANSWERING.
IS EVERYTHING OKAY FOR VIOLIN THIS MORNING?

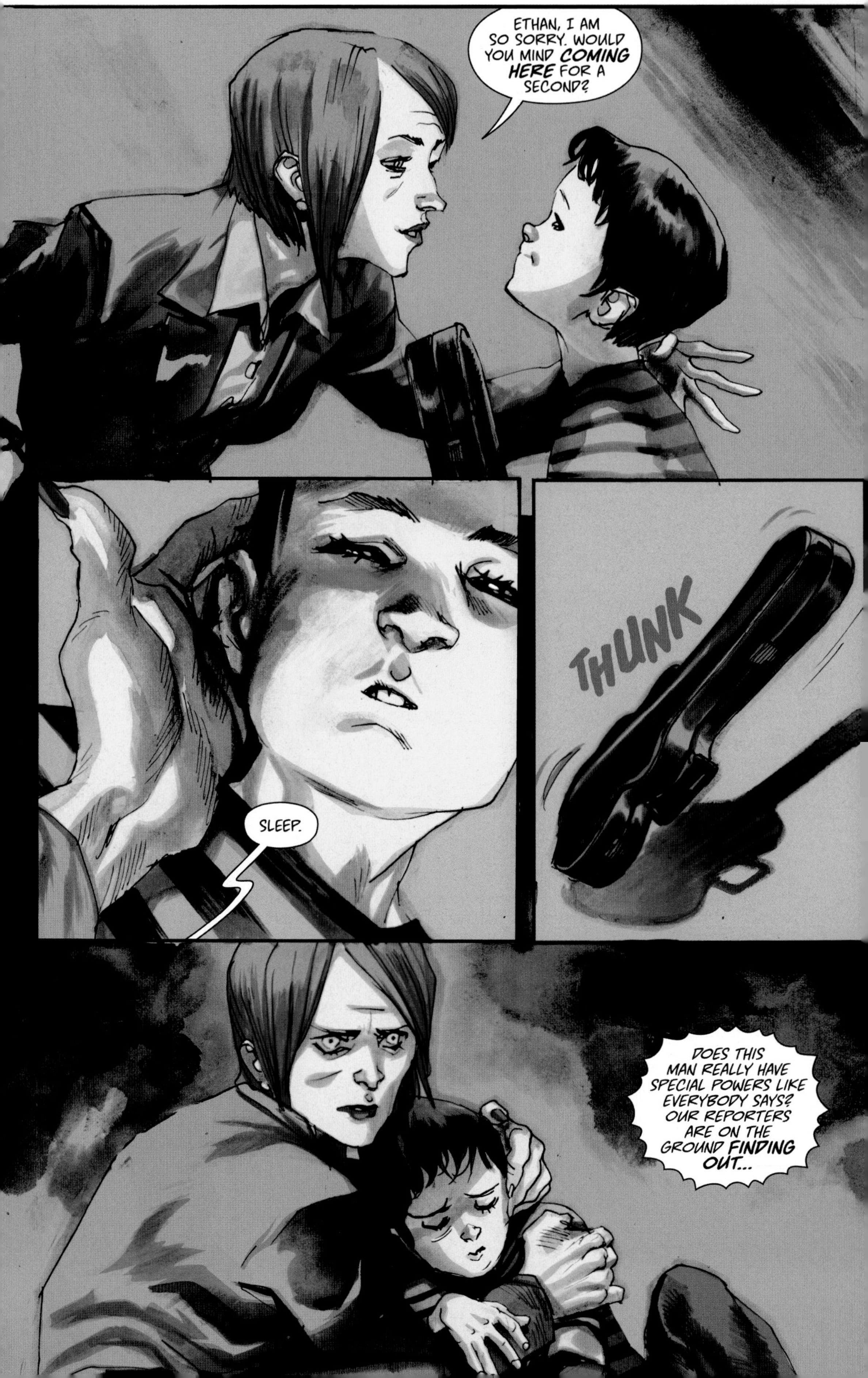
ETHAN, I AM SO SORRY. WOULD YOU MIND COMING HERE FOR A SECOND?
SLEEP.
THUNK
DOES THIS MAN REALLY HAVE SPECIAL POWERS LIKE EVERYBODY SAYS? OUR REPORTERS ARE ON THE GROUND FINDING OUT...

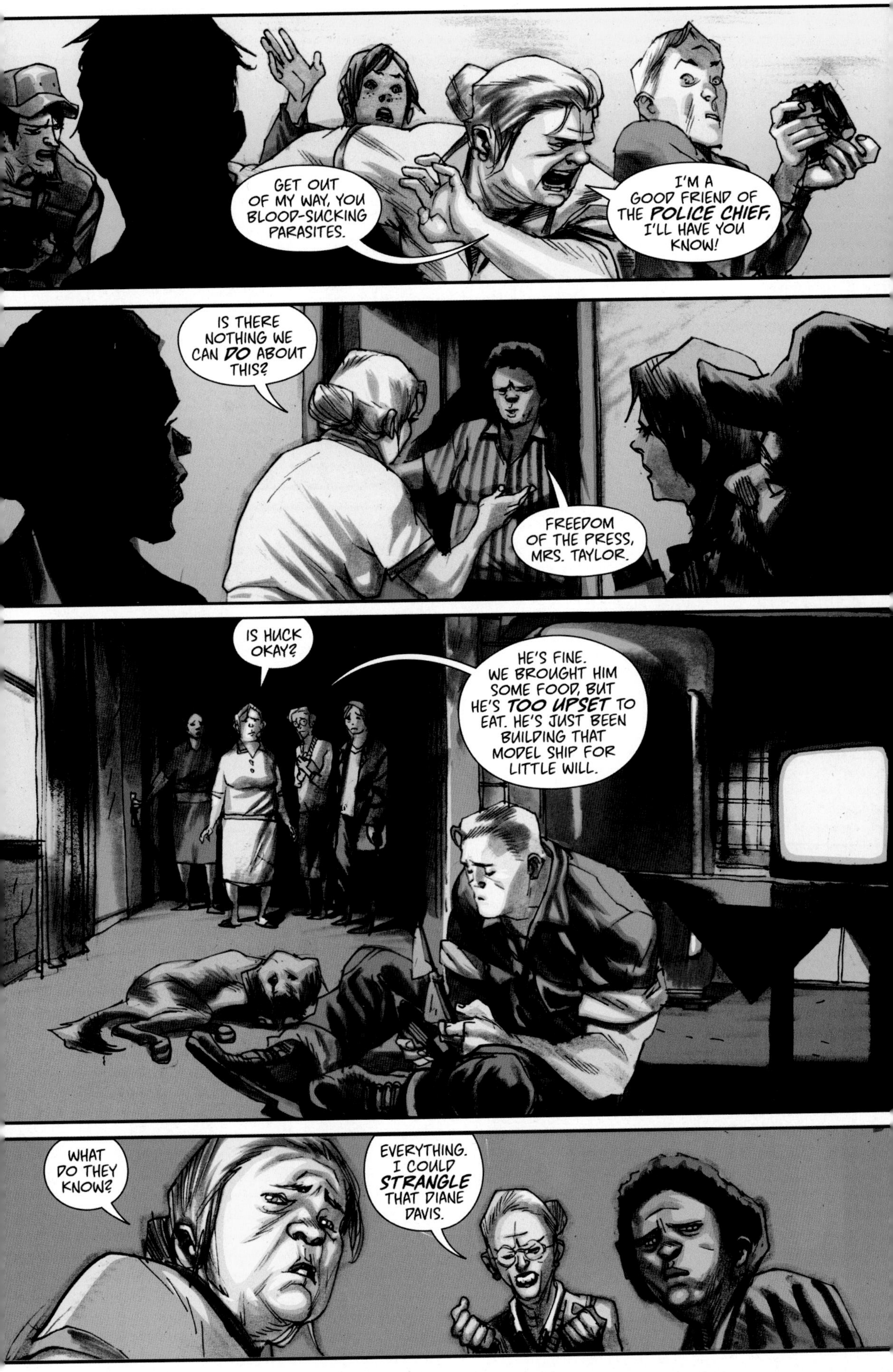
GET OUT OF MY WAY, YOU BLOOD-SUCKING PARASITES.
I'M A GOOD FRIEND OF THE POLICE CHIEF, I'LL HAVE YOU KNOW!
IS THERE NOTHING WE CAN DO ABOUT THIS?
FREEDOM OF THE PRESS, MRS. TAYLOR.
IS HUCK OKAY?
HE'S FINE. WE BROUGHT HIM SOME FOOD, BUT HE'S TOO UPSET TO EAT. HE'S JUST BEEN BUILDING THAT MODEL SHIP FOR LITTLE WILL.
WHAT DO THEY KNOW?
EVERYTHING. I COULD STRANGLE THAT DIANE DAVIS.

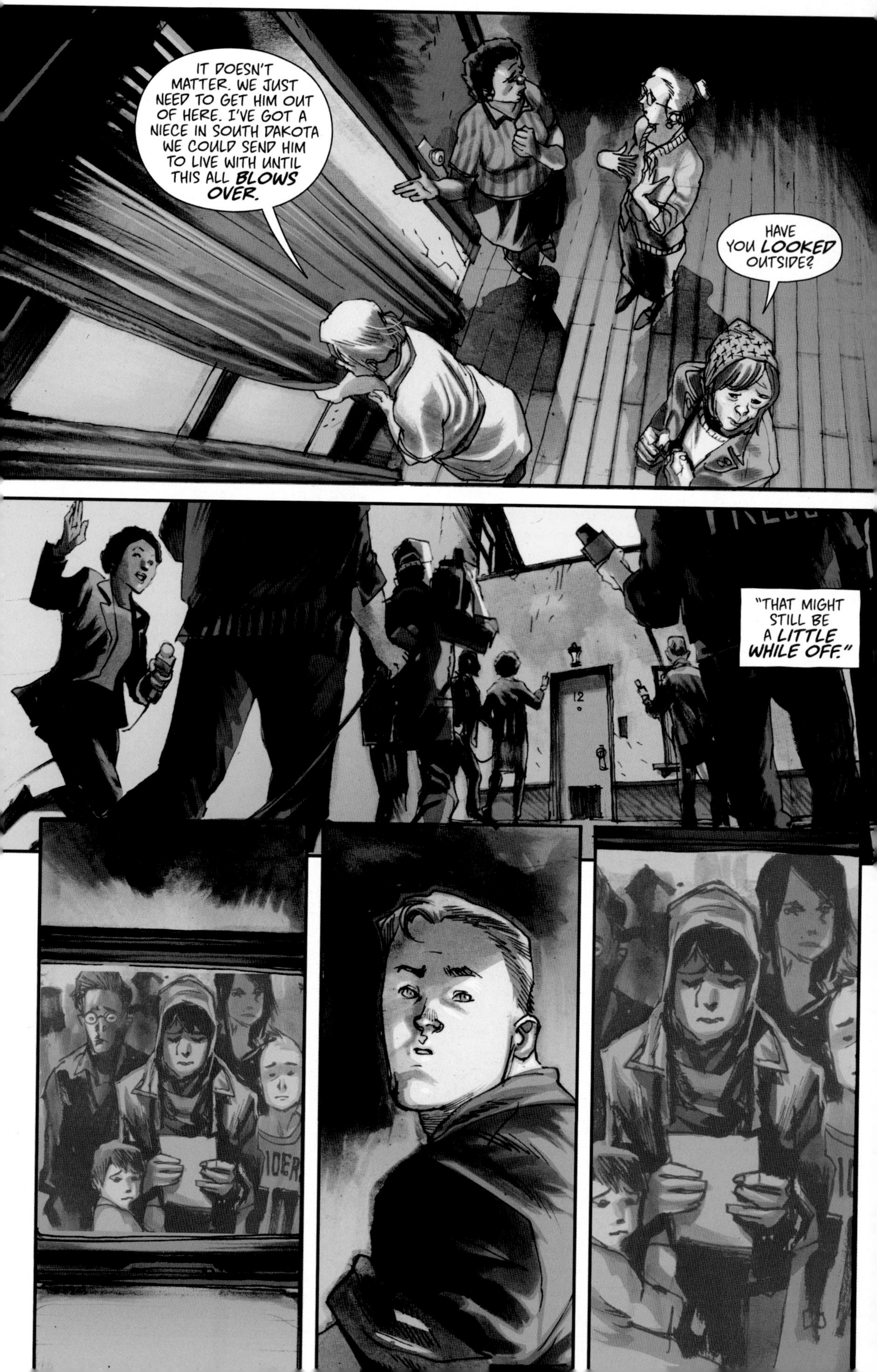
IT DOESN'T MATTER. WE JUST NEED TO GET HIM OUT OF HERE. I'VE GOT A NIECE IN SOUTH DAKOTA WE COULD SEND HIM TO LIVE WITH UNTIL THIS ALL BLOWS OVER.
HAVE YOU LOOKED OUTSIDE?
"THAT MIGHT STILL BE A LITTLE WHILE OFF."
12

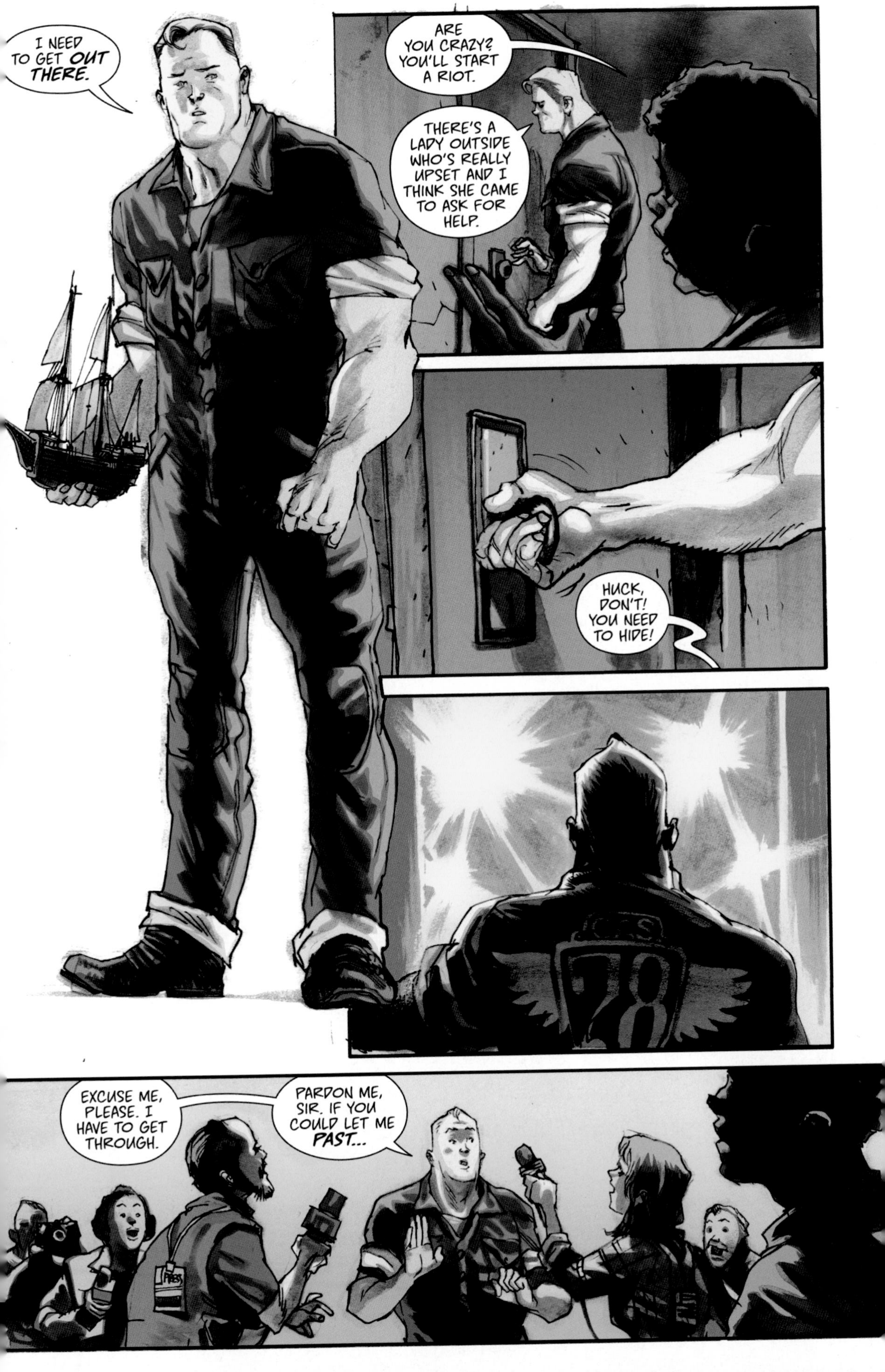
I NEED TO GET OUT THERE.
ARE YOU CRAZY? YOU'LL START A RIOT.
THERE'S A LADY OUTSIDE WHO'S REALLY UPSET AND I THINK SHE CAME TO ASK FOR HELP.
HUCK, DON'T! YOU NEED TO HIDE!
EXCUSE ME, PLEASE. I HAVE TO GET THROUGH.
PARDON ME, SIR. IF YOU COULD LET ME PAST...

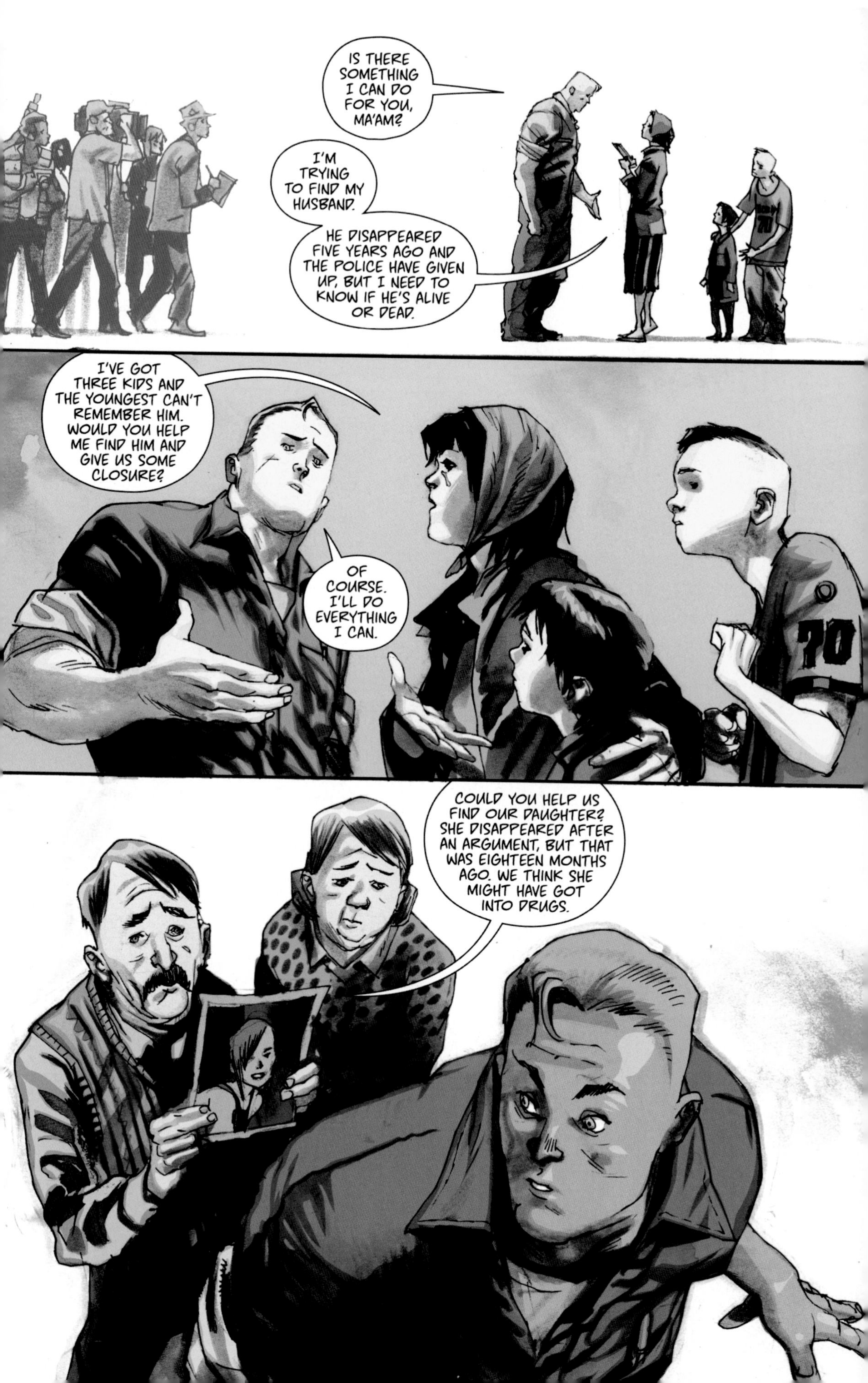
IS THERE SOMETHING I CAN DO FOR YOU, MA'AM?
I'M TRYING TO FIND MY HUSBAND.
HE DISAPPEARED FIVE YEARS AGO AND THE POLICE HAVE GIVEN UP, BUT I NEED TO KNOW IF HE'S ALIVE OR DEAD.
I'VE GOT THREE KIDS AND THE YOUNGEST CAN'T REMEMBER HIM. WOULD YOU HELP ME FIND HIM AND GIVE US SOME CLOSURE?
OF COURSE. I'LL DO EVERYTHING I CAN.
COULD YOU HELP US FIND OUR DAUGHTER? SHE DISAPPEARED AFTER AN ARGUMENT, BUT THAT WAS EIGHTEEN MONTHS AGO. WE THINK SHE MIGHT HAVE GOT INTO DRUGS.

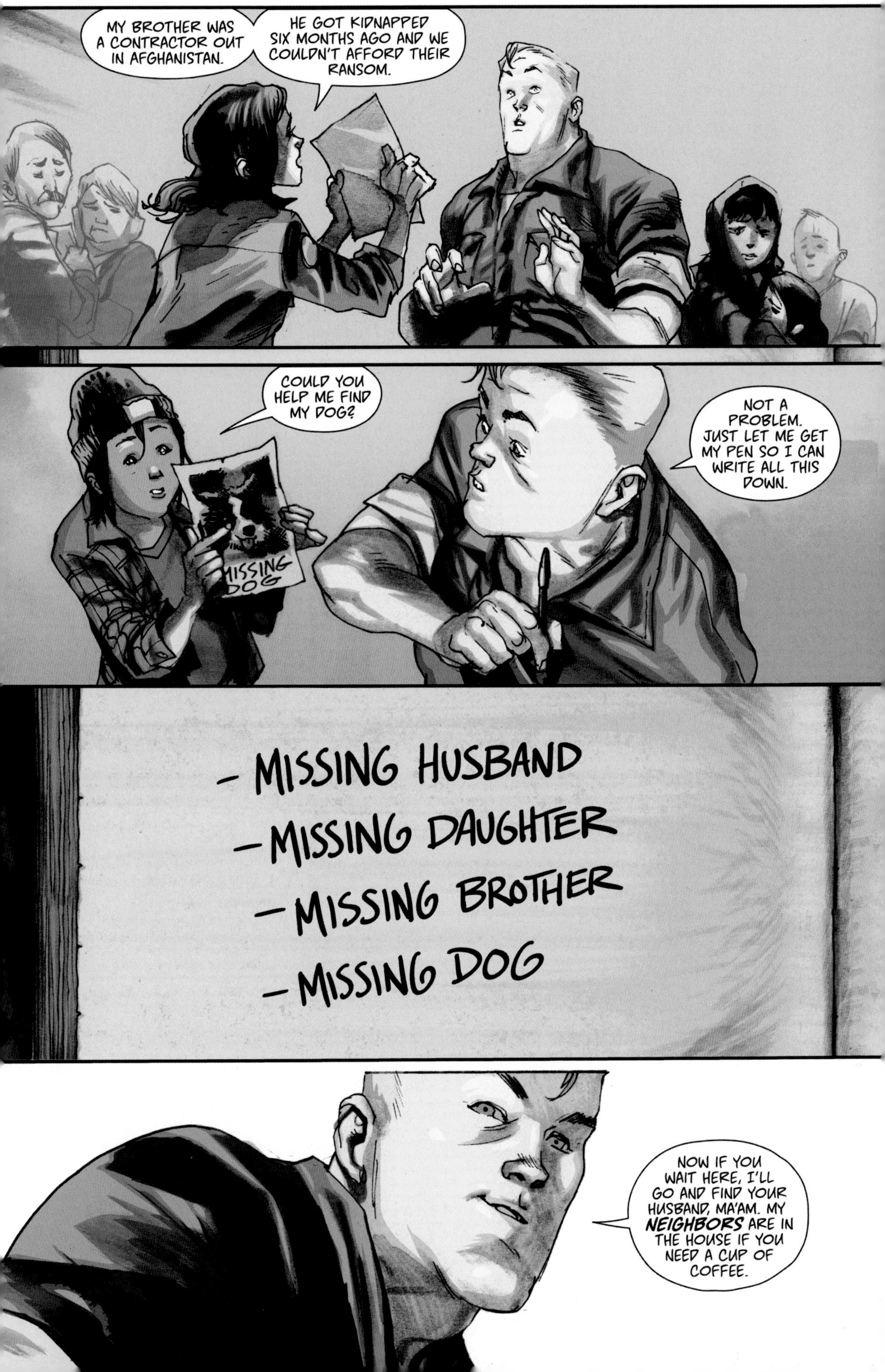
MY BROTHER WAS A CONTRACTOR OUT IN AFGHANISTAN.
HE GOT KIDNAPPED SIX MONTHS AGO AND WE COULDN'T AFFORD THEIR RANSOM.
COULD YOU HELP ME FIND MY DOG?
MISSING DOG
NOT A PROBLEM. JUST LET ME GET MY PEN SO I CAN WRITE ALL THIS DOWN.
- MISSING HUSBAND
- MISSING DAUGHTER
- MISSING BROTHER
- MISSING DOG
NOW IF YOU WAIT HERE, I'LL GO AND FIND YOUR HUSBAND, MA'AM. MY **NEIGHBORS** ARE IN THE HOUSE IF YOU NEED A CUP OF COFFEE.

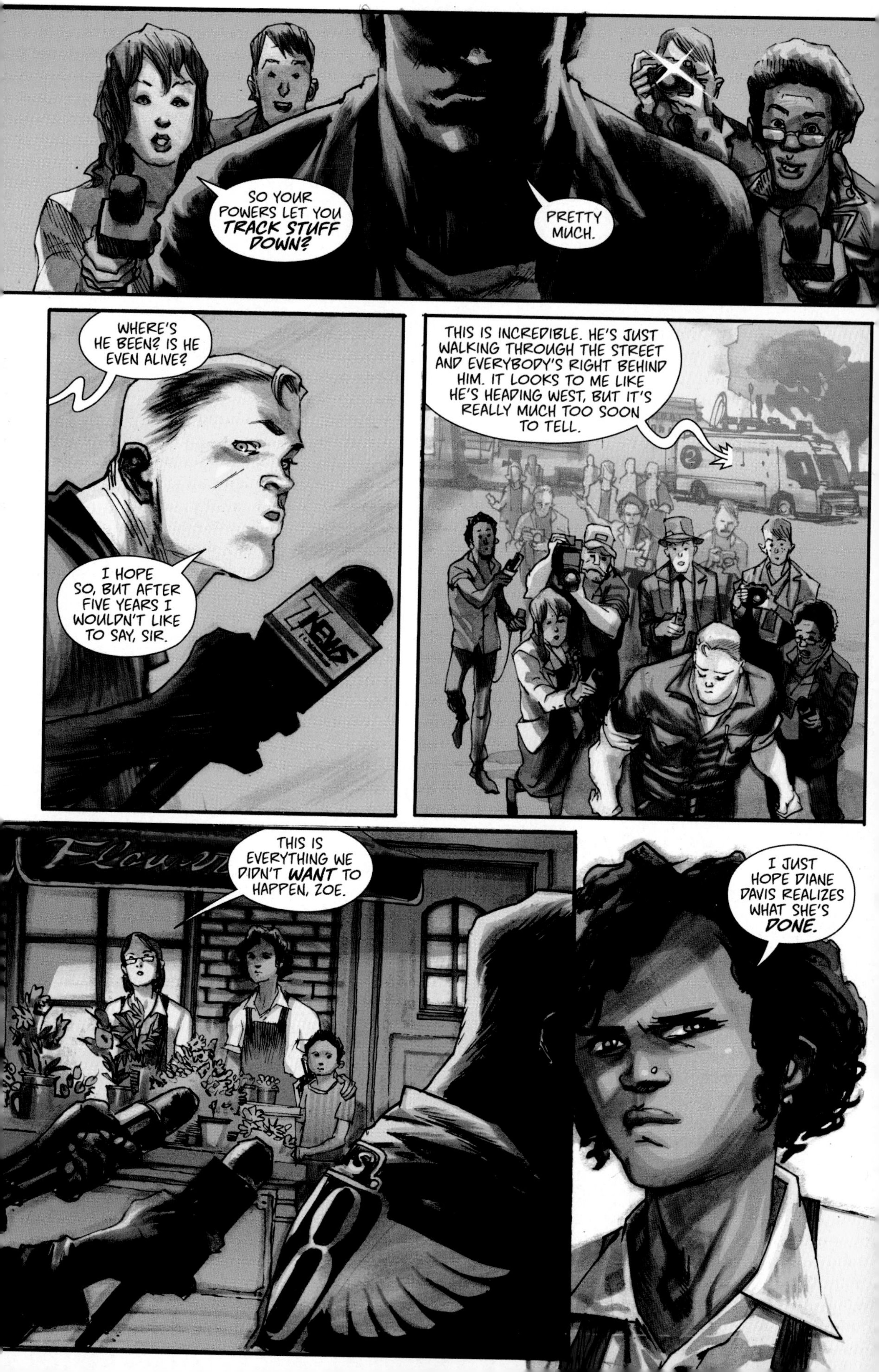
SO YOUR POWERS LET YOU TRACK STUFF DOWN?
PRETTY MUCH.
WHERE'S HE BEEN? IS HE EVEN ALIVE?
I HOPE SO, BUT AFTER FIVE YEARS I WOULDN'T LIKE TO SAY, SIR.
NEWS
THIS IS INCREDIBLE. HE'S JUST WALKING THROUGH THE STREET AND EVERYBODY'S RIGHT BEHIND HIM. IT LOOKS TO ME LIKE HE'S HEADING WEST, BUT IT'S REALLY MUCH TOO SOON TO TELL.
THIS IS EVERYTHING WE DIDN'T WANT TO HAPPEN, ZOE.
I JUST HOPE DIANE DAVIS REALIZES WHAT SHE'S DONE.

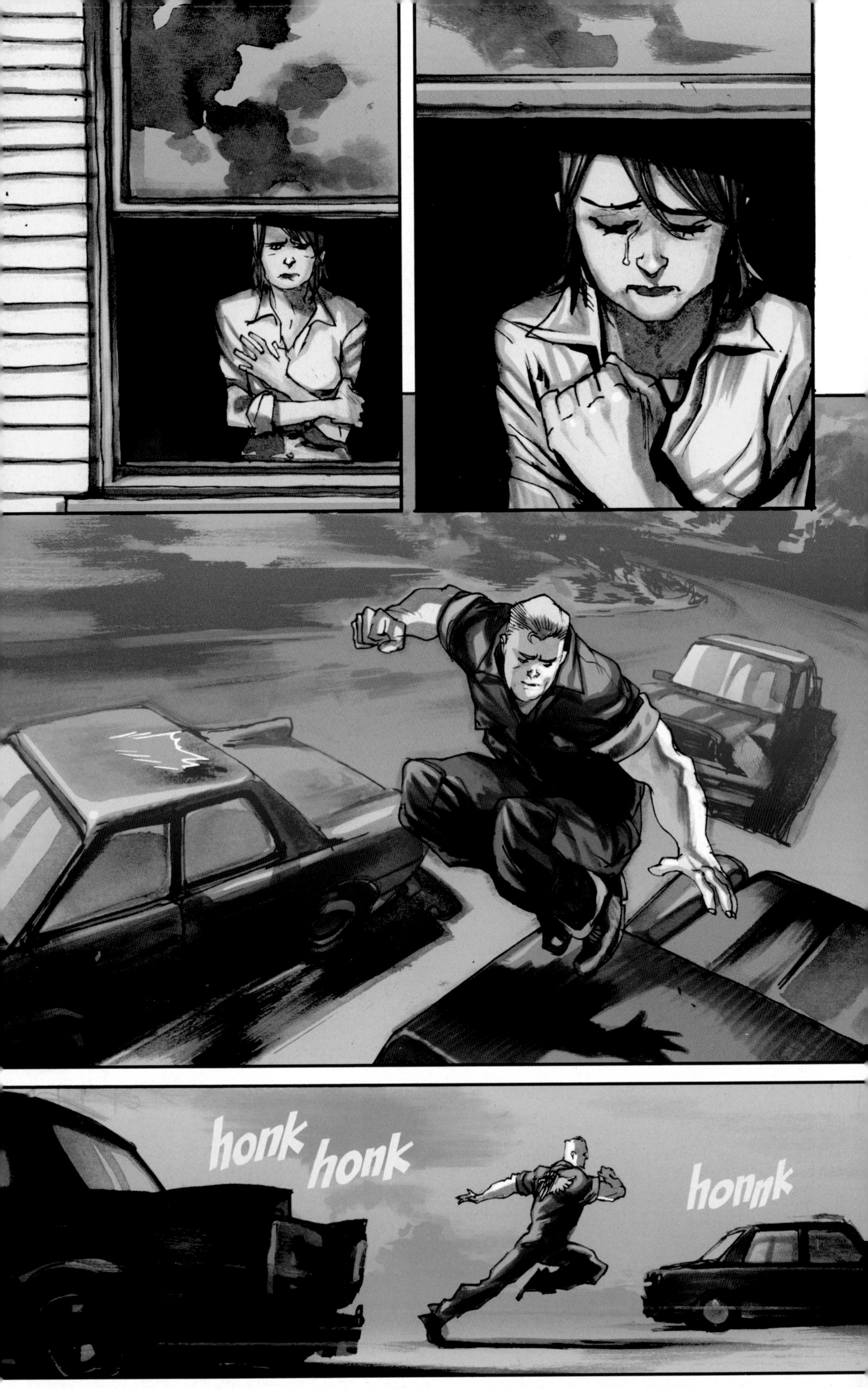
honk
honk
honnk

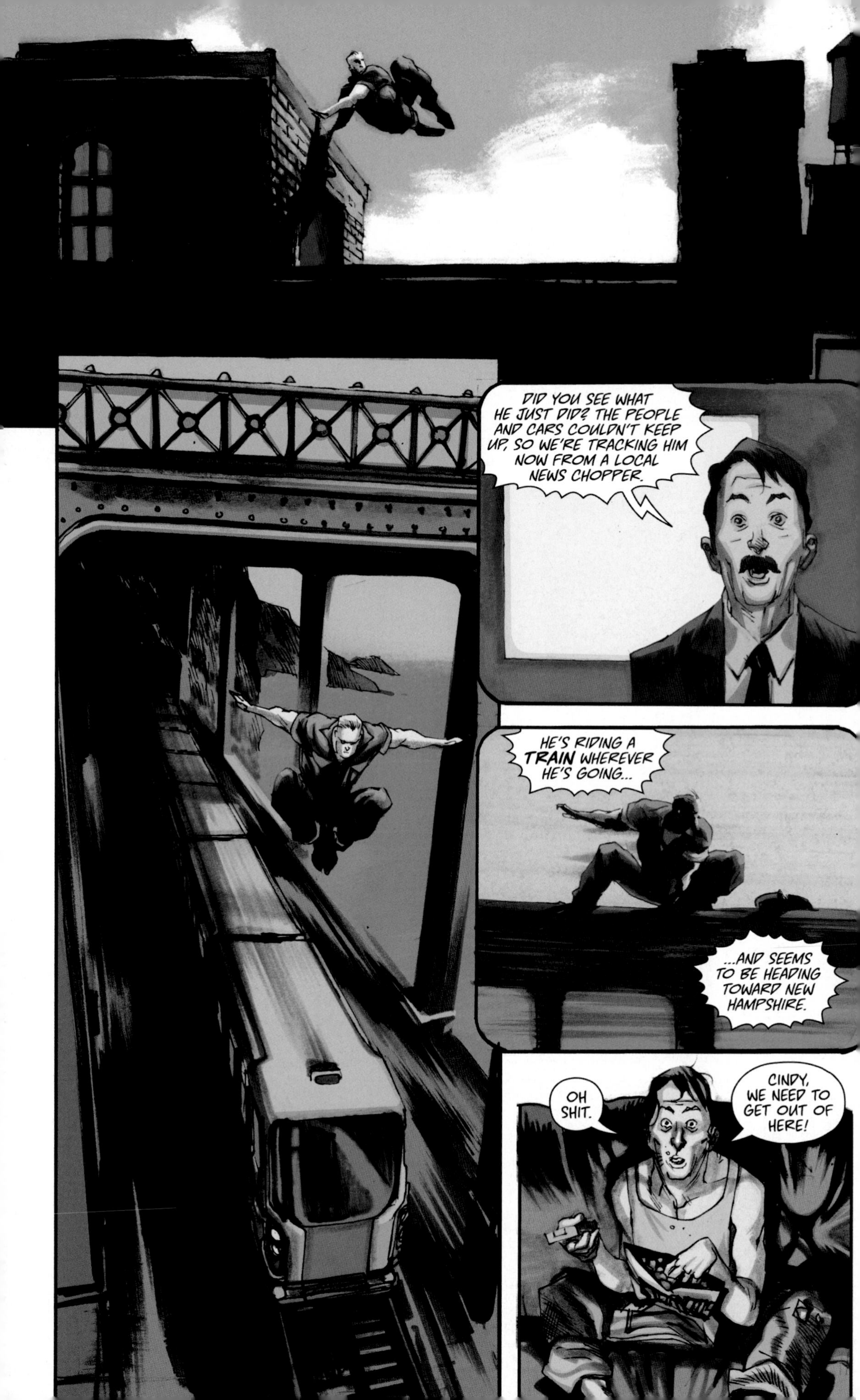
DID YOU SEE WHAT HE JUST DID? THE PEOPLE AND CARS COULDN'T KEEP UP, SO WE'RE TRACKING HIM NOW FROM A LOCAL NEWS CHOPPER.
HE'S RIDING A TRAIN WHEREVER HE'S GOING...
...AND SEEMS TO BE HEADING TOWARD NEW HAMPSHIRE.
OH SHIT.
CINDY, WE NEED TO GET OUT OF HERE!

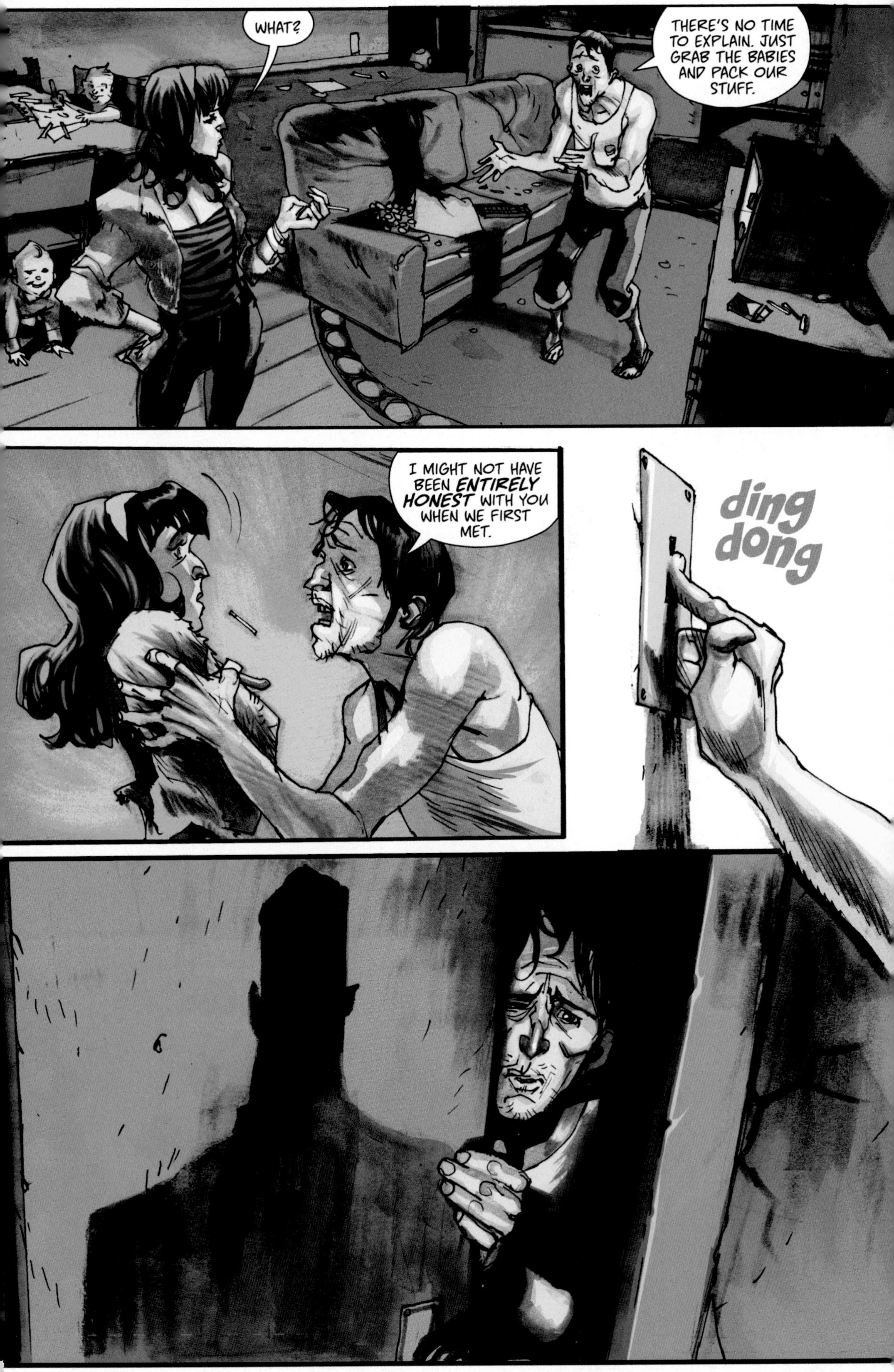
WHAT?
THERE'S NO TIME TO EXPLAIN. JUST GRAB THE BABIES AND PACK OUR STUFF.
I MIGHT NOT HAVE BEEN ENTIRELY HONEST WITH YOU WHEN WE FIRST MET.
ding dong

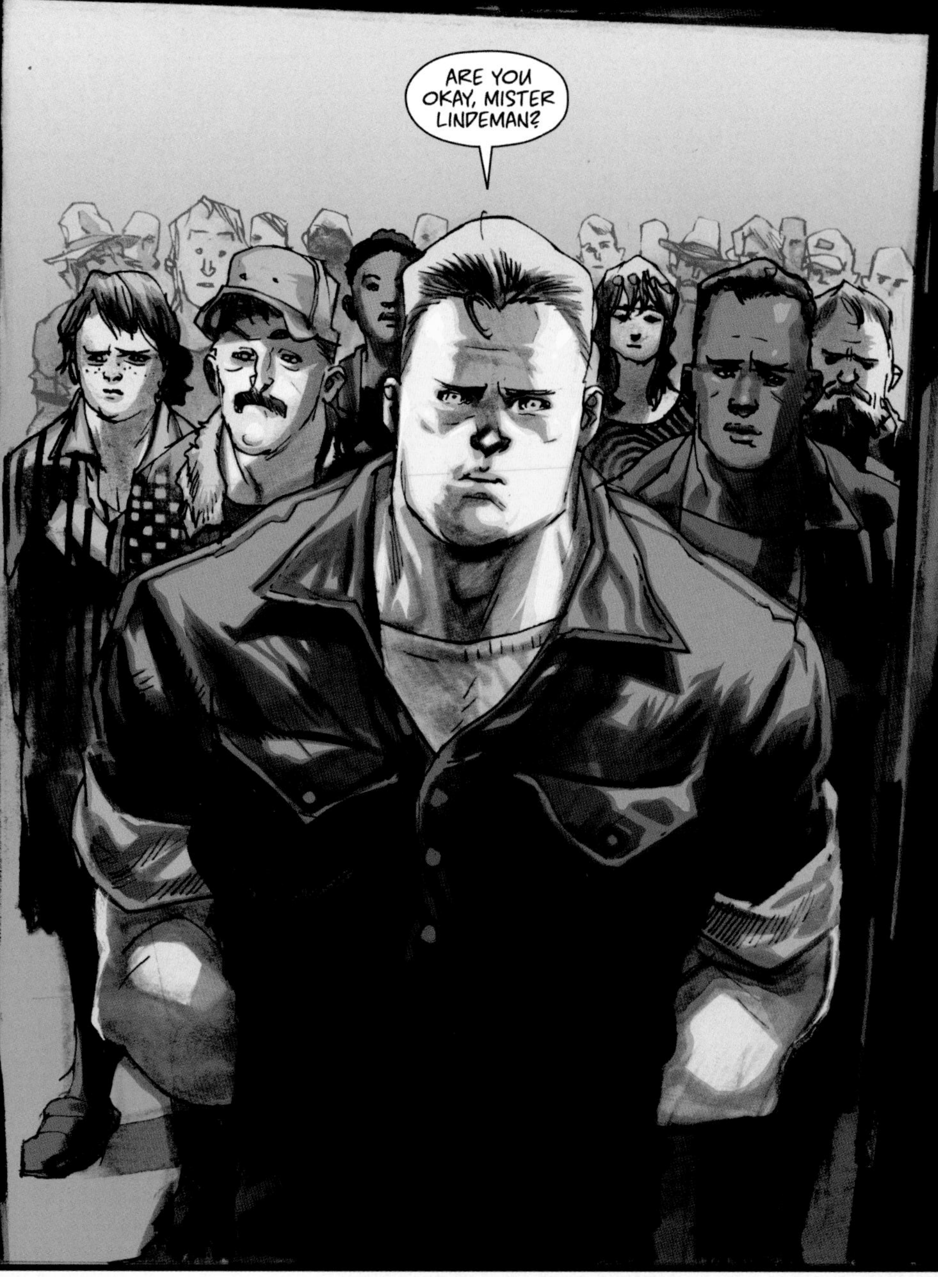
ARE YOU OKAY, MISTER LINDEMAN?

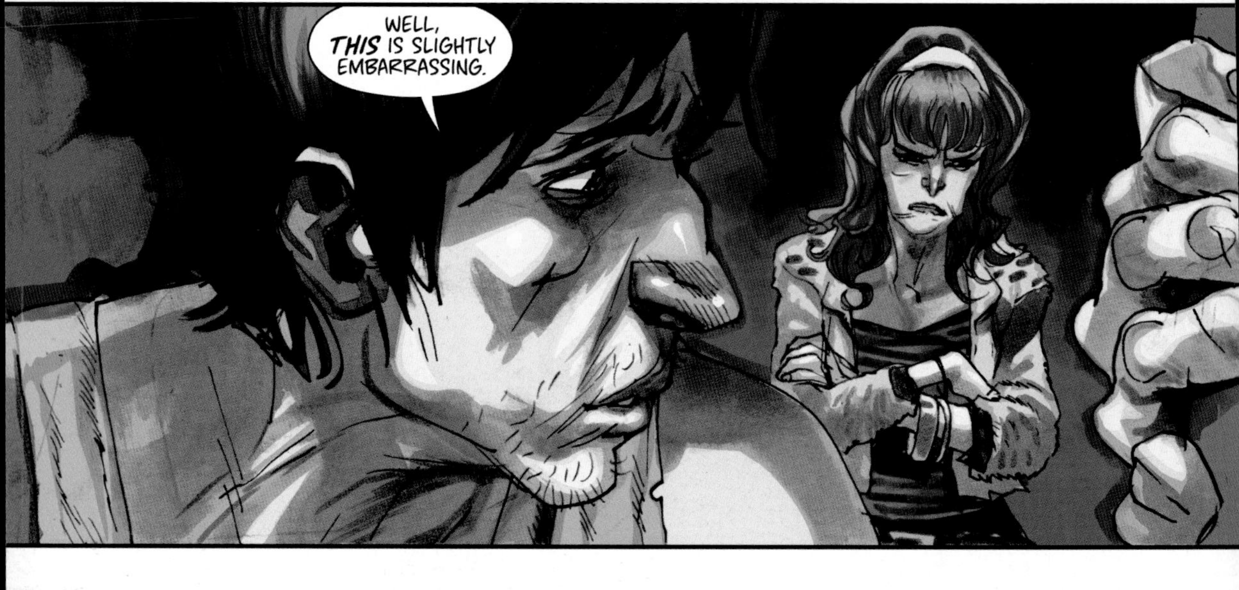
WELL, *THIS* IS SLIGHTLY EMBARRASSING.

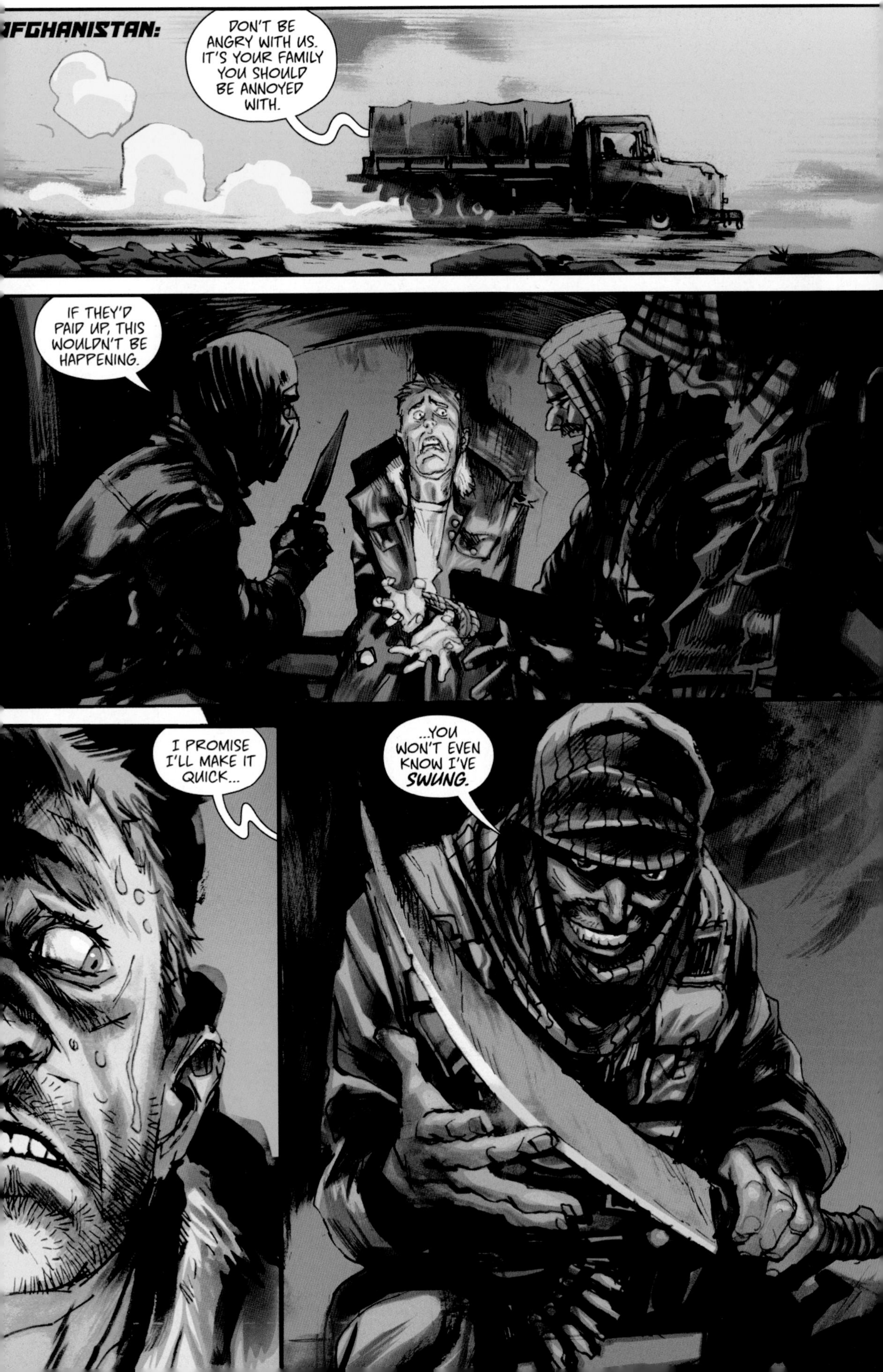
AFGHANISTAN:
DON'T BE ANGRY WITH US. IT'S YOUR FAMILY YOU SHOULD BE ANNOYED WITH.
IF THEY'D PAID UP, THIS WOULDN'T BE HAPPENING.
I PROMISE I'LL MAKE IT QUICK...
...YOU WON'T EVEN KNOW I'VE SWUNG.

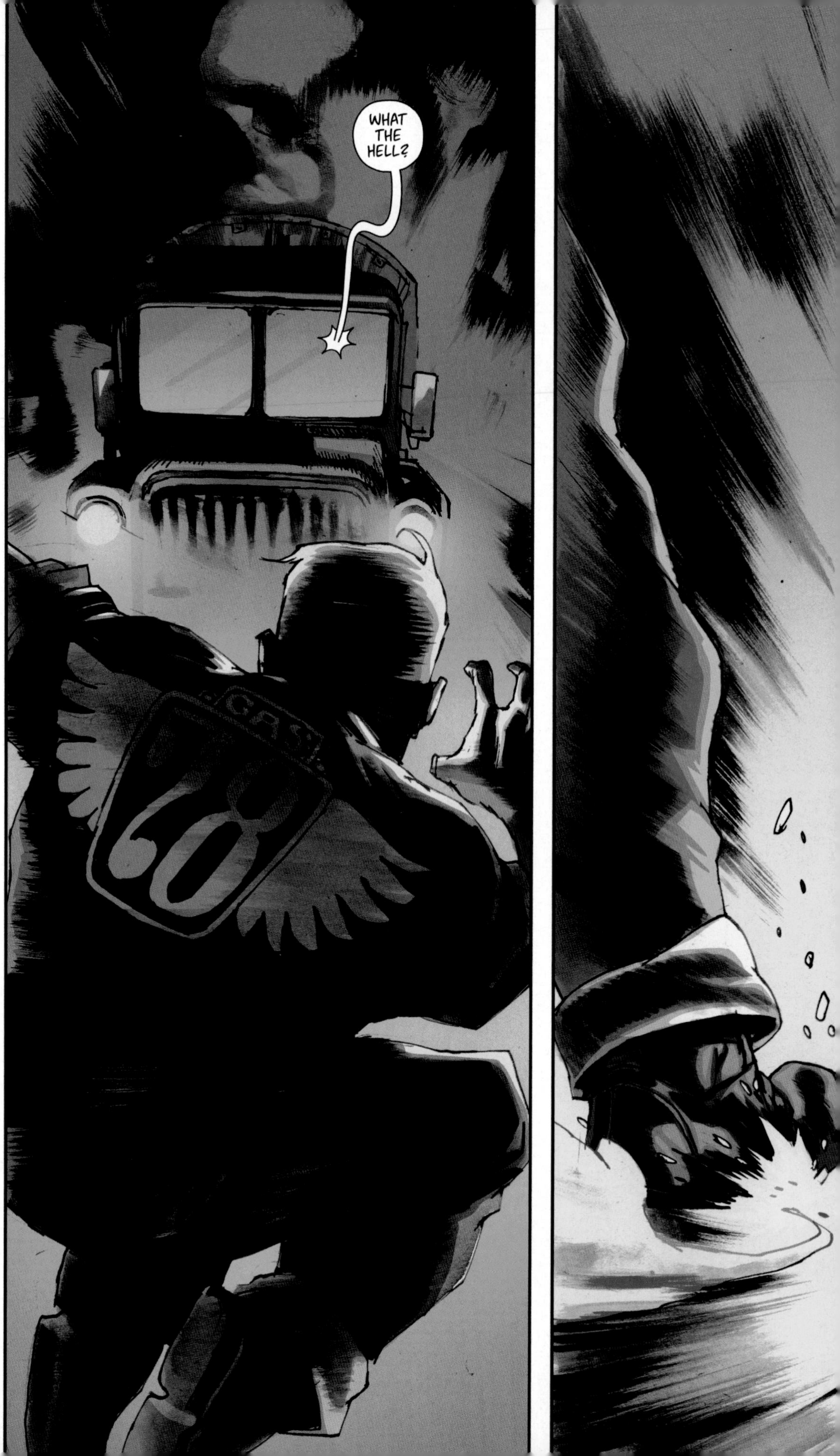
WHAT THE HELL?

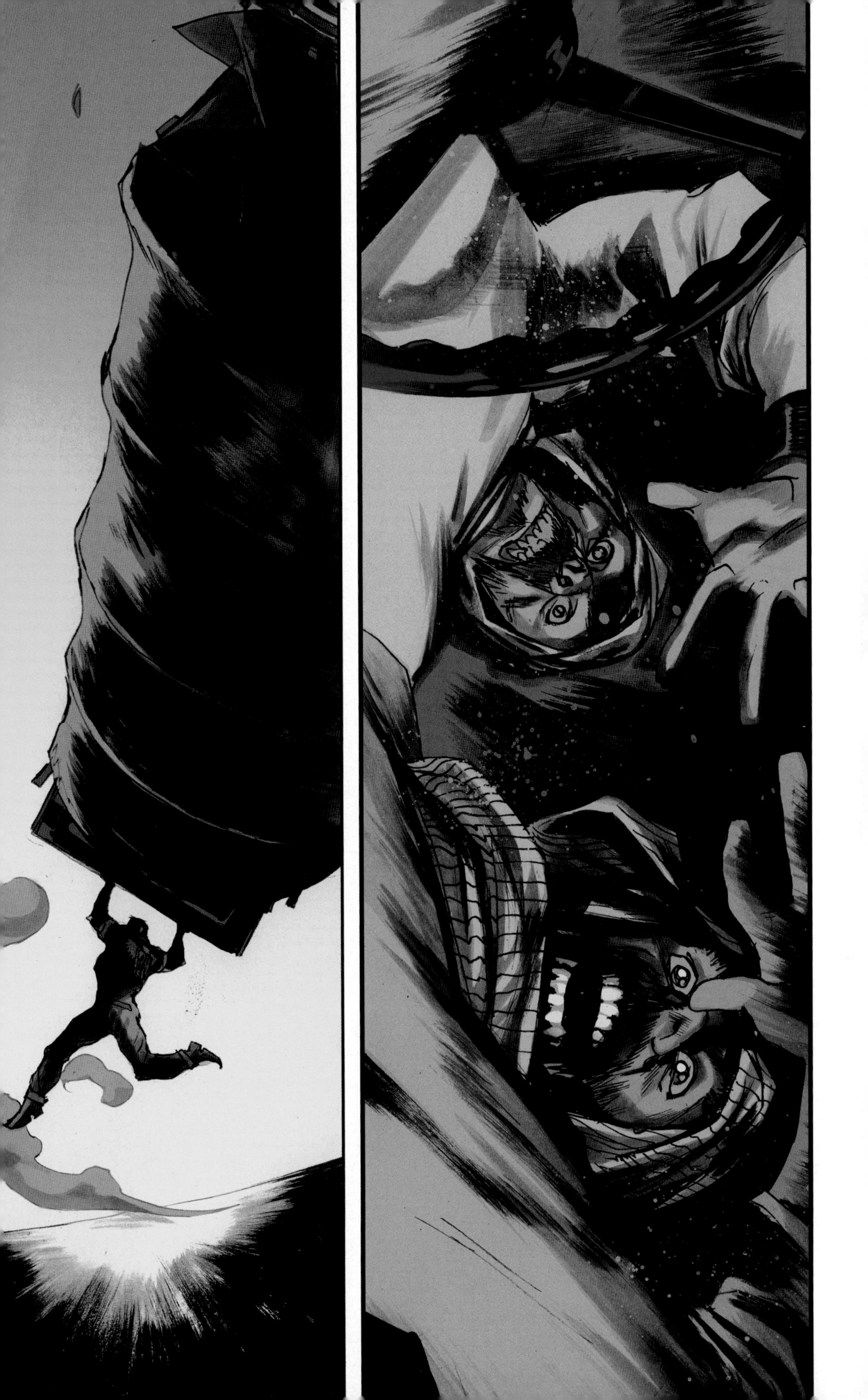

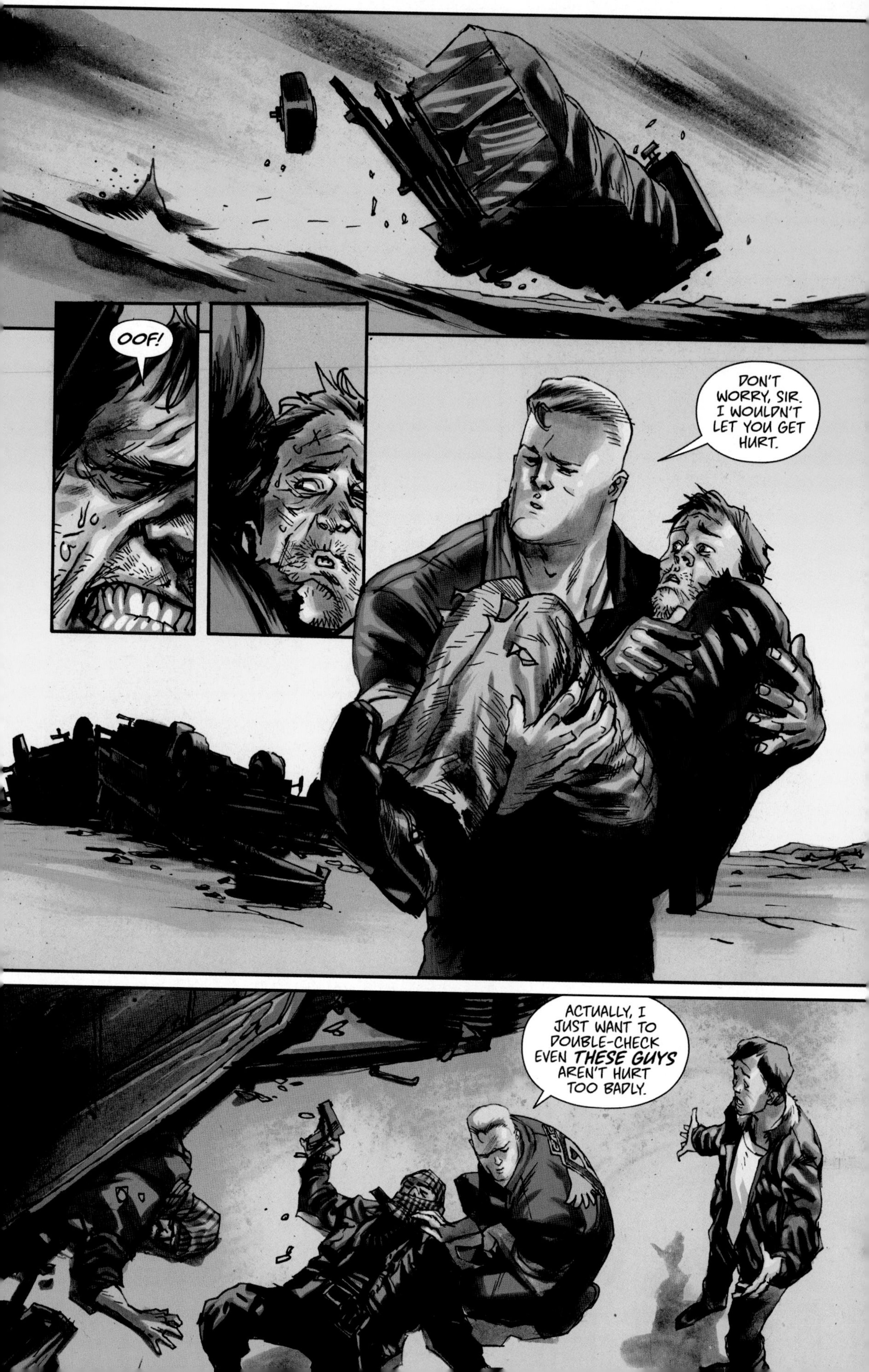
OOF!
DON'T WORRY, SIR. I WOULDN'T LET YOU GET HURT.
ACTUALLY, I JUST WANT TO DOUBLE-CHECK EVEN THESE GUYS AREN'T HURT TOO BADLY.

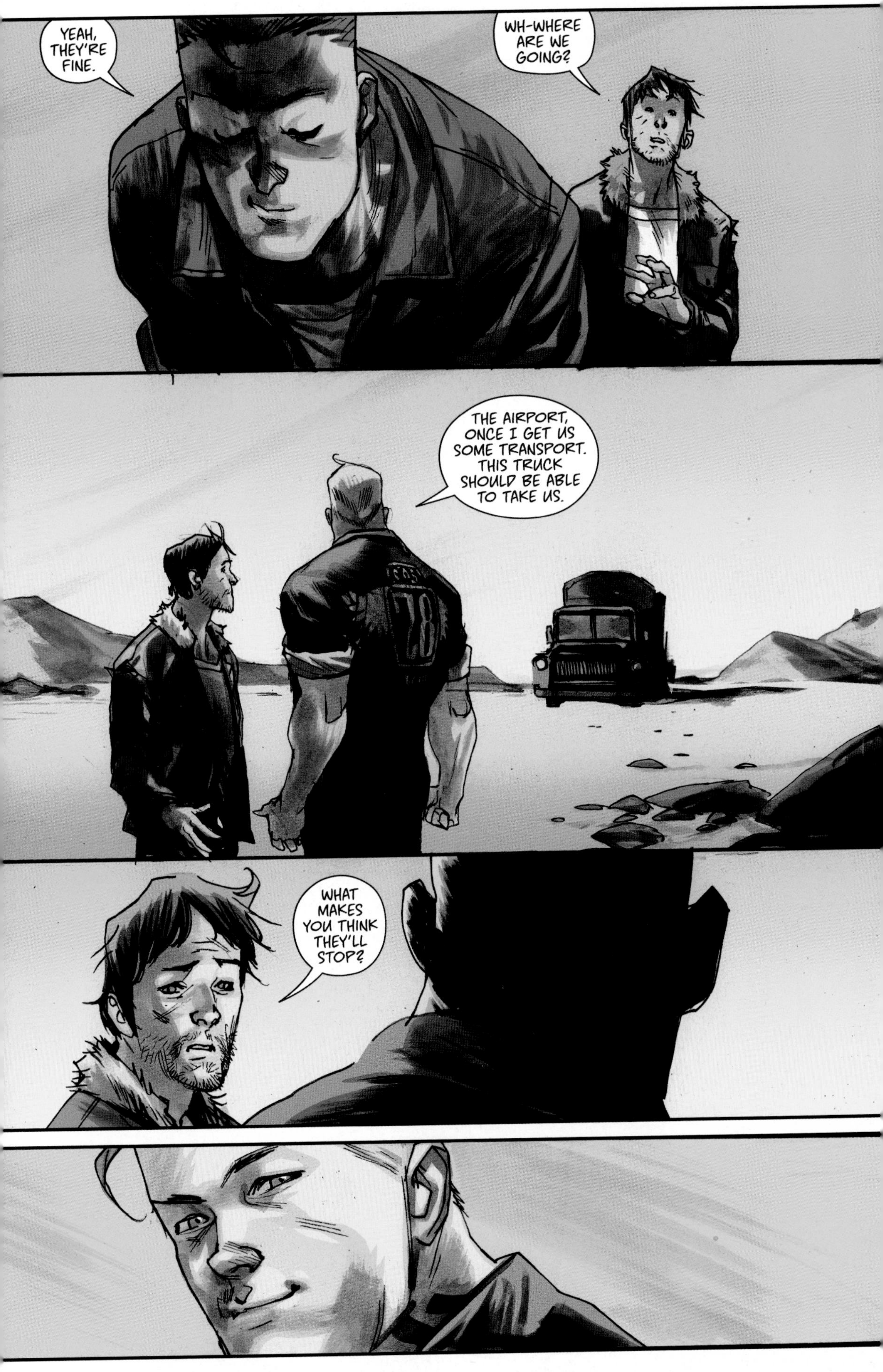
YEAH, THEY'RE FINE.
WH-WHERE ARE WE GOING?
THE AIRPORT, ONCE I GET US SOME TRANSPORT. THIS TRUCK SHOULD BE ABLE TO TAKE US.
WHAT MAKES YOU THINK THEY'LL STOP?

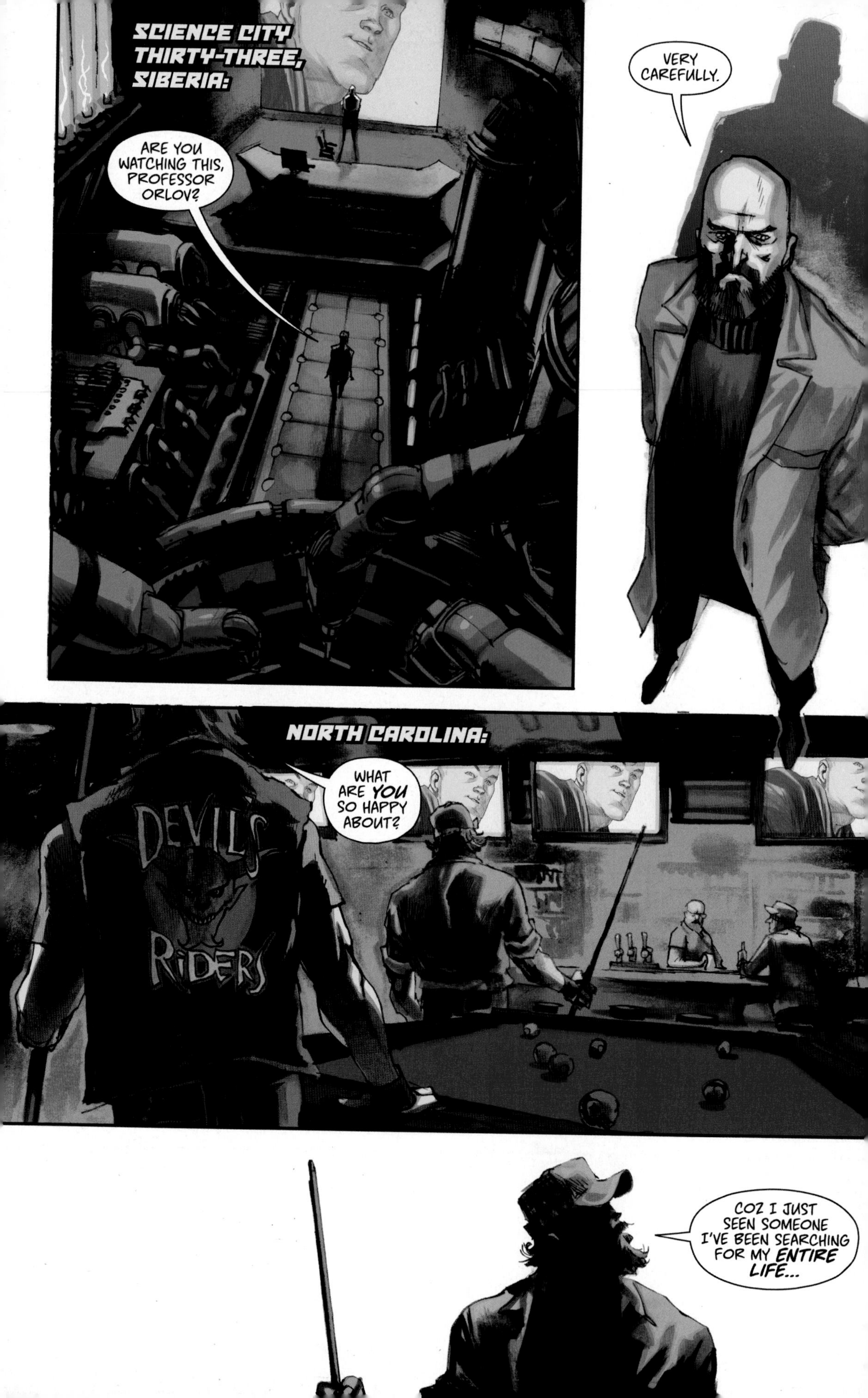
SCIENCE CITY THIRTY-THREE, SIBERIA:
ARE YOU WATCHING THIS, PROFESSOR ORLOV?
VERY CAREFULLY.
NORTH CAROLINA:
DEVILS RIDERS
WHAT ARE YOU SO HAPPY ABOUT?
COZ I JUST SEEN SOMEONE I'VE BEEN SEARCHING FOR MY ENTIRE LIFE...

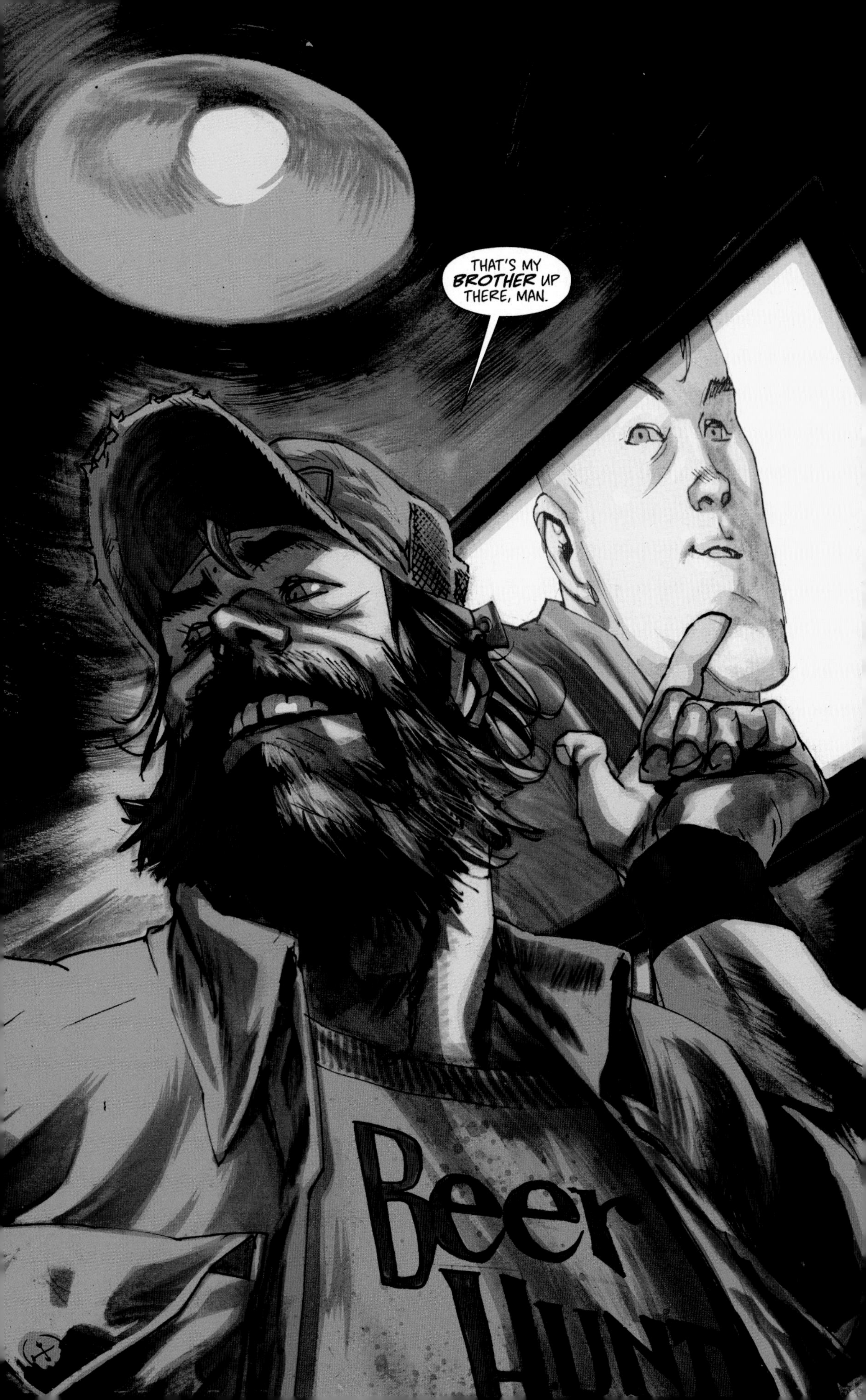
THAT'S MY **BROTHER** UP THERE, MAN.
Beer

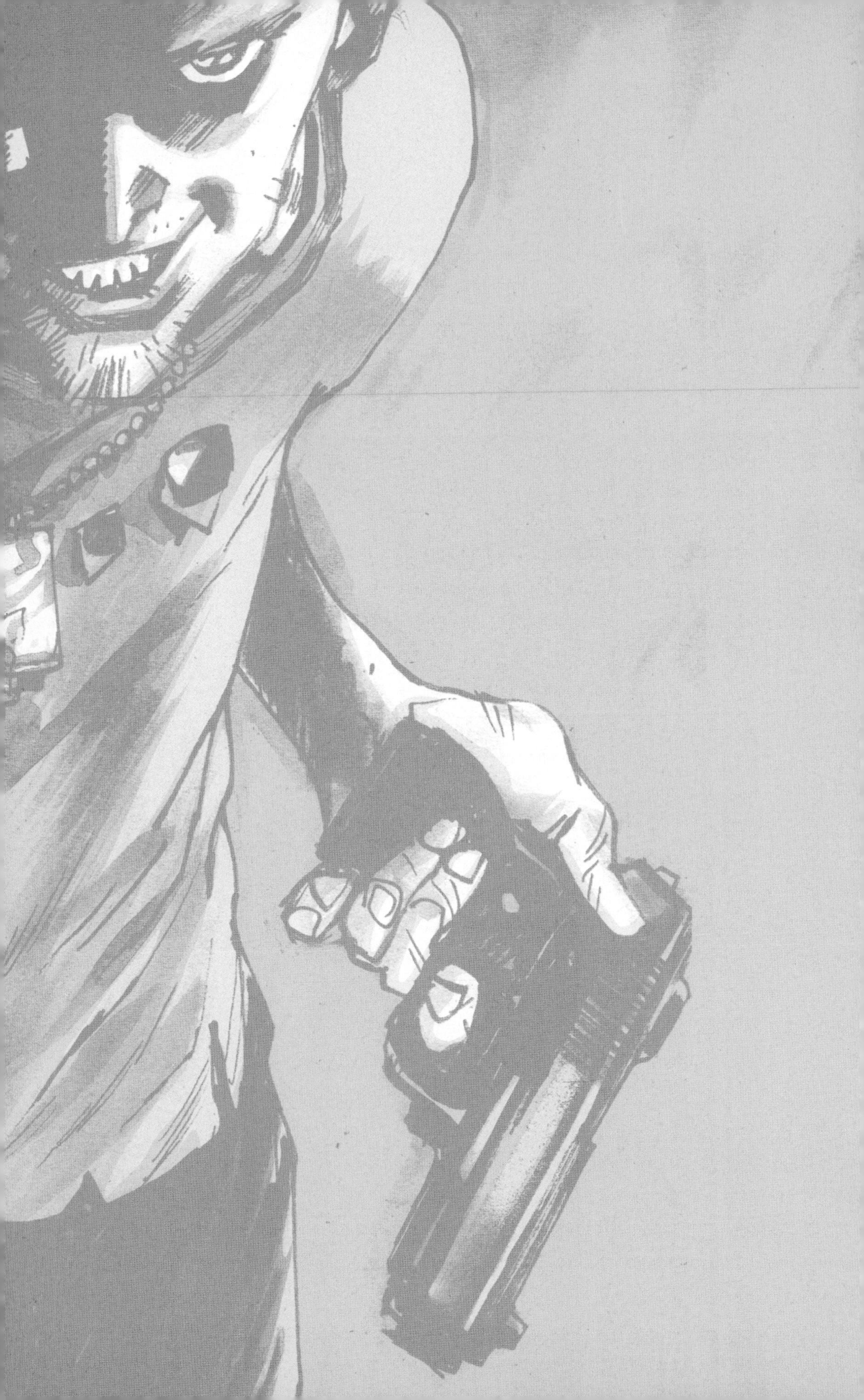

THREE

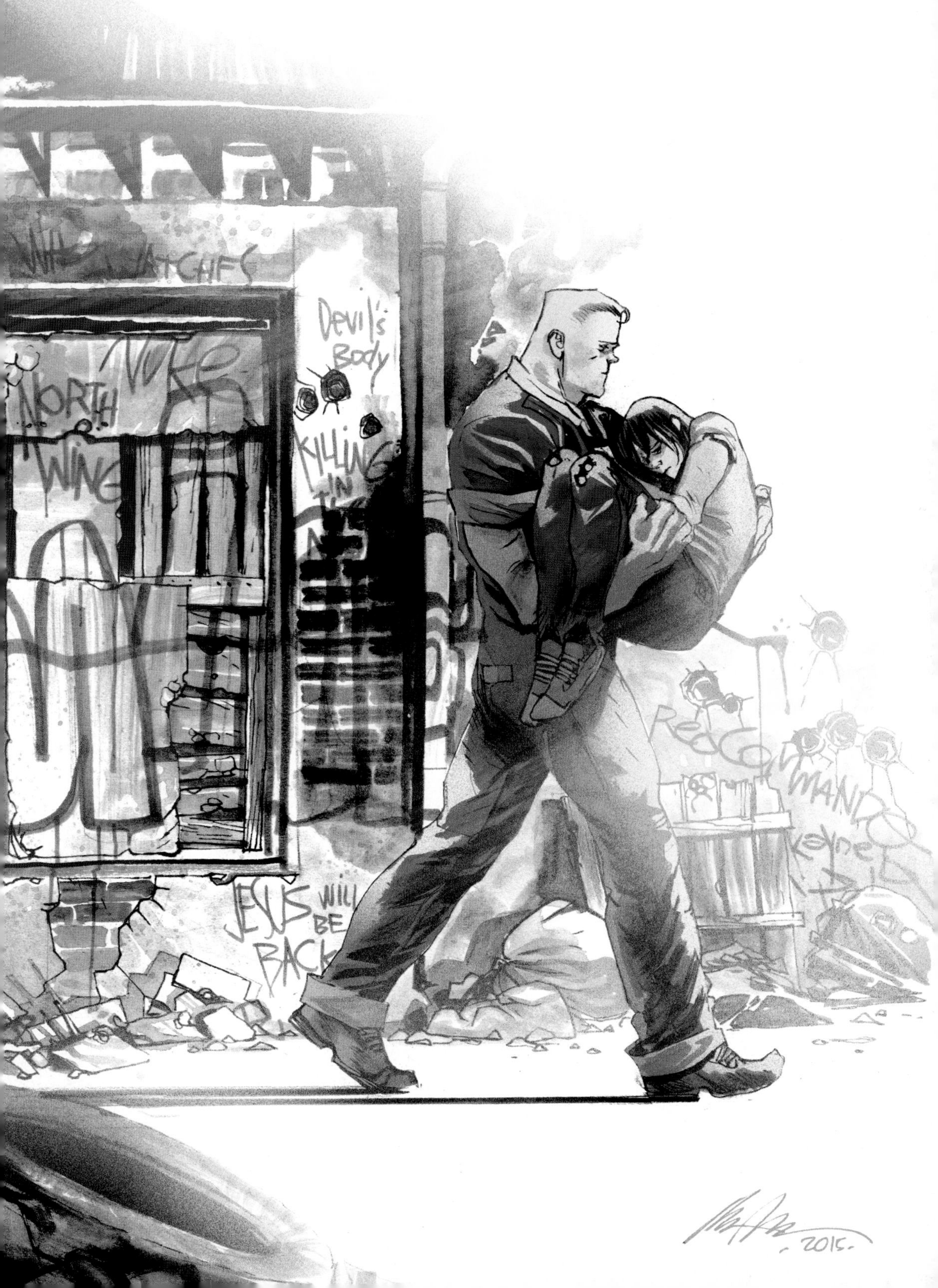
Devil's Body
NORTH
WING
KILLING IN
JESUS WILL BE BACK
2015

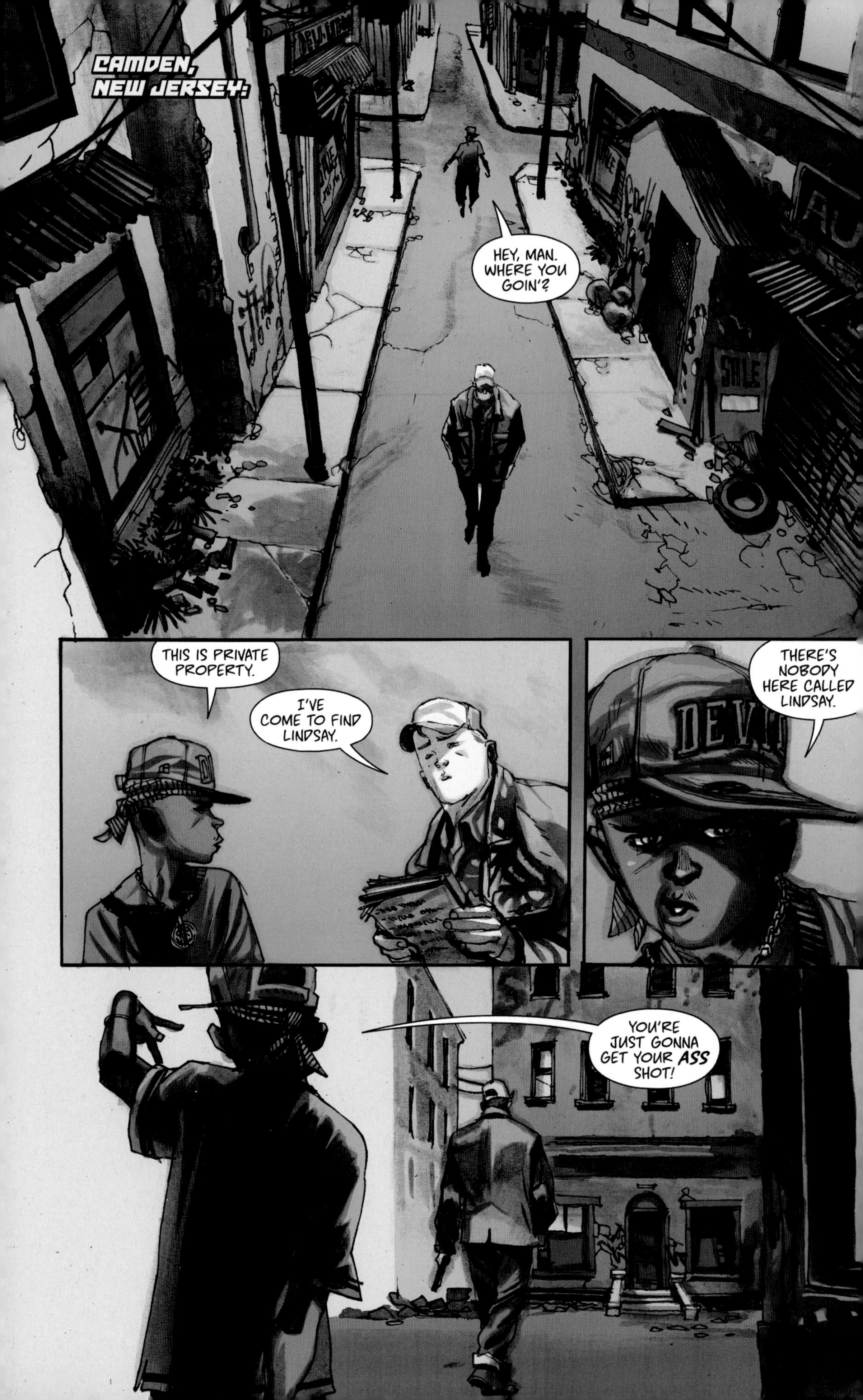
CAMDEN, NEW JERSEY:
HEY, MAN. WHERE YOU GOIN'?
THIS IS PRIVATE PROPERTY.
I'VE COME TO FIND LINDSAY.
THERE'S NOBODY HERE CALLED LINDSAY.
YOU'RE JUST GONNA GET YOUR ASS SHOT!

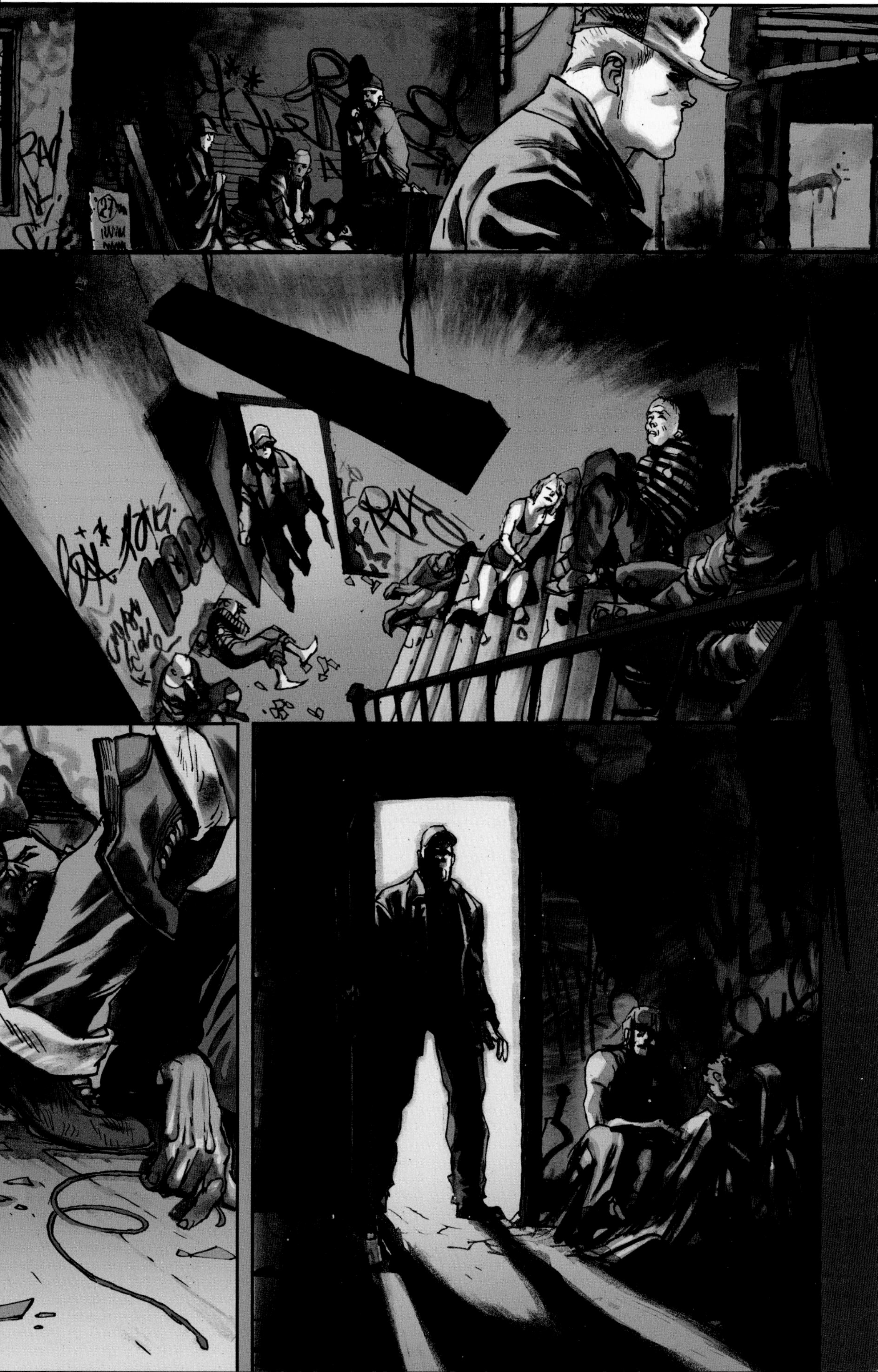

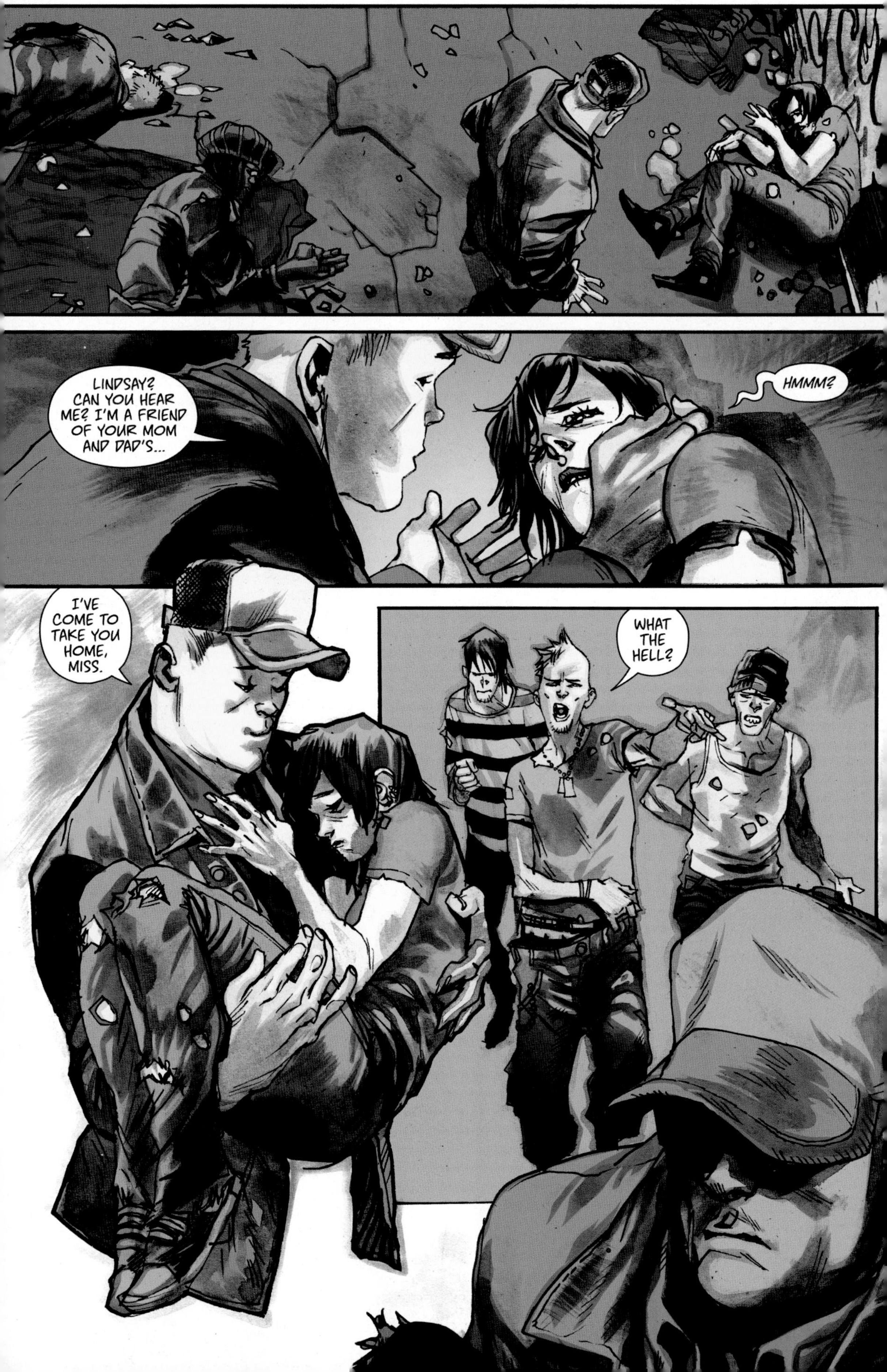
LINDSAY? CAN YOU HEAR ME? I'M A FRIEND OF YOUR MOM AND DAD'S...
HMMM?
I'VE COME TO TAKE YOU HOME, MISS.
WHAT THE HELL?

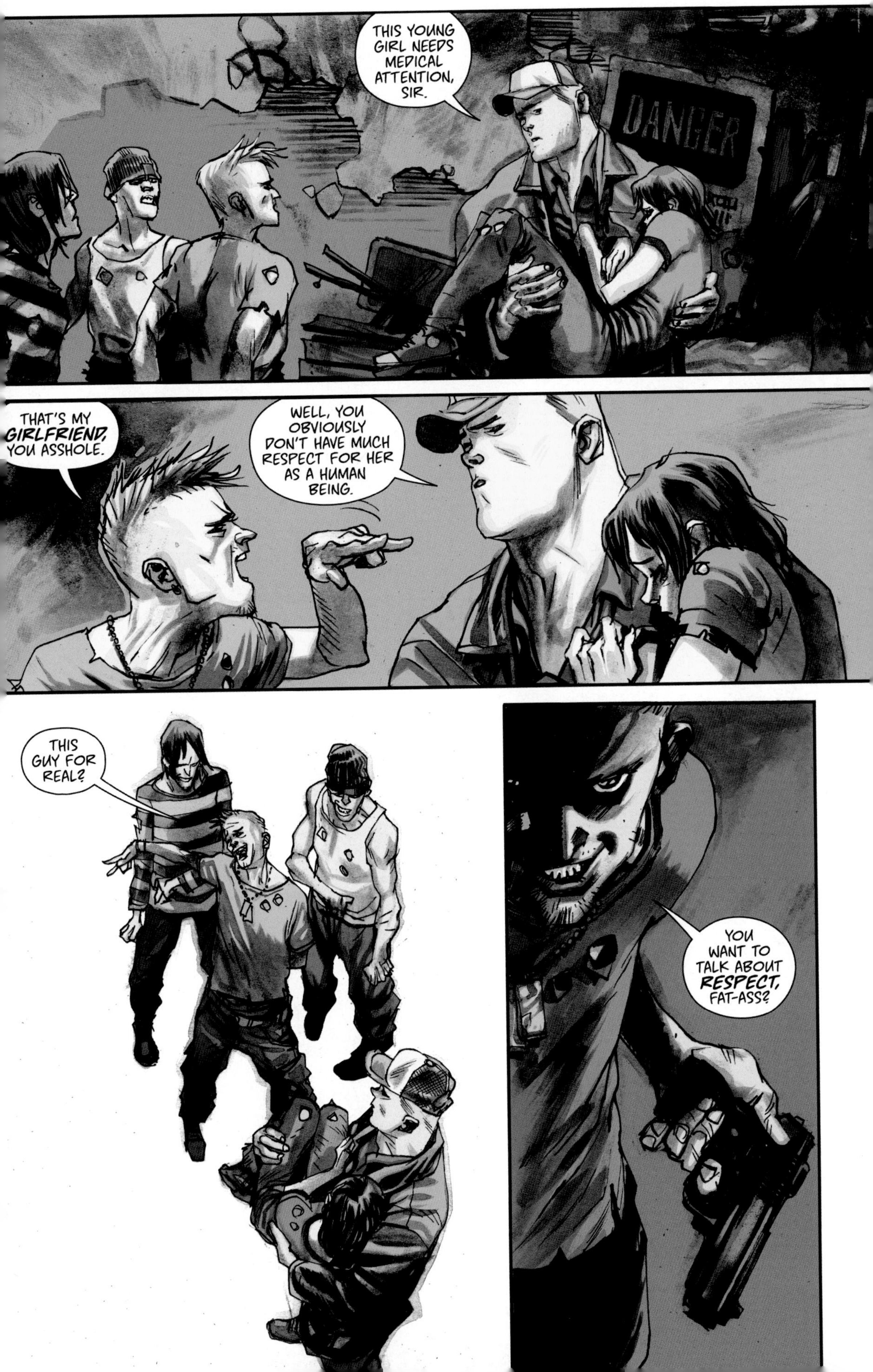
THIS YOUNG GIRL NEEDS MEDICAL ATTENTION, SIR.
DANGER
THAT'S MY GIRLFRIEND, YOU ASSHOLE.
WELL, YOU OBVIOUSLY DON'T HAVE MUCH RESPECT FOR HER AS A HUMAN BEING.
THIS GUY FOR REAL?
YOU WANT TO TALK ABOUT RESPECT, FAT-ASS?

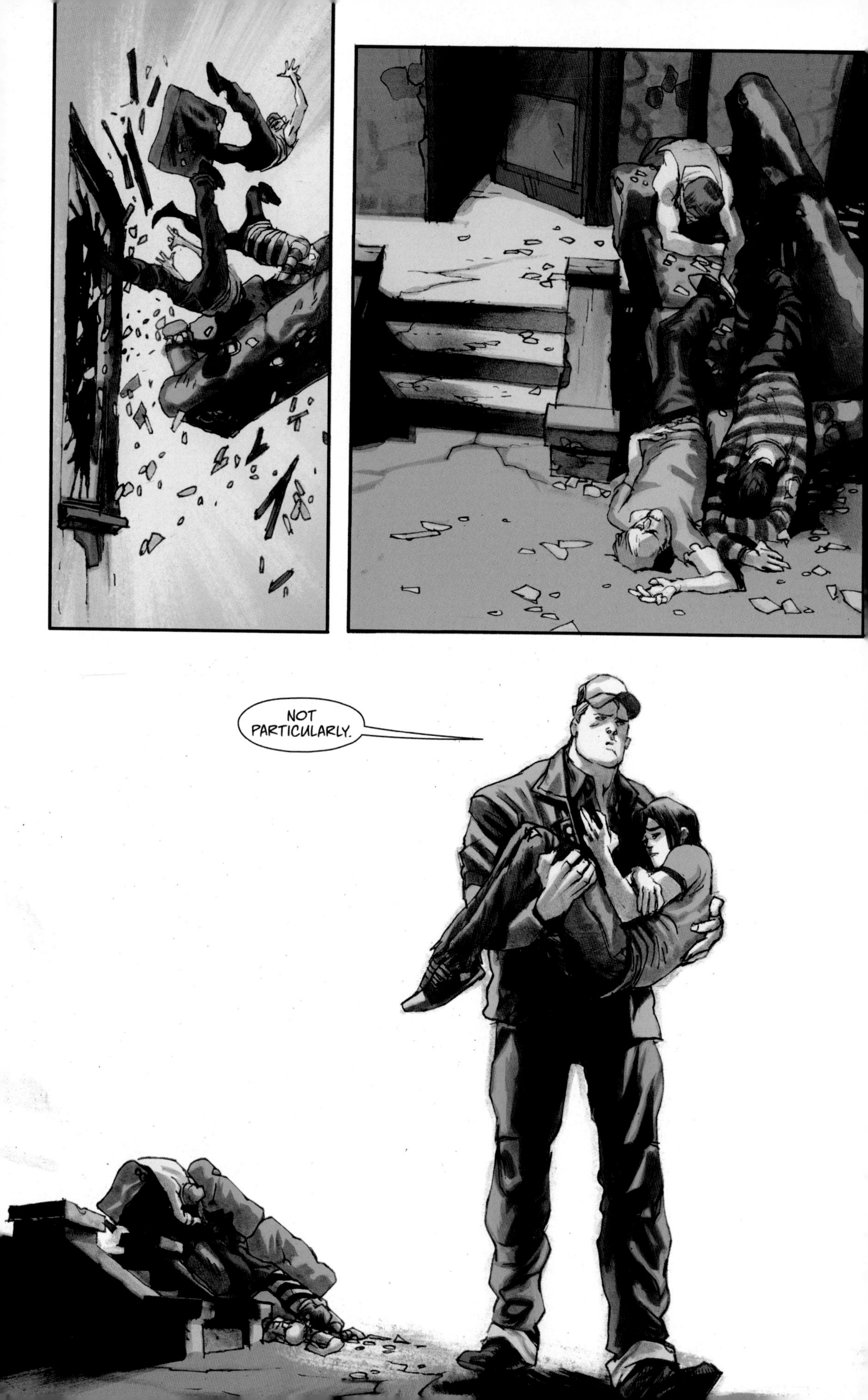
NOT PARTICULARLY.

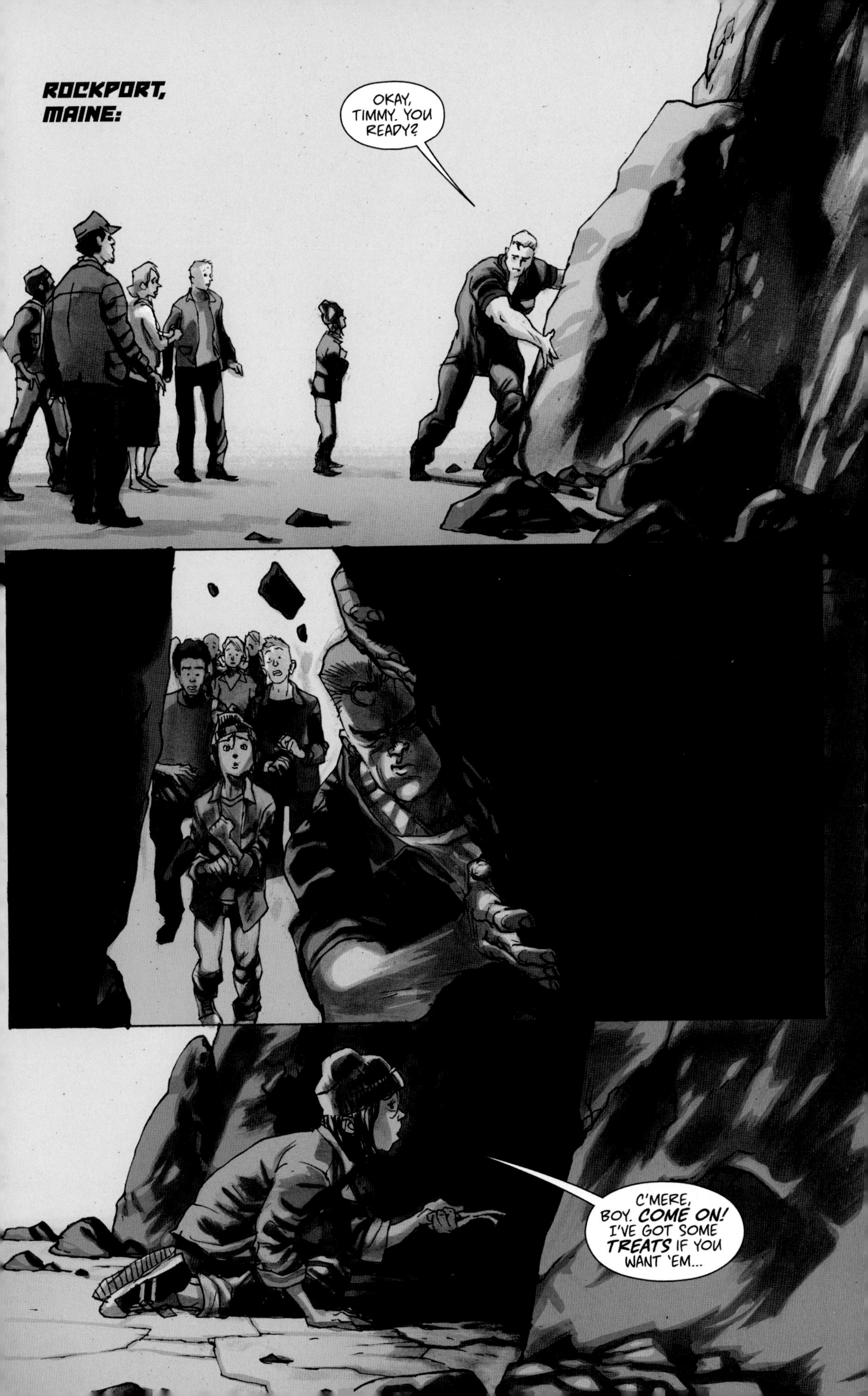
ROCKPORT, MAINE:
OKAY, TIMMY. YOU READY?
C'MERE, BOY. COME ON! I'VE GOT SOME TREATS IF YOU WANT 'EM...

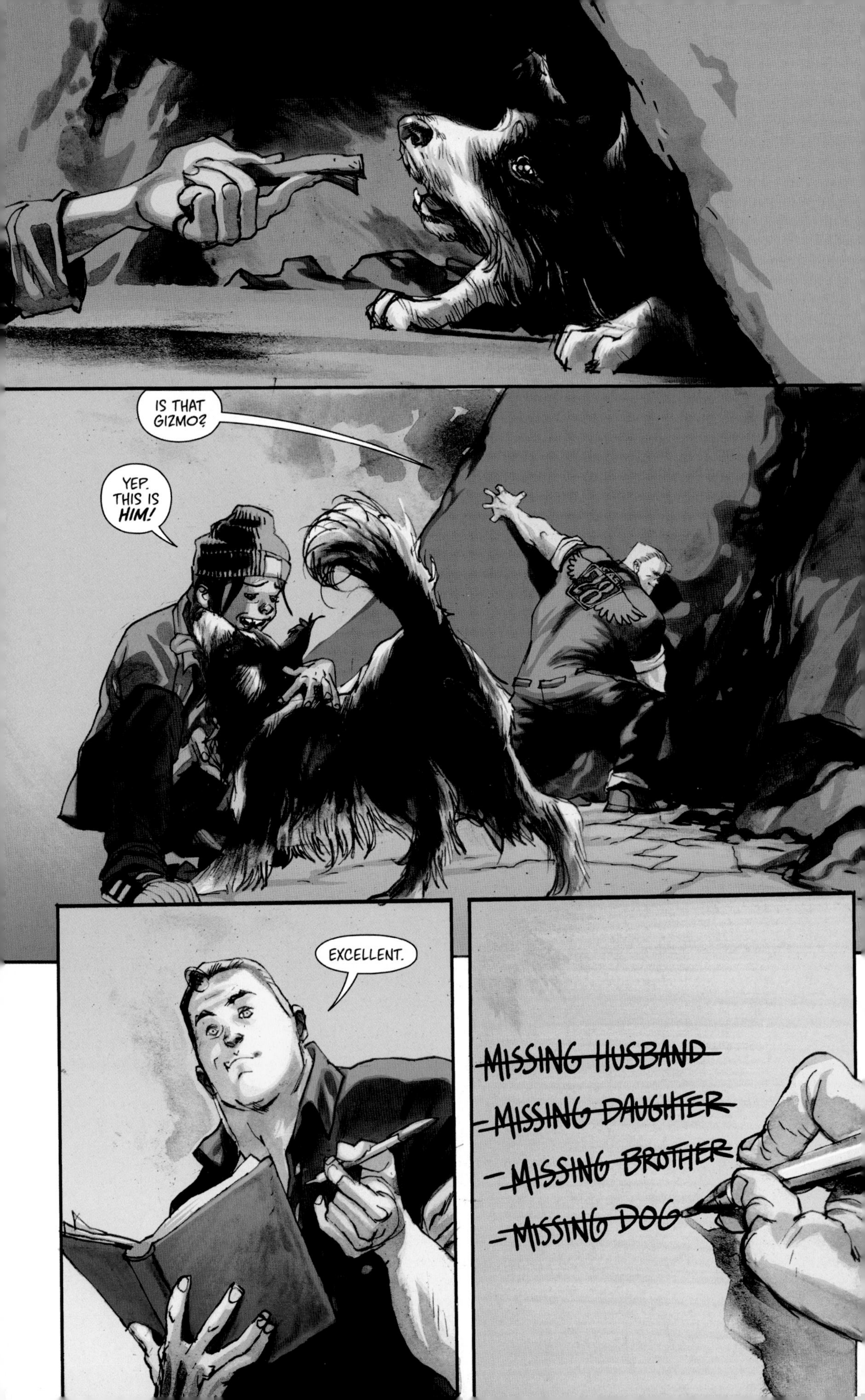
IS THAT GIZMO?
YEP. THIS IS *HIM!*
EXCELLENT.
~~MISSING HUSBAND~~
~~MISSING DAUGHTER~~
~~MISSING BROTHER~~
~~MISSING DOG~~

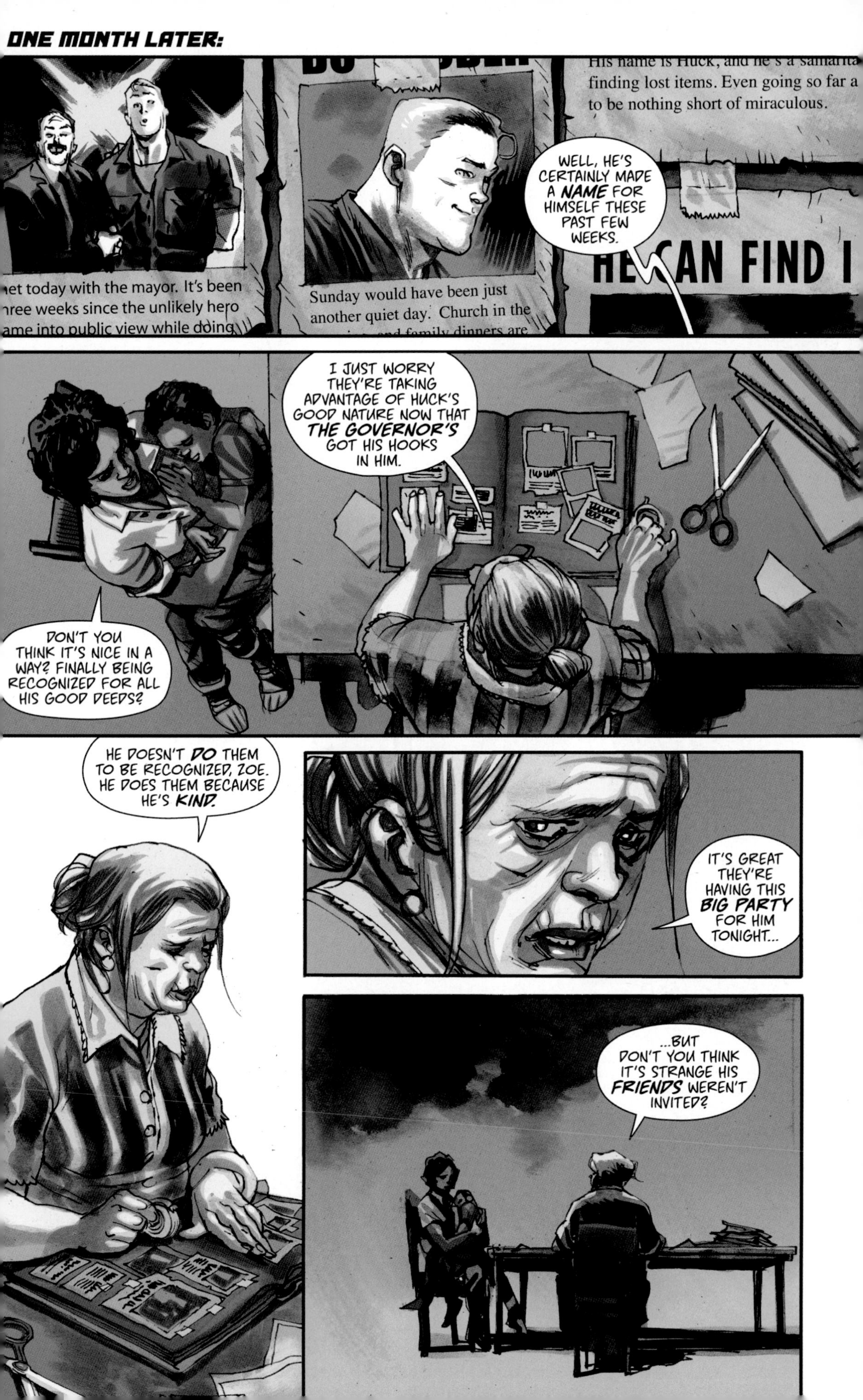
ONE MONTH LATER:
His name is Huck, and he's a samarita
finding lost items. Even going so far a
to be nothing short of miraculous.
WELL, HE'S CERTAINLY MADE A NAME FOR HIMSELF THESE PAST FEW WEEKS.
HE CAN FIND I
met today with the mayor. It's been
hree weeks since the unlikely hero
ame into public view while doing
Sunday would have been just
another quiet day. Church in the
I JUST WORRY THEY'RE TAKING ADVANTAGE OF HUCK'S GOOD NATURE NOW THAT THE GOVERNOR'S GOT HIS HOOKS IN HIM.
DON'T YOU THINK IT'S NICE IN A WAY? FINALLY BEING RECOGNIZED FOR ALL HIS GOOD DEEDS?
HE DOESN'T DO THEM TO BE RECOGNIZED, ZOE. HE DOES THEM BECAUSE HE'S KIND.
IT'S GREAT THEY'RE HAVING THIS BIG PARTY FOR HIM TONIGHT...
...BUT DON'T YOU THINK IT'S STRANGE HIS FRIENDS WEREN'T INVITED?

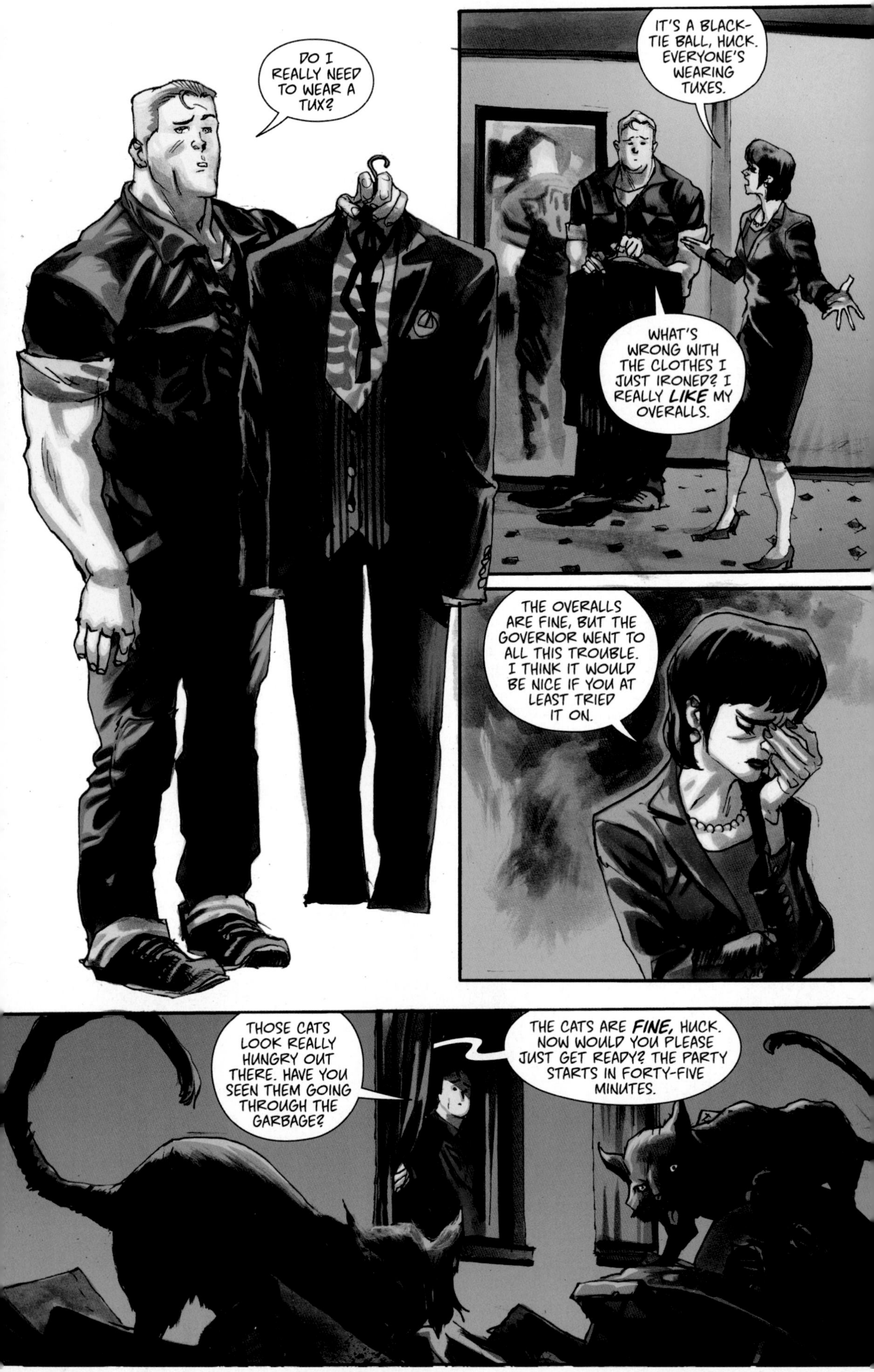
DO I REALLY NEED TO WEAR A TUX?
IT'S A BLACK-TIE BALL, HUCK. EVERYONE'S WEARING TUXES.
WHAT'S WRONG WITH THE CLOTHES I JUST IRONED? I REALLY **LIKE** MY OVERALLS.
THE OVERALLS ARE FINE, BUT THE GOVERNOR WENT TO ALL THIS TROUBLE. I THINK IT WOULD BE NICE IF YOU AT LEAST TRIED IT ON.
THOSE CATS LOOK REALLY HUNGRY OUT THERE. HAVE YOU SEEN THEM GOING THROUGH THE GARBAGE?
THE CATS ARE ***FINE,*** HUCK. NOW WOULD YOU PLEASE JUST GET READY? THE PARTY STARTS IN FORTY-FIVE MINUTES.

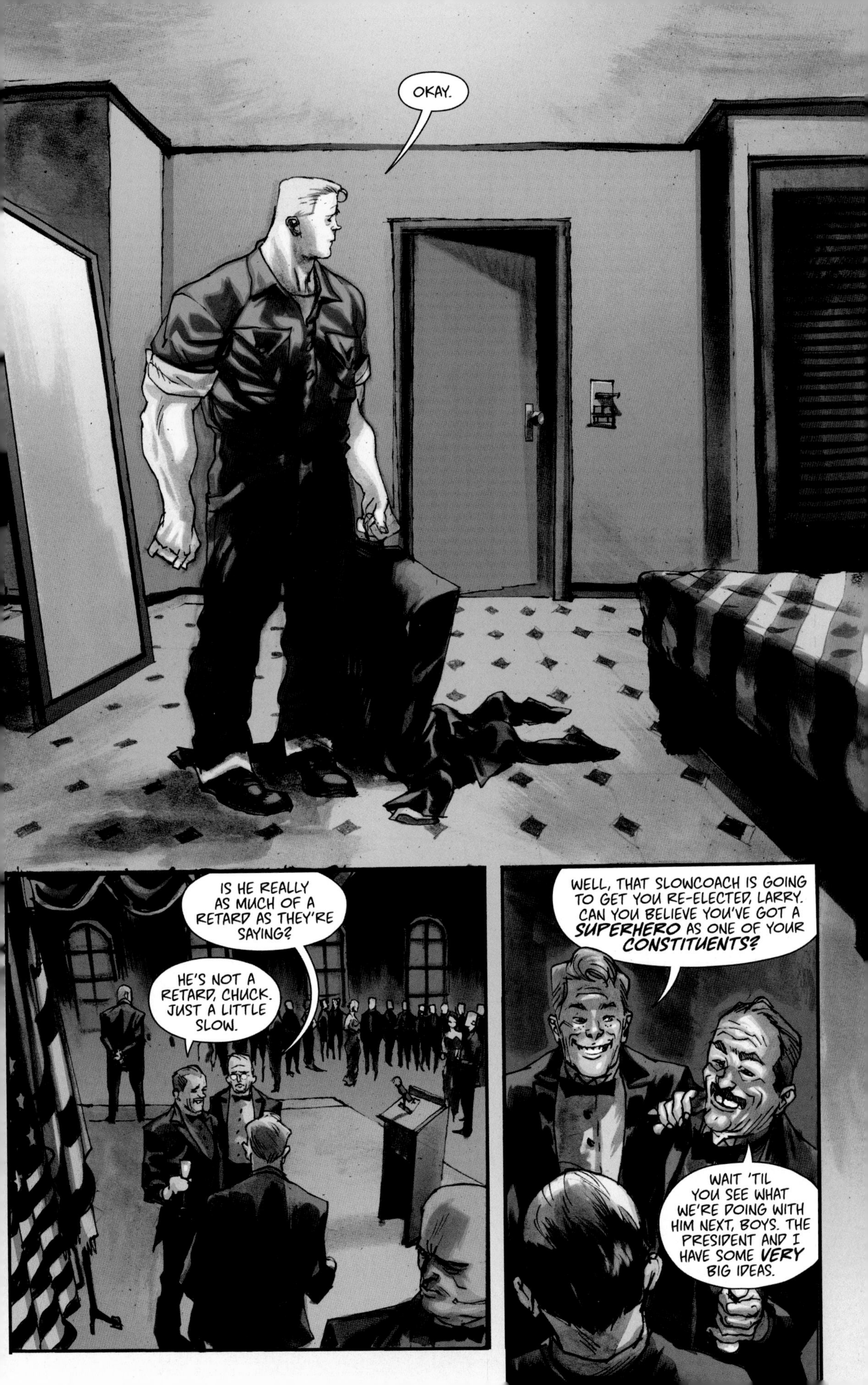
OKAY.
IS HE REALLY AS MUCH OF A RETARD AS THEY'RE SAYING?
HE'S NOT A RETARD, CHUCK. JUST A LITTLE SLOW.
WELL, THAT SLOWCOACH IS GOING TO GET YOU RE-ELECTED, LARRY. CAN YOU BELIEVE YOU'VE GOT A SUPERHERO AS ONE OF YOUR CONSTITUENTS?
WAIT 'TIL YOU SEE WHAT WE'RE DOING WITH HIM NEXT, BOYS. THE PRESIDENT AND I HAVE SOME VERY BIG IDEAS.

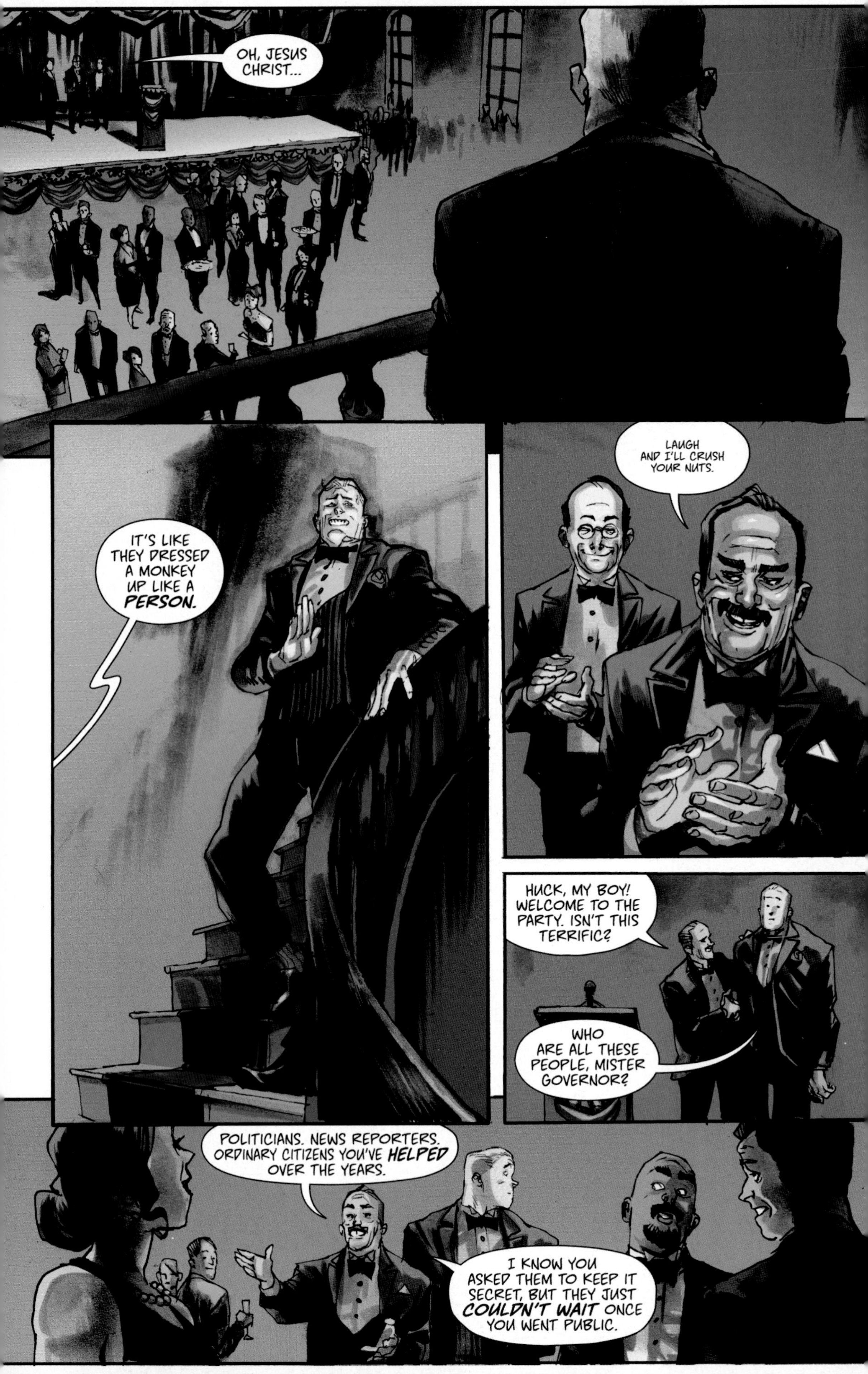
OH, JESUS CHRIST...
IT'S LIKE THEY DRESSED A MONKEY UP LIKE A PERSON.
LAUGH AND I'LL CRUSH YOUR NUTS.
HUCK, MY BOY! WELCOME TO THE PARTY. ISN'T THIS TERRIFIC?
WHO ARE ALL THESE PEOPLE, MISTER GOVERNOR?
POLITICIANS. NEWS REPORTERS. ORDINARY CITIZENS YOU'VE HELPED OVER THE YEARS.
I KNOW YOU ASKED THEM TO KEEP IT SECRET, BUT THEY JUST COULDN'T WAIT ONCE YOU WENT PUBLIC.

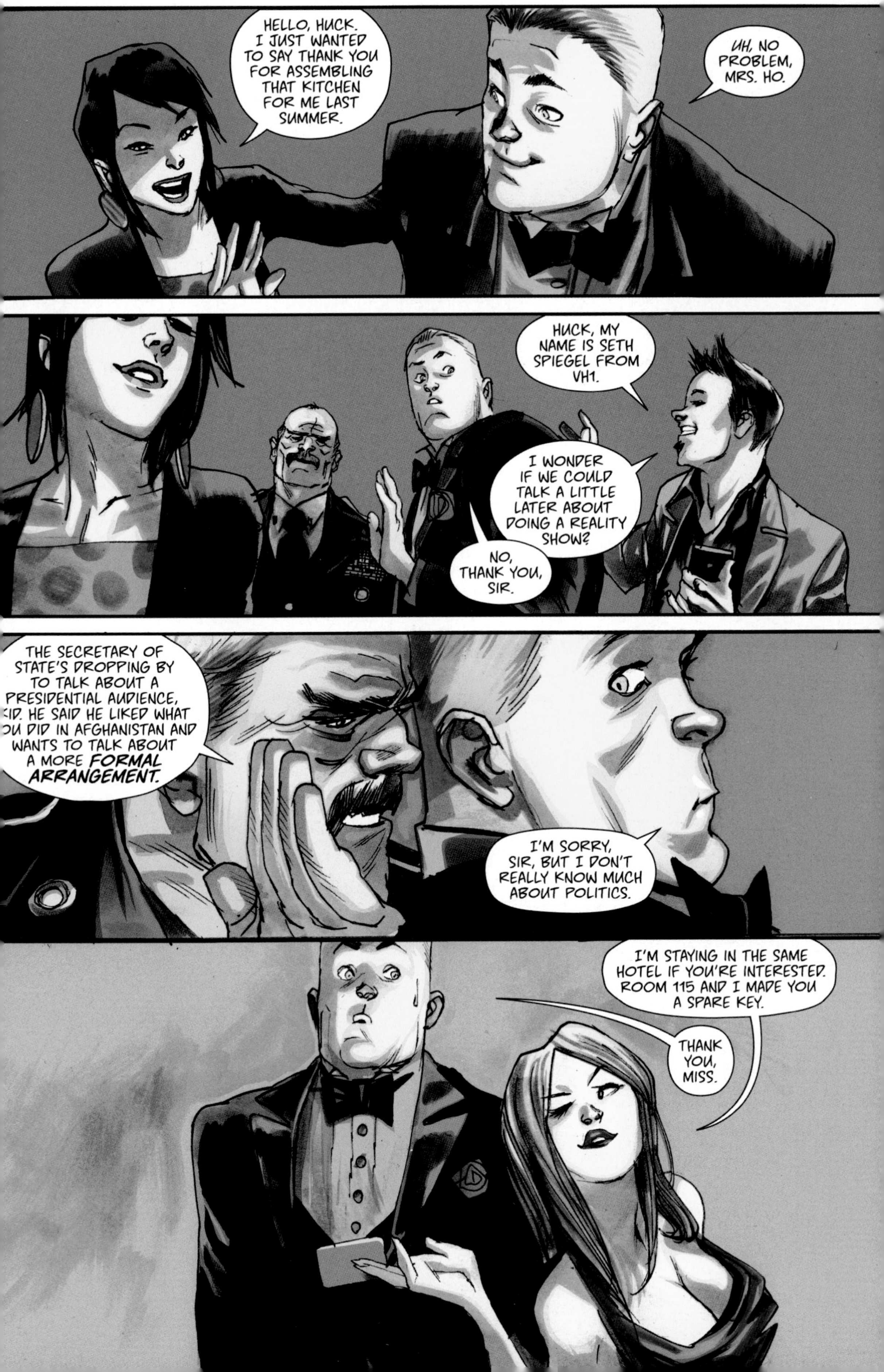
HELLO, HUCK. I JUST WANTED TO SAY THANK YOU FOR ASSEMBLING THAT KITCHEN FOR ME LAST SUMMER.
UH, NO PROBLEM, MRS. HO.
HUCK, MY NAME IS SETH SPIEGEL FROM VH1.
I WONDER IF WE COULD TALK A LITTLE LATER ABOUT DOING A REALITY SHOW?
NO, THANK YOU, SIR.
THE SECRETARY OF STATE'S DROPPING BY TO TALK ABOUT A PRESIDENTIAL AUDIENCE, ID. HE SAID HE LIKED WHAT OU DID IN AFGHANISTAN AND WANTS TO TALK ABOUT A MORE *FORMAL ARRANGEMENT.*
I'M SORRY, SIR, BUT I DON'T REALLY KNOW MUCH ABOUT POLITICS.
I'M STAYING IN THE SAME HOTEL IF YOU'RE INTERESTED. ROOM 115 AND I MADE YOU A SPARE KEY.
THANK YOU, MISS.

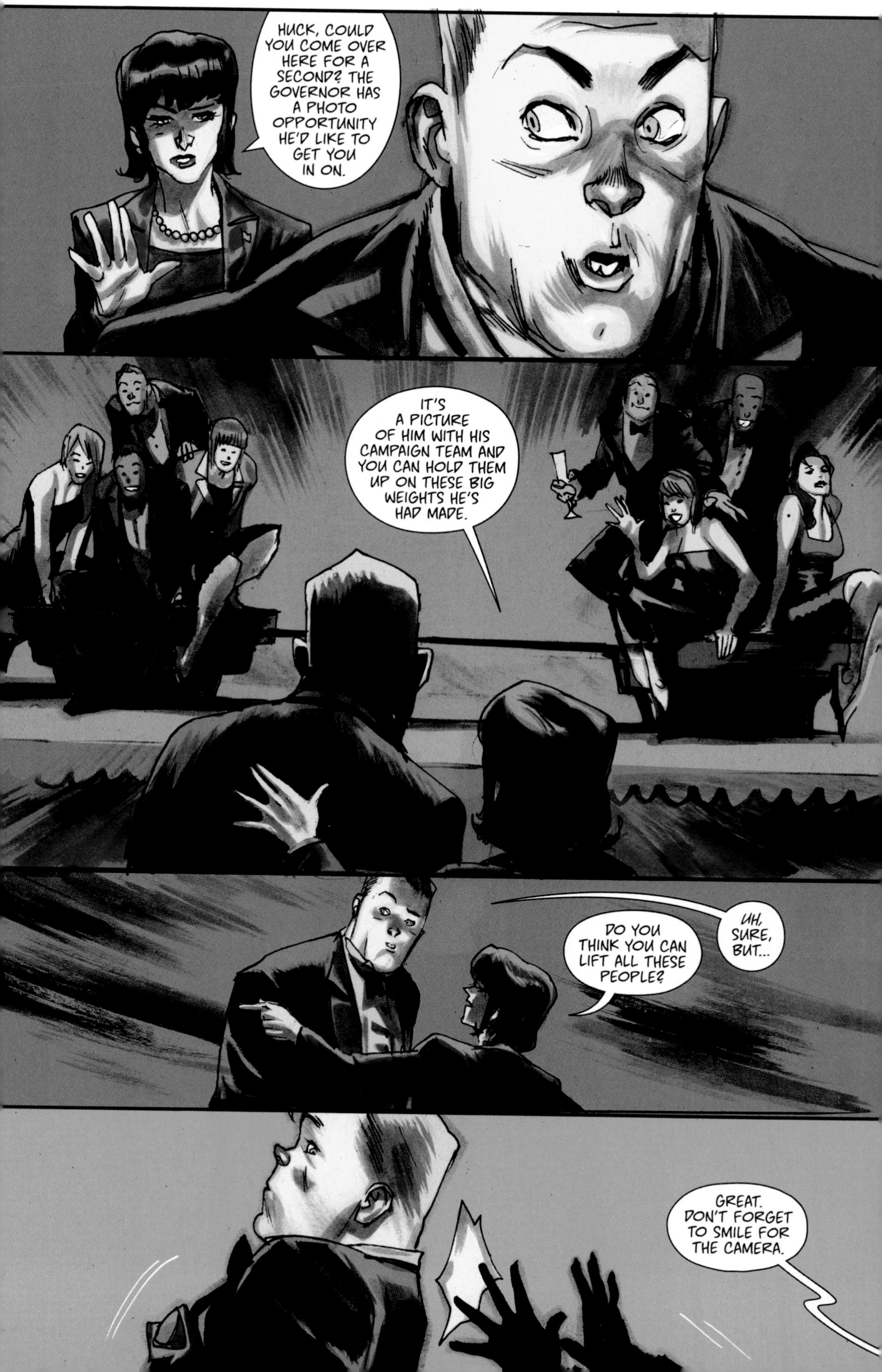
HUCK, COULD YOU COME OVER HERE FOR A SECOND? THE GOVERNOR HAS A PHOTO OPPORTUNITY HE'D LIKE TO GET YOU IN ON.
IT'S A PICTURE OF HIM WITH HIS CAMPAIGN TEAM AND YOU CAN HOLD THEM UP ON THESE BIG WEIGHTS HE'S HAD MADE.
DO YOU THINK YOU CAN LIFT ALL THESE PEOPLE?
UH, SURE, BUT...
GREAT. DON'T FORGET TO SMILE FOR THE CAMERA.

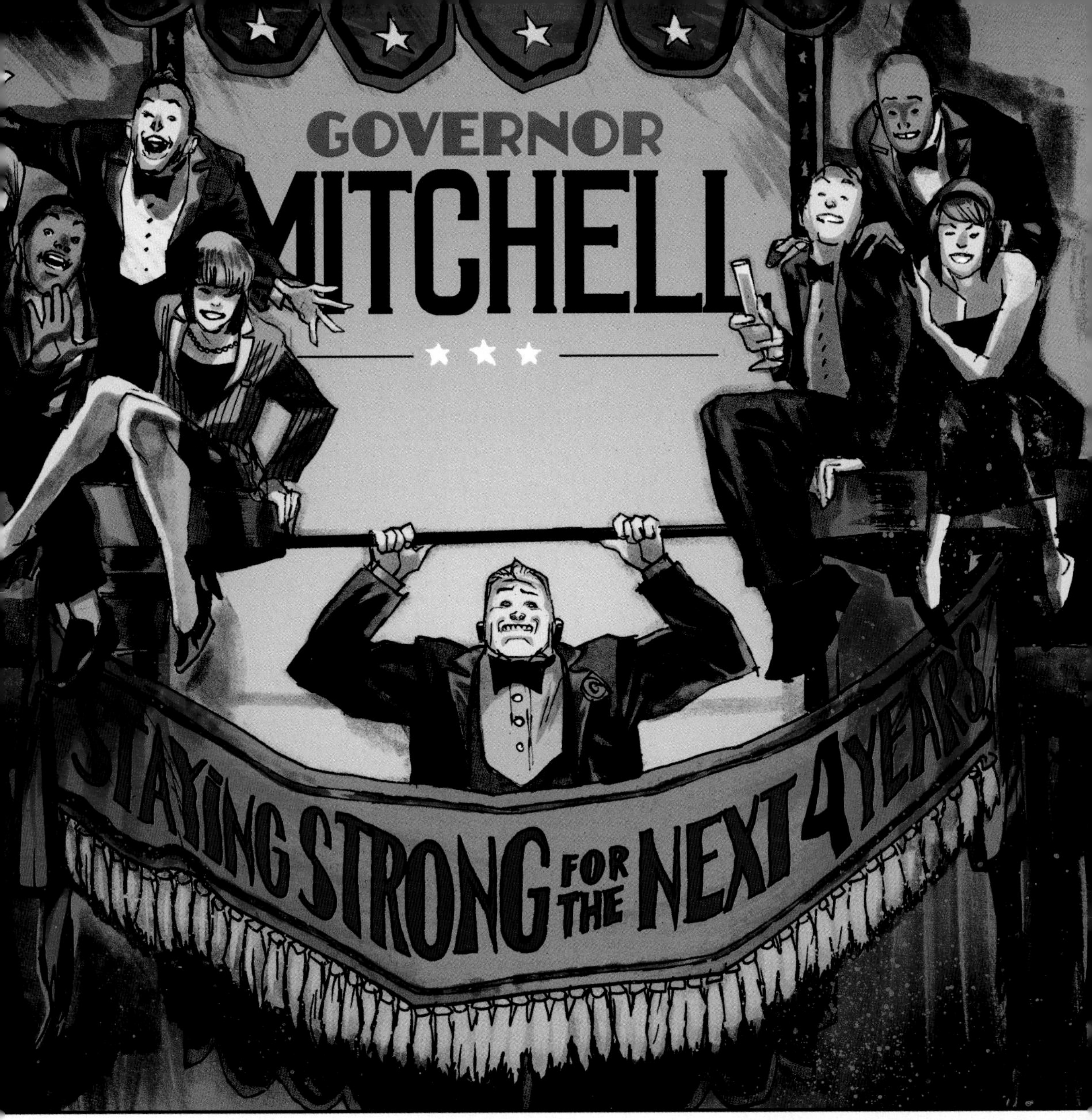
GOVERNOR
MITCHELL
STAYING STRONG FOR THE NEXT 4 YEARS

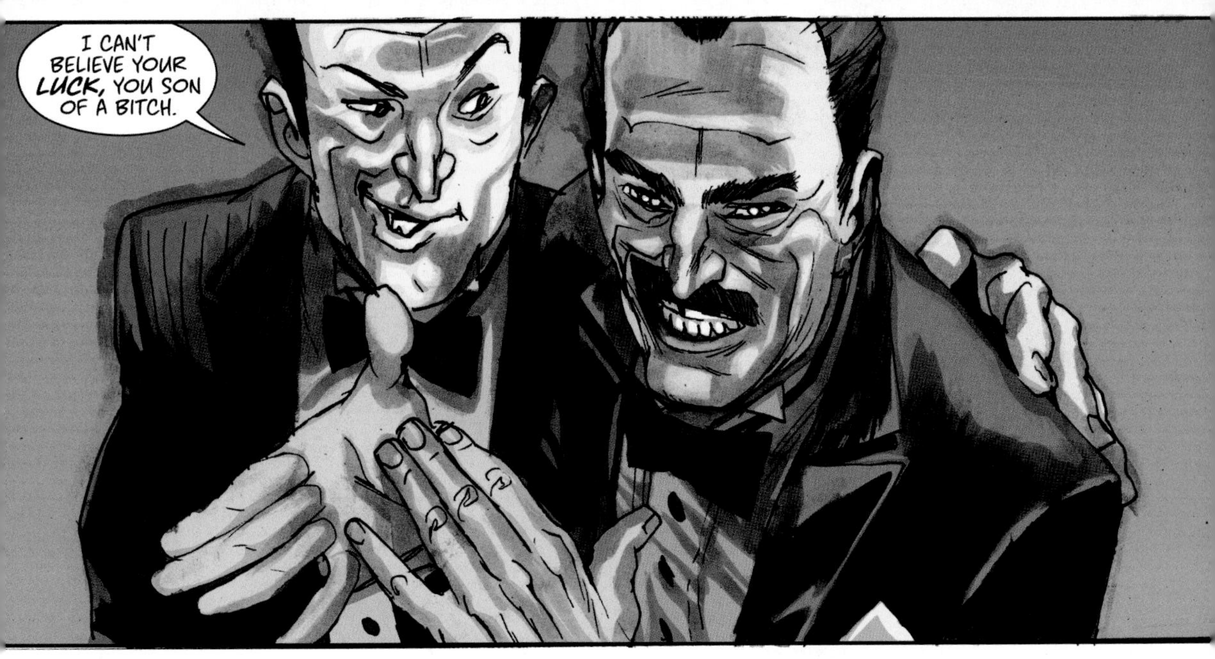
I CAN'T BELIEVE YOUR LUCK, YOU SON OF A BITCH.

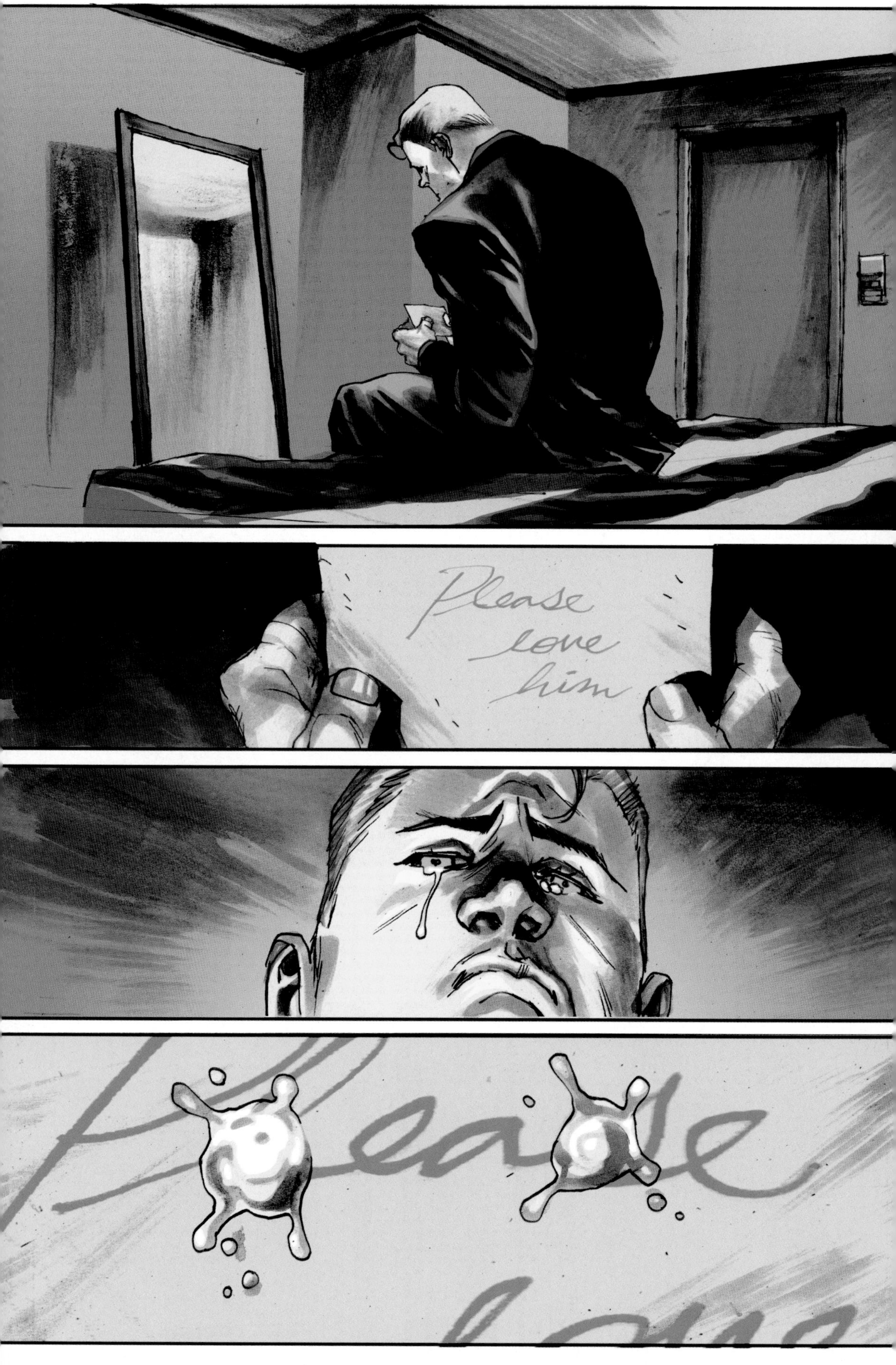
Please love him

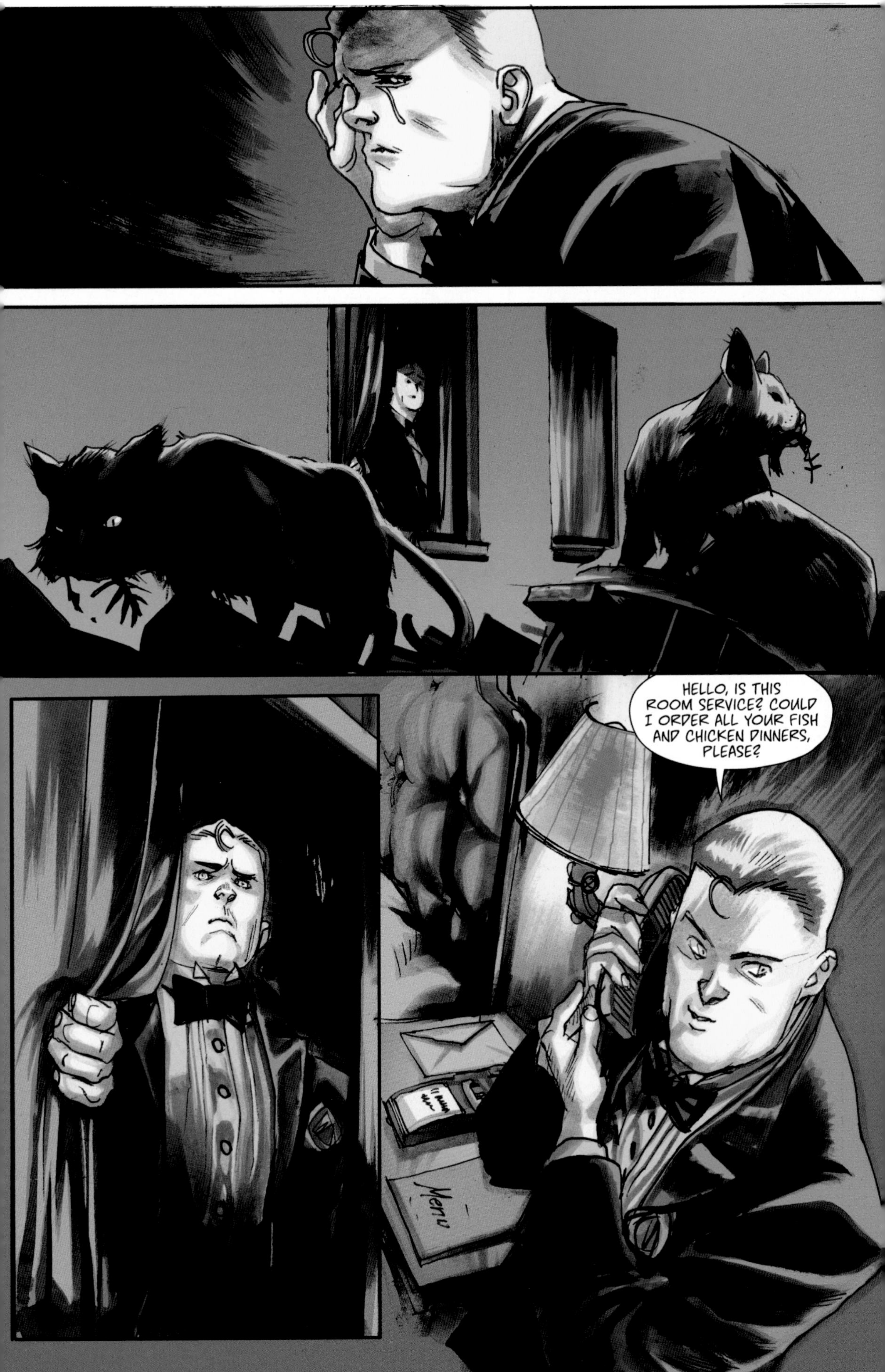
HELLO, IS THIS ROOM SERVICE? COULD I ORDER ALL YOUR FISH AND CHICKEN DINNERS, PLEASE?
Menu

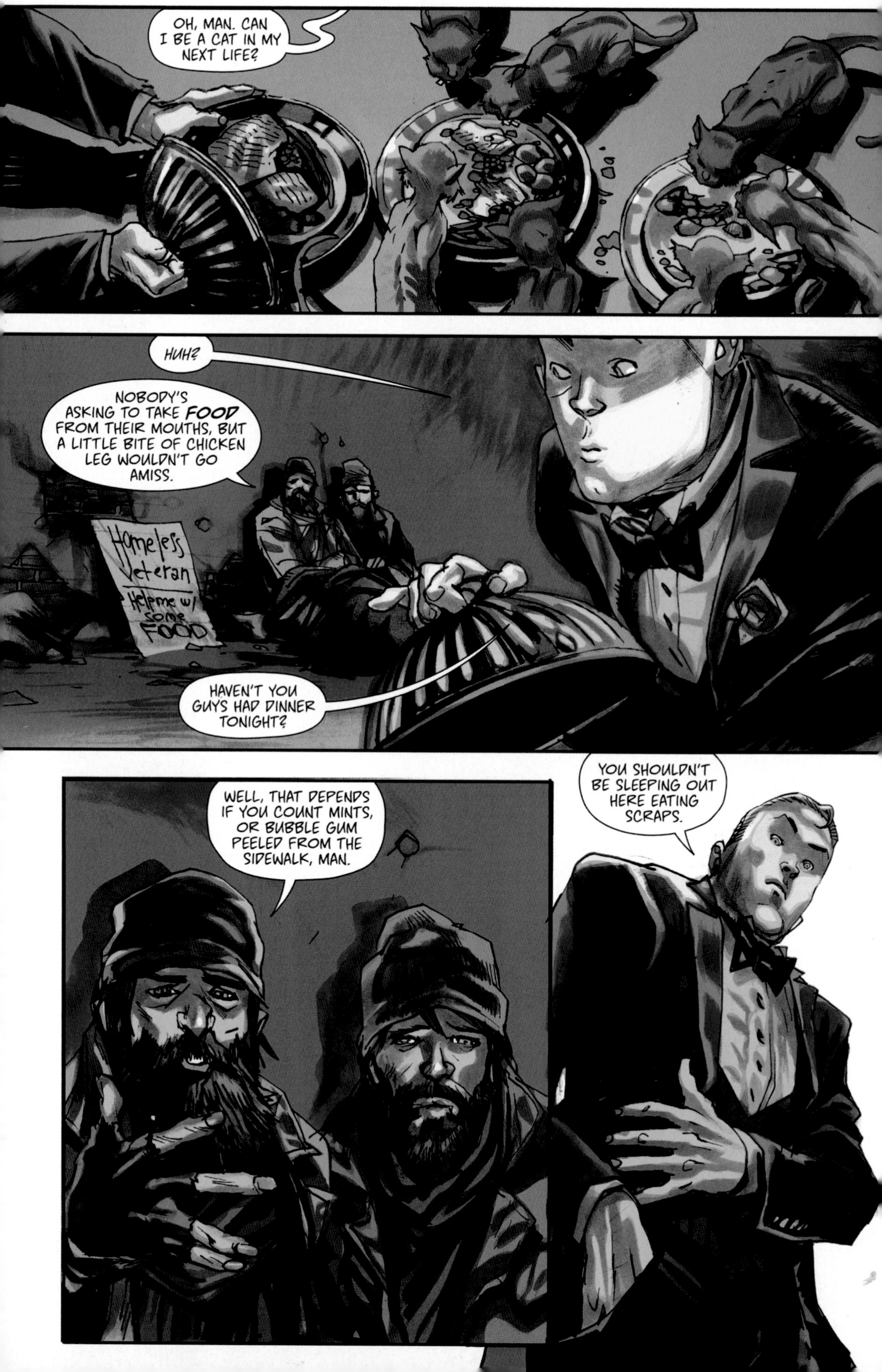
OH, MAN. CAN I BE A CAT IN MY NEXT LIFE?
HUH?
NOBODY'S ASKING TO TAKE FOOD FROM THEIR MOUTHS, BUT A LITTLE BITE OF CHICKEN LEG WOULDN'T GO AMISS.
Homeless Veteran Help me w/ some FOOD
HAVEN'T YOU GUYS HAD DINNER TONIGHT?
WELL, THAT DEPENDS IF YOU COUNT MINTS, OR BUBBLE GUM PEELED FROM THE SIDEWALK, MAN.
YOU SHOULDN'T BE SLEEPING OUT HERE EATING SCRAPS.

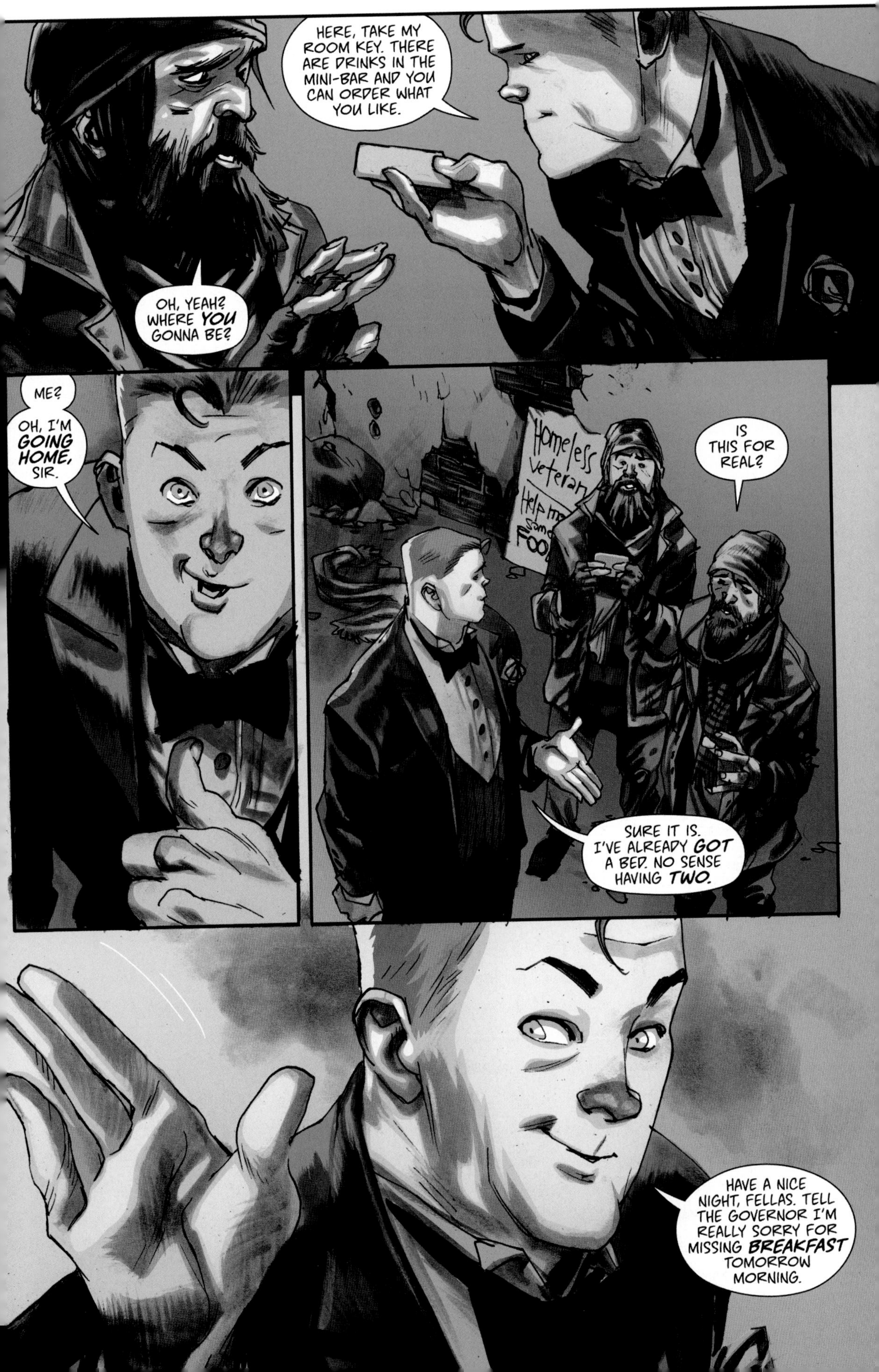
HERE, TAKE MY ROOM KEY. THERE ARE DRINKS IN THE MINI-BAR AND YOU CAN ORDER WHAT YOU LIKE.
OH, YEAH? WHERE YOU GONNA BE?
ME?
OH, I'M GOING HOME, SIR.
Homeless Veteran
IS THIS FOR REAL?
SURE IT IS. I'VE ALREADY GOT A BED. NO SENSE HAVING TWO.
HAVE A NICE NIGHT, FELLAS. TELL THE GOVERNOR I'M REALLY SORRY FOR MISSING BREAKFAST TOMORROW MORNING.

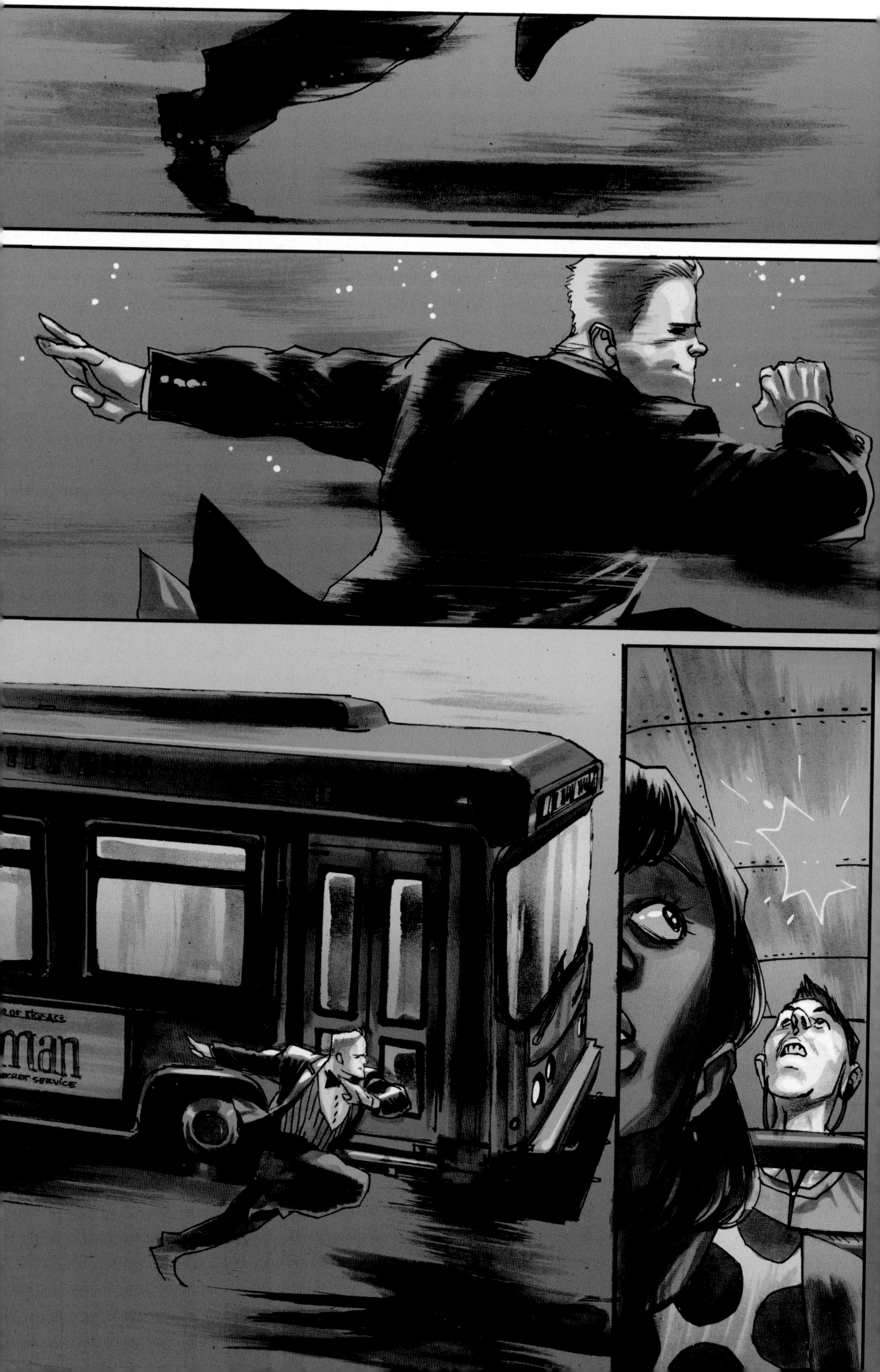

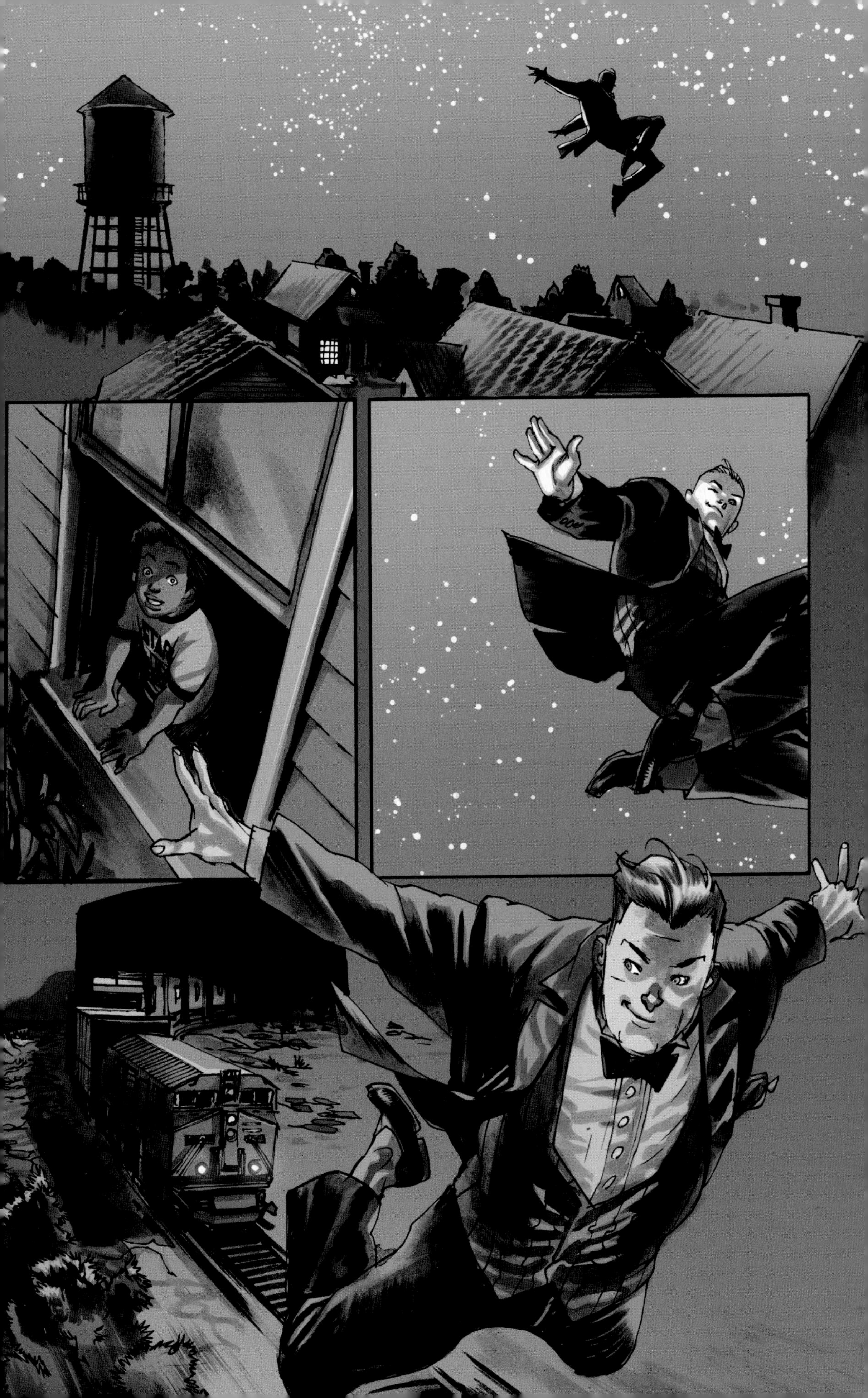

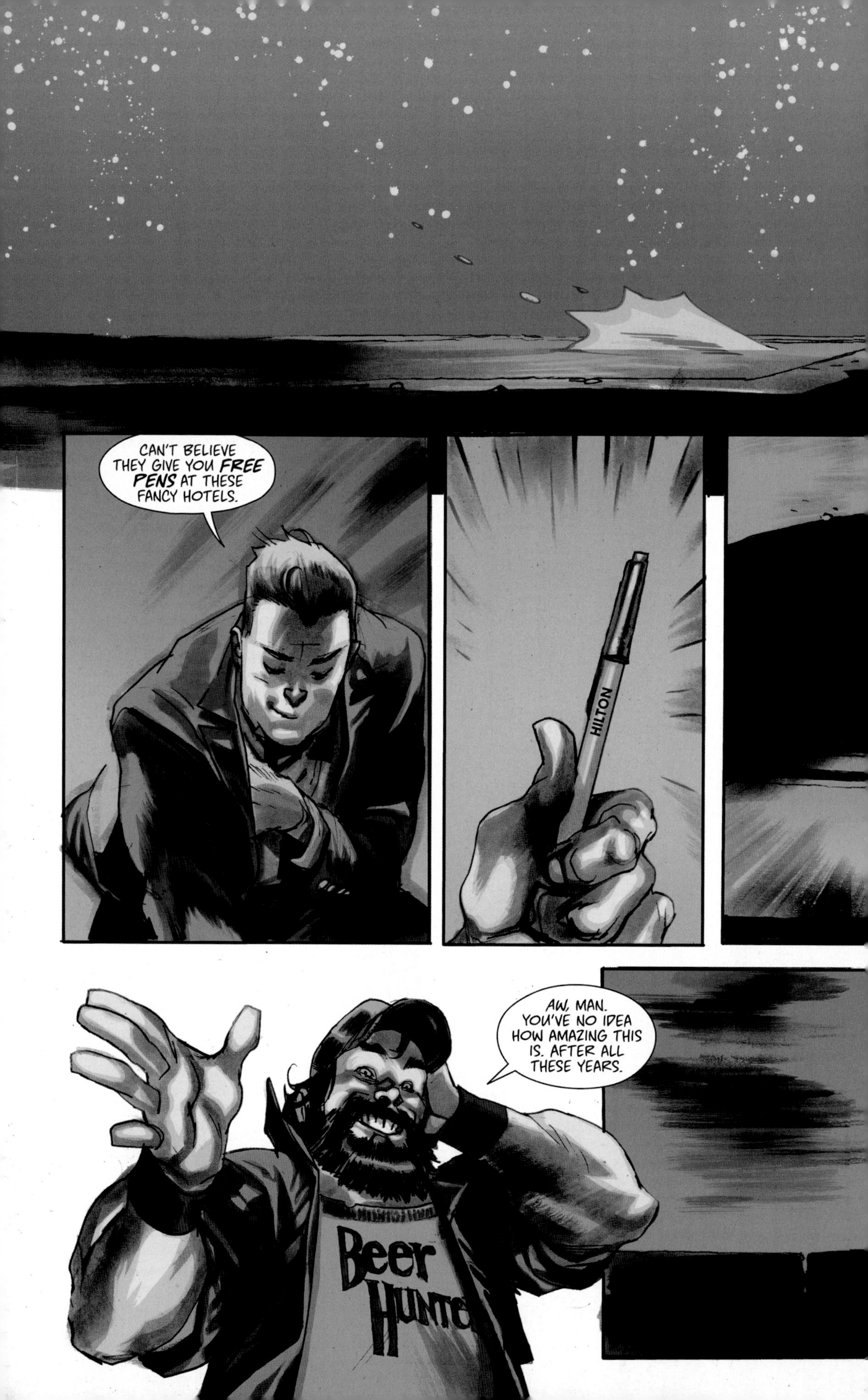
CAN'T BELIEVE THEY GIVE YOU FREE PENS AT THESE FANCY HOTELS.
HILTON
AW, MAN. YOU'VE NO IDEA HOW AMAZING THIS IS. AFTER ALL THESE YEARS.
Beer Hunte

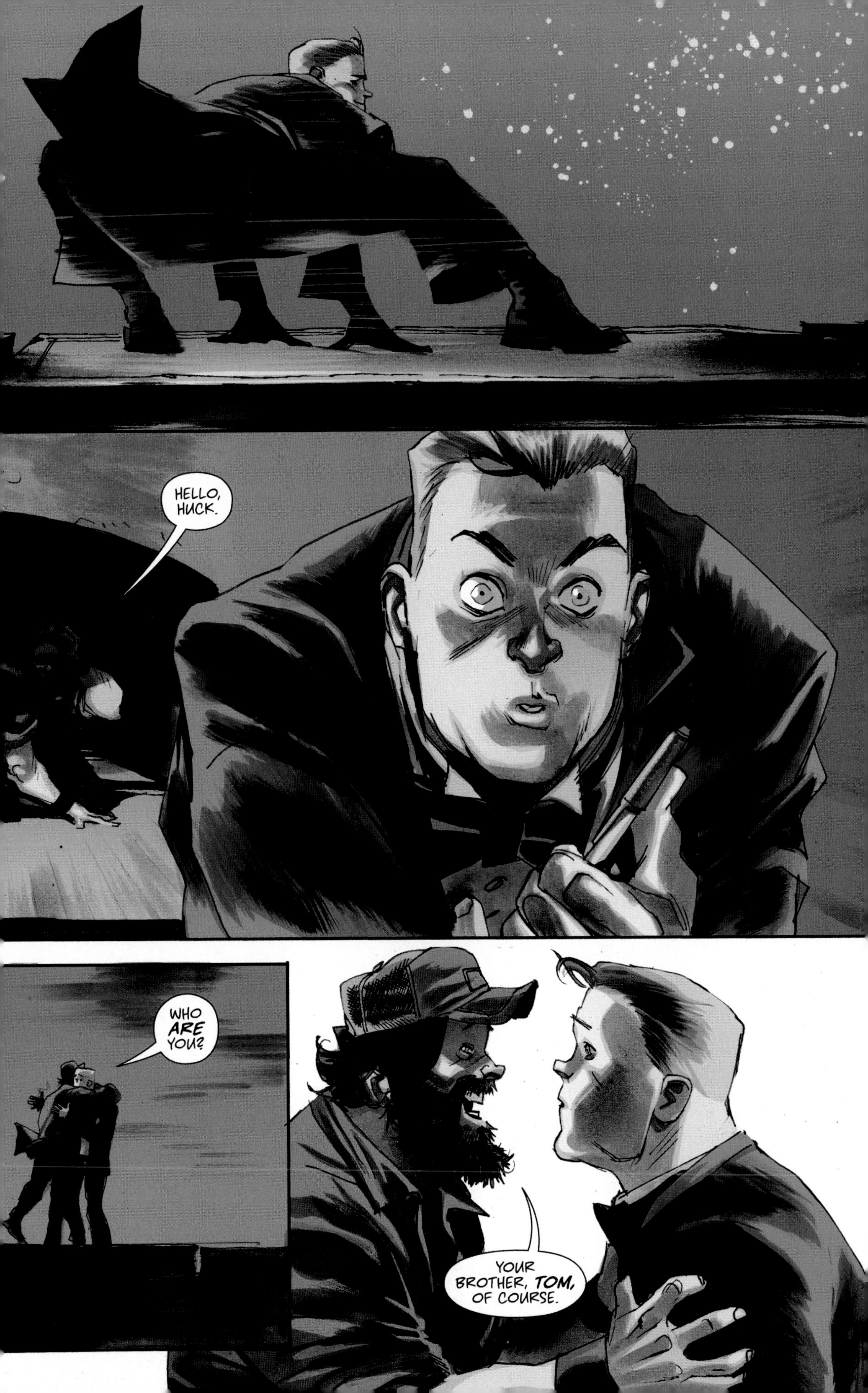
HELLO, HUCK.
WHO ARE YOU?
YOUR BROTHER, TOM, OF COURSE.

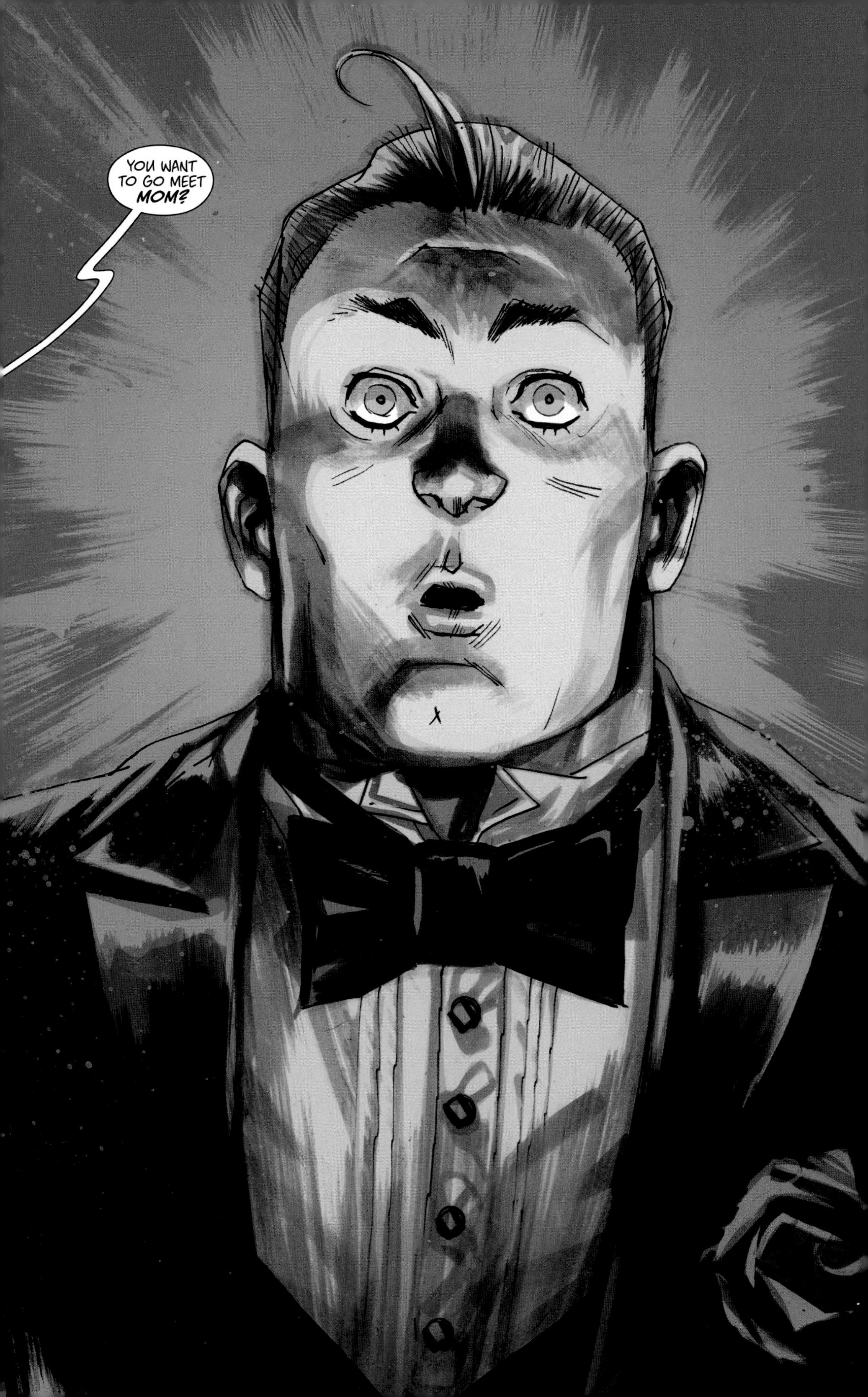
YOU WANT TO GO MEET MOM?

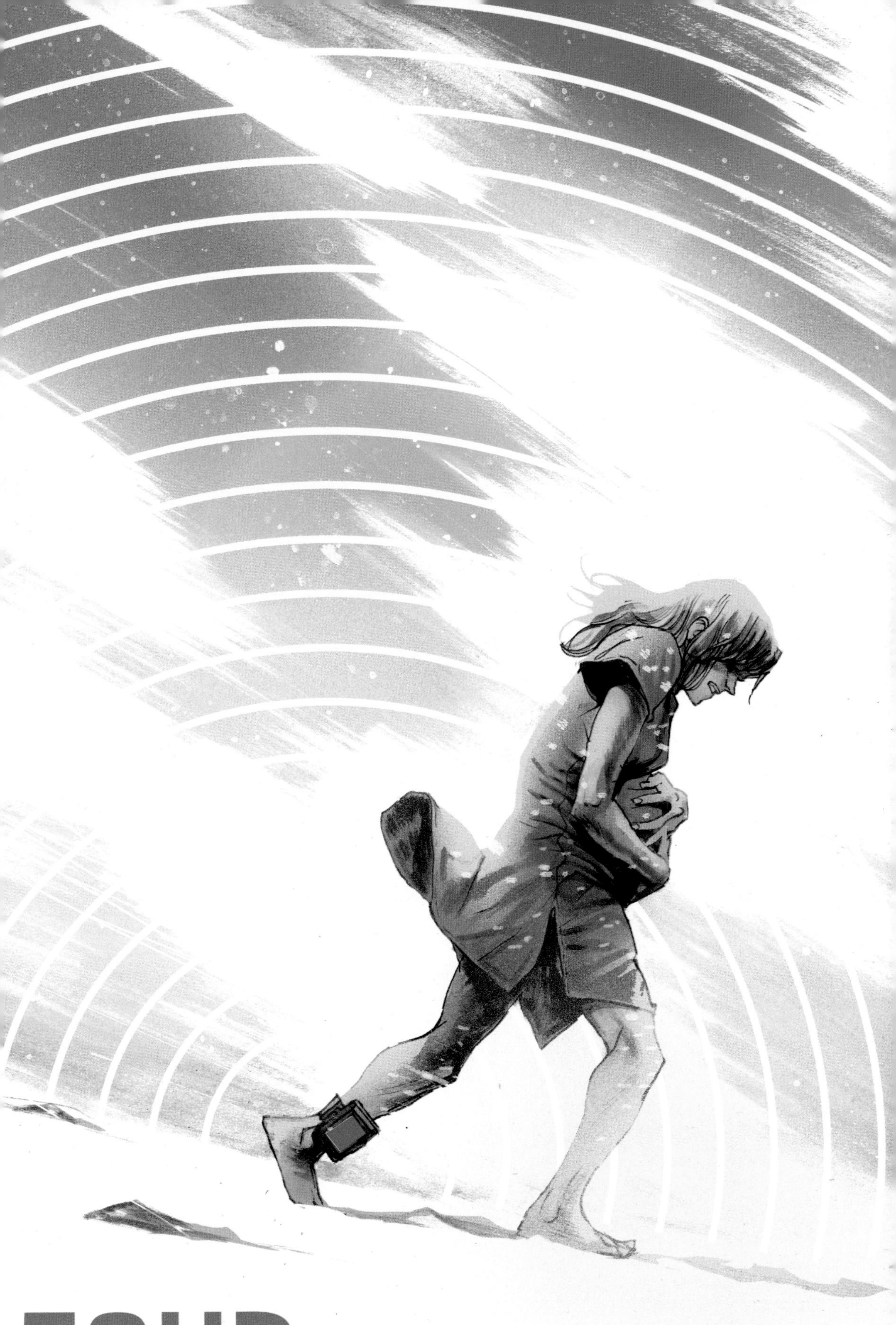

FOUR

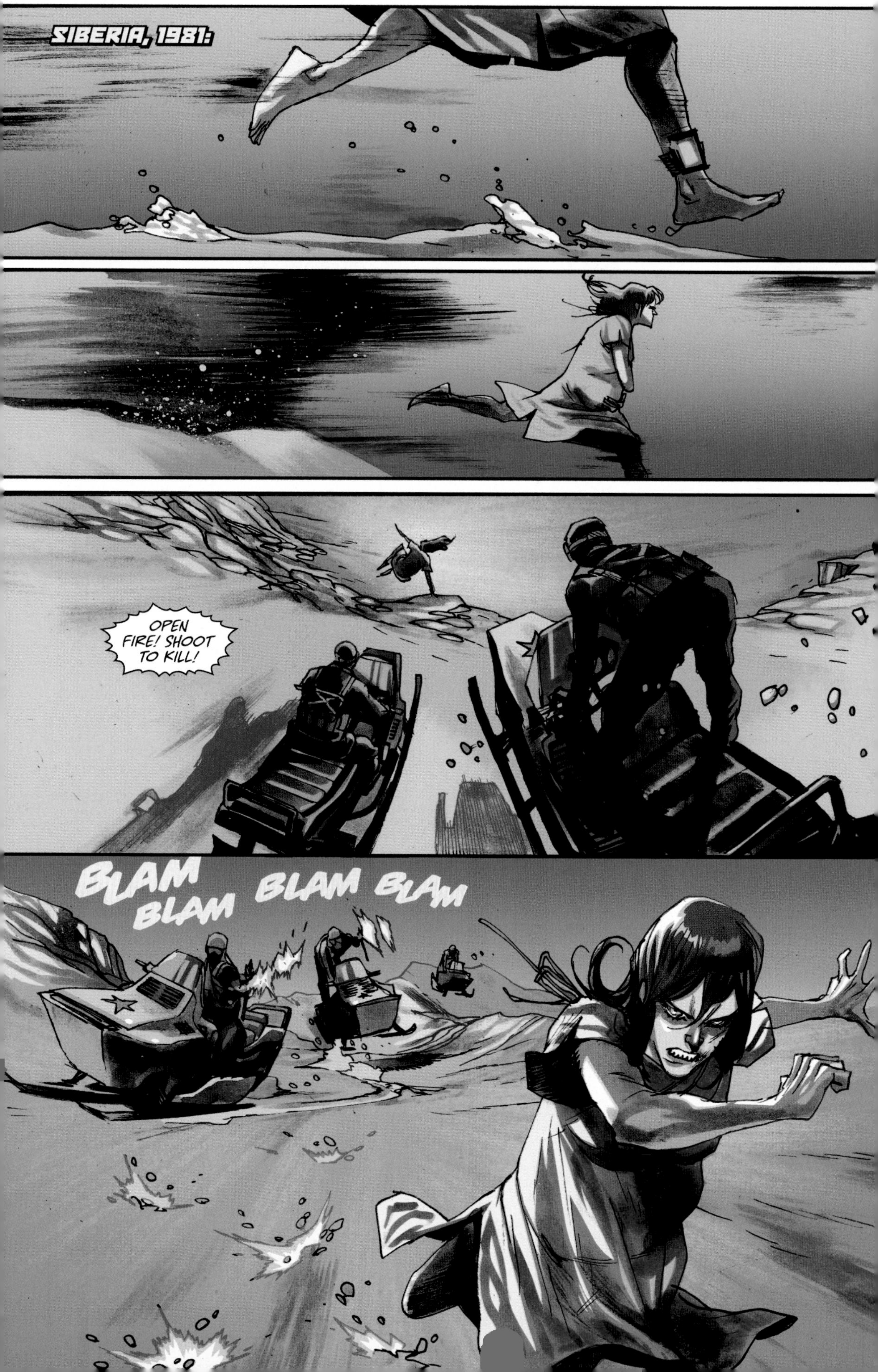
SIBERIA, 1981:
OPEN FIRE! SHOOT TO KILL!
BLAM BLAM BLAM BLAM

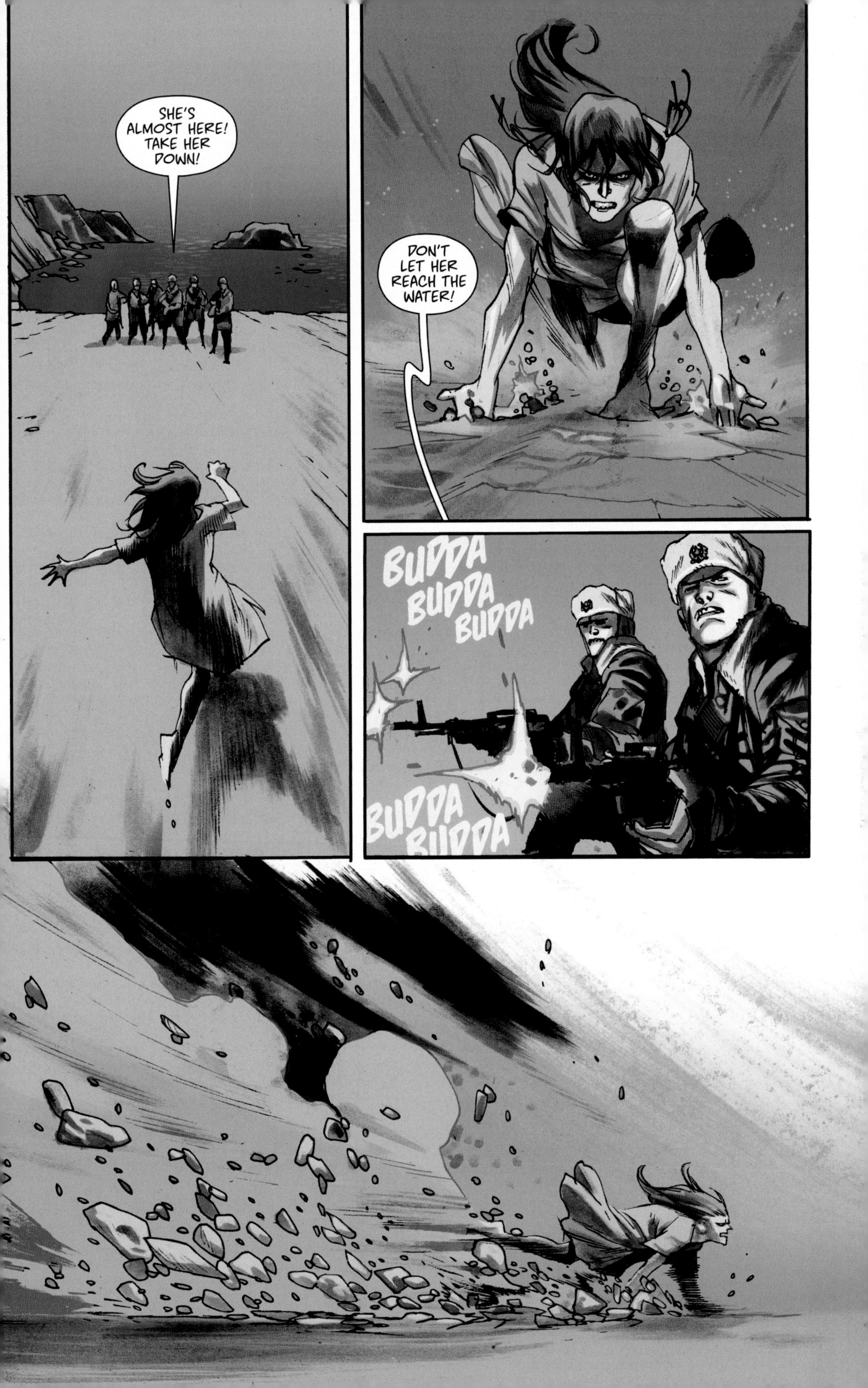
SHE'S ALMOST HERE! TAKE HER DOWN!
DON'T LET HER REACH THE WATER!
BUDDA BUDDA BUDDA
BUDDA BUDDA

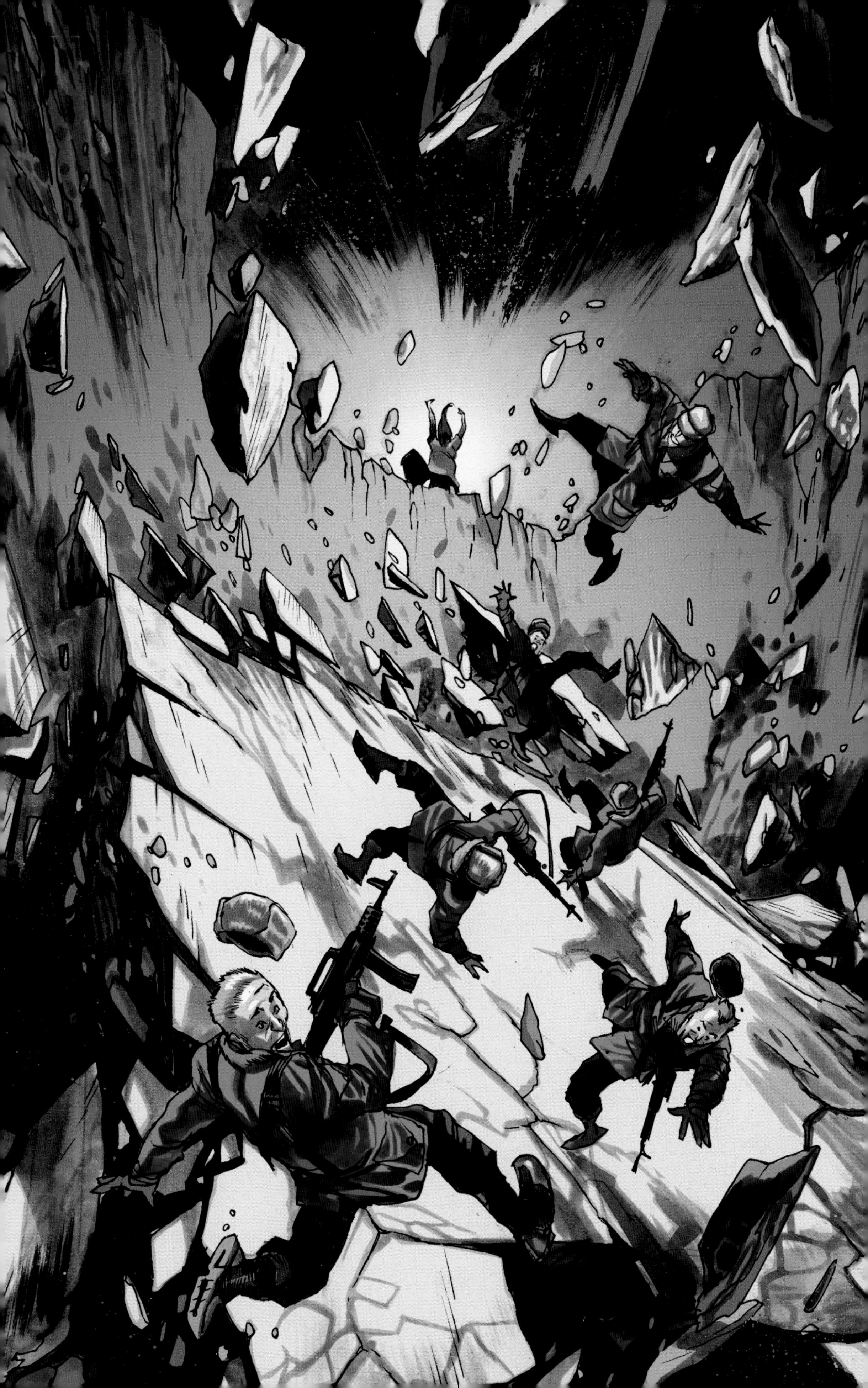

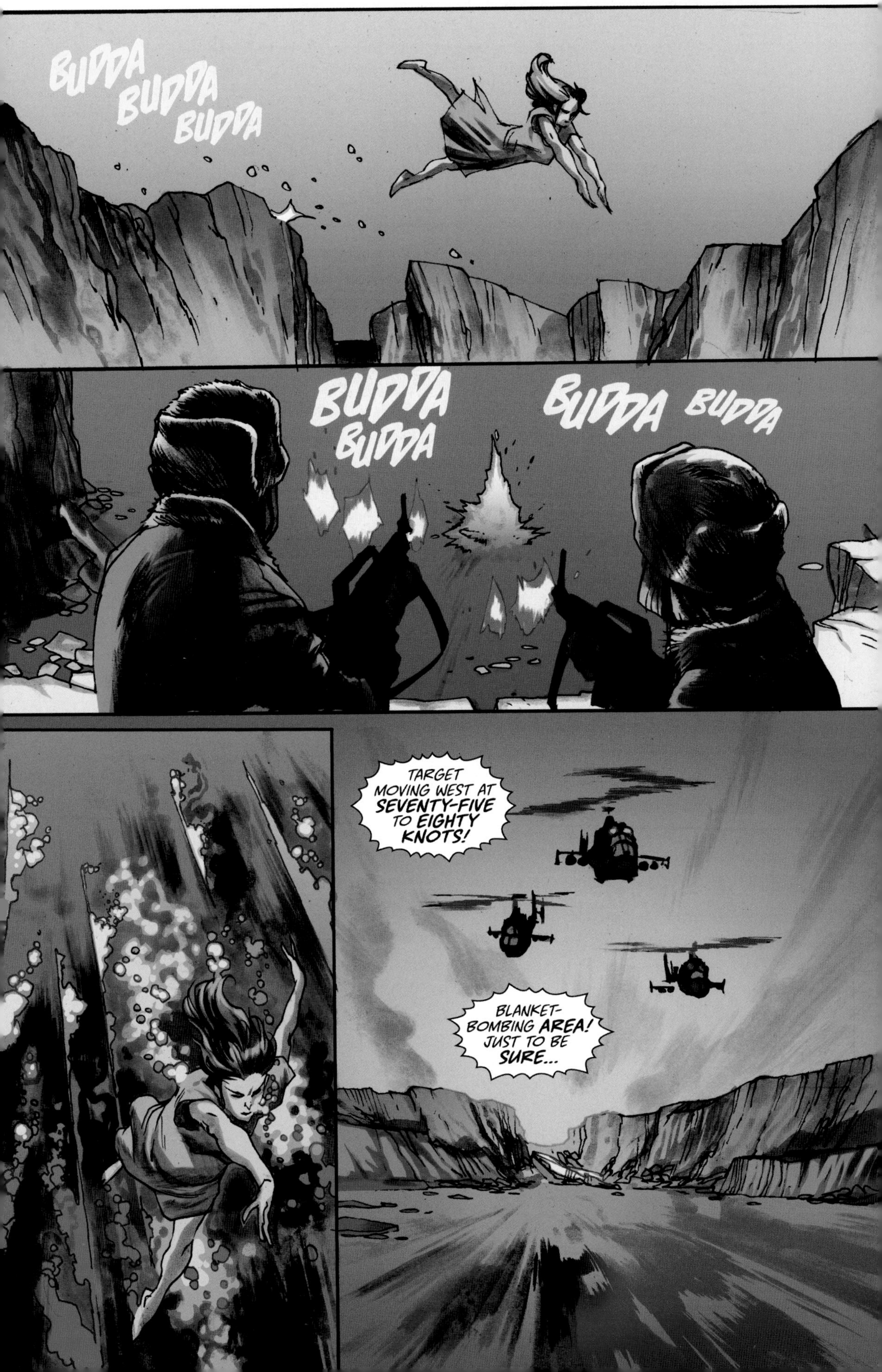
BUDDA BUDDA BUDDA
BUDDA BUDDA
BUDDA BUDDA
TARGET MOVING WEST AT SEVENTY-FIVE TO EIGHTY KNOTS!
BLANKET-BOMBING AREA! JUST TO BE SURE...

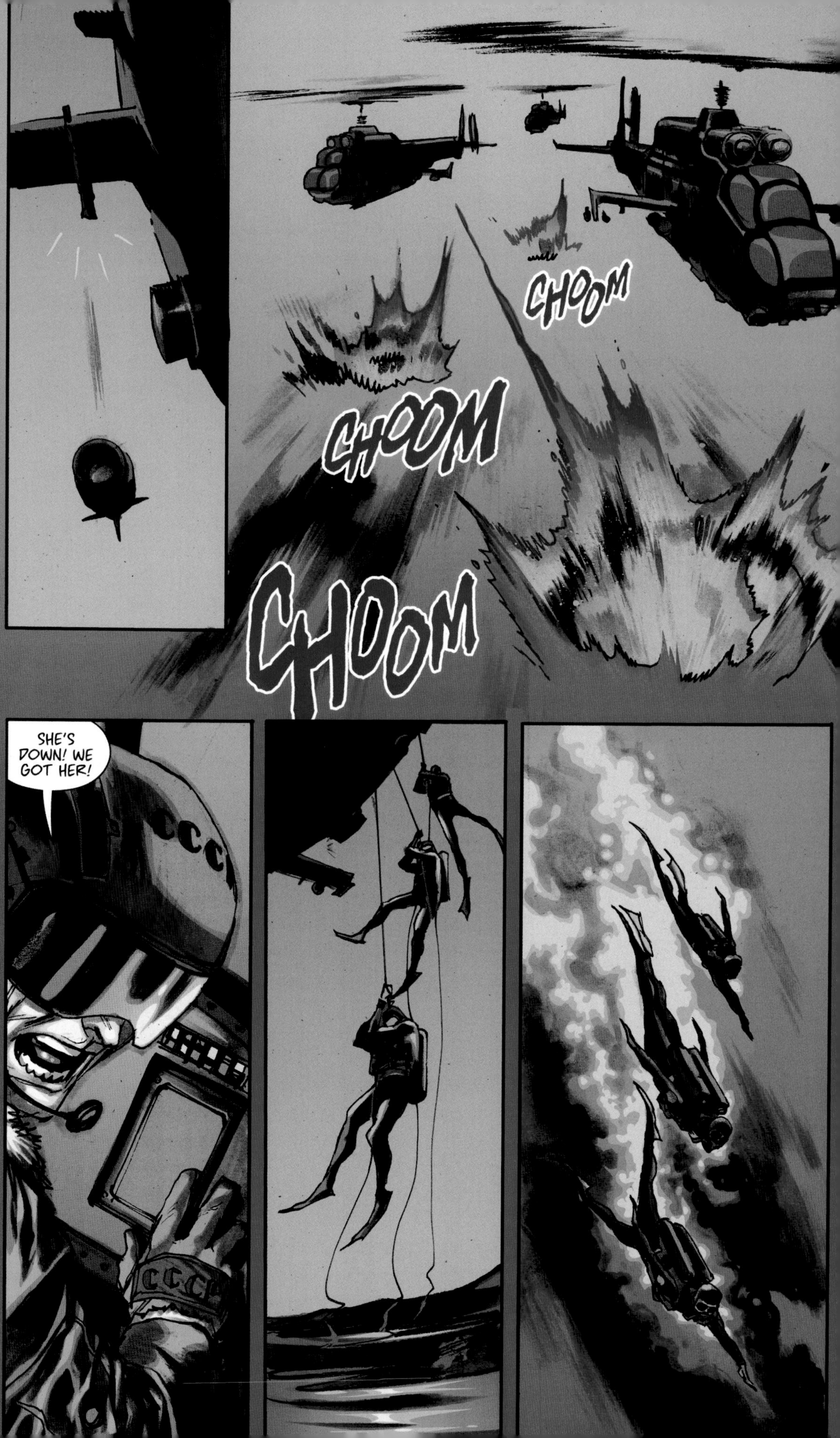
CHOOM
CHOOM
CHOOM
SHE'S DOWN! WE GOT HER!

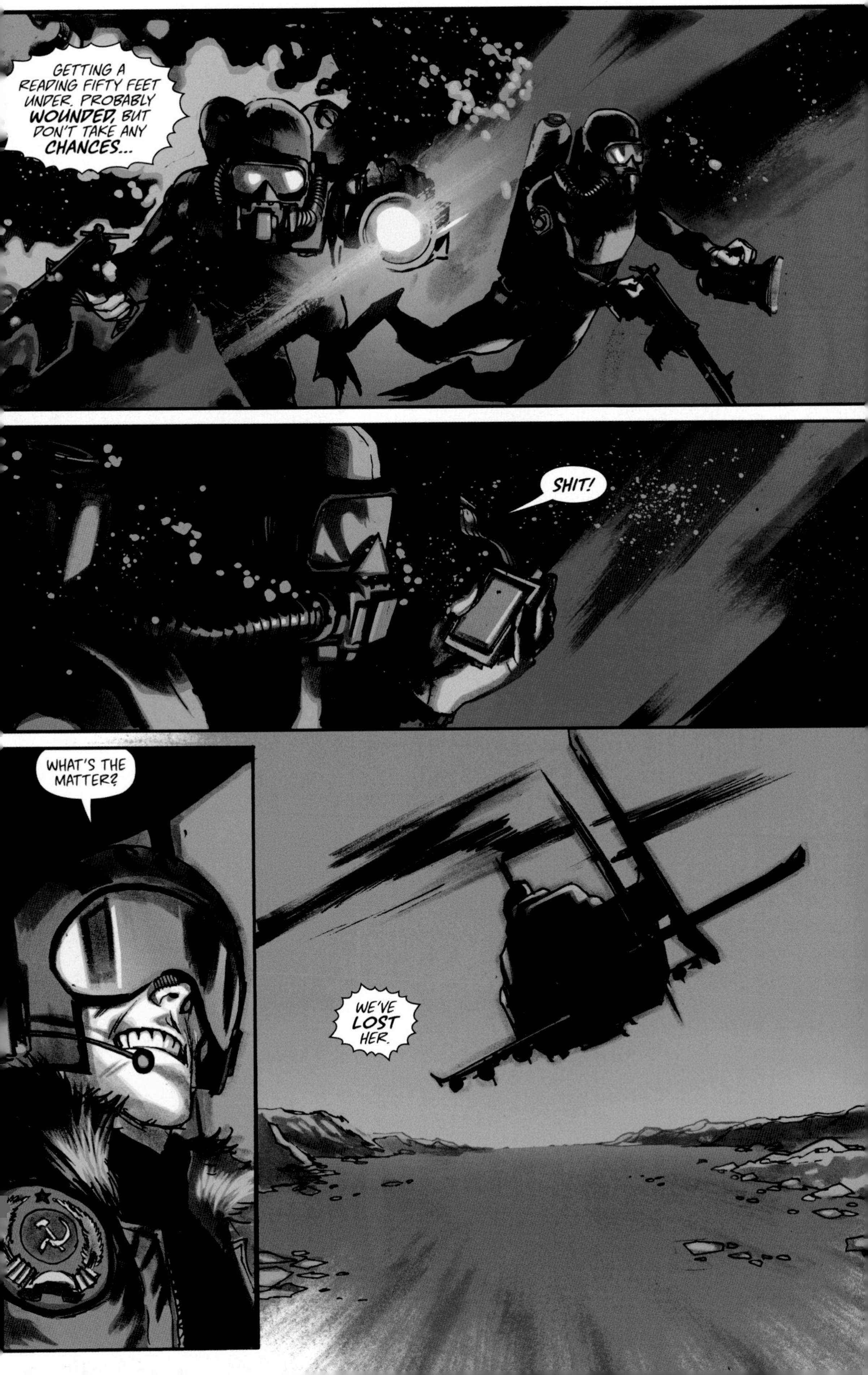
GETTING A READING FIFTY FEET UNDER. PROBABLY **WOUNDED**, BUT DON'T TAKE ANY **CHANCES...**
SHIT!
WHAT'S THE MATTER?
WE'VE **LOST** HER.

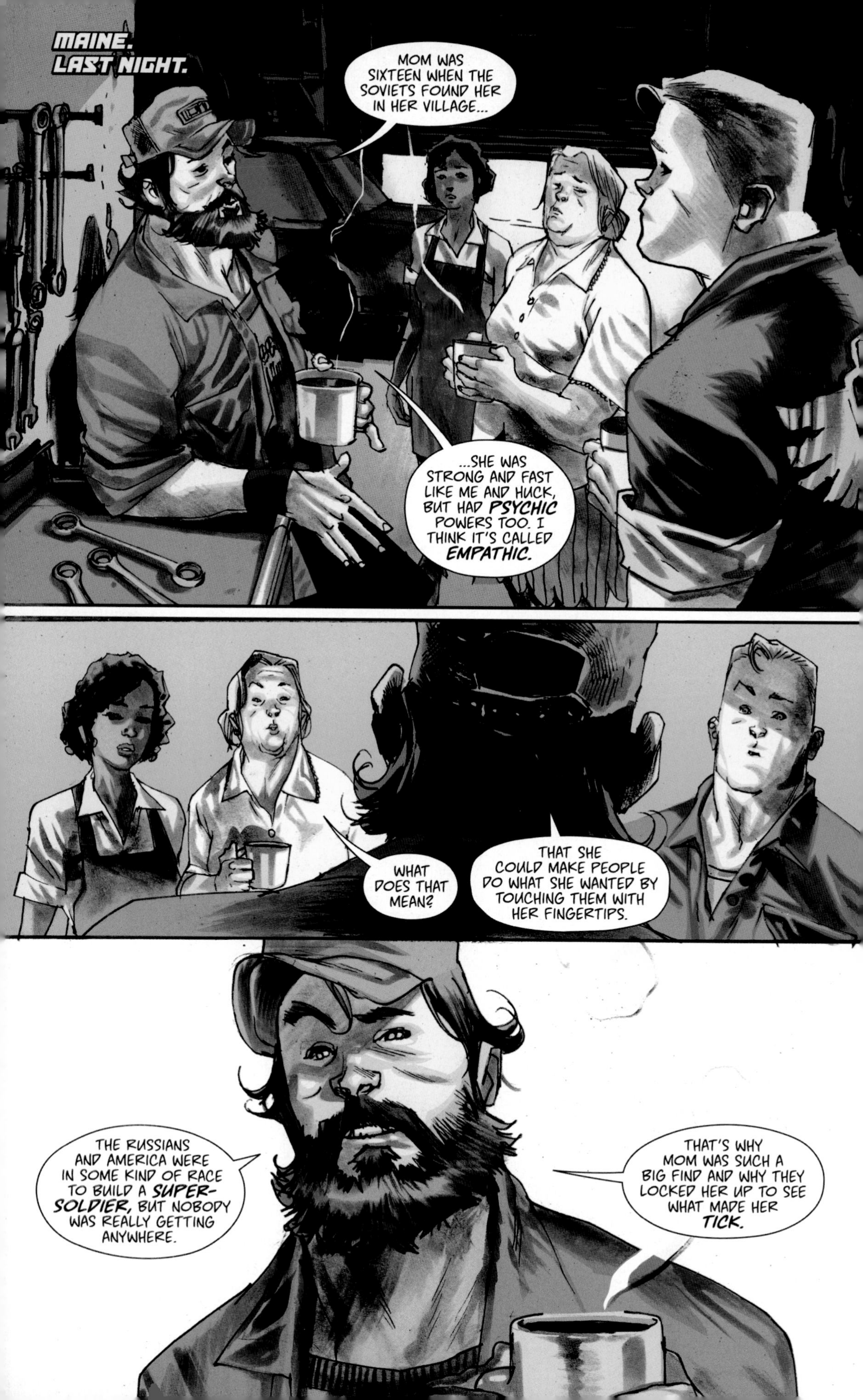
MAINE. LAST NIGHT.
MOM WAS SIXTEEN WHEN THE SOVIETS FOUND HER IN HER VILLAGE...
...SHE WAS STRONG AND FAST LIKE ME AND HUCK, BUT HAD PSYCHIC POWERS TOO. I THINK IT'S CALLED EMPATHIC.
WHAT DOES THAT MEAN?
THAT SHE COULD MAKE PEOPLE DO WHAT SHE WANTED BY TOUCHING THEM WITH HER FINGERTIPS.
THE RUSSIANS AND AMERICA WERE IN SOME KIND OF RACE TO BUILD A SUPER-SOLDIER, BUT NOBODY WAS REALLY GETTING ANYWHERE.
THAT'S WHY MOM WAS SUCH A BIG FIND AND WHY THEY LOCKED HER UP TO SEE WHAT MADE HER TICK.

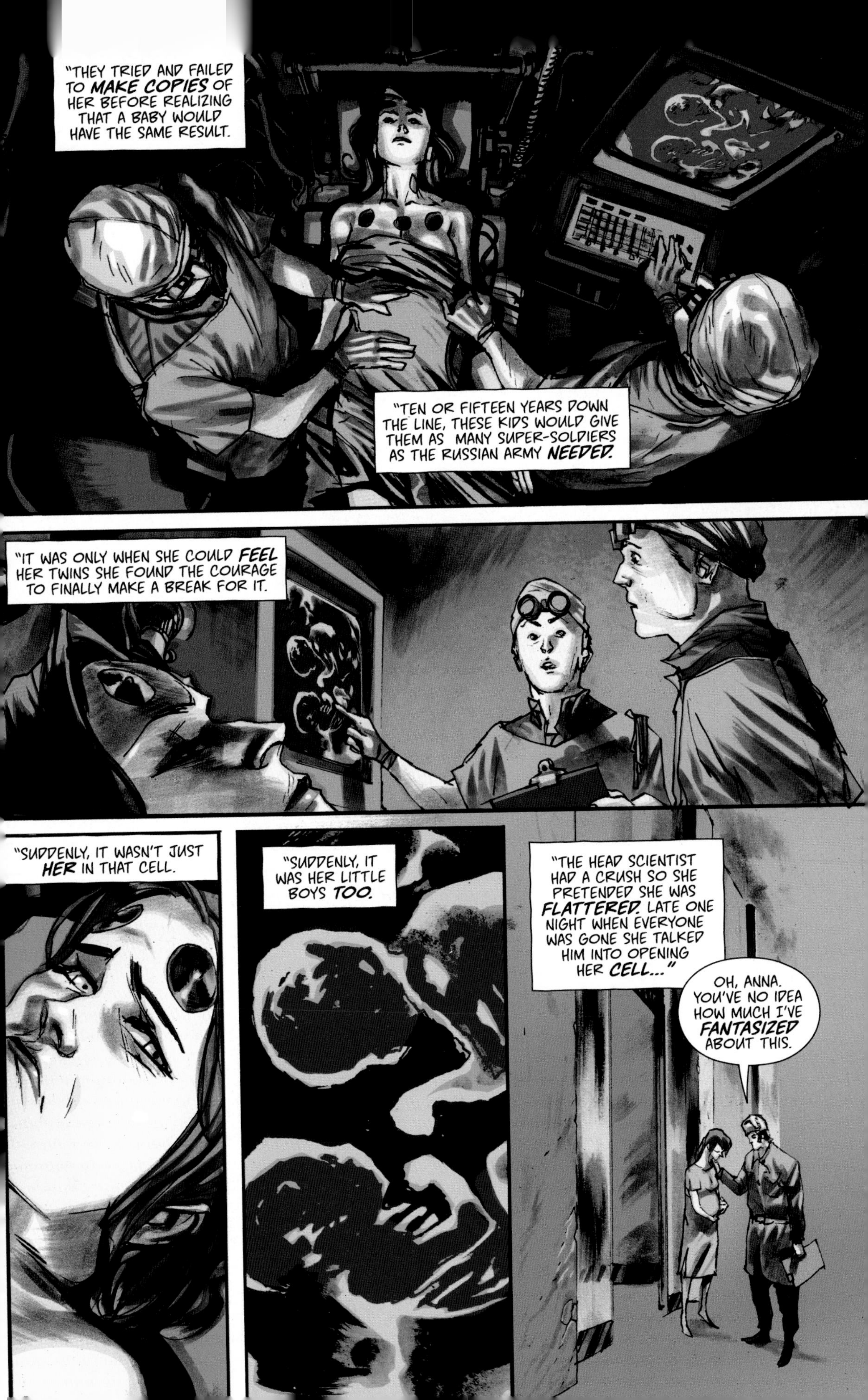
"THEY TRIED AND FAILED TO MAKE COPIES OF HER BEFORE REALIZING THAT A BABY WOULD HAVE THE SAME RESULT.
"TEN OR FIFTEEN YEARS DOWN THE LINE, THESE KIDS WOULD GIVE THEM AS MANY SUPER-SOLDIERS AS THE RUSSIAN ARMY NEEDED.
"IT WAS ONLY WHEN SHE COULD FEEL HER TWINS SHE FOUND THE COURAGE TO FINALLY MAKE A BREAK FOR IT.
"SUDDENLY, IT WASN'T JUST HER IN THAT CELL.
"SUDDENLY, IT WAS HER LITTLE BOYS TOO.
"THE HEAD SCIENTIST HAD A CRUSH SO SHE PRETENDED SHE WAS FLATTERED. LATE ONE NIGHT WHEN EVERYONE WAS GONE SHE TALKED HIM INTO OPENING HER CELL..."
OH, ANNA. YOU'VE NO IDEA HOW MUCH I'VE FANTASIZED ABOUT THIS.

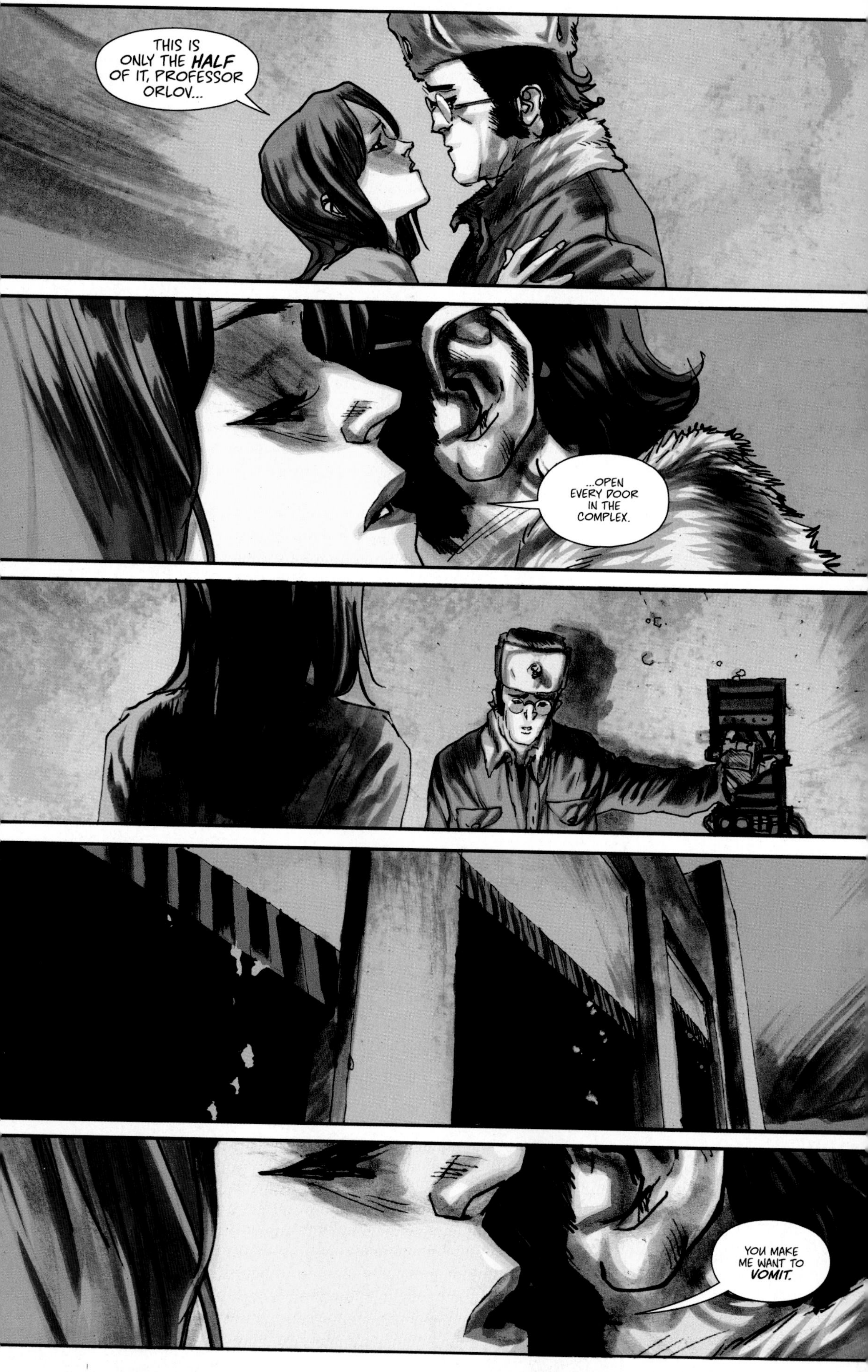
THIS IS ONLY THE HALF OF IT, PROFESSOR ORLOV...
...OPEN EVERY DOOR IN THE COMPLEX.
YOU MAKE ME WANT TO VOMIT.

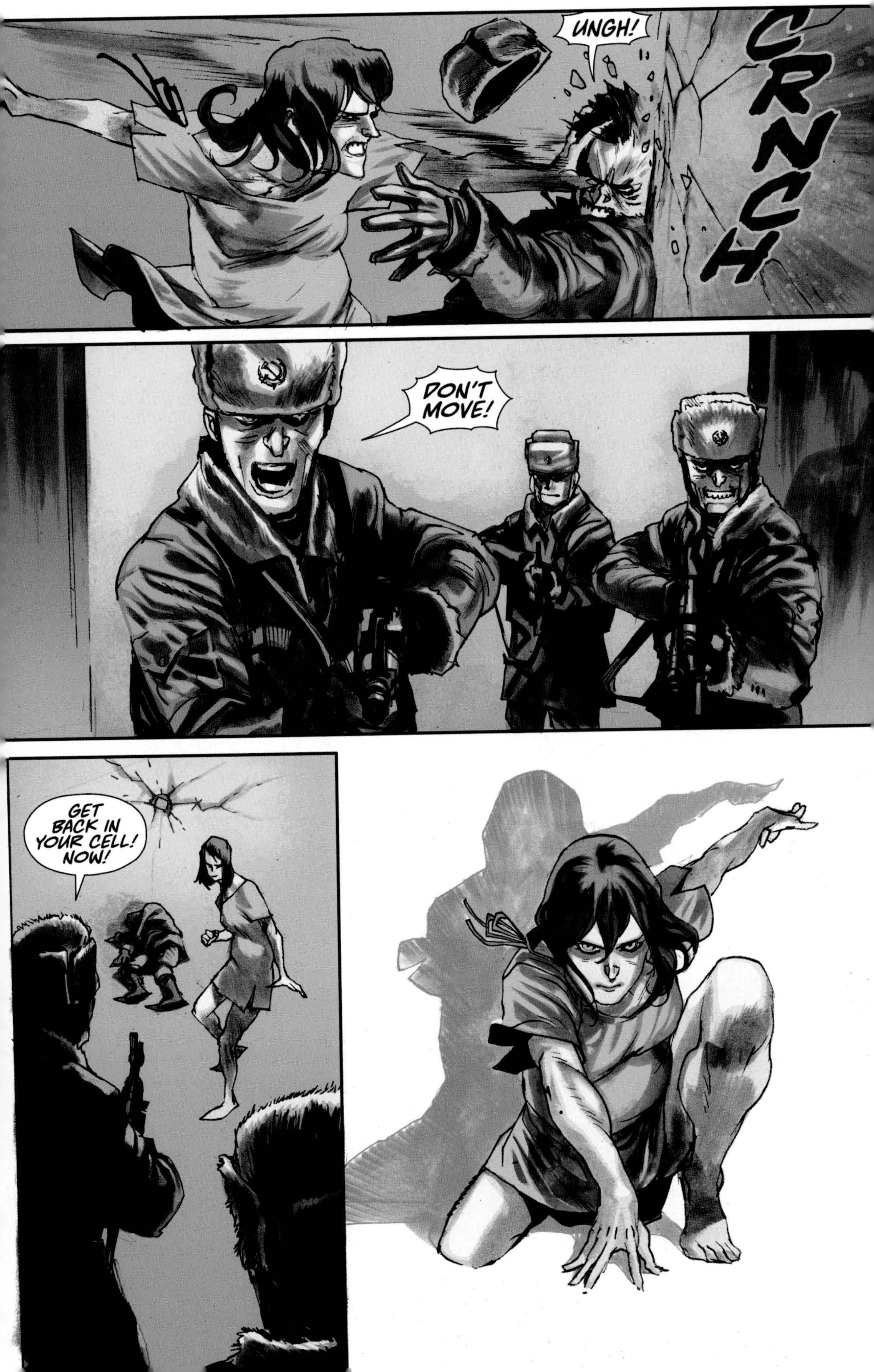
UNGH!
CRNCH
DON'T MOVE!
GET BACK IN YOUR CELL! NOW!

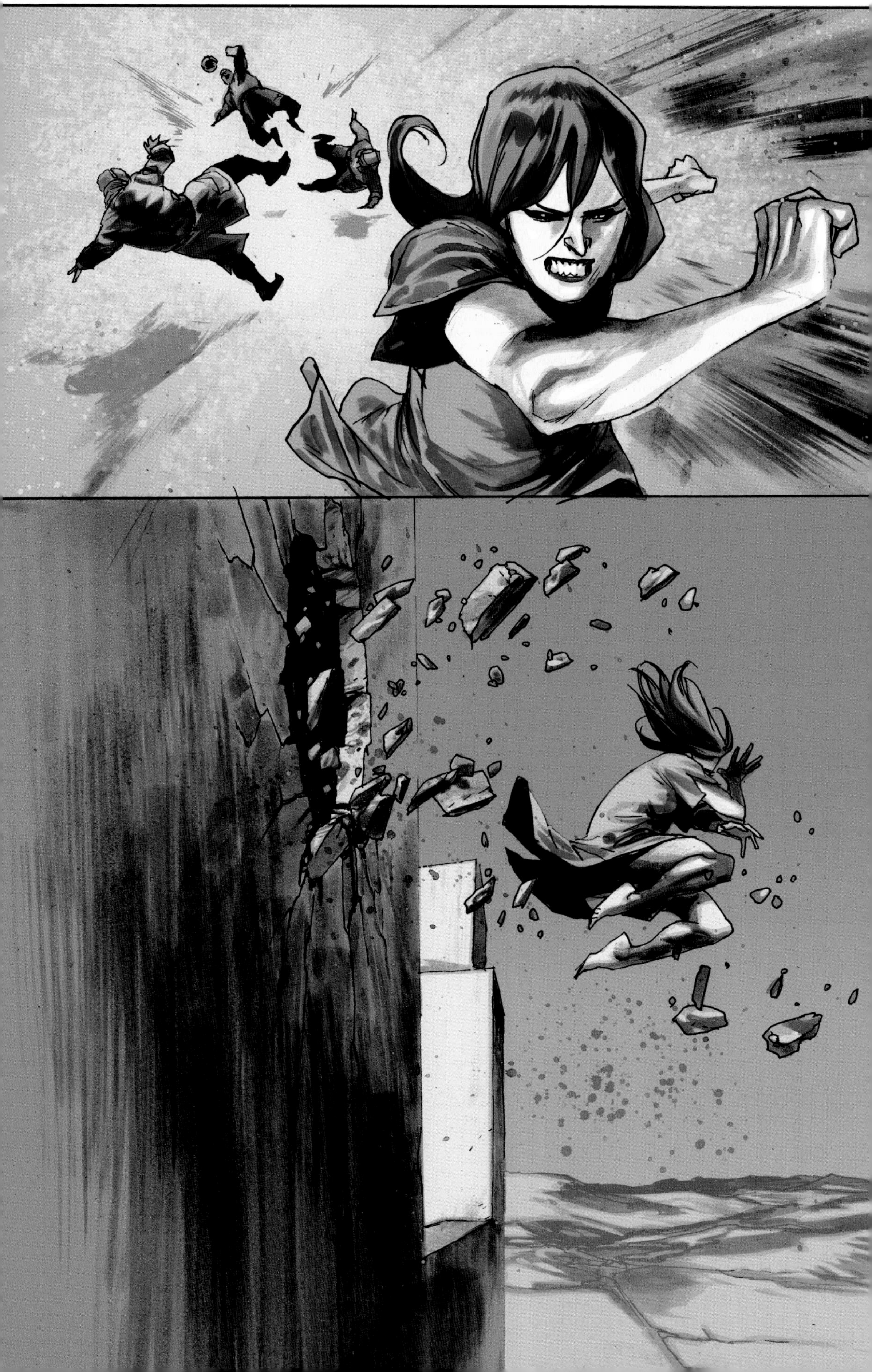

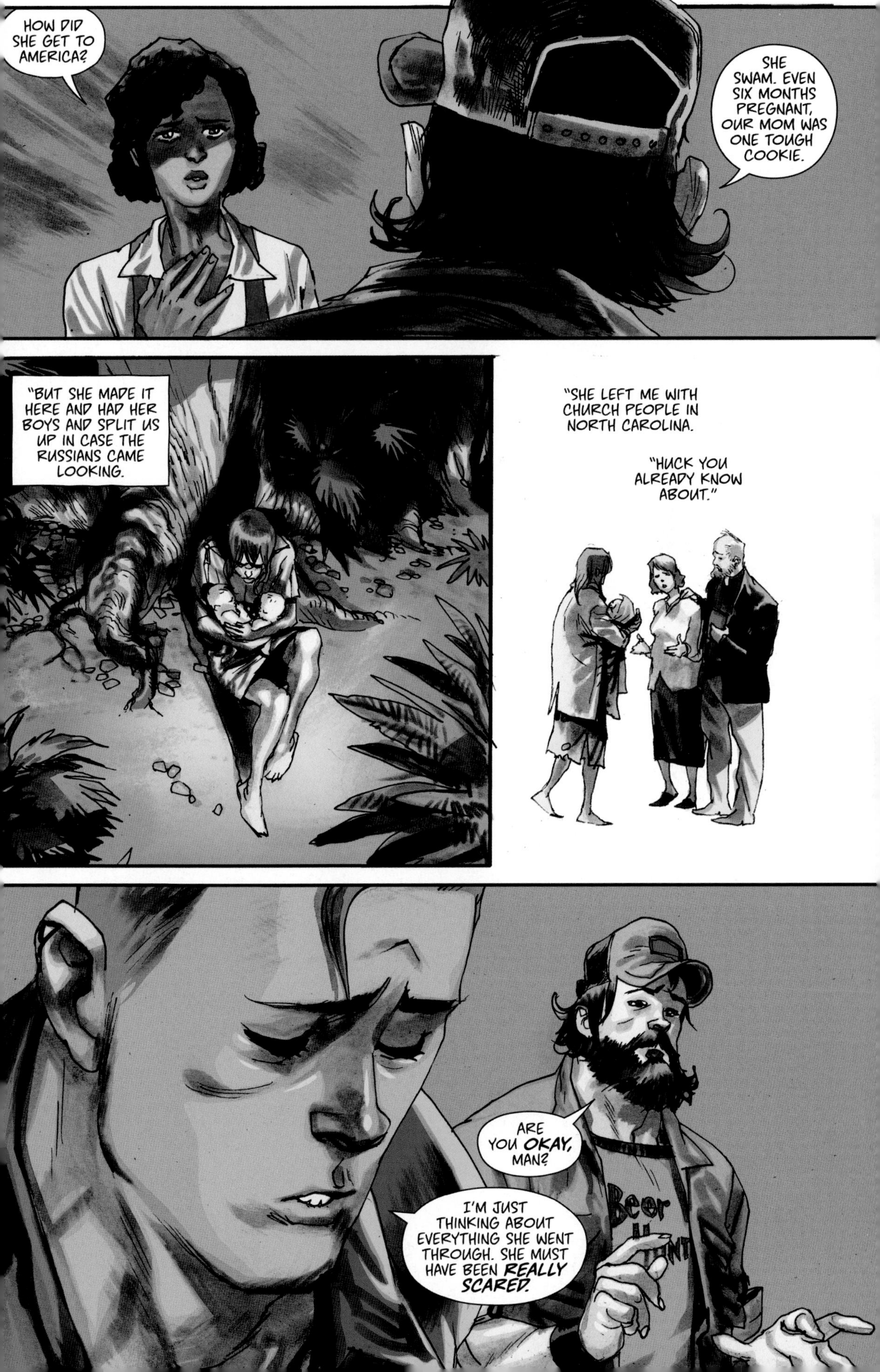
HOW DID SHE GET TO AMERICA?
SHE SWAM. EVEN SIX MONTHS PREGNANT, OUR MOM WAS ONE TOUGH COOKIE.
"BUT SHE MADE IT HERE AND HAD HER BOYS AND SPLIT US UP IN CASE THE RUSSIANS CAME LOOKING.
"SHE LEFT ME WITH CHURCH PEOPLE IN NORTH CAROLINA.
"HUCK YOU ALREADY KNOW ABOUT."
ARE YOU **OKAY,** MAN?
I'M JUST THINKING ABOUT EVERYTHING SHE WENT THROUGH. SHE MUST HAVE BEEN **REALLY SCARED.**

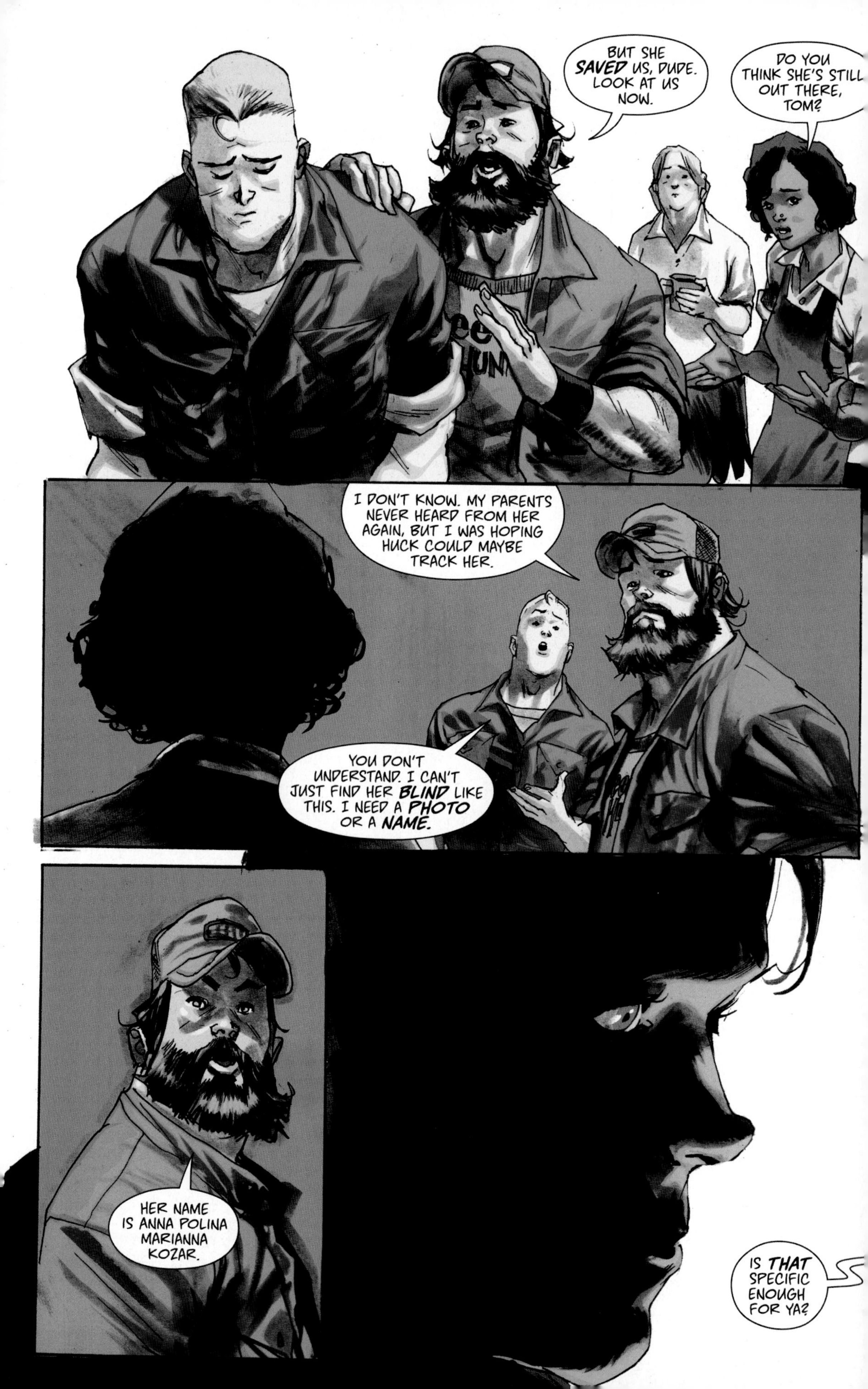
BUT SHE SAVED US, DUDE. LOOK AT US NOW.
DO YOU THINK SHE'S STILL OUT THERE, TOM?
I DON'T KNOW. MY PARENTS NEVER HEARD FROM HER AGAIN, BUT I WAS HOPING HUCK COULD MAYBE TRACK HER.
YOU DON'T UNDERSTAND. I CAN'T JUST FIND HER BLIND LIKE THIS. I NEED A PHOTO OR A NAME.
HER NAME IS ANNA POLINA MARIANNA KOZAR.
IS THAT SPECIFIC ENOUGH FOR YA?

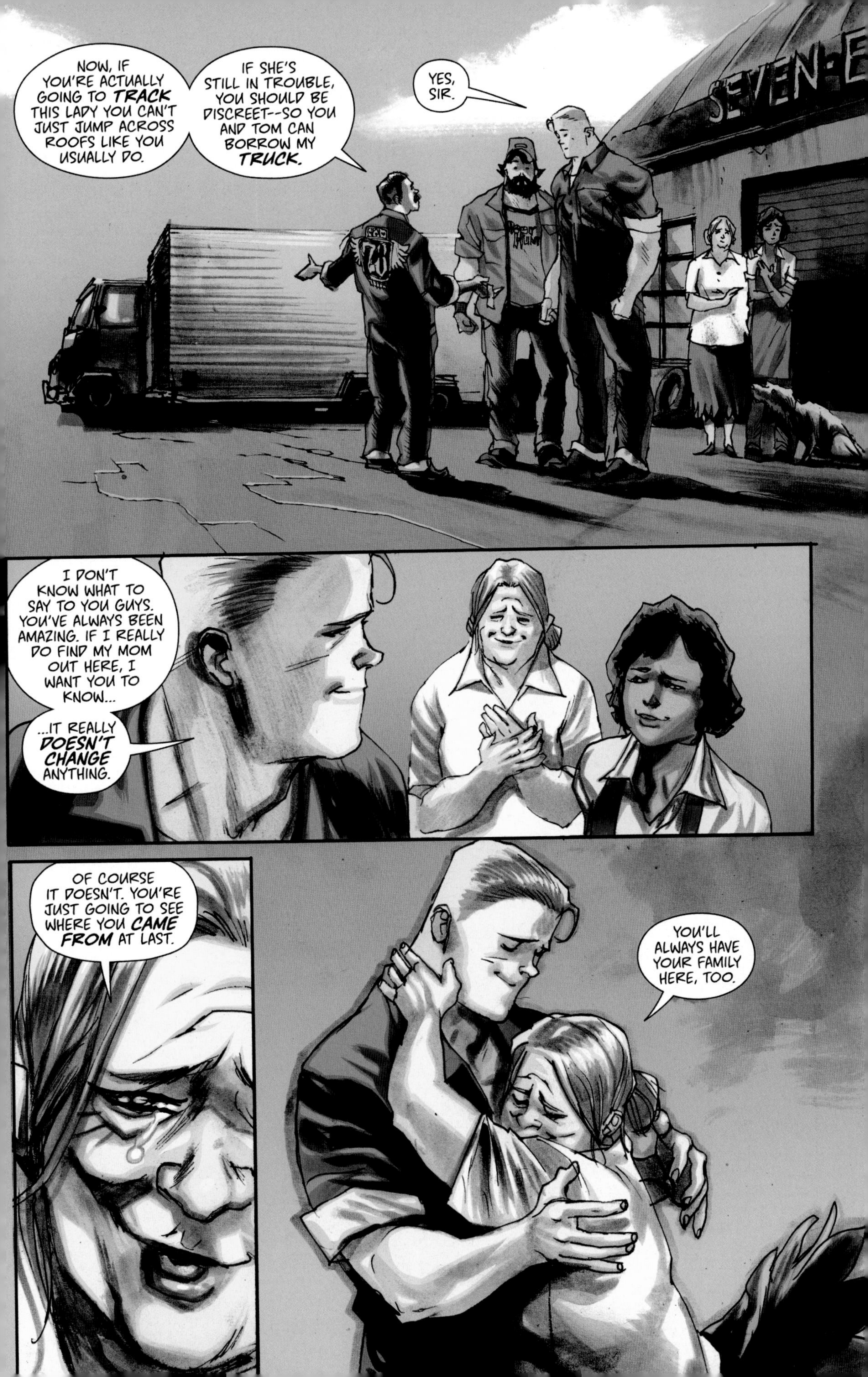
SEVEN-E
NOW, IF YOU'RE ACTUALLY GOING TO TRACK THIS LADY YOU CAN'T JUST JUMP ACROSS ROOFS LIKE YOU USUALLY DO.
IF SHE'S STILL IN TROUBLE, YOU SHOULD BE DISCREET--SO YOU AND TOM CAN BORROW MY TRUCK.
YES, SIR.
I DON'T KNOW WHAT TO SAY TO YOU GUYS. YOU'VE ALWAYS BEEN AMAZING. IF I REALLY DO FIND MY MOM OUT HERE, I WANT YOU TO KNOW...
...IT REALLY DOESN'T CHANGE ANYTHING.
OF COURSE IT DOESN'T. YOU'RE JUST GOING TO SEE WHERE YOU CAME FROM AT LAST.
YOU'LL ALWAYS HAVE YOUR FAMILY HERE, TOO.

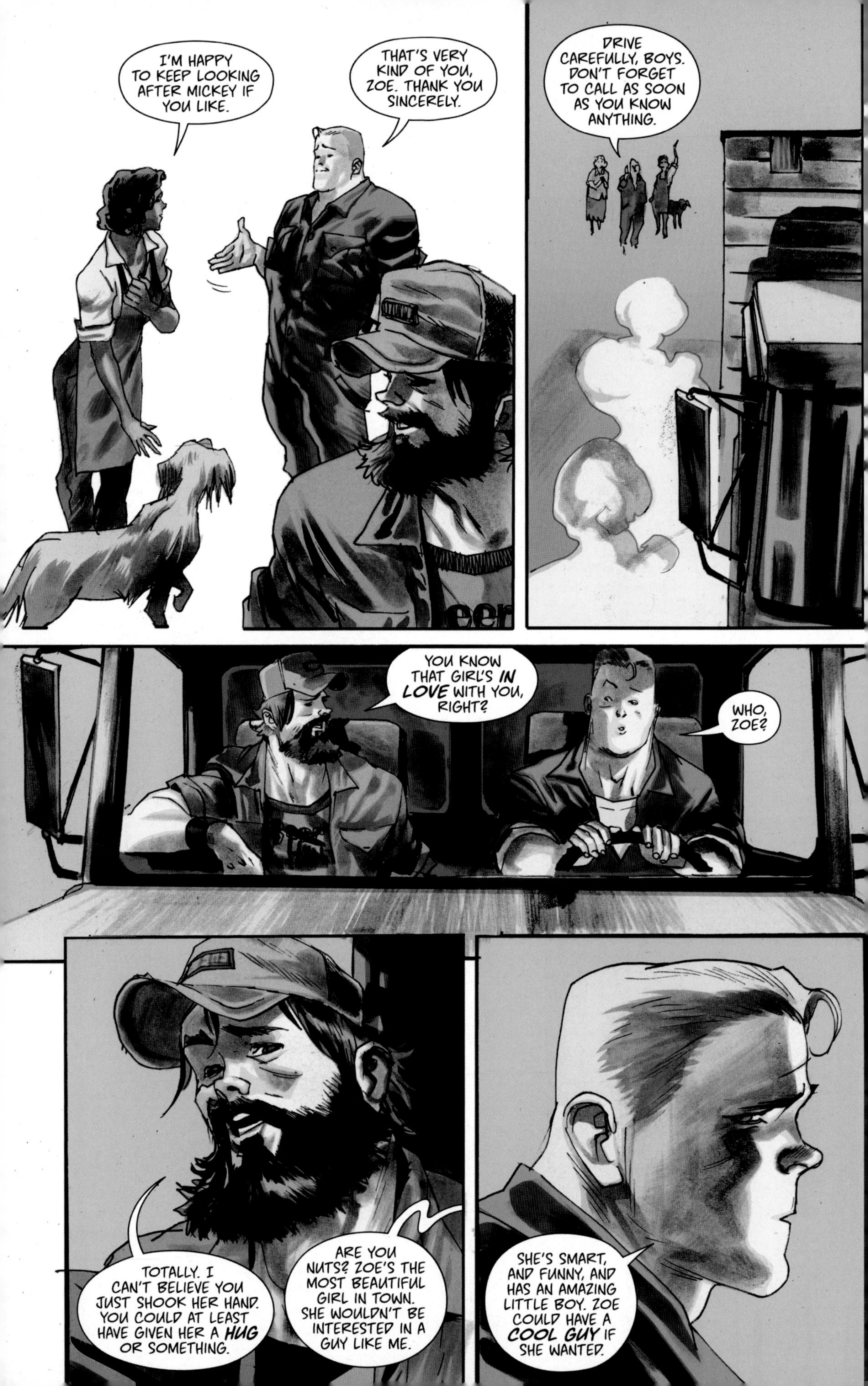
I'M HAPPY TO KEEP LOOKING AFTER MICKEY IF YOU LIKE.
THAT'S VERY KIND OF YOU, ZOE. THANK YOU SINCERELY.
DRIVE CAREFULLY, BOYS. DON'T FORGET TO CALL AS SOON AS YOU KNOW ANYTHING.
YOU KNOW THAT GIRL'S IN LOVE WITH YOU, RIGHT?
WHO, ZOE?
TOTALLY. I CAN'T BELIEVE YOU JUST SHOOK HER HAND. YOU COULD AT LEAST HAVE GIVEN HER A HUG OR SOMETHING.
ARE YOU NUTS? ZOE'S THE MOST BEAUTIFUL GIRL IN TOWN. SHE WOULDN'T BE INTERESTED IN A GUY LIKE ME.
SHE'S SMART, AND FUNNY, AND HAS AN AMAZING LITTLE BOY. ZOE COULD HAVE A COOL GUY IF SHE WANTED.

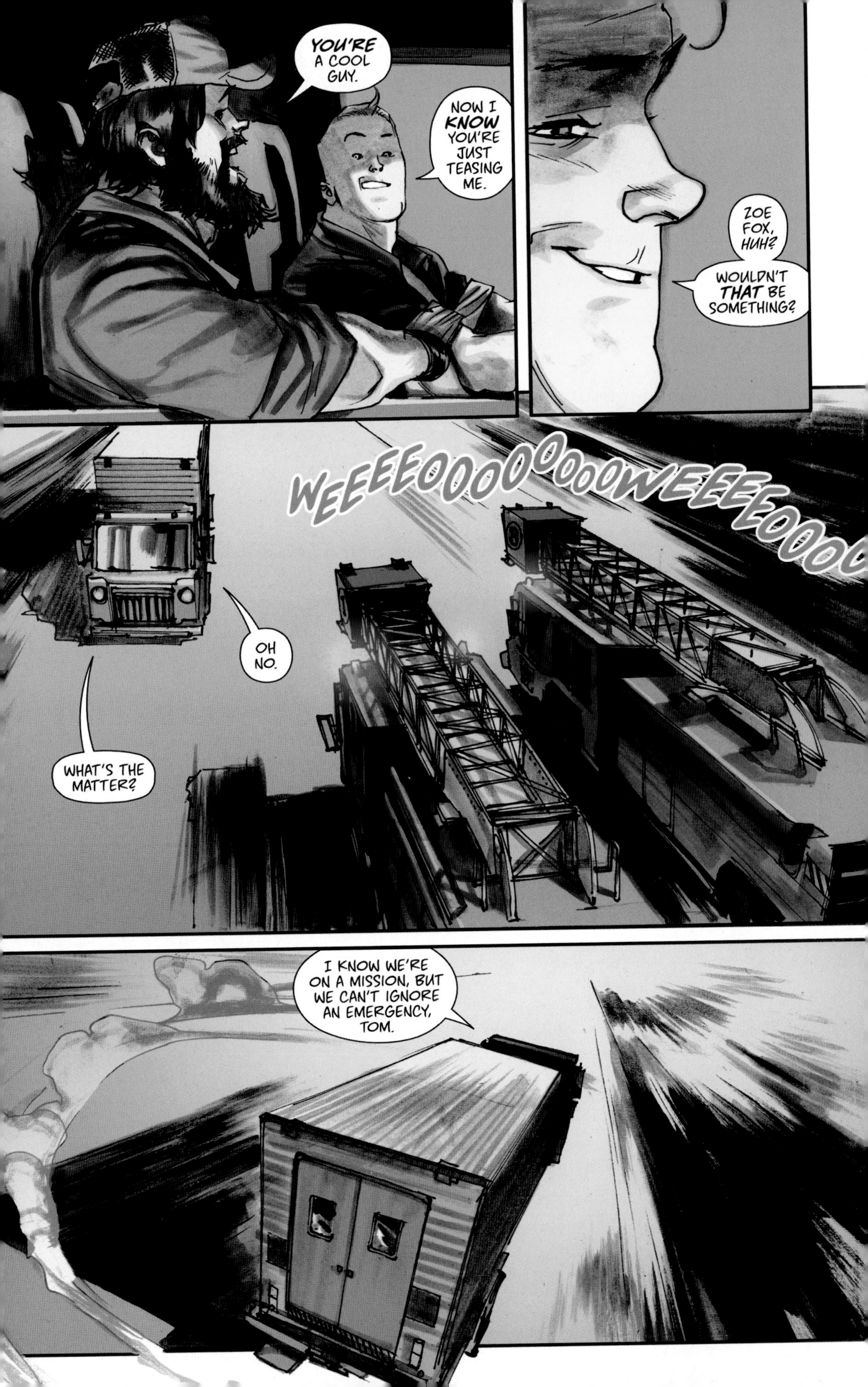
YOU'RE A COOL GUY.
NOW I KNOW YOU'RE JUST TEASING ME.
ZOE FOX, HUH?
WOULDN'T THAT BE SOMETHING?
WEEEEOOOOOoooOWEEEEOOOO
OH NO.
WHAT'S THE MATTER?
I KNOW WE'RE ON A MISSION, BUT WE CAN'T IGNORE AN EMERGENCY, TOM.

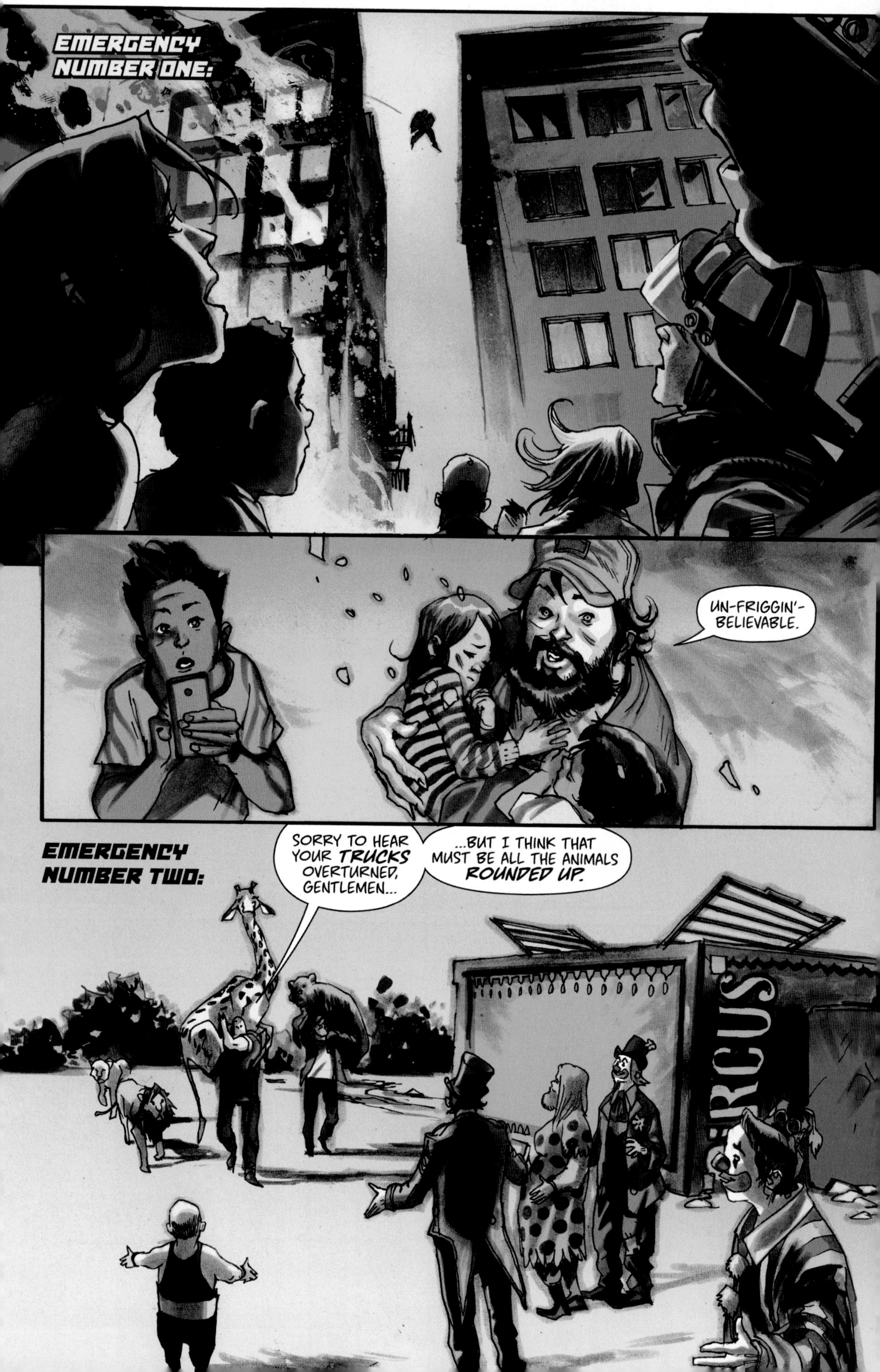
EMERGENCY NUMBER ONE:
UN-FRIGGIN'-BELIEVABLE.
EMERGENCY NUMBER TWO:
SORRY TO HEAR YOUR TRUCKS OVERTURNED, GENTLEMEN...
...BUT I THINK THAT MUST BE ALL THE ANIMALS ROUNDED UP.
CIRCUS

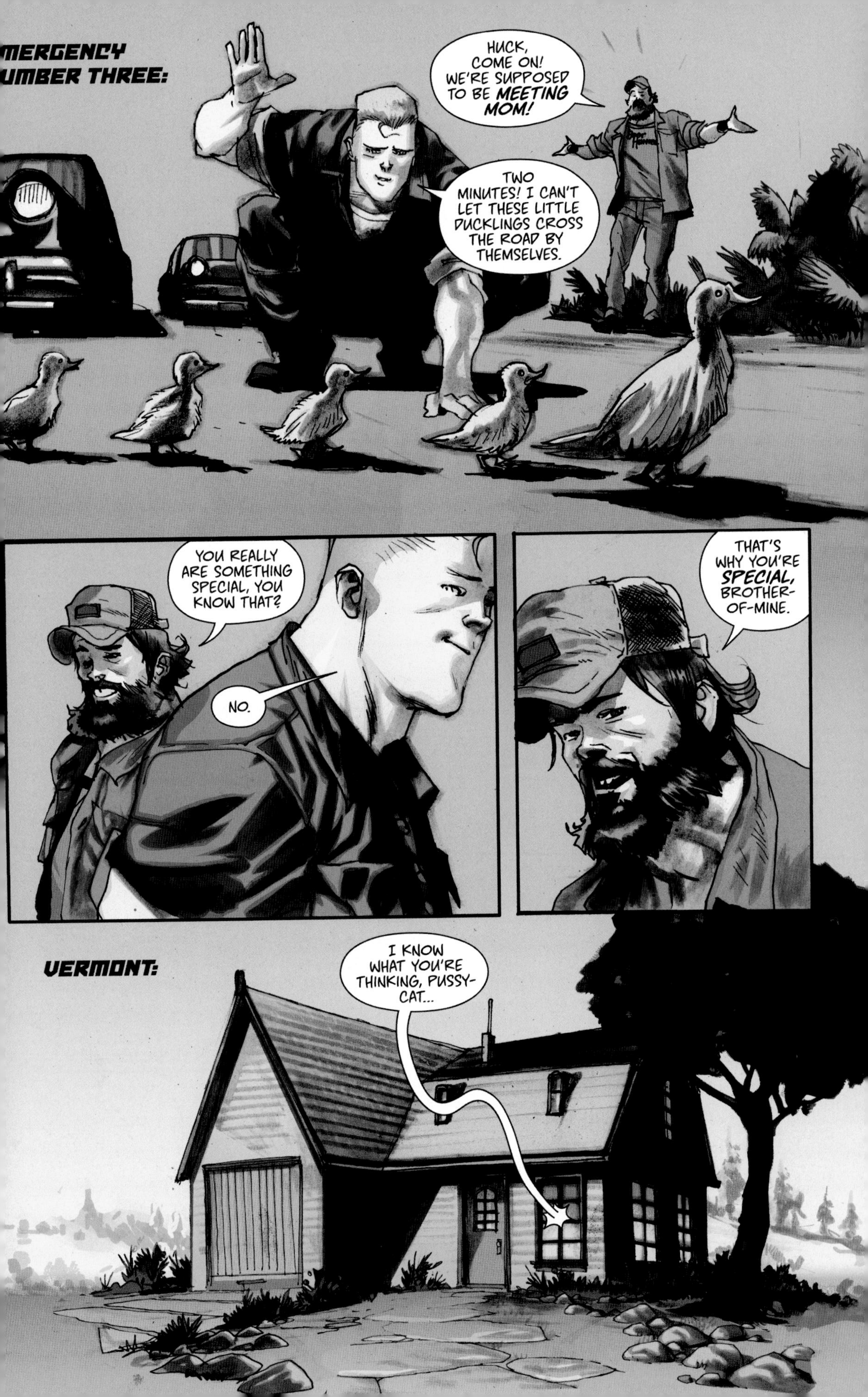

MERGENCY
UMBER THREE:
HUCK, COME ON! WE'RE SUPPOSED TO BE MEETING MOM!
TWO MINUTES! I CAN'T LET THESE LITTLE DUCKLINGS CROSS THE ROAD BY THEMSELVES.
YOU REALLY ARE SOMETHING SPECIAL, YOU KNOW THAT?
NO.
THAT'S WHY YOU'RE SPECIAL, BROTHER-OF-MINE.
VERMONT:
I KNOW WHAT YOU'RE THINKING, PUSSY-CAT...

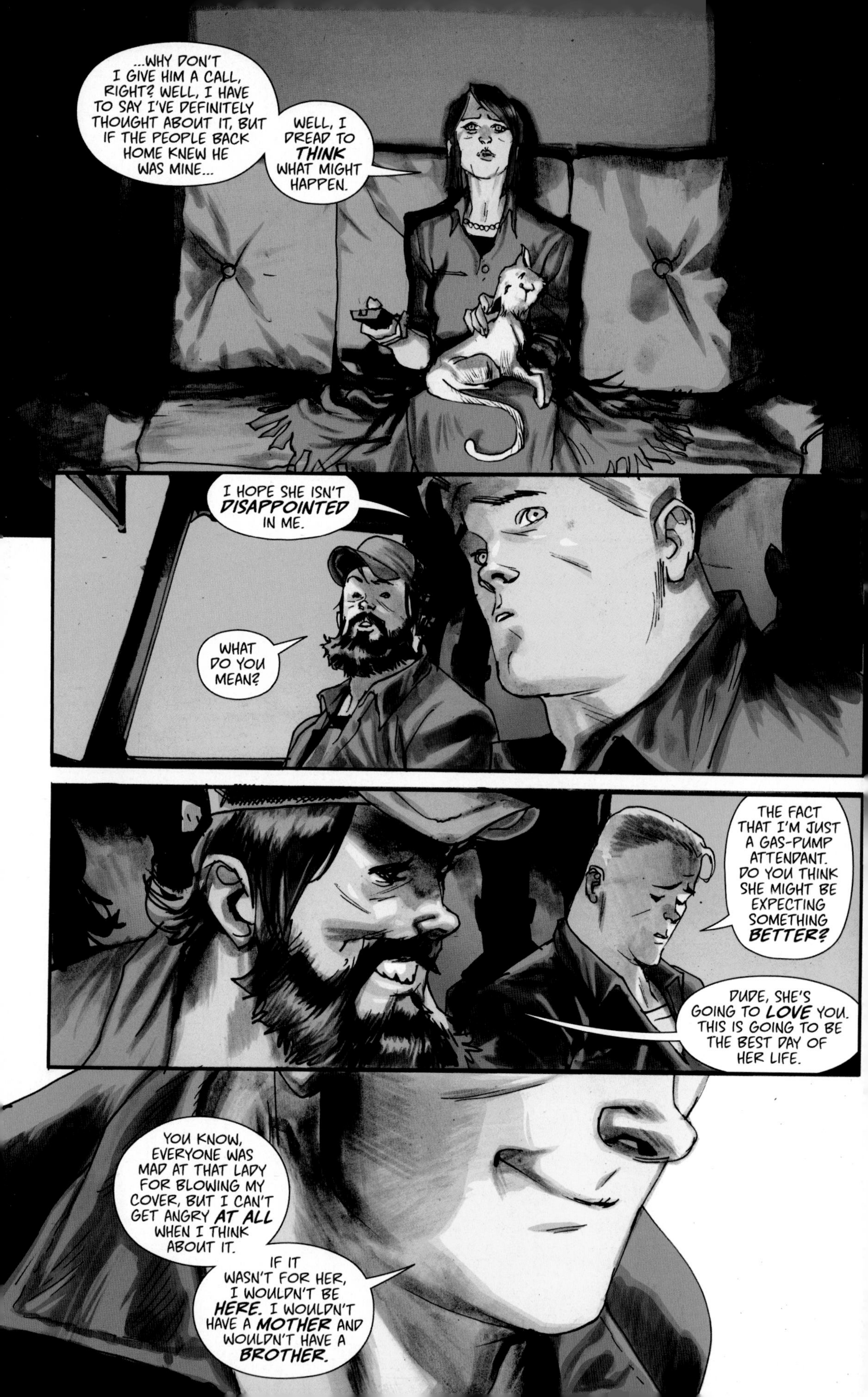
...WHY DON'T I GIVE HIM A CALL, RIGHT? WELL, I HAVE TO SAY I'VE DEFINITELY THOUGHT ABOUT IT, BUT IF THE PEOPLE BACK HOME KNEW HE WAS MINE...
WELL, I DREAD TO THINK WHAT MIGHT HAPPEN.
I HOPE SHE ISN'T DISAPPOINTED IN ME.
WHAT DO YOU MEAN?
THE FACT THAT I'M JUST A GAS-PUMP ATTENDANT. DO YOU THINK SHE MIGHT BE EXPECTING SOMETHING BETTER?
DUDE, SHE'S GOING TO LOVE YOU. THIS IS GOING TO BE THE BEST DAY OF HER LIFE.
YOU KNOW, EVERYONE WAS MAD AT THAT LADY FOR BLOWING MY COVER, BUT I CAN'T GET ANGRY AT ALL WHEN I THINK ABOUT IT.
IF IT WASN'T FOR HER, I WOULDN'T BE HERE. I WOULDN'T HAVE A MOTHER AND WOULDN'T HAVE A BROTHER.

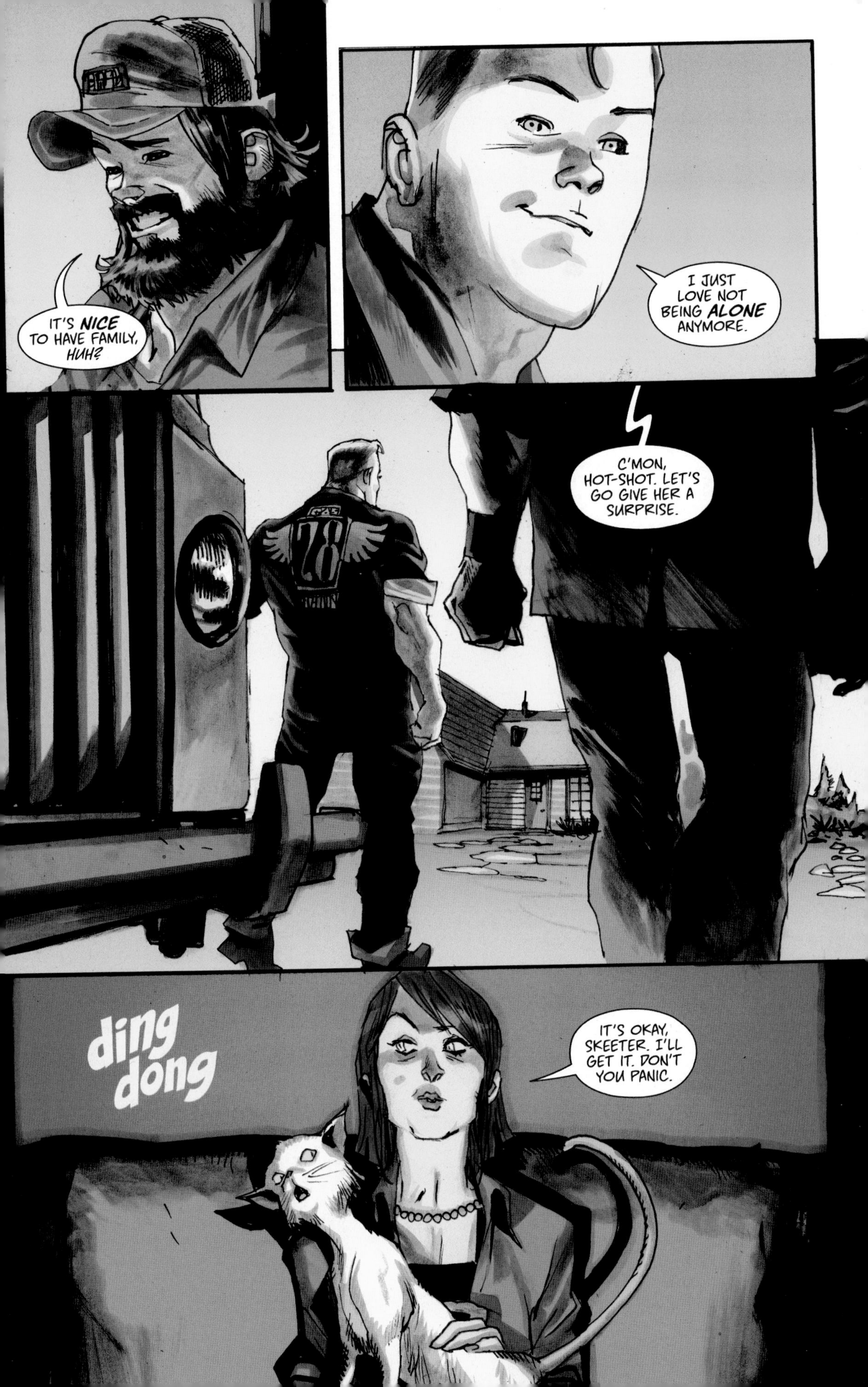
IT'S NICE TO HAVE FAMILY, HUH?
I JUST LOVE NOT BEING ALONE ANYMORE.
C'MON, HOT-SHOT. LET'S GO GIVE HER A SURPRISE.
ding dong
IT'S OKAY, SKEETER. I'LL GET IT. DON'T YOU PANIC.

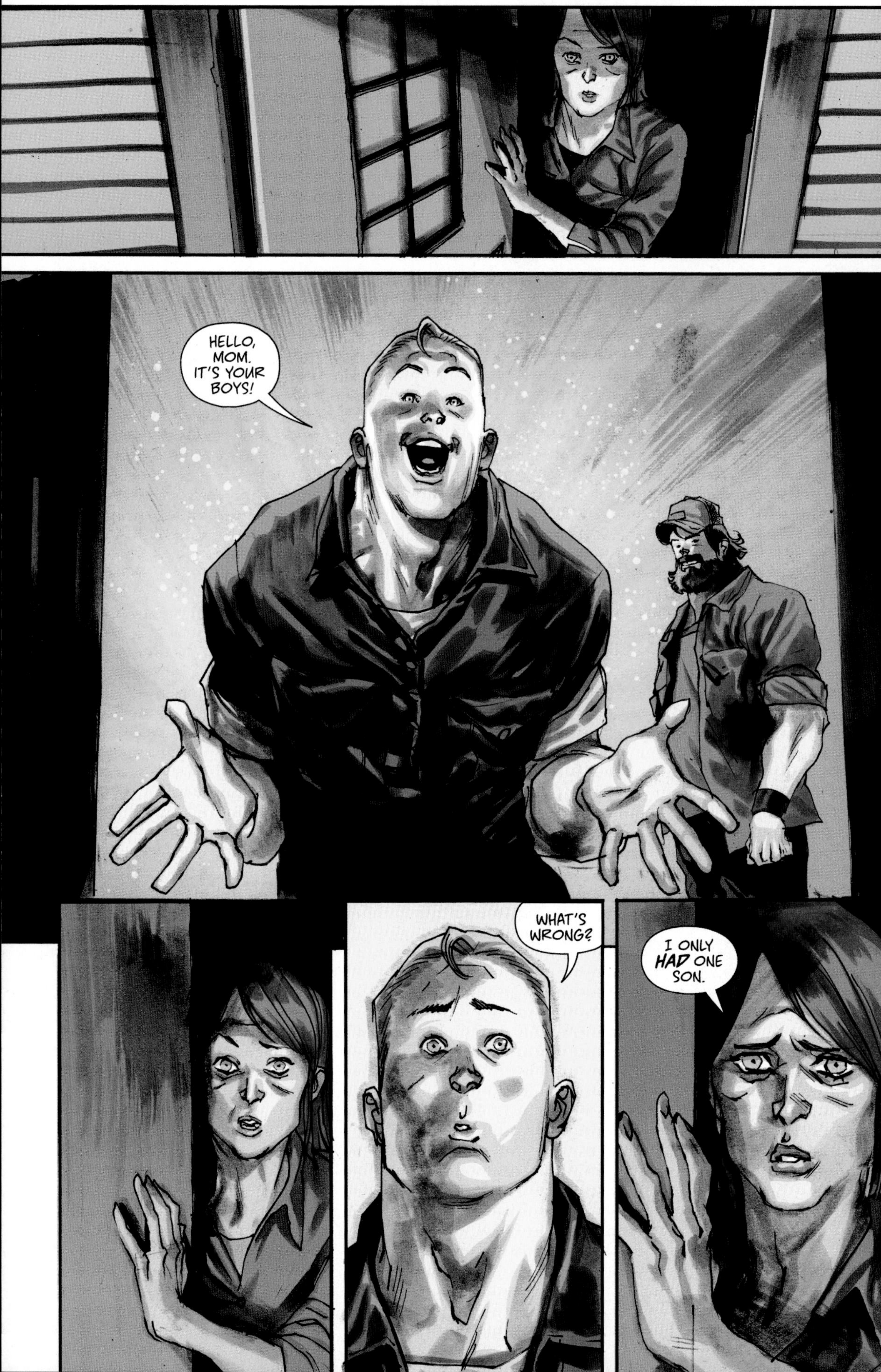
HELLO, MOM. IT'S YOUR BOYS!
WHAT'S WRONG?
I ONLY HAD ONE SON.

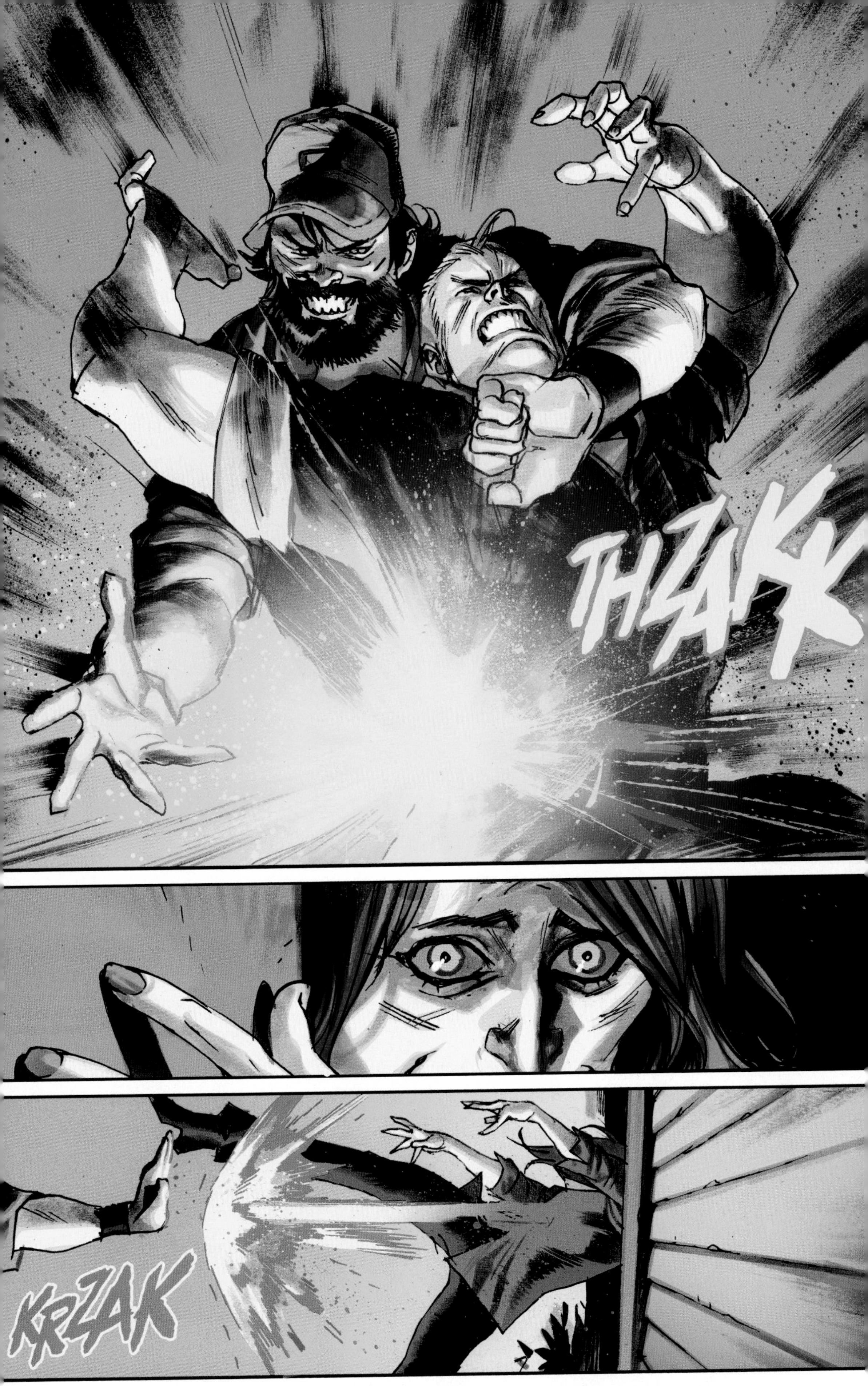
THZAKK
KRZAK

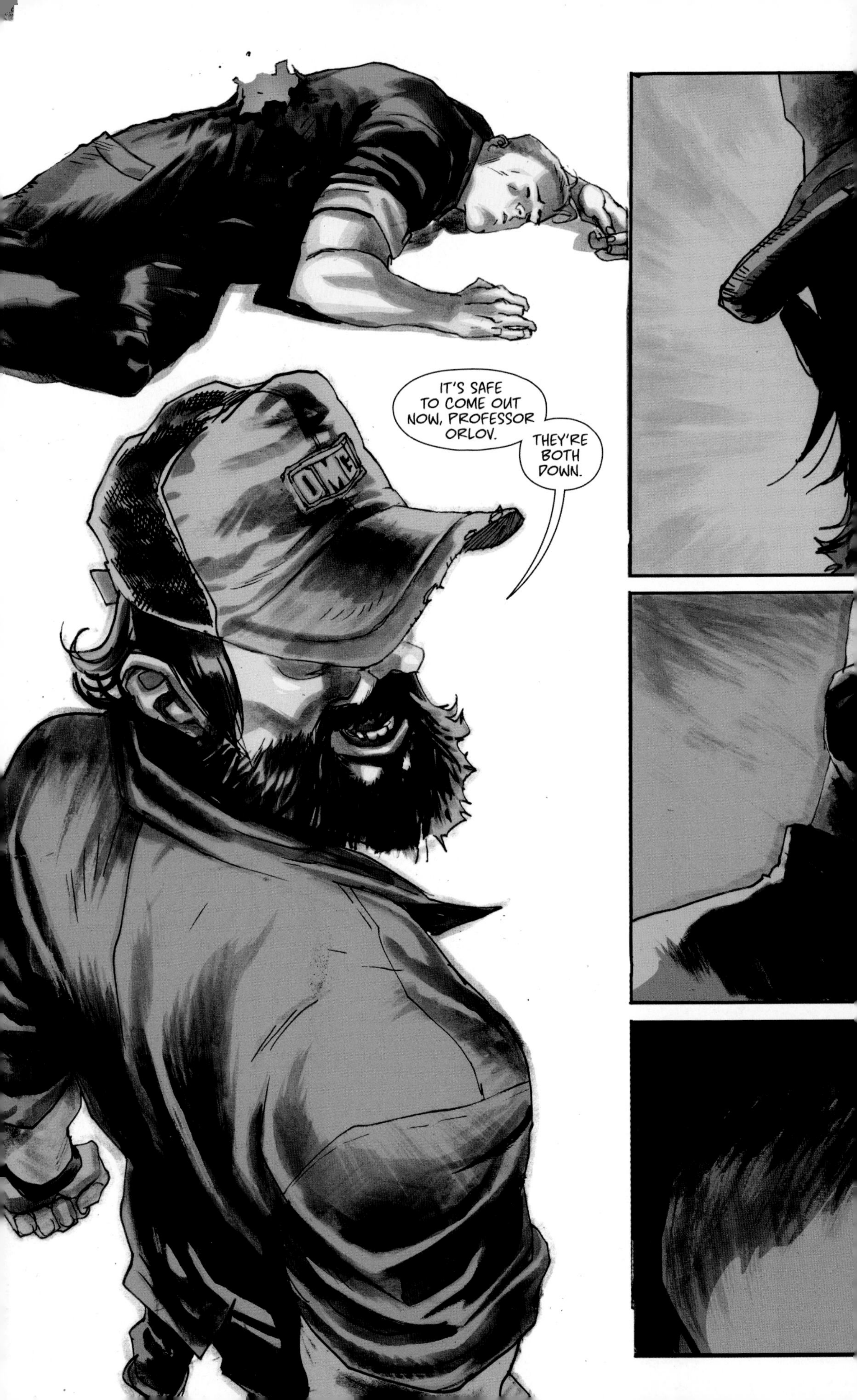
IT'S SAFE TO COME OUT NOW, PROFESSOR ORLOV.
THEY'RE BOTH DOWN.
OMEGA

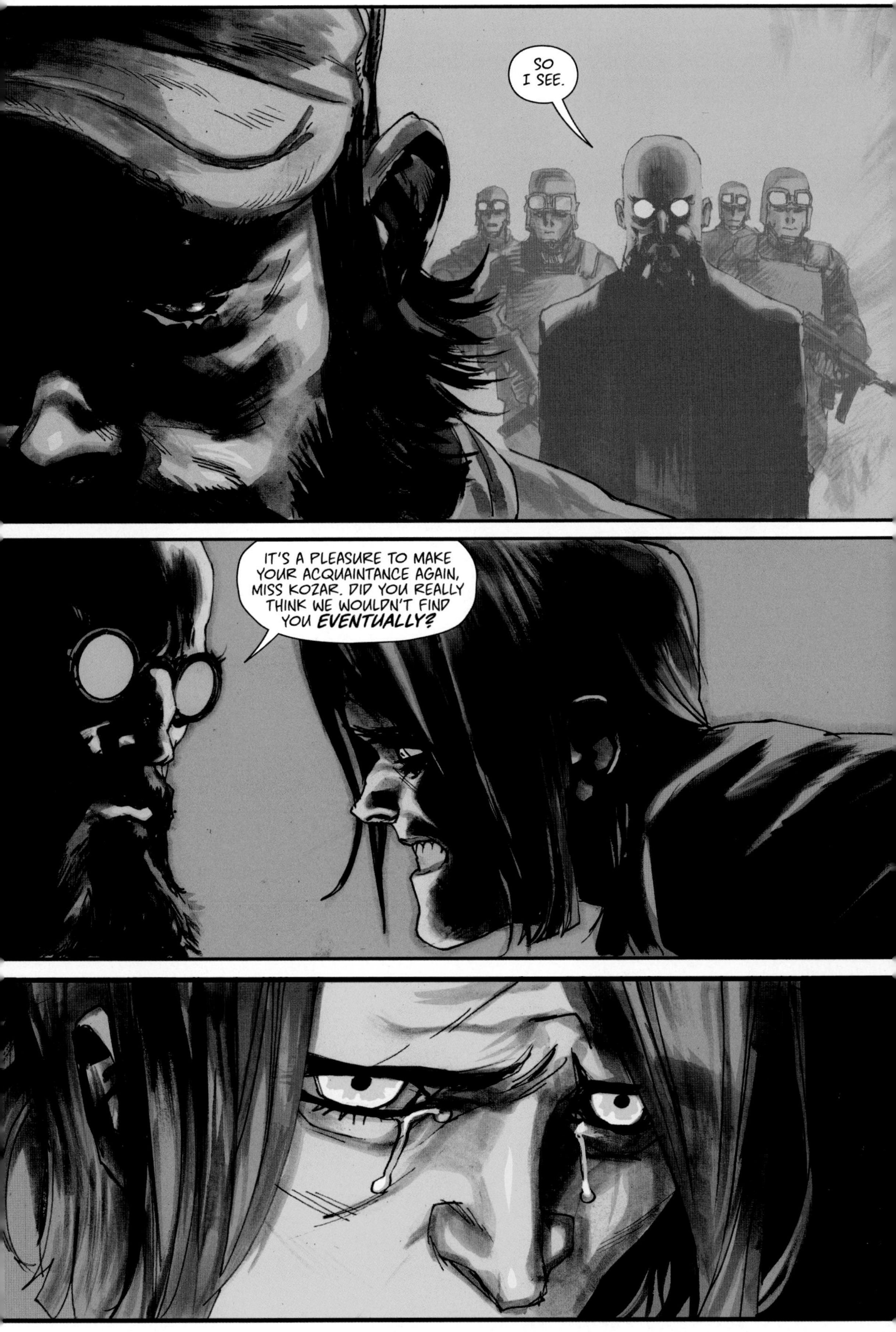
SO I SEE.
IT'S A PLEASURE TO MAKE YOUR ACQUAINTANCE AGAIN, MISS KOZAR. DID YOU REALLY THINK WE WOULDN'T FIND YOU EVENTUALLY?

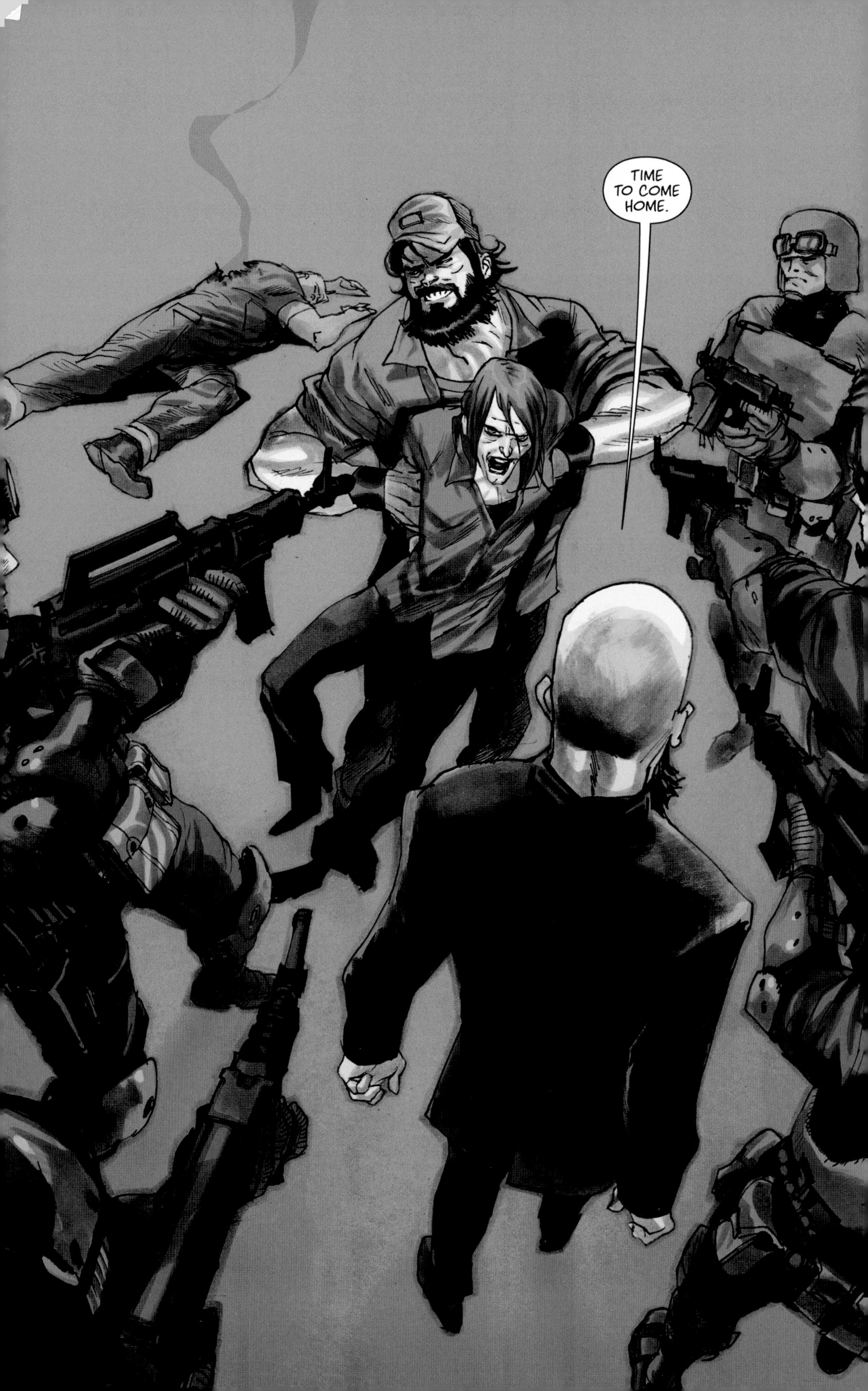
TIME TO COME HOME.

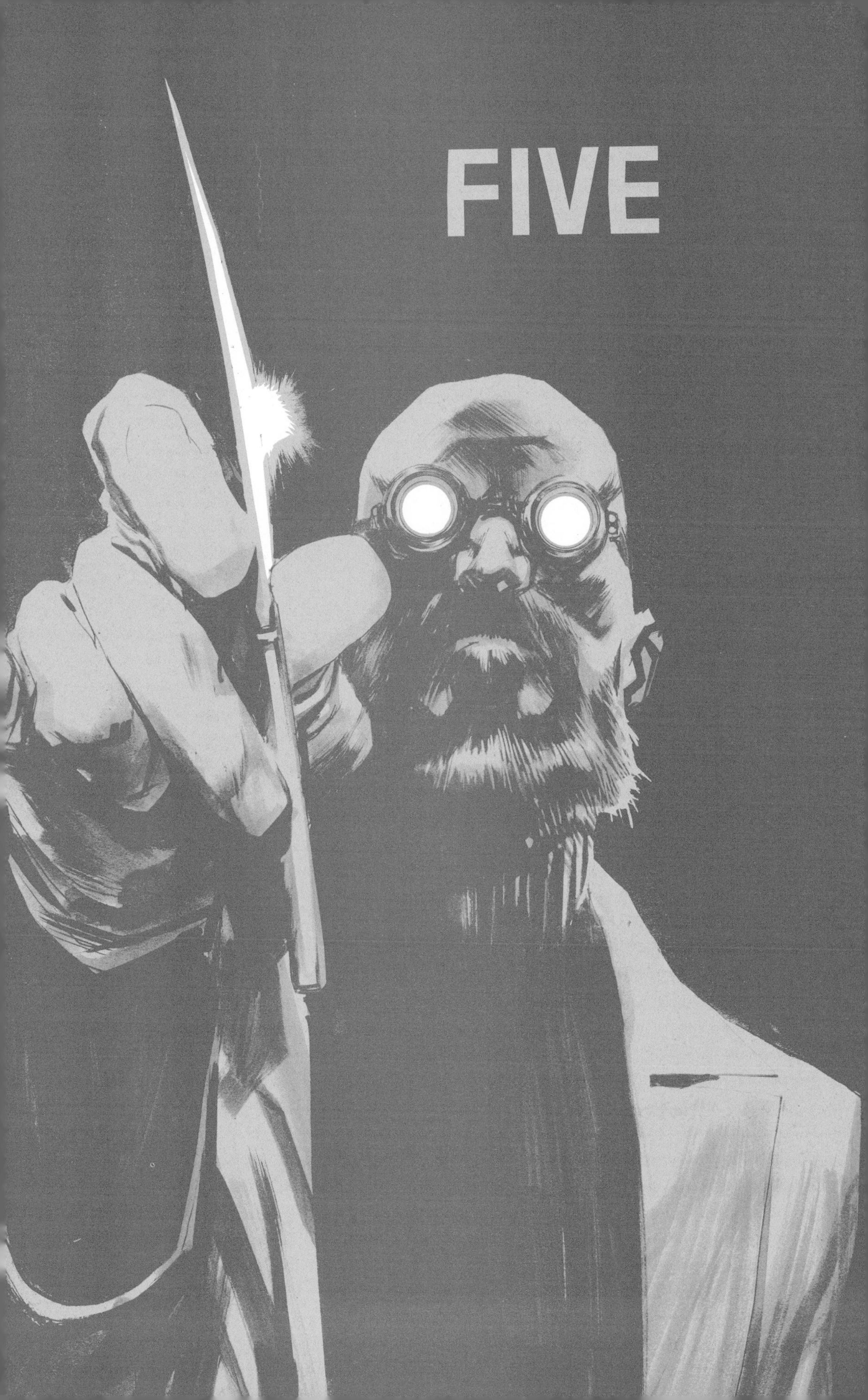
FIVE

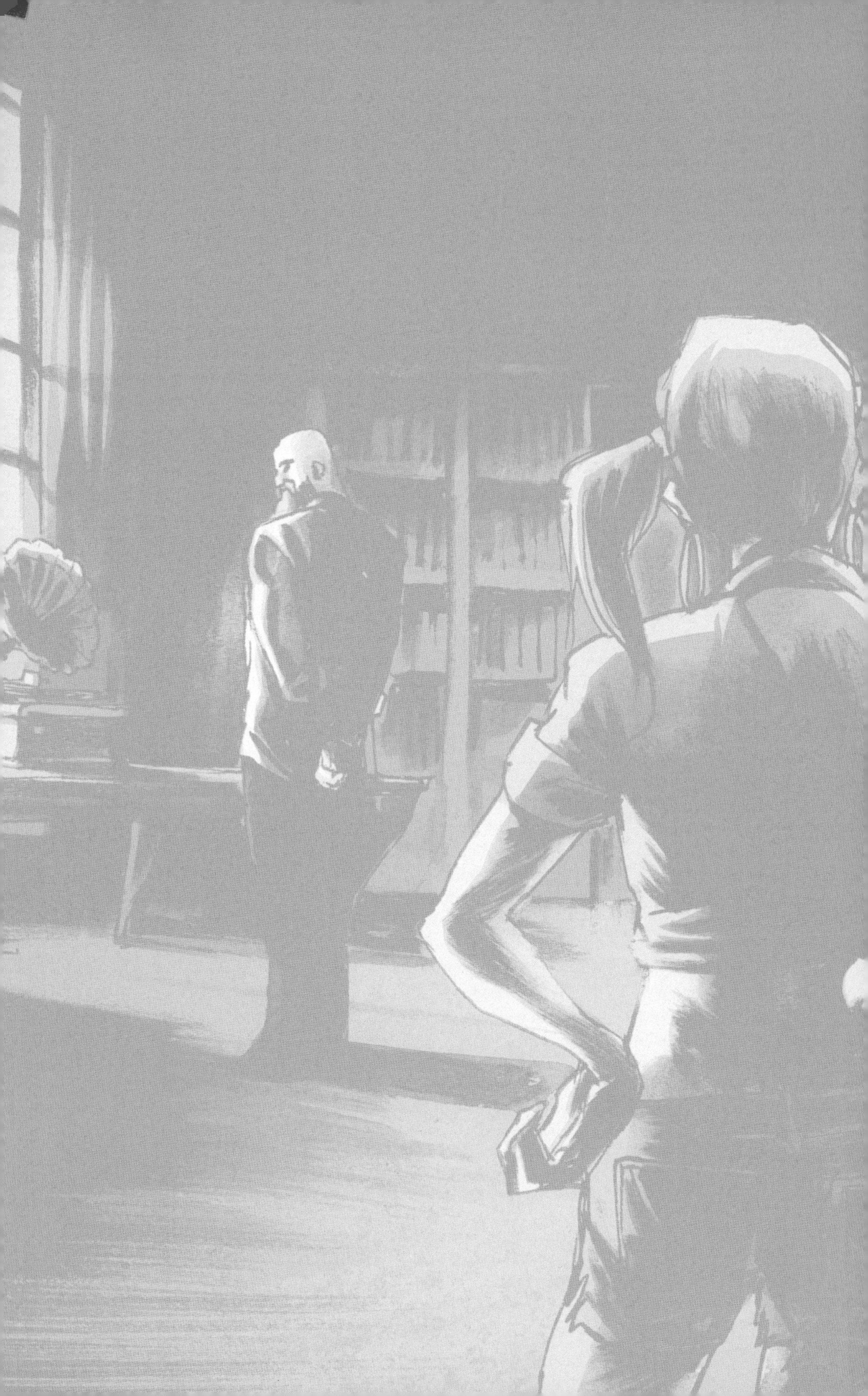

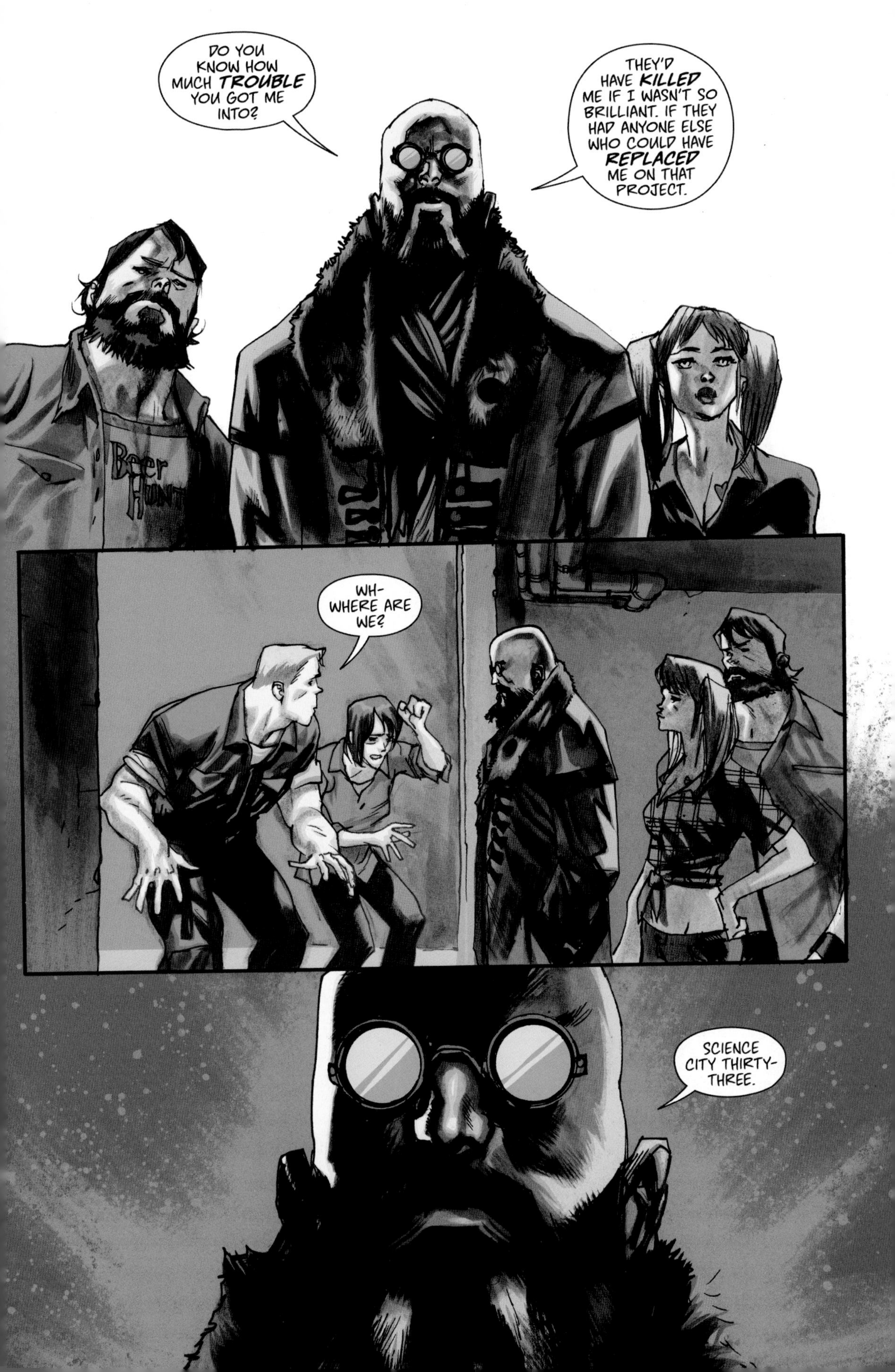
DO YOU KNOW HOW MUCH TROUBLE YOU GOT ME INTO?
THEY'D HAVE KILLED ME IF I WASN'T SO BRILLIANT. IF THEY HAD ANYONE ELSE WHO COULD HAVE REPLACED ME ON THAT PROJECT.
WH- WHERE ARE WE?
SCIENCE CITY THIRTY-THREE.

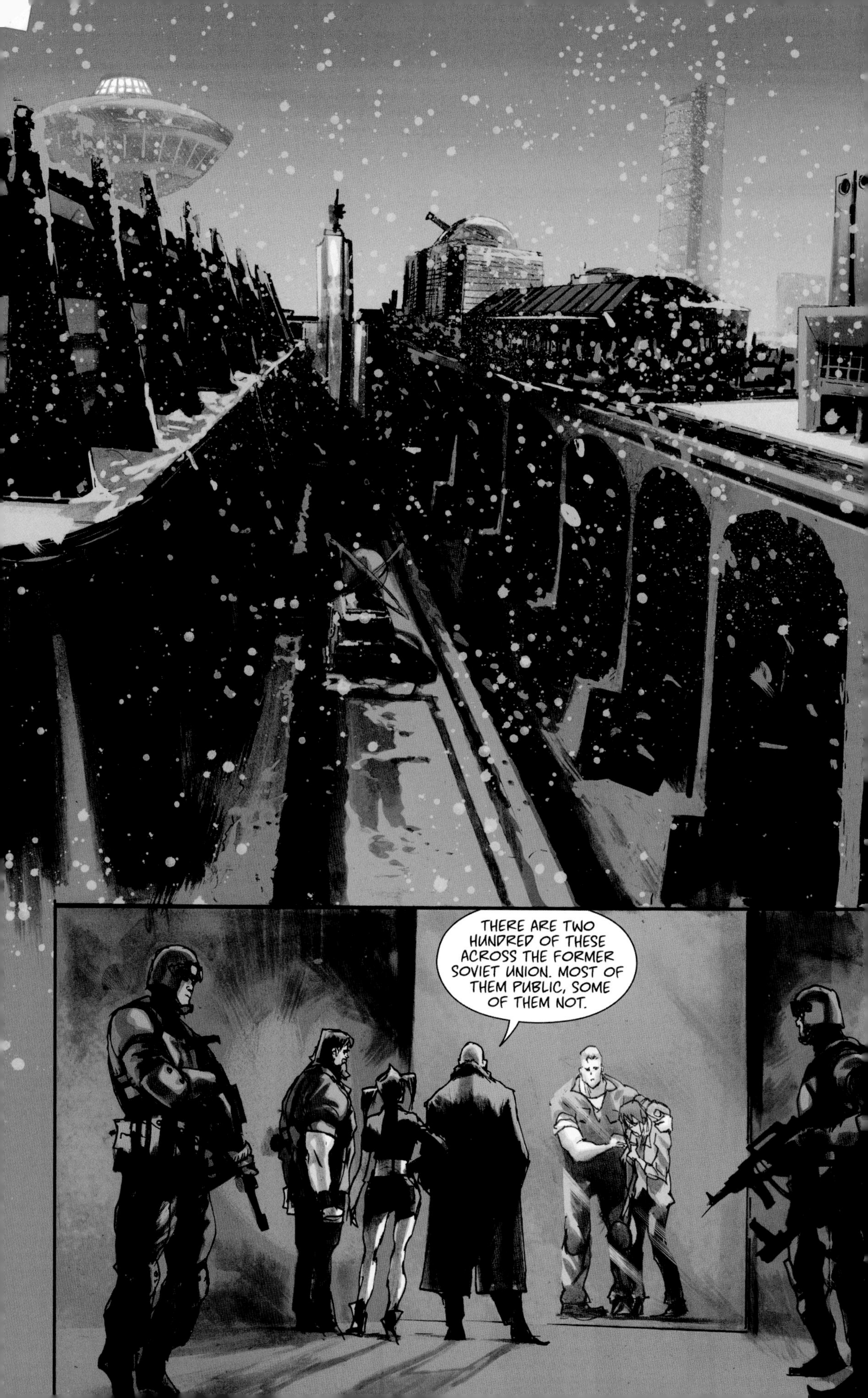
THERE ARE TWO HUNDRED OF THESE ACROSS THE FORMER SOVIET UNION. MOST OF THEM PUBLIC, SOME OF THEM NOT.

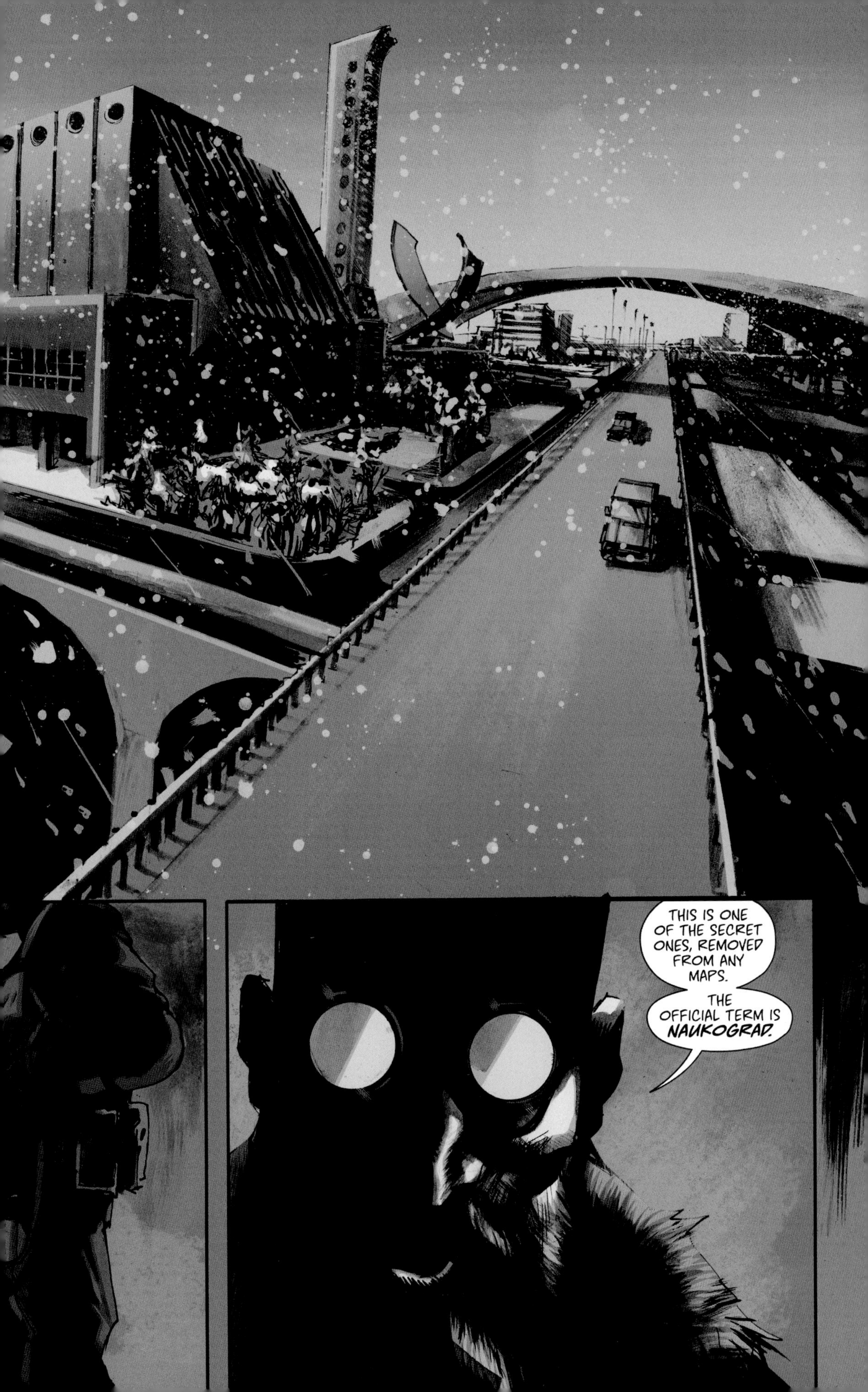
THIS IS ONE OF THE SECRET ONES, REMOVED FROM ANY MAPS.
THE OFFICIAL TERM IS *NAUKOGRAD.*

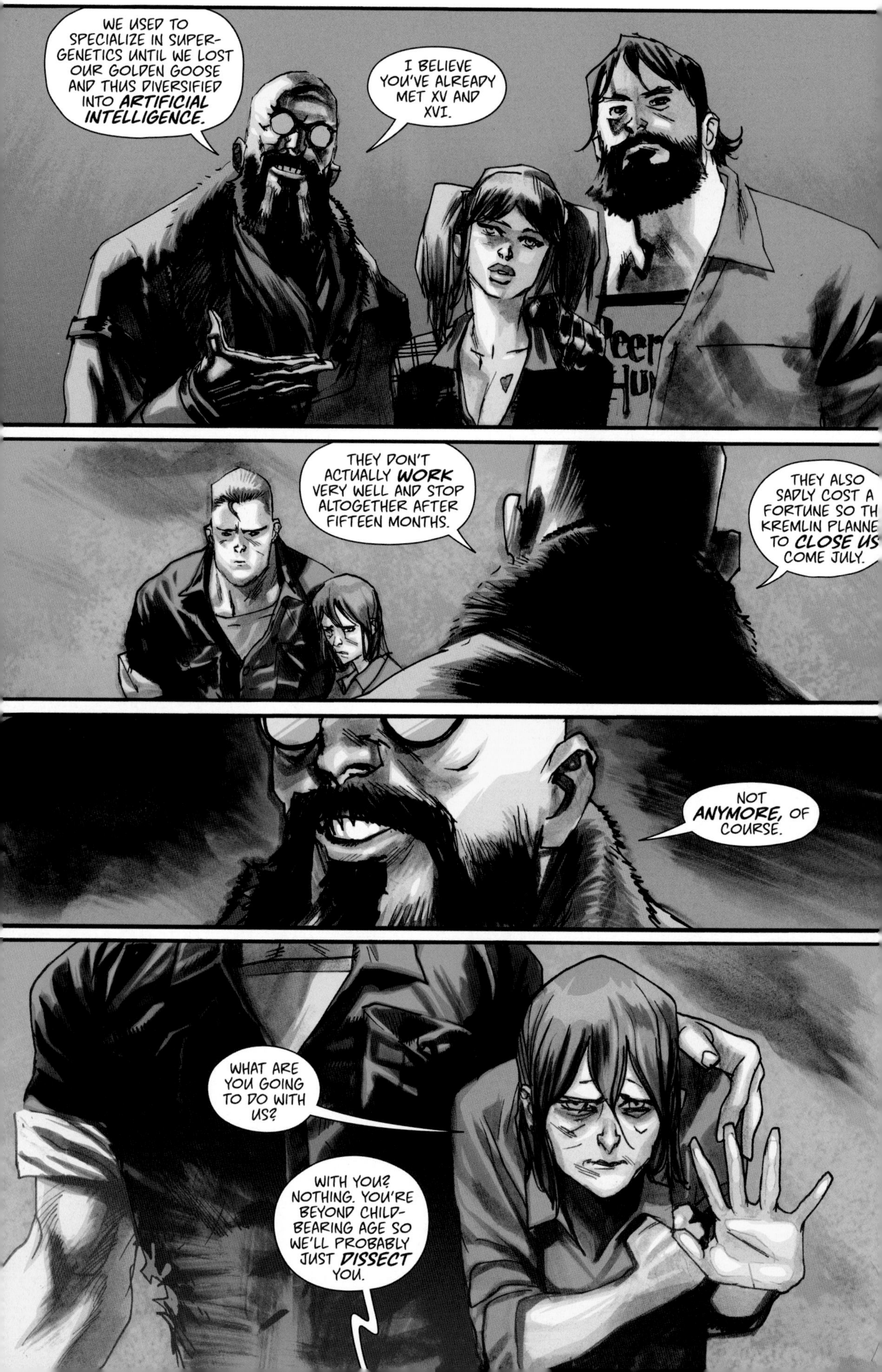
WE USED TO SPECIALIZE IN SUPER-GENETICS UNTIL WE LOST OUR GOLDEN GOOSE AND THUS DIVERSIFIED INTO ARTIFICIAL INTELLIGENCE.
I BELIEVE YOU'VE ALREADY MET XV AND XVI.
THEY DON'T ACTUALLY WORK VERY WELL AND STOP ALTOGETHER AFTER FIFTEEN MONTHS.
THEY ALSO SADLY COST A FORTUNE SO TH KREMLIN PLANNE TO CLOSE US COME JULY.
NOT ANYMORE, OF COURSE.
WHAT ARE YOU GOING TO DO WITH US?
WITH YOU? NOTHING. YOU'RE BEYOND CHILD-BEARING AGE SO WE'LL PROBABLY JUST DISSECT YOU.

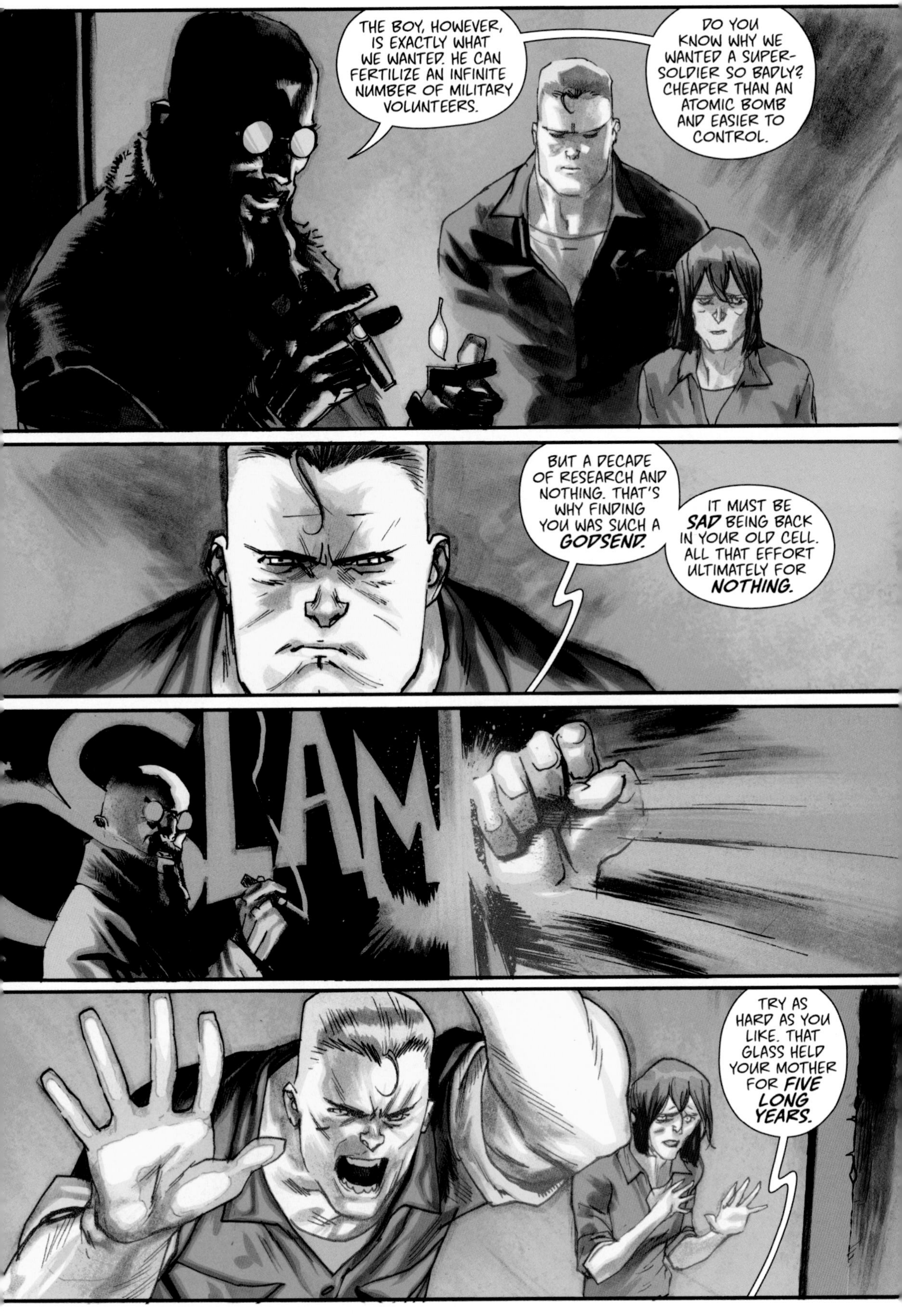
THE BOY, HOWEVER, IS EXACTLY WHAT WE WANTED. HE CAN FERTILIZE AN INFINITE NUMBER OF MILITARY VOLUNTEERS.
DO YOU KNOW WHY WE WANTED A SUPER-SOLDIER SO BADLY? CHEAPER THAN AN ATOMIC BOMB AND EASIER TO CONTROL.
BUT A DECADE OF RESEARCH AND NOTHING. THAT'S WHY FINDING YOU WAS SUCH A GODSEND.
IT MUST BE SAD BEING BACK IN YOUR OLD CELL. ALL THAT EFFORT ULTIMATELY FOR NOTHING.
SLAM
TRY AS HARD AS YOU LIKE. THAT GLASS HELD YOUR MOTHER FOR FIVE LONG YEARS.

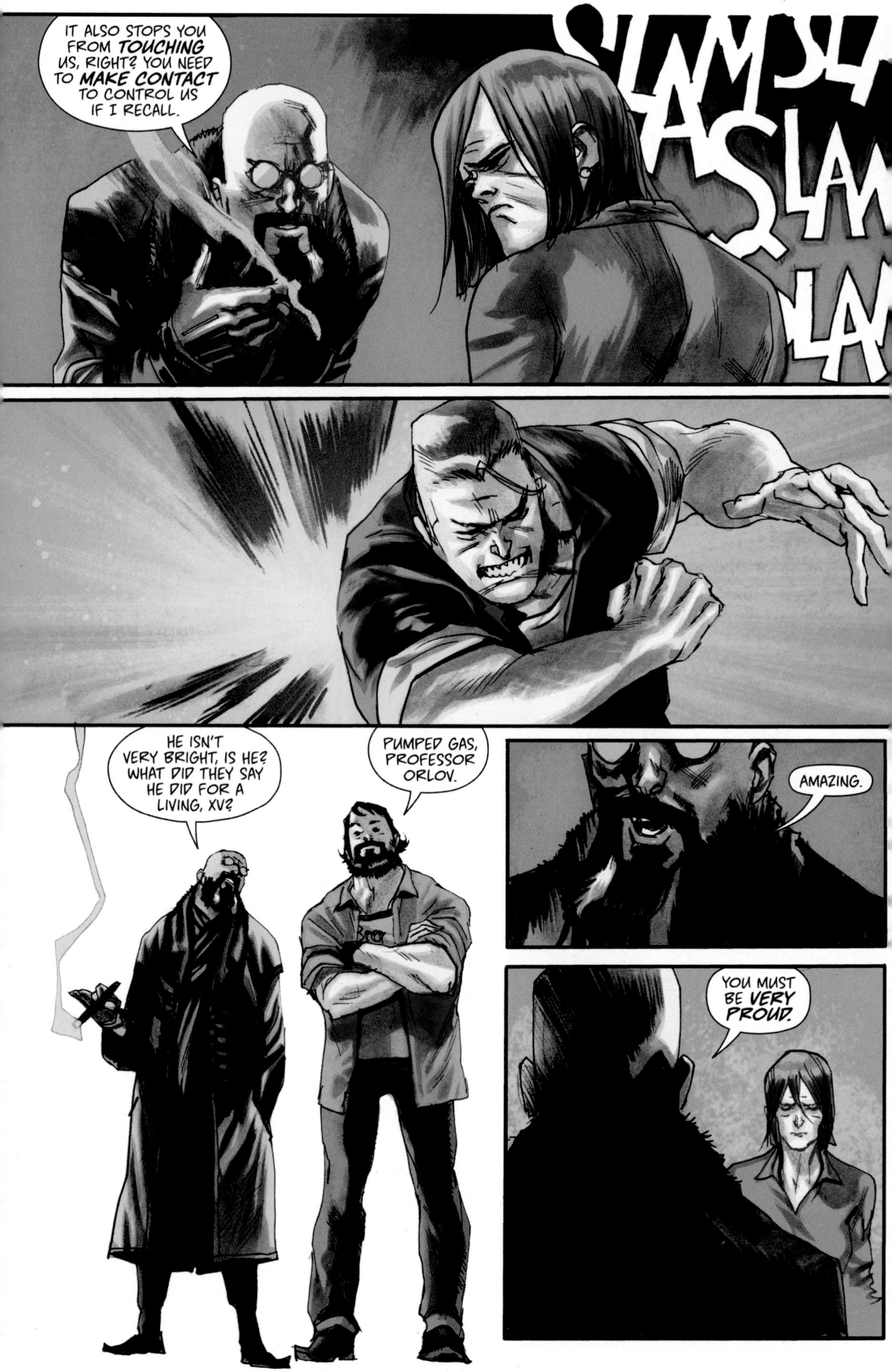

IT ALSO STOPS YOU FROM **TOUCHING** US, RIGHT? YOU NEED TO **MAKE CONTACT** TO CONTROL US IF I RECALL.
HE ISN'T VERY BRIGHT, IS HE? WHAT DID THEY SAY HE DID FOR A LIVING, XV?
PUMPED GAS, PROFESSOR ORLOV.
AMAZING.
YOU MUST BE ***VERY PROUD.***

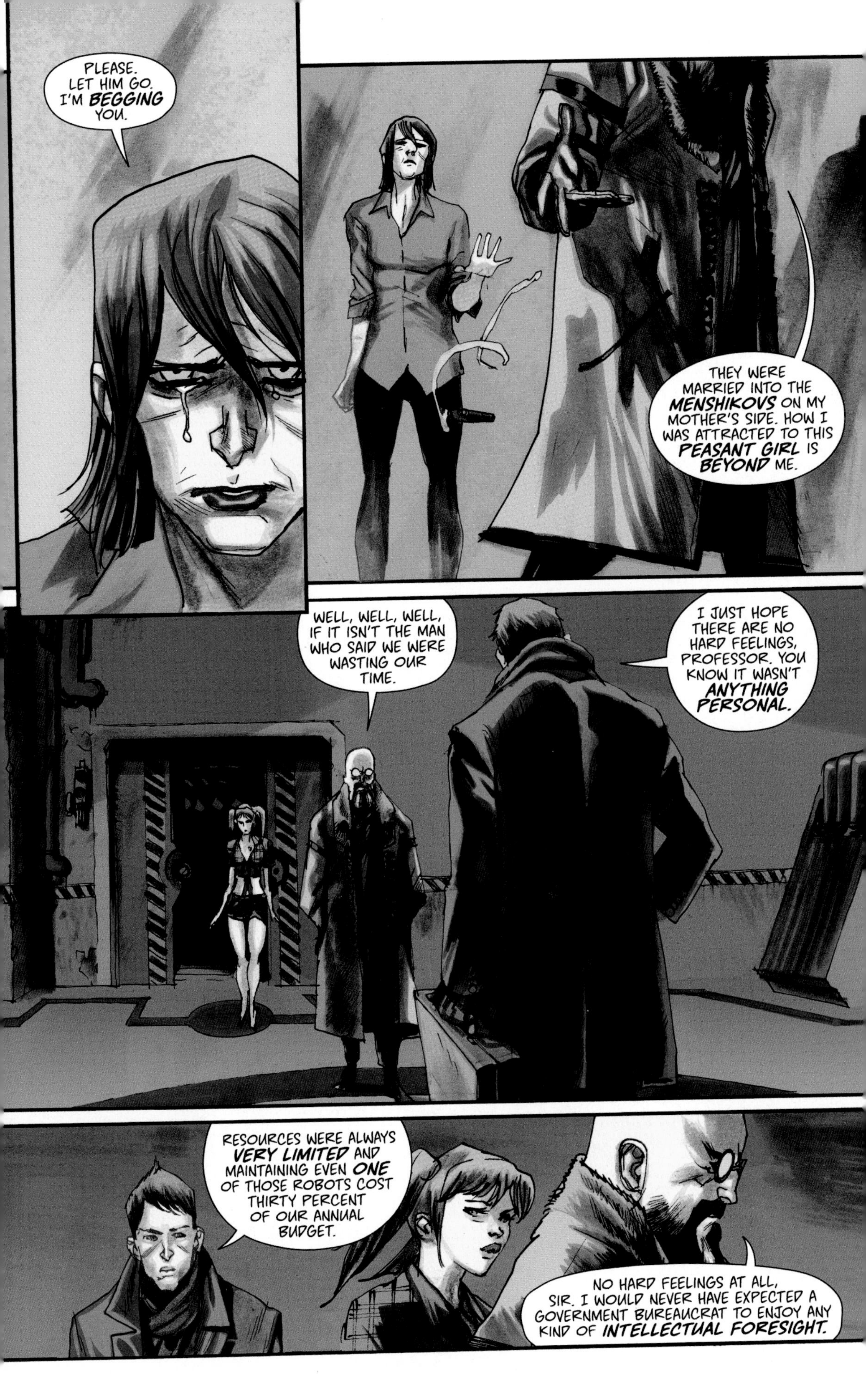
PLEASE. LET HIM GO. I'M BEGGING YOU.
THEY WERE MARRIED INTO THE MENSHIKOVS ON MY MOTHER'S SIDE. HOW I WAS ATTRACTED TO THIS PEASANT GIRL IS BEYOND ME.
WELL, WELL, WELL, IF IT ISN'T THE MAN WHO SAID WE WERE WASTING OUR TIME.
I JUST HOPE THERE ARE NO HARD FEELINGS, PROFESSOR. YOU KNOW IT WASN'T ANYTHING PERSONAL.
RESOURCES WERE ALWAYS VERY LIMITED AND MAINTAINING EVEN ONE OF THOSE ROBOTS COST THIRTY PERCENT OF OUR ANNUAL BUDGET.
NO HARD FEELINGS AT ALL, SIR. I WOULD NEVER HAVE EXPECTED A GOVERNMENT BUREAUCRAT TO ENJOY ANY KIND OF INTELLECTUAL FORESIGHT.

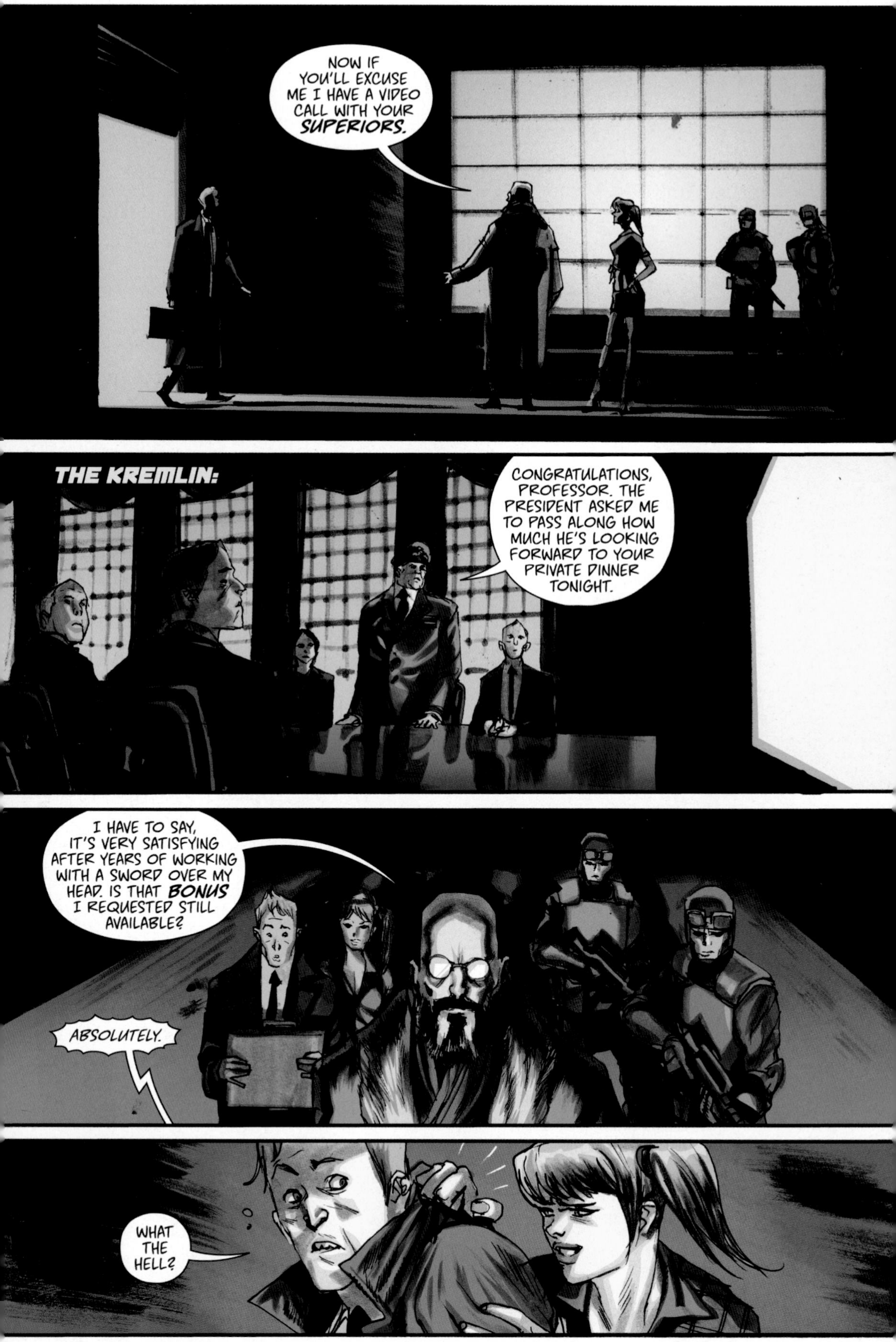
NOW IF YOU'LL EXCUSE ME I HAVE A VIDEO CALL WITH YOUR SUPERIORS.
THE KREMLIN:
CONGRATULATIONS, PROFESSOR. THE PRESIDENT ASKED ME TO PASS ALONG HOW MUCH HE'S LOOKING FORWARD TO YOUR PRIVATE DINNER TONIGHT.
I HAVE TO SAY, IT'S VERY SATISFYING AFTER YEARS OF WORKING WITH A SWORD OVER MY HEAD. IS THAT BONUS I REQUESTED STILL AVAILABLE?
ABSOLUTELY.
WHAT THE HELL?

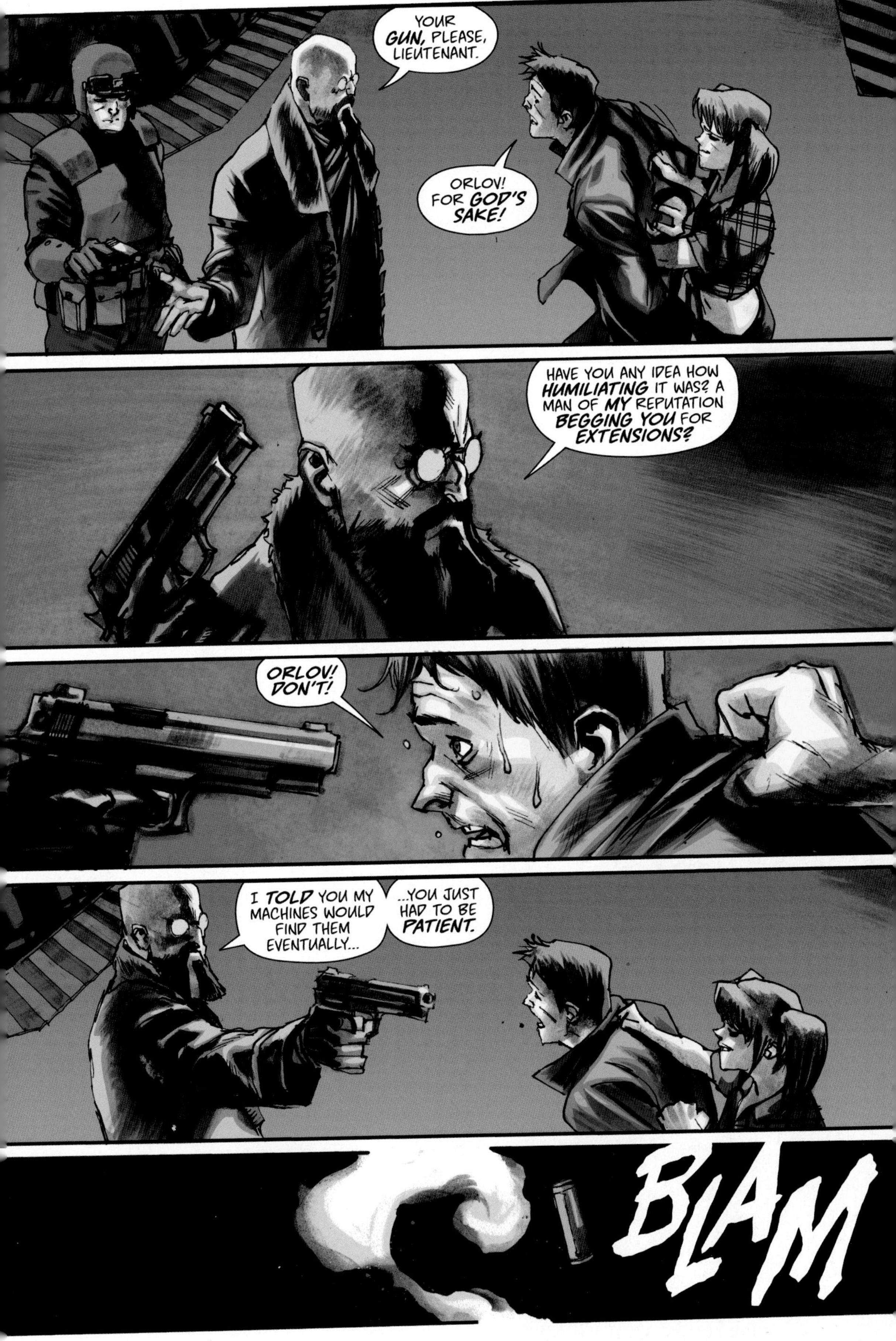
YOUR GUN, PLEASE, LIEUTENANT.
ORLOV! FOR GOD'S SAKE!
HAVE YOU ANY IDEA HOW HUMILIATING IT WAS? A MAN OF MY REPUTATION BEGGING YOU FOR EXTENSIONS?
ORLOV! DON'T!
I TOLD YOU MY MACHINES WOULD FIND THEM EVENTUALLY...
...YOU JUST HAD TO BE PATIENT.
BLAM

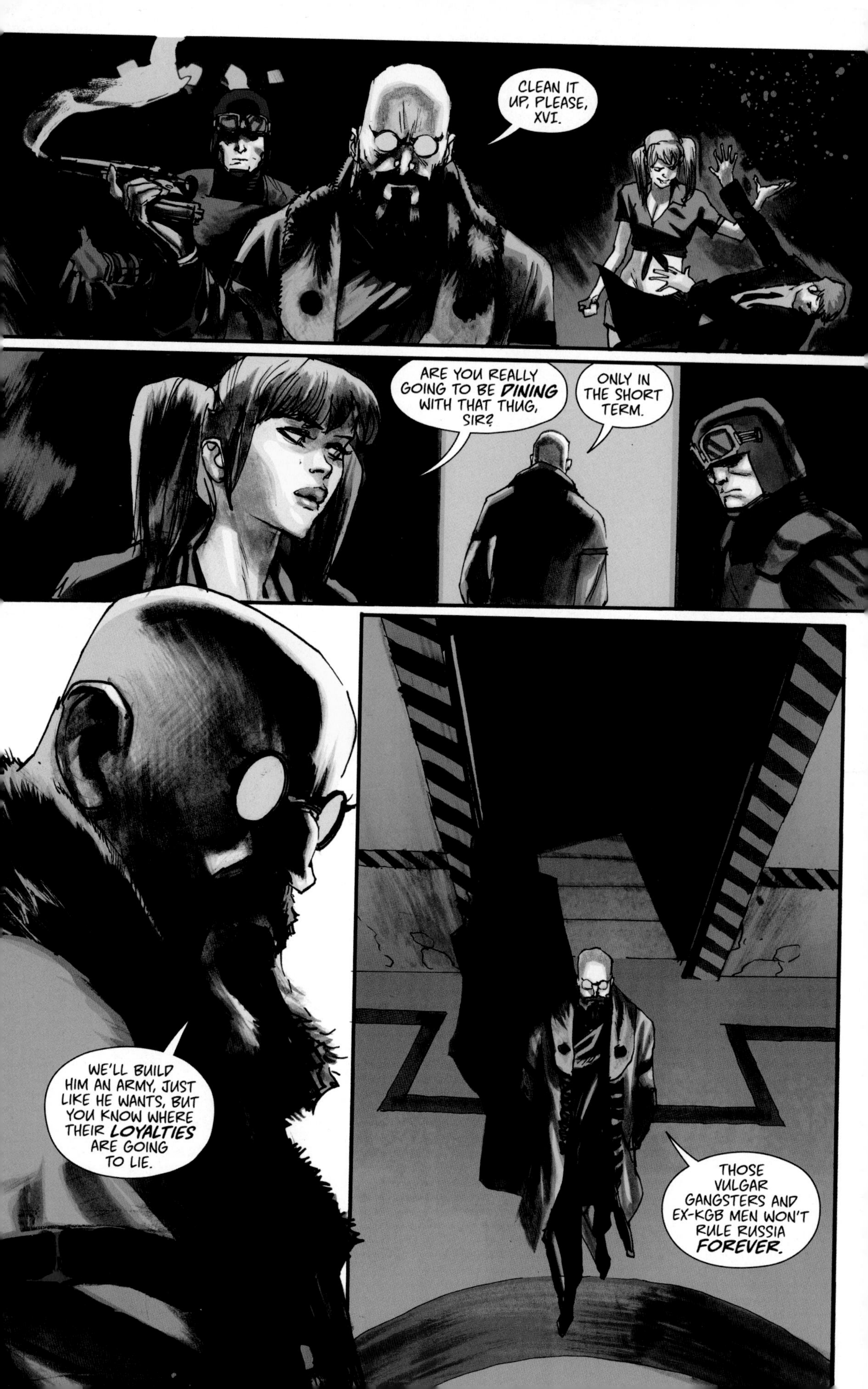
CLEAN IT UP, PLEASE, XVI.
ARE YOU REALLY GOING TO BE **DINING** WITH THAT THUG, SIR?
ONLY IN THE SHORT TERM.
WE'LL BUILD HIM AN ARMY, JUST LIKE HE WANTS, BUT YOU KNOW WHERE THEIR **LOYALTIES** ARE GOING TO LIE.
THOSE VULGAR GANGSTERS AND EX-KGB MEN WON'T RULE RUSSIA **FOREVER**.

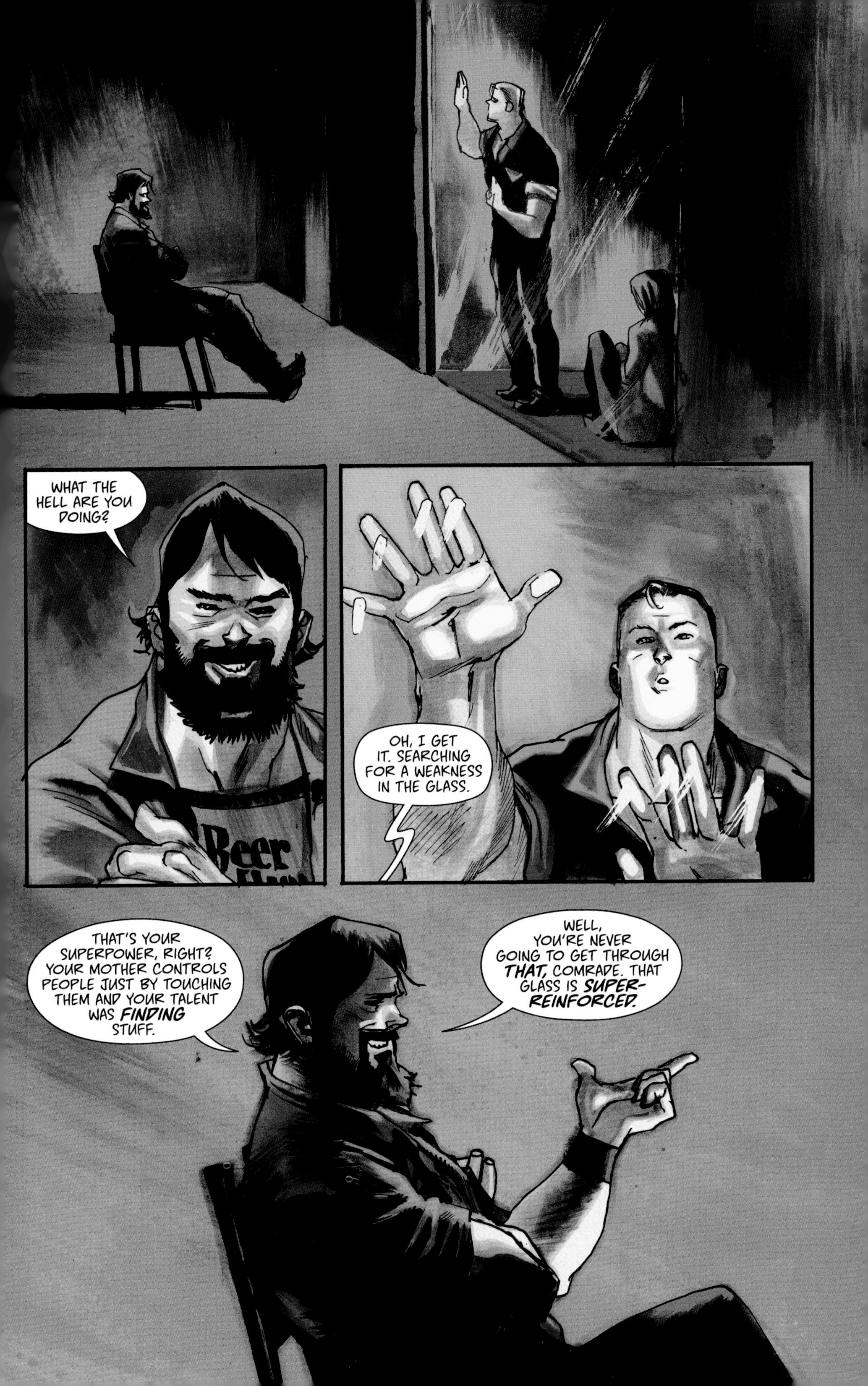
WHAT THE HELL ARE YOU DOING?
OH, I GET IT. SEARCHING FOR A WEAKNESS IN THE GLASS.
Beer
THAT'S YOUR SUPERPOWER, RIGHT? YOUR MOTHER CONTROLS PEOPLE JUST BY TOUCHING THEM AND YOUR TALENT WAS *FINDING* STUFF.
WELL, YOU'RE NEVER GOING TO GET THROUGH *THAT,* COMRADE. THAT GLASS IS *SUPER-REINFORCED.*

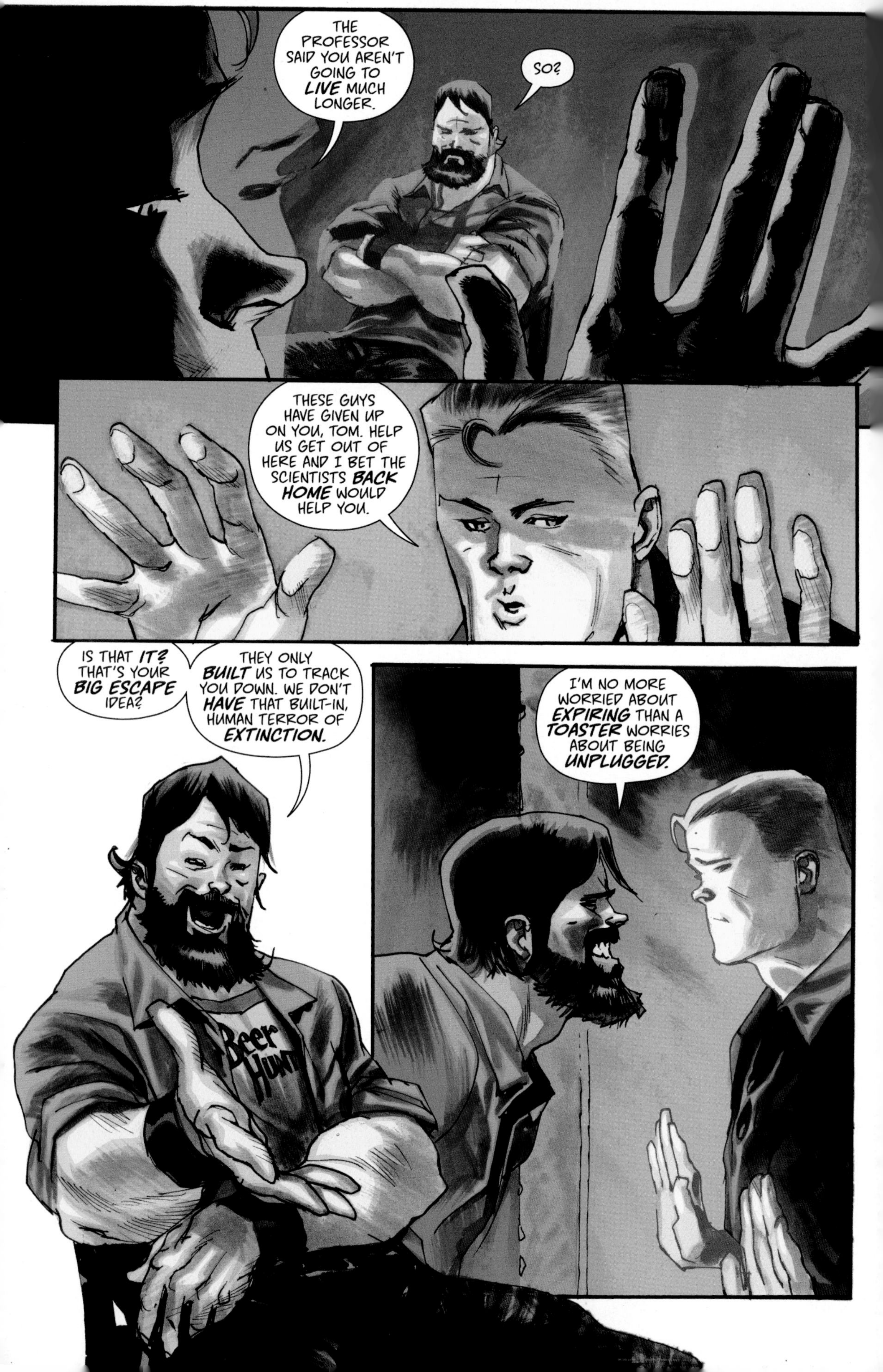

THE PROFESSOR SAID YOU AREN'T GOING TO LIVE MUCH LONGER.
SO?
THESE GUYS HAVE GIVEN UP ON YOU, TOM. HELP US GET OUT OF HERE AND I BET THE SCIENTISTS BACK HOME WOULD HELP YOU.
IS THAT IT? THAT'S YOUR BIG ESCAPE IDEA?
THEY ONLY BUILT US TO TRACK YOU DOWN. WE DON'T HAVE THAT BUILT-IN, HUMAN TERROR OF EXTINCTION.
I'M NO MORE WORRIED ABOUT EXPIRING THAN A TOASTER WORRIES ABOUT BEING UNPLUGGED.
Beer Hunt

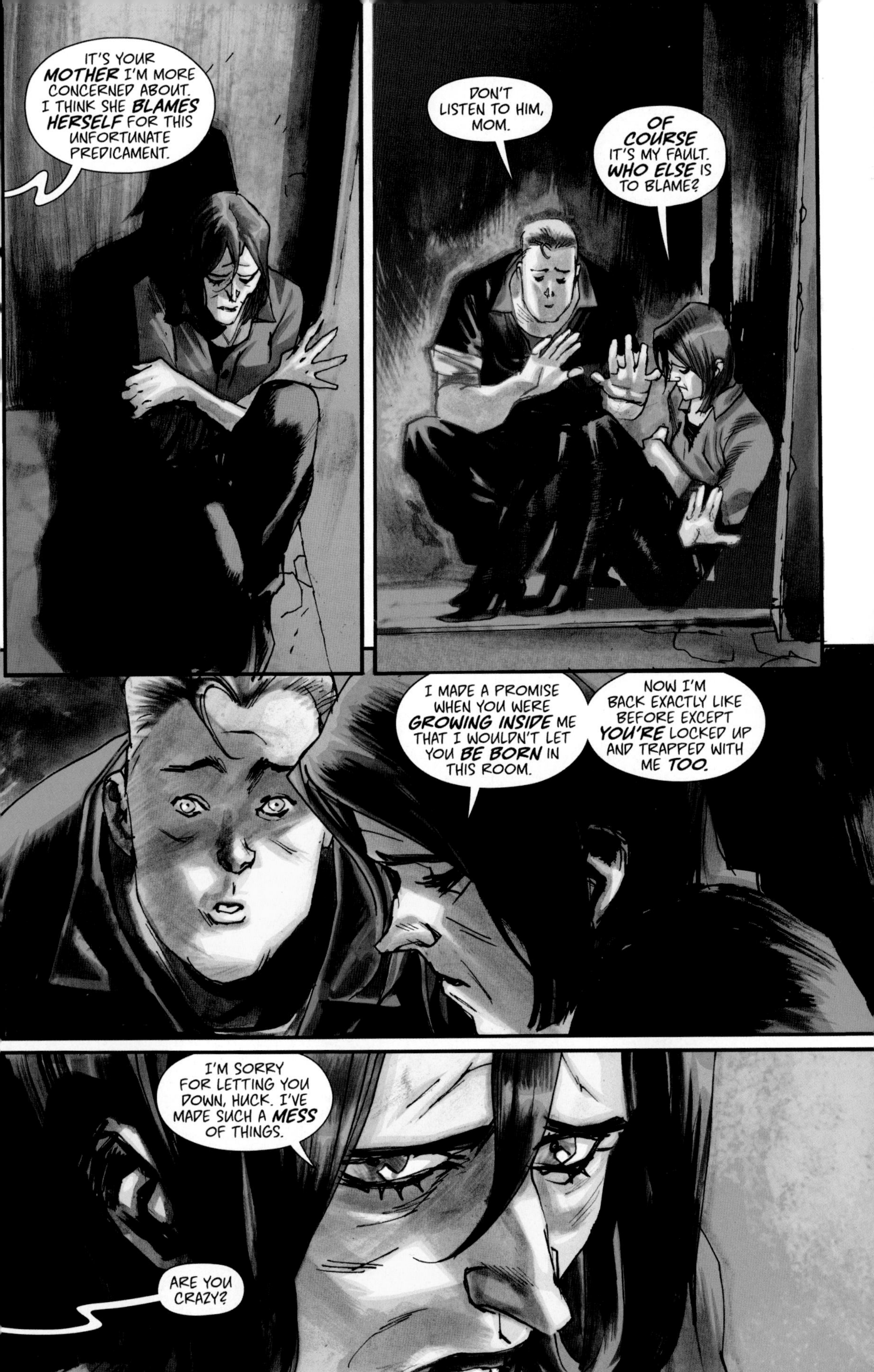
IT'S YOUR MOTHER I'M MORE CONCERNED ABOUT. I THINK SHE BLAMES HERSELF FOR THIS UNFORTUNATE PREDICAMENT.
DON'T LISTEN TO HIM, MOM.
OF COURSE IT'S MY FAULT. WHO ELSE IS TO BLAME?
I MADE A PROMISE WHEN YOU WERE GROWING INSIDE ME THAT I WOULDN'T LET YOU BE BORN IN THIS ROOM.
NOW I'M BACK EXACTLY LIKE BEFORE EXCEPT YOU'RE LOCKED UP AND TRAPPED WITH ME TOO.
I'M SORRY FOR LETTING YOU DOWN, HUCK. I'VE MADE SUCH A MESS OF THINGS.
ARE YOU CRAZY?

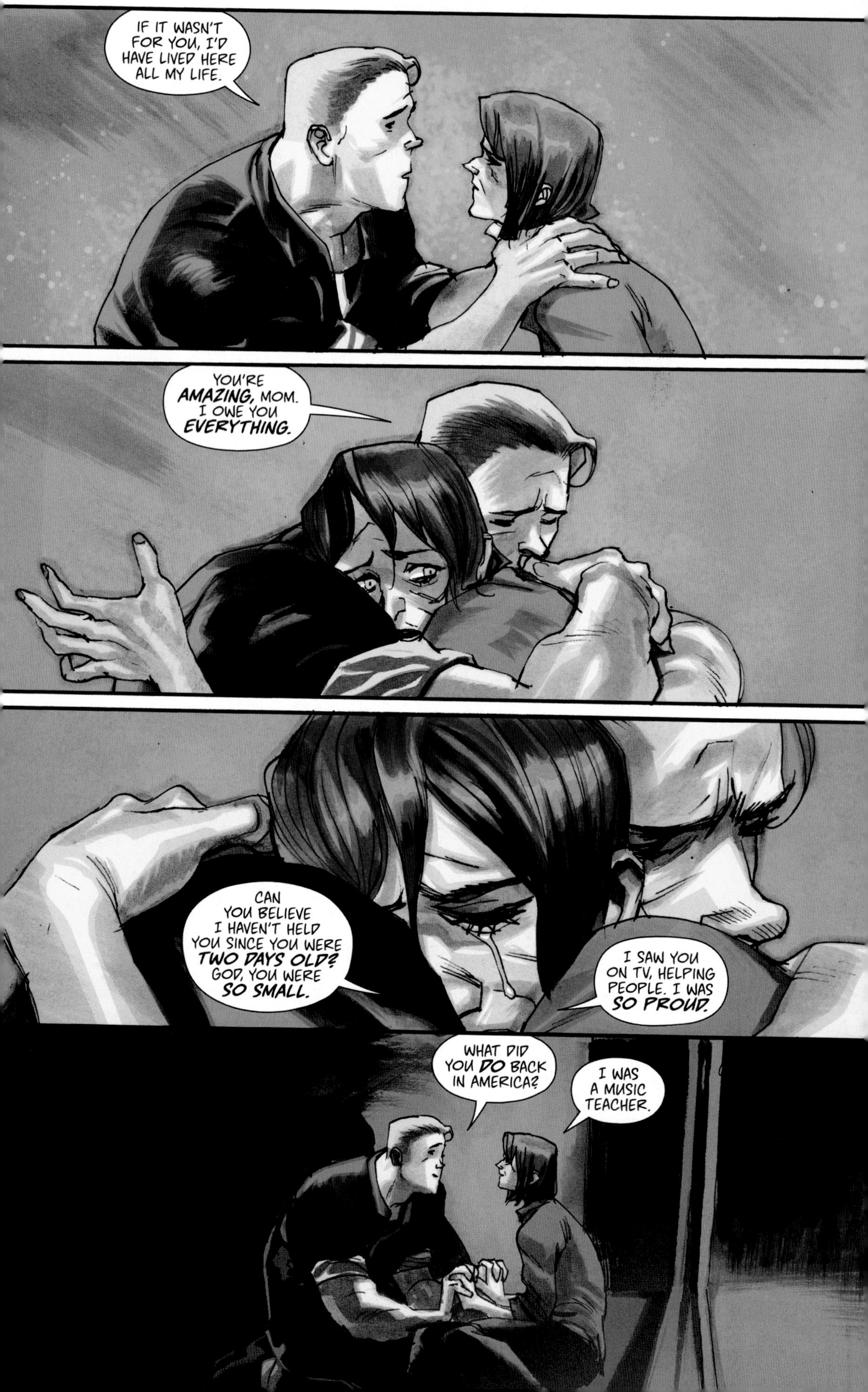
IF IT WASN'T FOR YOU, I'D HAVE LIVED HERE ALL MY LIFE.
YOU'RE AMAZING, MOM. I OWE YOU EVERYTHING.
CAN YOU BELIEVE I HAVEN'T HELD YOU SINCE YOU WERE TWO DAYS OLD? GOD, YOU WERE SO SMALL.
I SAW YOU ON TV, HELPING PEOPLE. I WAS SO PROUD.
WHAT DID YOU DO BACK IN AMERICA?
I WAS A MUSIC TEACHER.

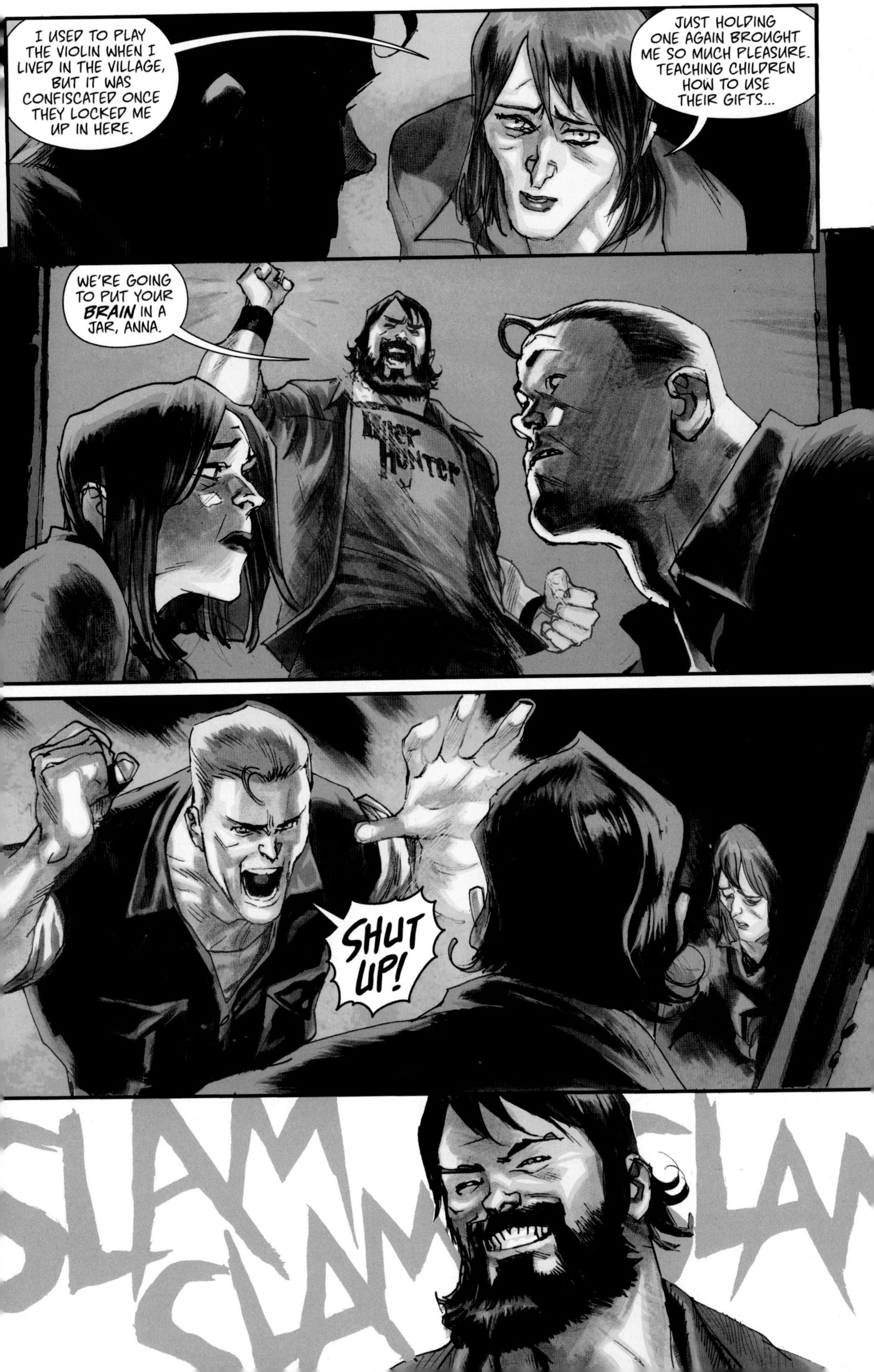
I USED TO PLAY THE VIOLIN WHEN I LIVED IN THE VILLAGE, BUT IT WAS CONFISCATED ONCE THEY LOCKED ME UP IN HERE.
JUST HOLDING ONE AGAIN BROUGHT ME SO MUCH PLEASURE. TEACHING CHILDREN HOW TO USE THEIR GIFTS...
WE'RE GOING TO PUT YOUR BRAIN IN A JAR, ANNA.
SHUT UP!
SLAM
SLAM
SLAM

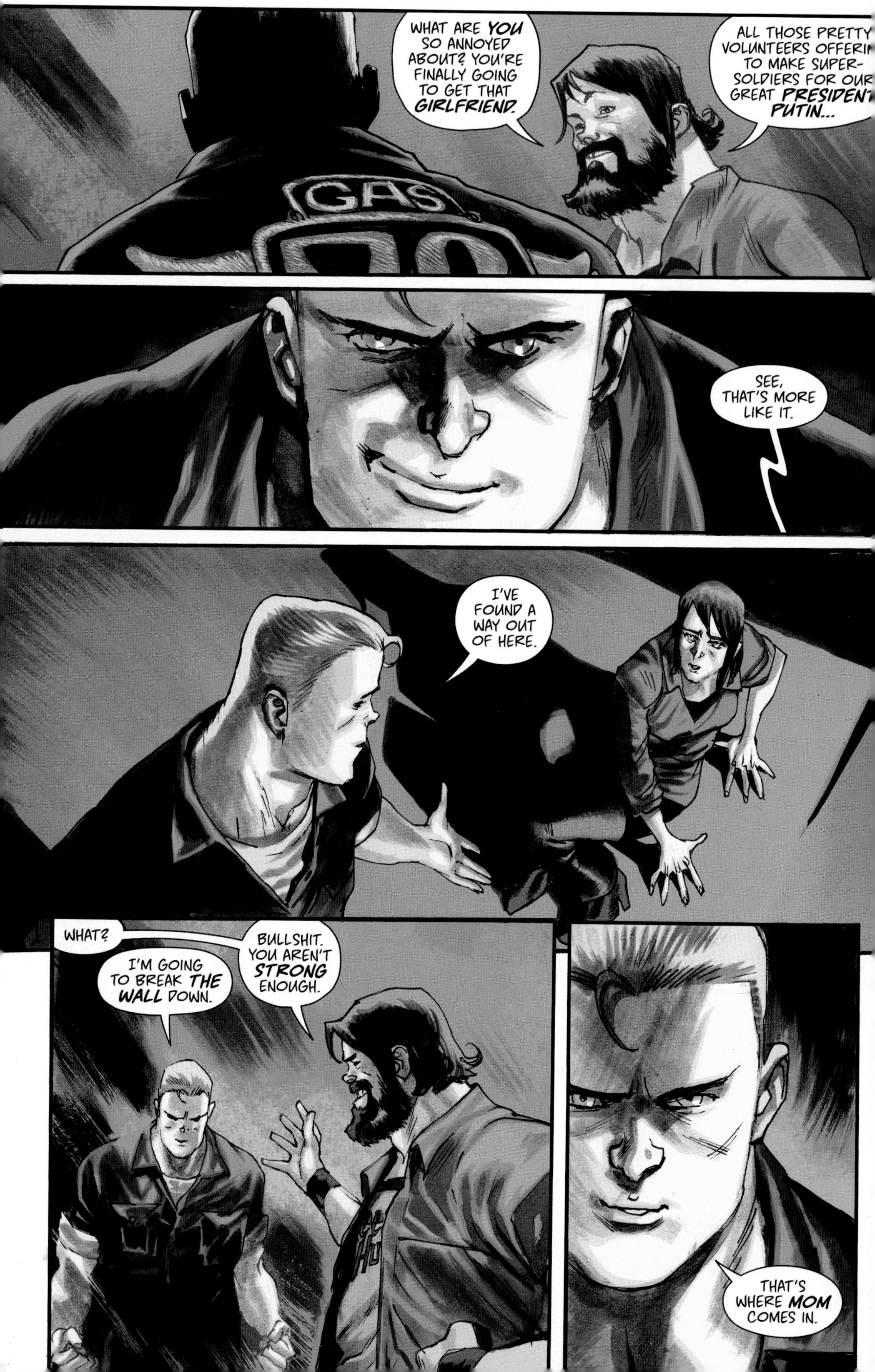

WHAT ARE YOU SO ANNOYED ABOUT? YOU'RE FINALLY GOING TO GET THAT GIRLFRIEND.
ALL THOSE PRETTY VOLUNTEERS OFFERI TO MAKE SUPER-SOLDIERS FOR OUR GREAT PRESIDENT PUTIN...
SEE, THAT'S MORE LIKE IT.
I'VE FOUND A WAY OUT OF HERE.
WHAT?
I'M GOING TO BREAK THE WALL DOWN.
BULLSHIT. YOU AREN'T STRONG ENOUGH.
THAT'S WHERE MOM COMES IN.

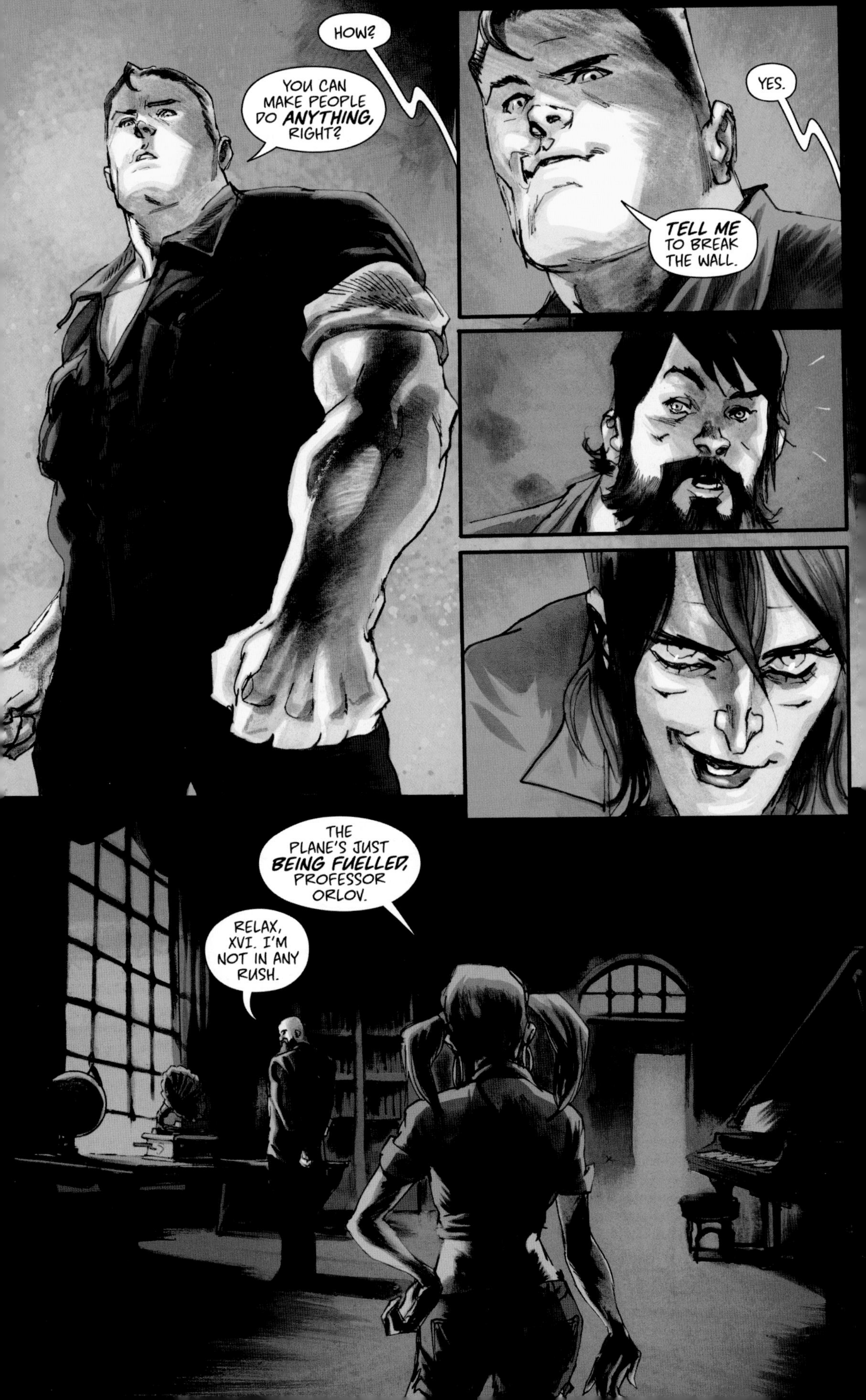

YOU CAN MAKE PEOPLE DO ANYTHING, RIGHT?
HOW?
YES.
TELL ME TO BREAK THE WALL.
THE PLANE'S JUST BEING FUELLED, PROFESSOR ORLOV.
RELAX, XVI. I'M NOT IN ANY RUSH.

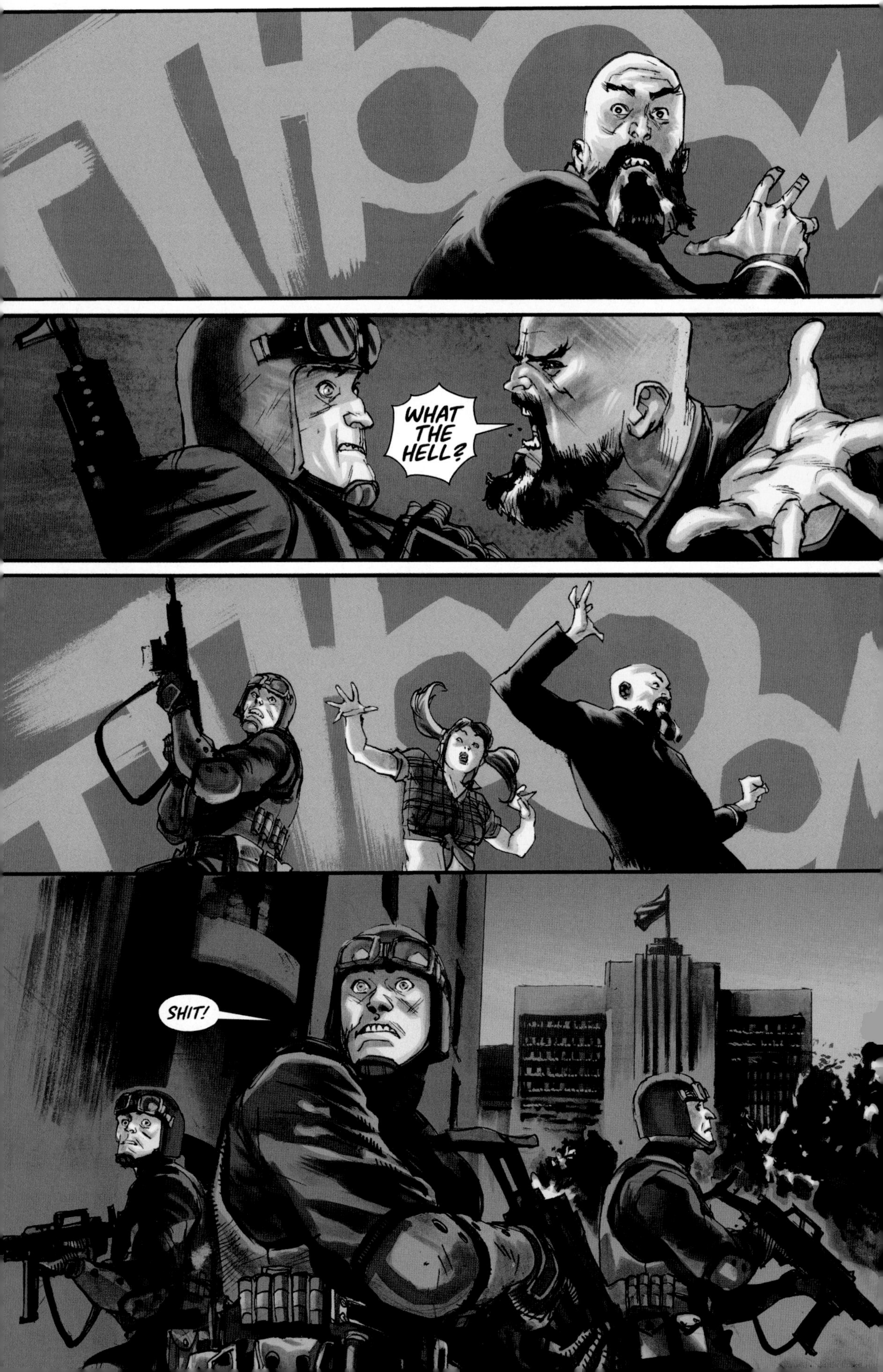
WHAT THE HELL?
SHIT!

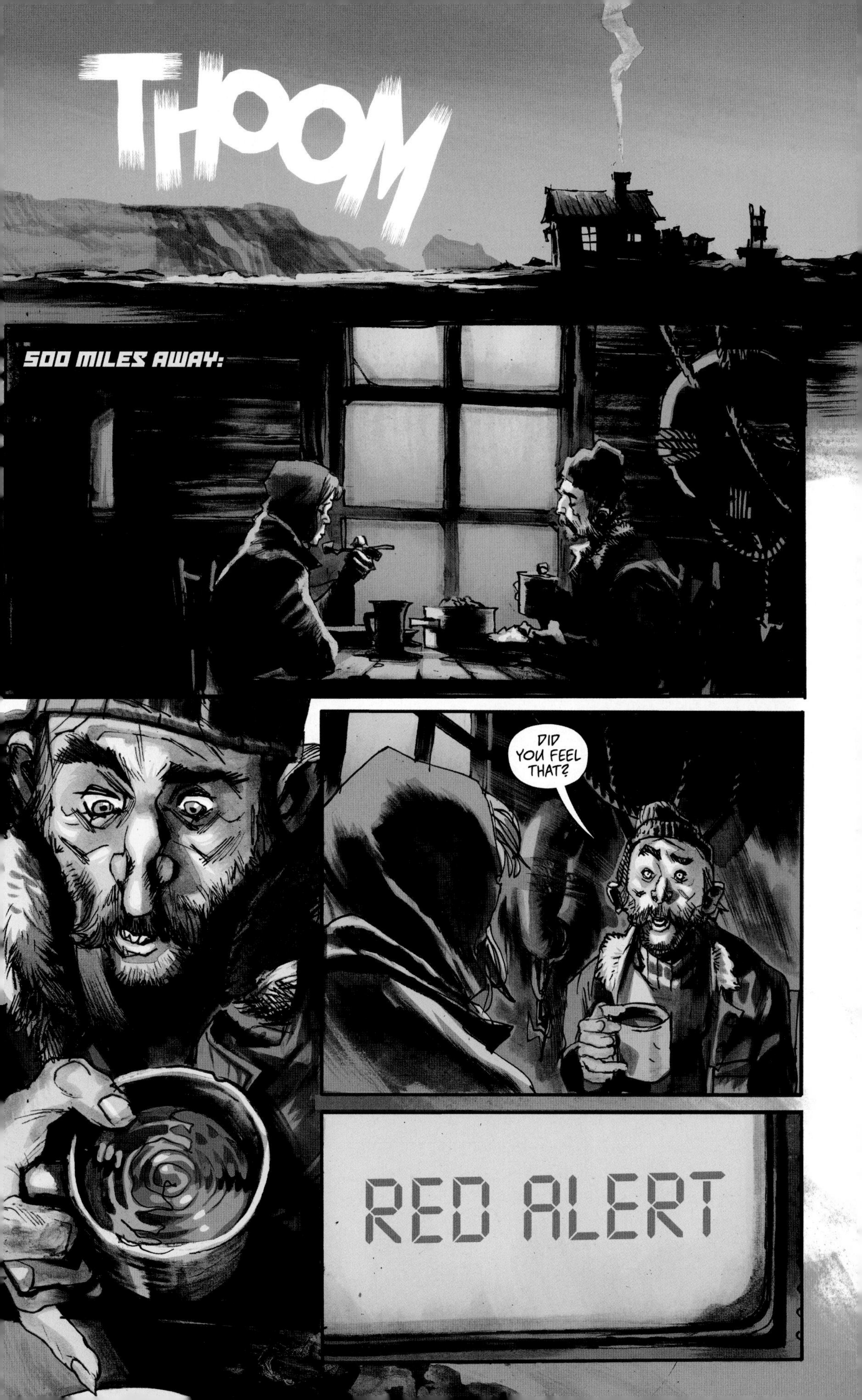
THOOM
500 MILES AWAY:
DID YOU FEEL THAT?
RED ALERT

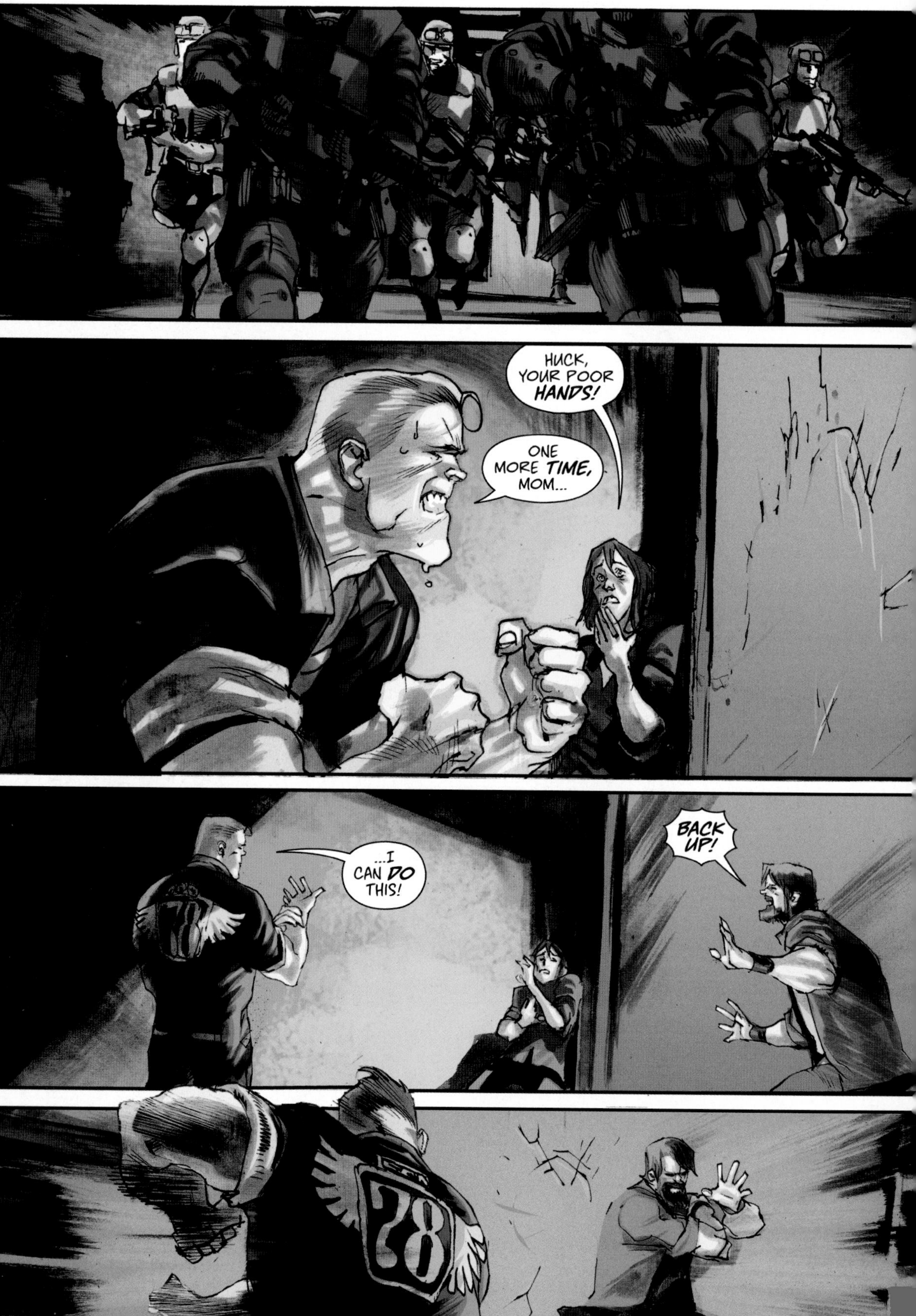
HUCK, YOUR POOR HANDS!
ONE MORE TIME, MOM...
...I CAN DO THIS!
BACK UP!

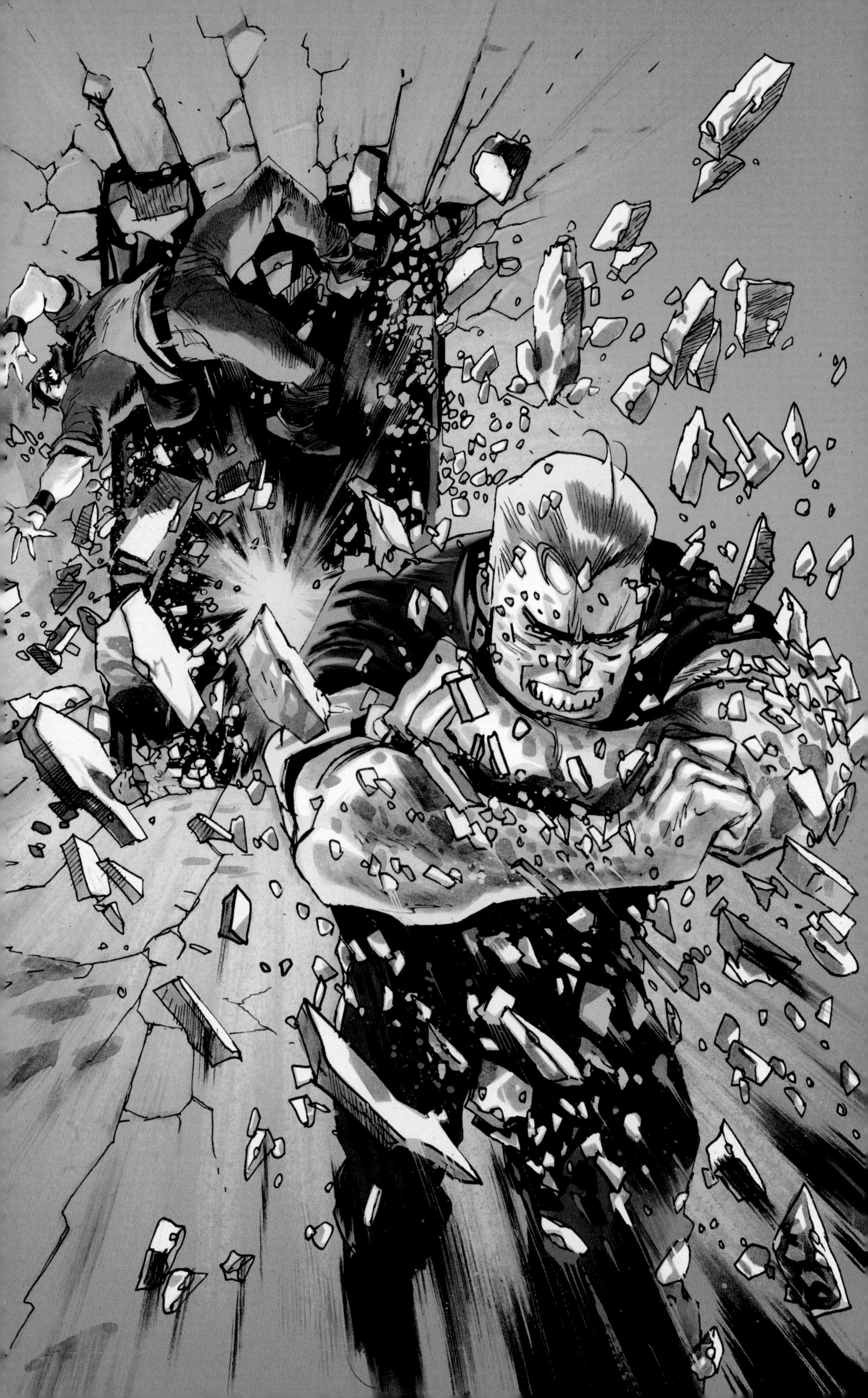

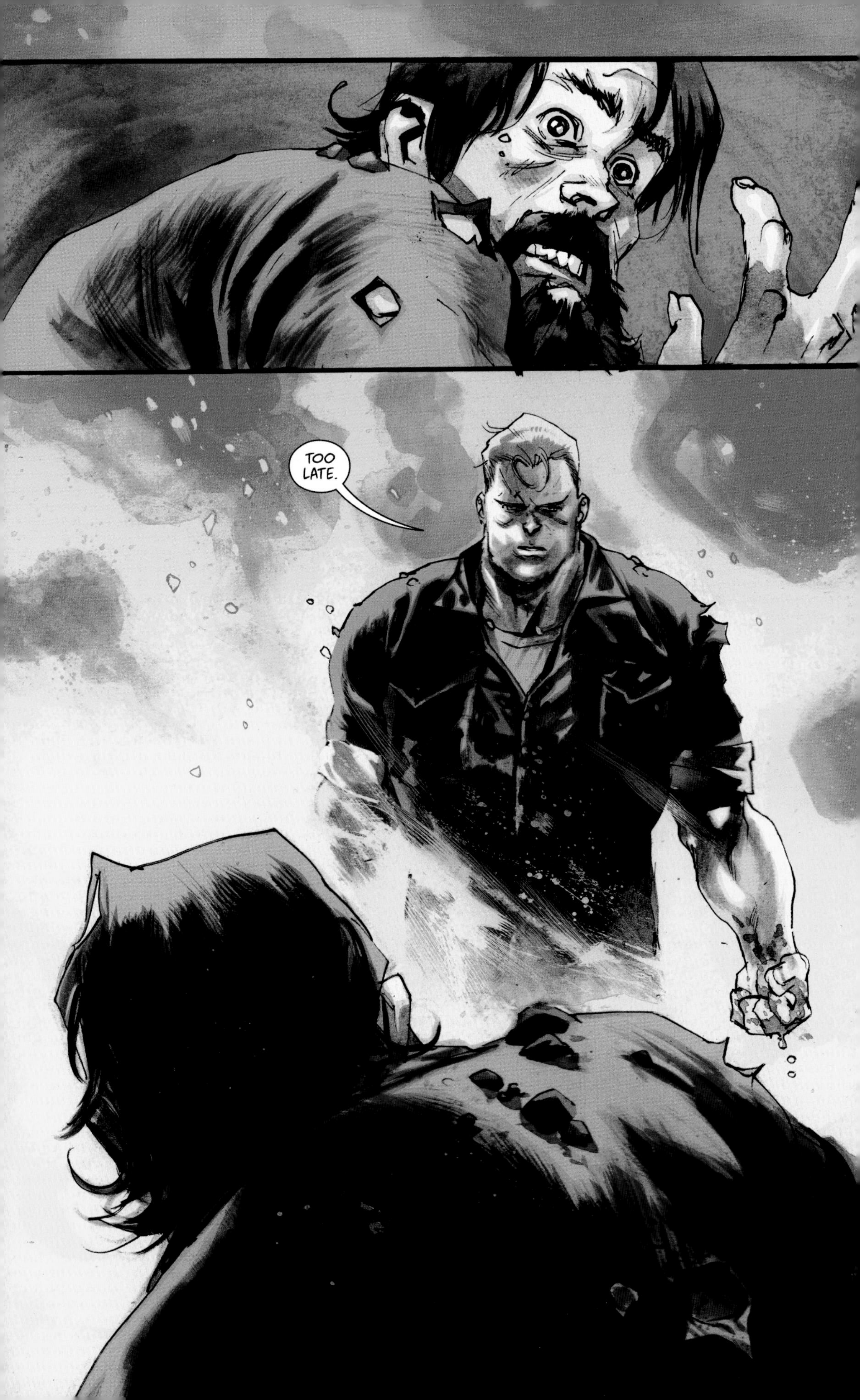
TOO LATE.

SIX

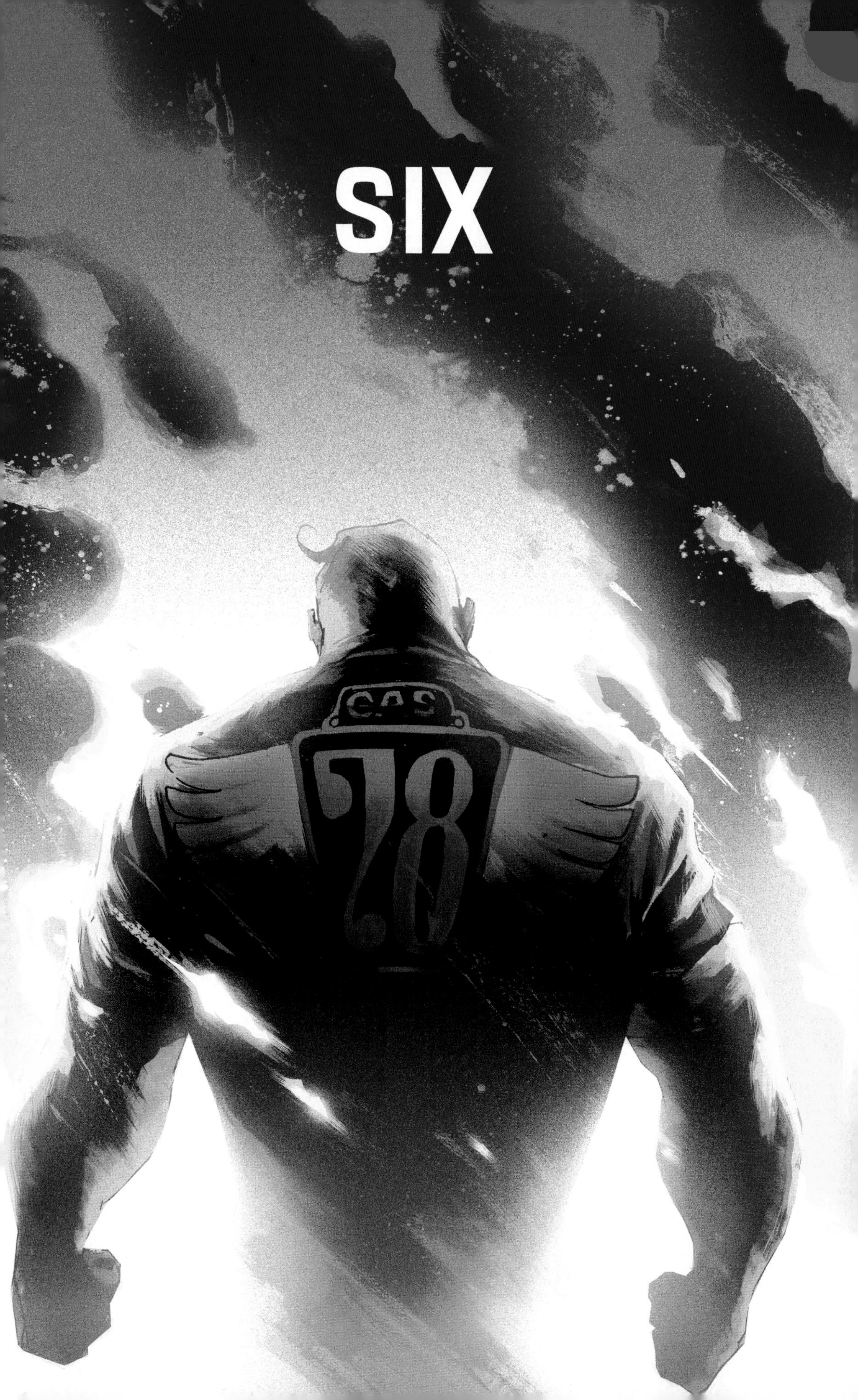
CAS
78

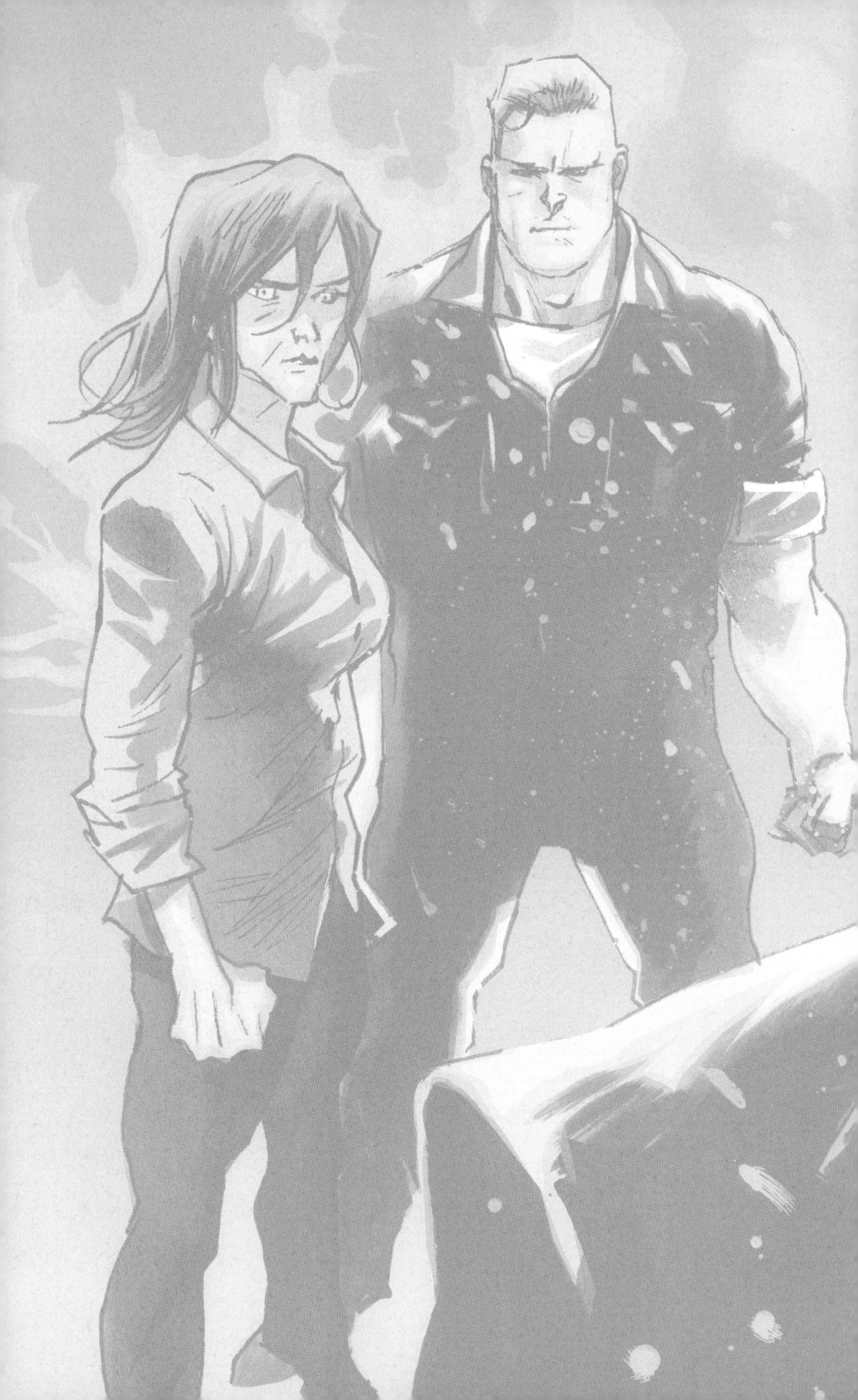

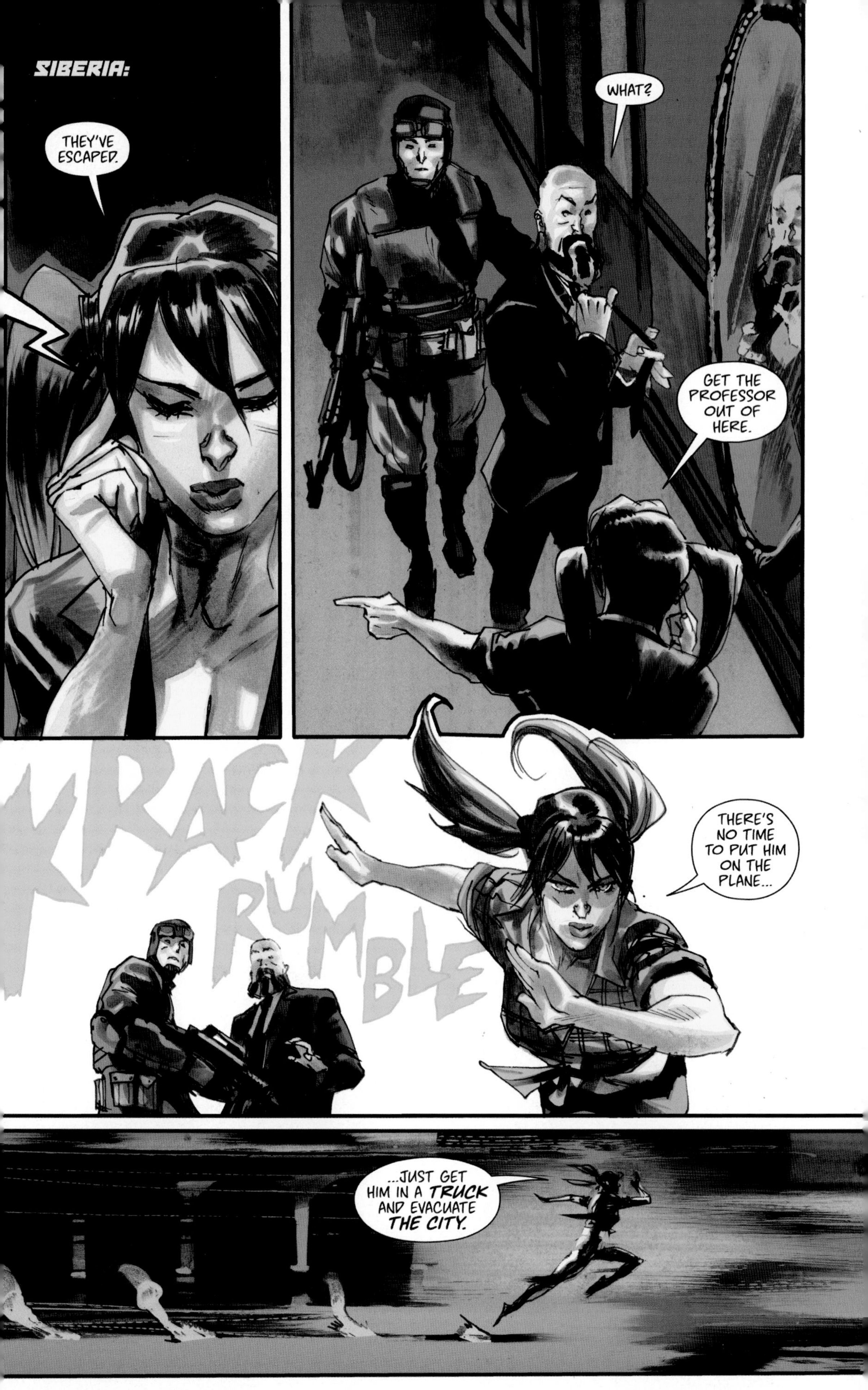
SIBERIA:
THEY'VE ESCAPED.
WHAT?
GET THE PROFESSOR OUT OF HERE.
KRACK
RUMBLE
THERE'S NO TIME TO PUT HIM ON THE PLANE...
...JUST GET HIM IN A TRUCK AND EVACUATE THE CITY.

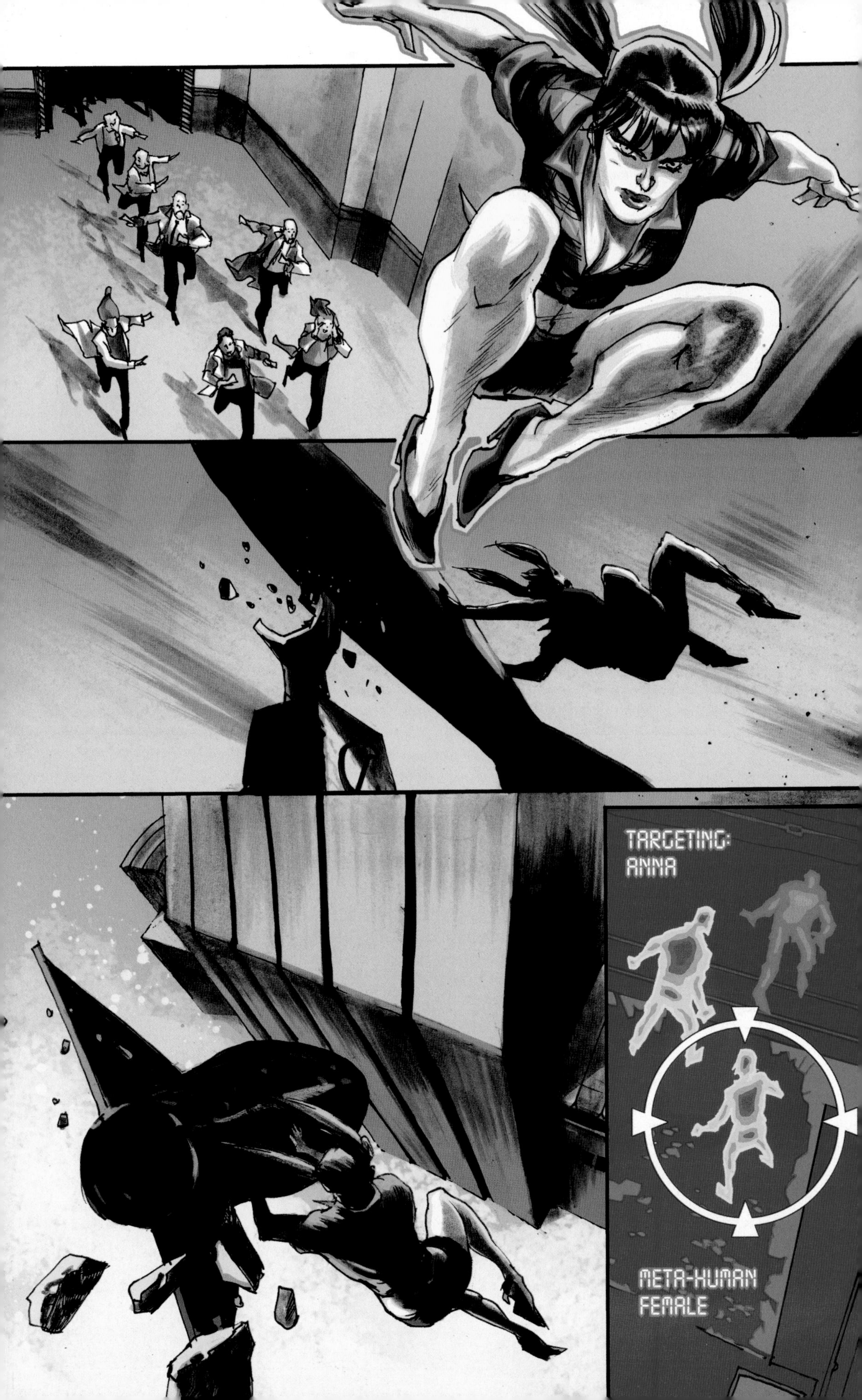
TARGETING:
ANNA
META-HUMAN
FEMALE

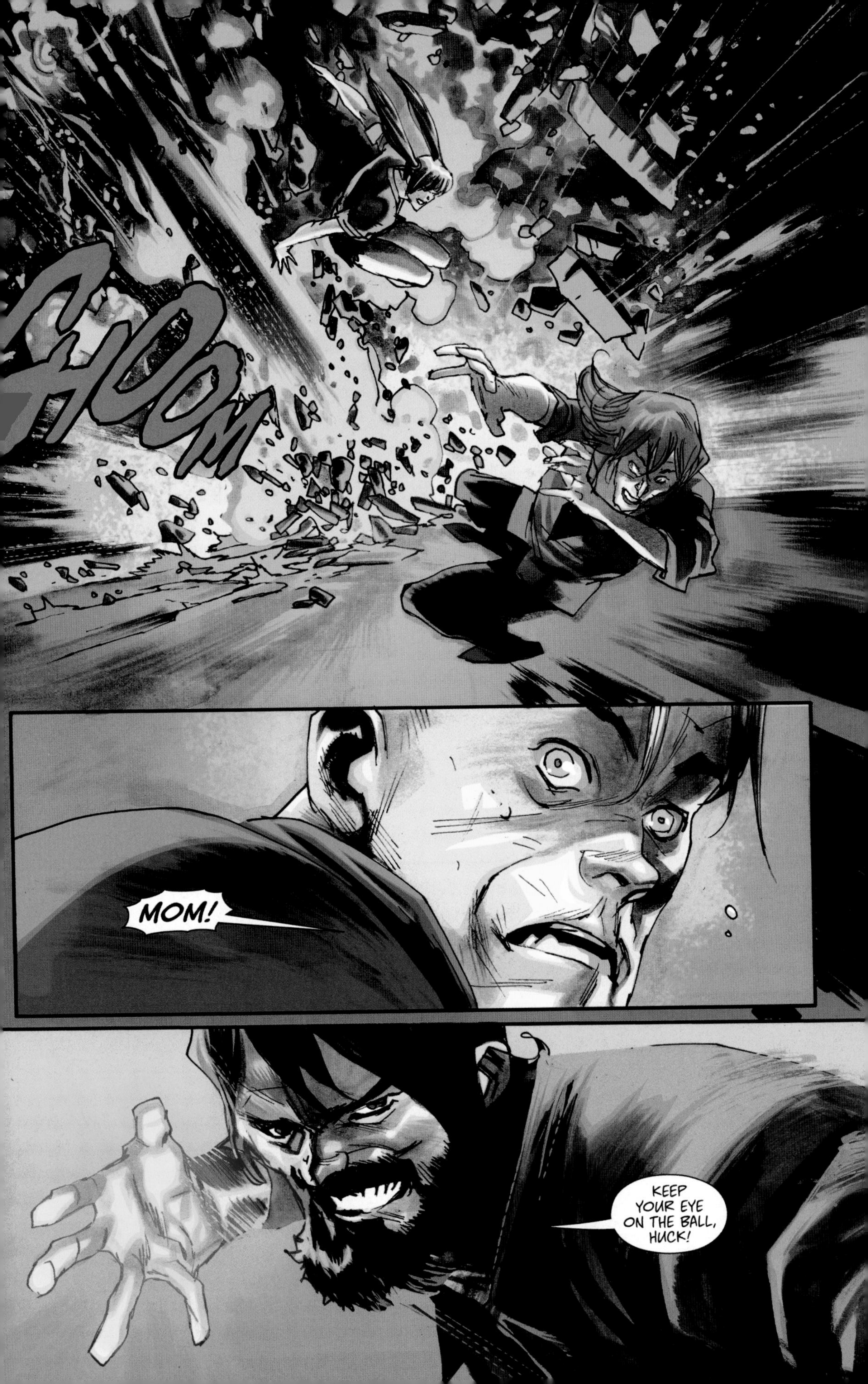
CHOOM
MOM!
KEEP YOUR EYE ON THE BALL, HUCK!

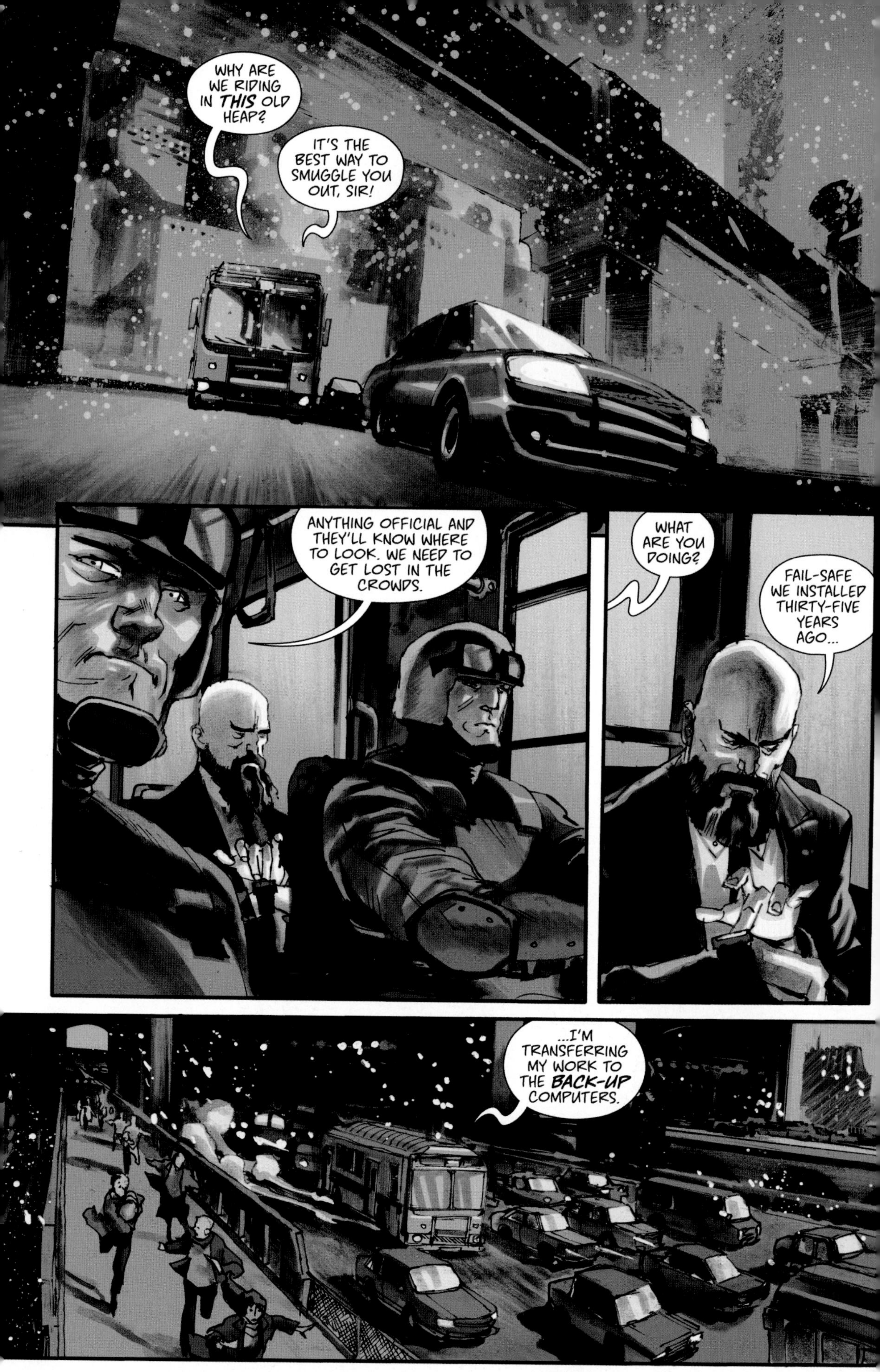

WHY ARE WE RIDING IN THIS OLD HEAP?
IT'S THE BEST WAY TO SMUGGLE YOU OUT, SIR!
ANYTHING OFFICIAL AND THEY'LL KNOW WHERE TO LOOK. WE NEED TO GET LOST IN THE CROWDS.
WHAT ARE YOU DOING?
FAIL-SAFE WE INSTALLED THIRTY-FIVE YEARS AGO...
...I'M TRANSFERRING MY WORK TO THE BACK-UP COMPUTERS.

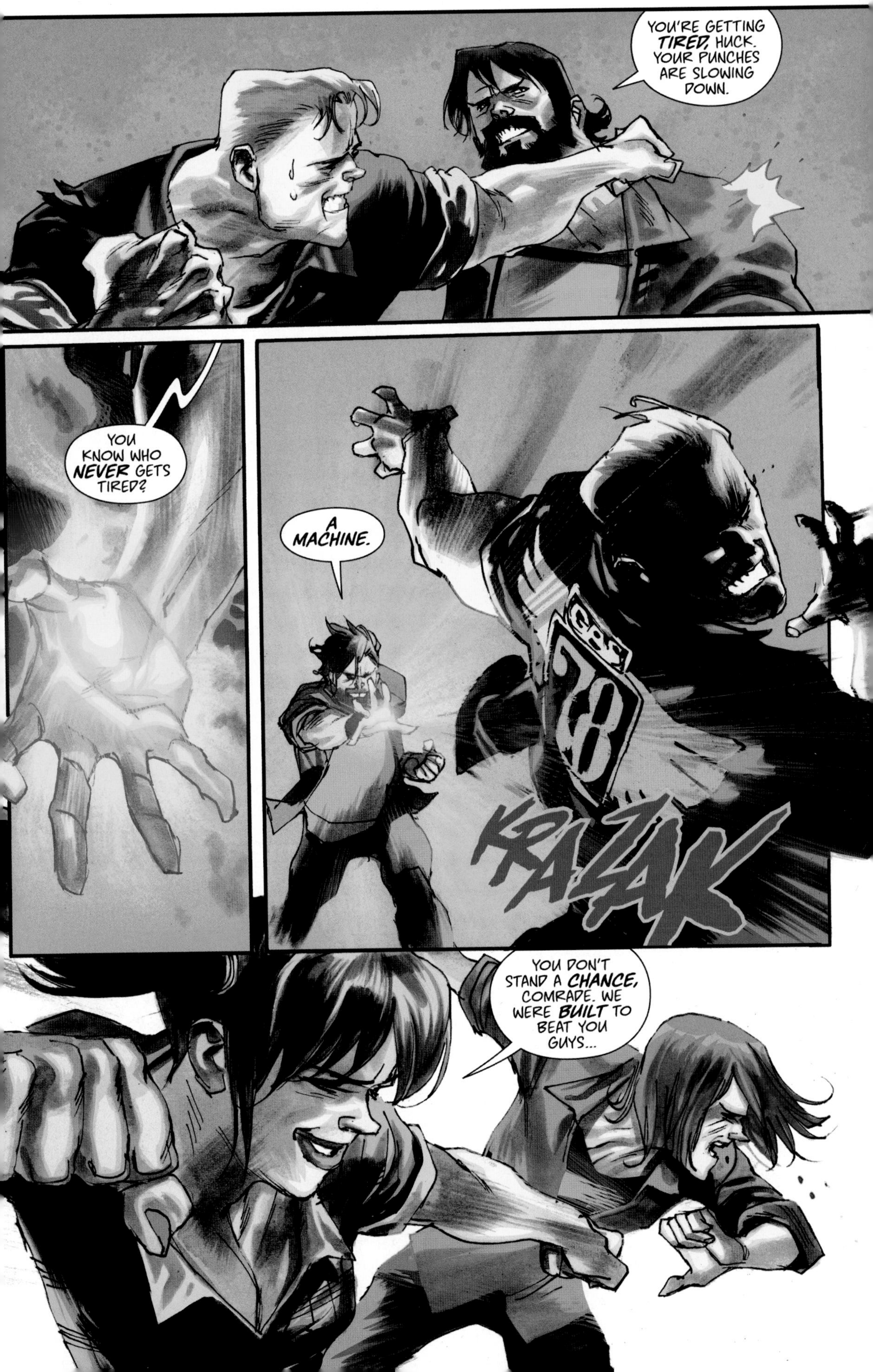
YOU'RE GETTING TIRED, HUCK. YOUR PUNCHES ARE SLOWING DOWN.
YOU KNOW WHO NEVER GETS TIRED?
A MACHINE.
KRAZAK
YOU DON'T STAND A CHANCE, COMRADE. WE WERE BUILT TO BEAT YOU GUYS...

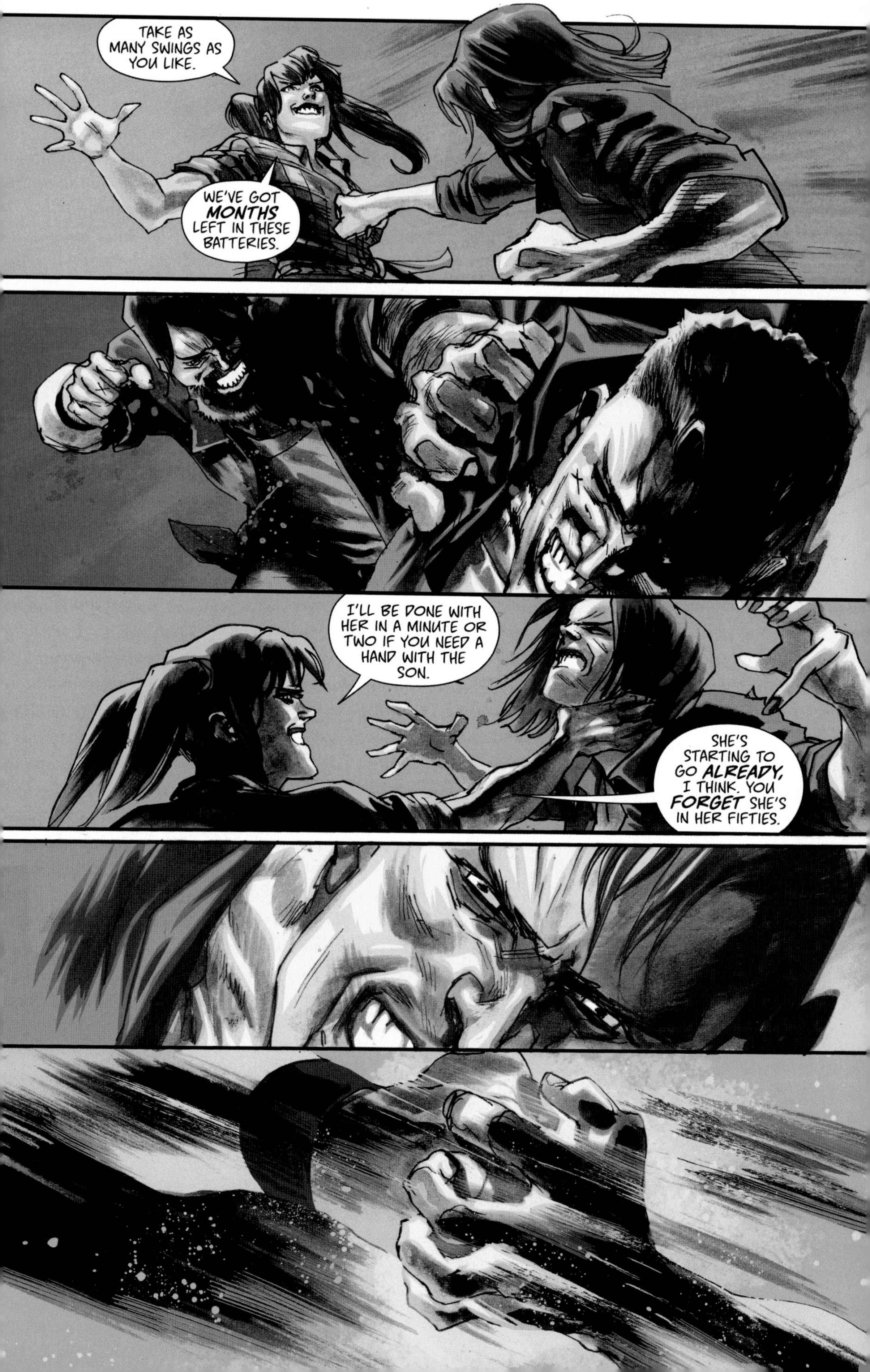
TAKE AS MANY SWINGS AS YOU LIKE.
WE'VE GOT **MONTHS** LEFT IN THESE BATTERIES.
I'LL BE DONE WITH HER IN A MINUTE OR TWO IF YOU NEED A HAND WITH THE SON.
SHE'S STARTING TO GO **ALREADY,** I THINK. YOU **FORGET** SHE'S IN HER FIFTIES.

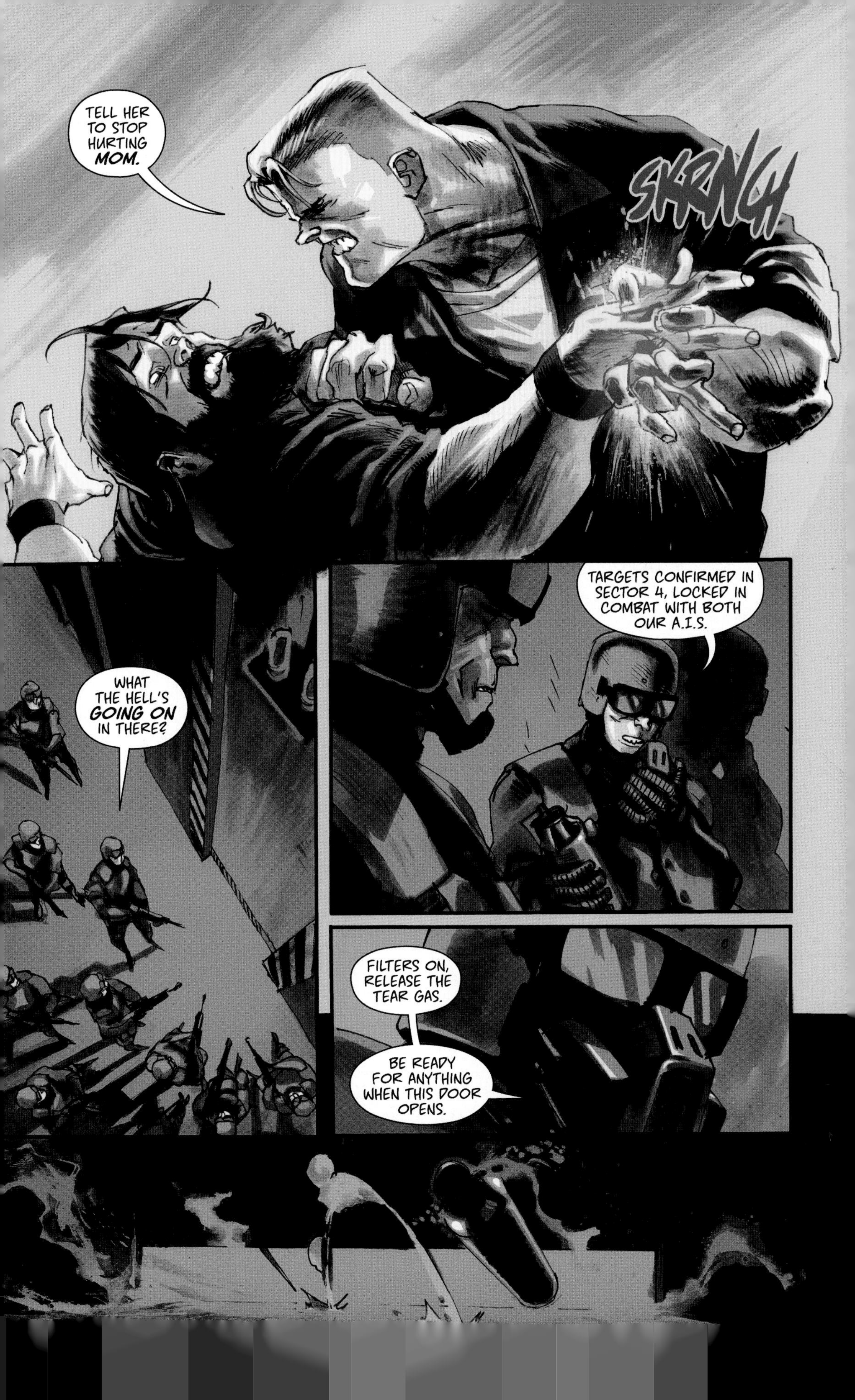
TELL HER TO STOP HURTING MOM.
SKRNCH
WHAT THE HELL'S GOING ON IN THERE?
TARGETS CONFIRMED IN SECTOR 4, LOCKED IN COMBAT WITH BOTH OUR A.I.S.
FILTERS ON, RELEASE THE TEAR GAS.
BE READY FOR ANYTHING WHEN THIS DOOR OPENS.

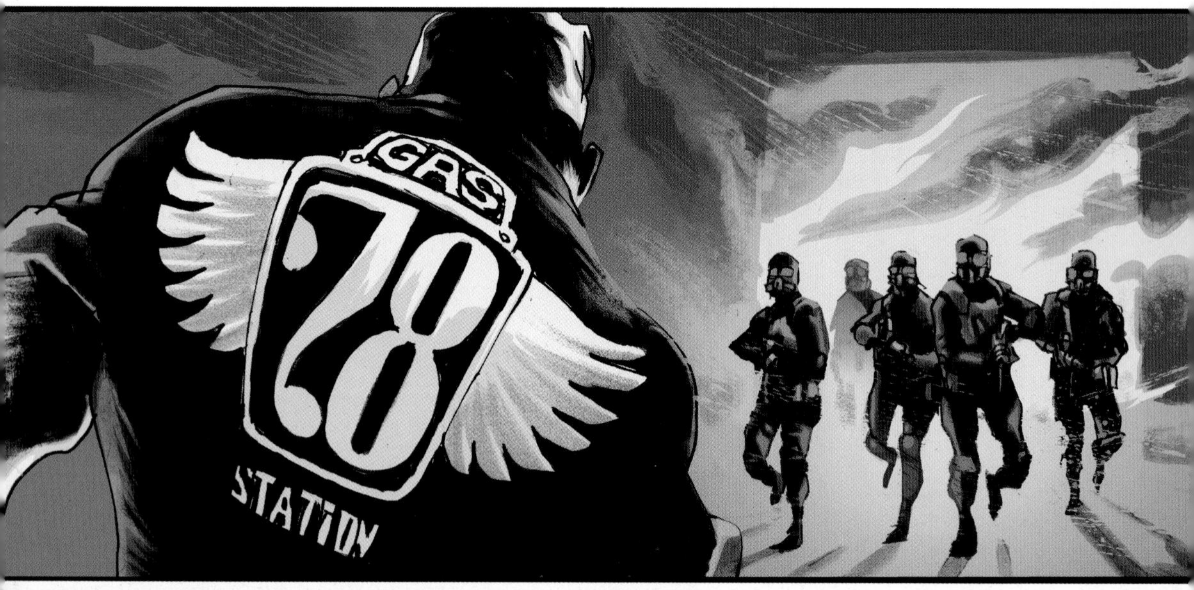
GAS
78
STATION

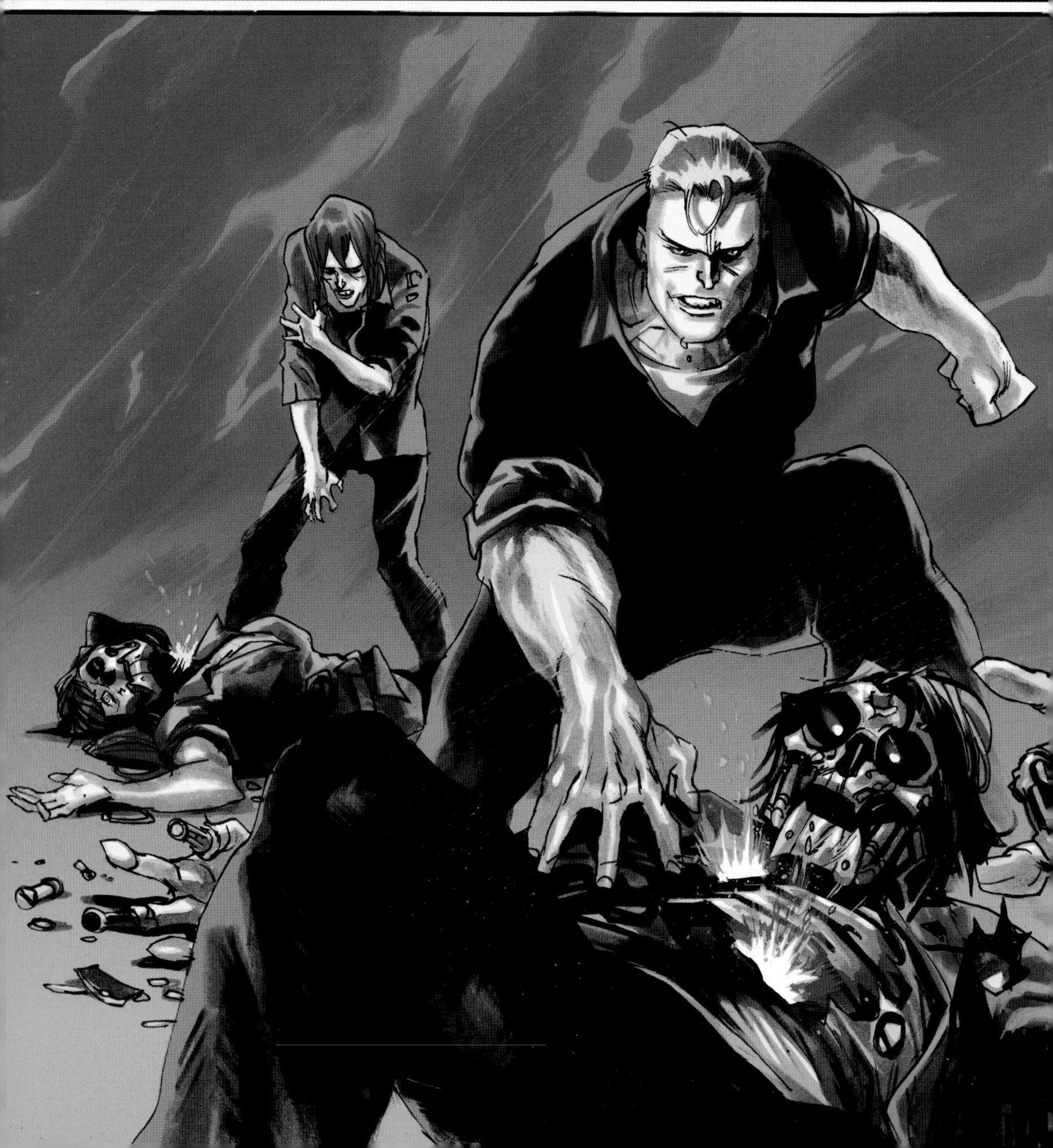

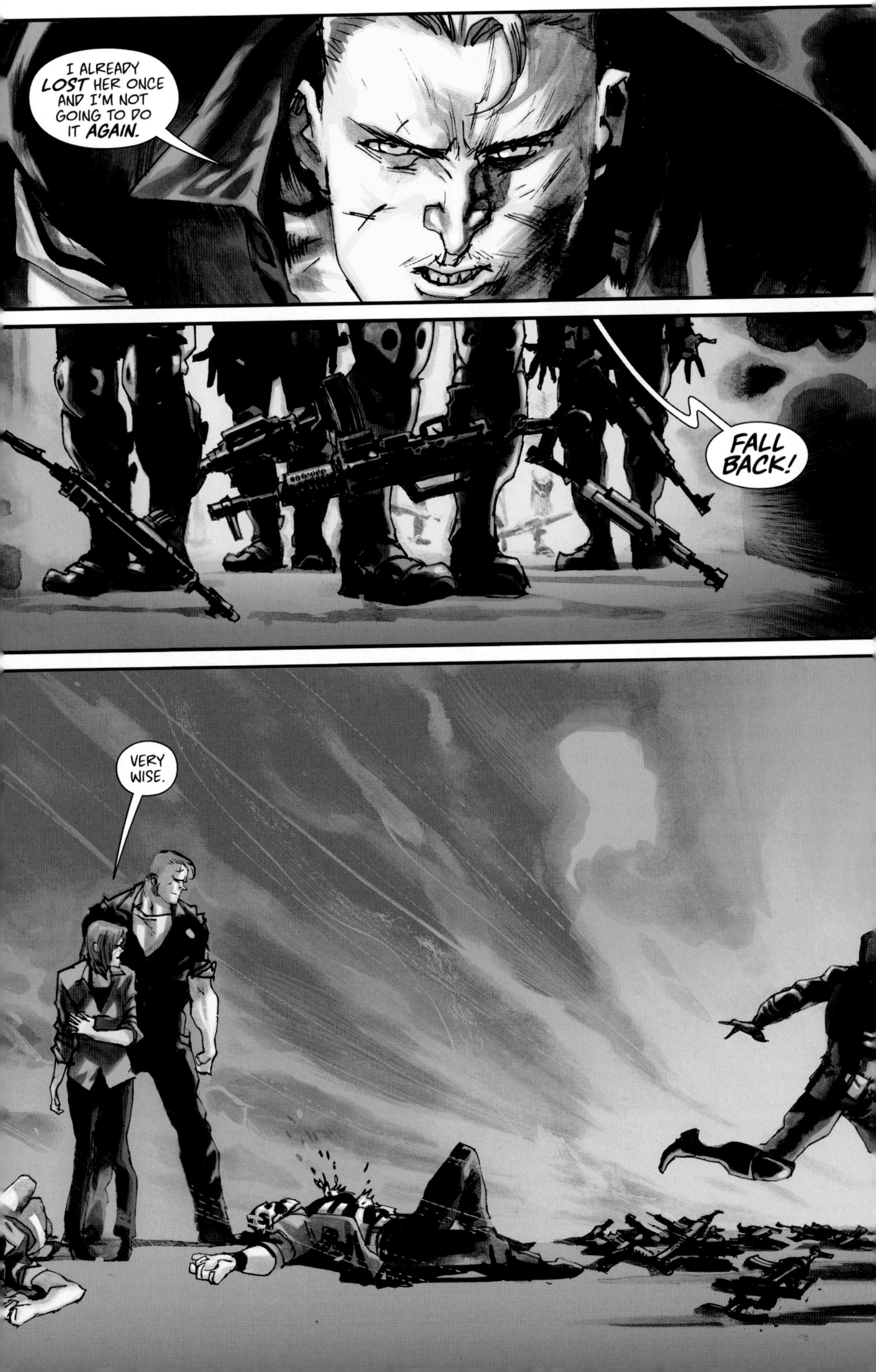
I ALREADY LOST HER ONCE AND I'M NOT GOING TO DO IT AGAIN.
FALL BACK!
VERY WISE.

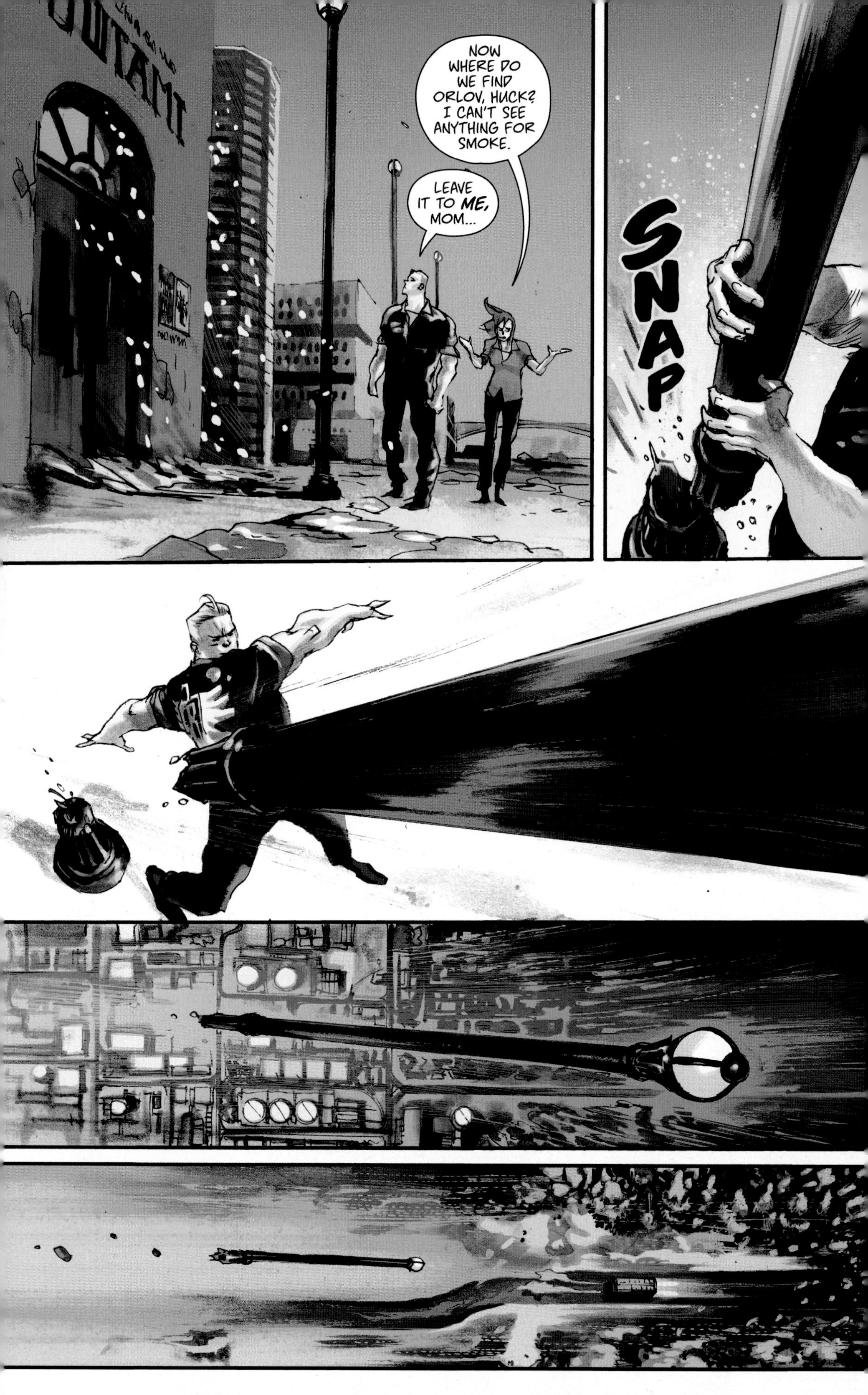
NOW WHERE DO WE FIND ORLOV, HUCK? I CAN'T SEE ANYTHING FOR SMOKE.
LEAVE IT TO ME, MOM...
SNAP

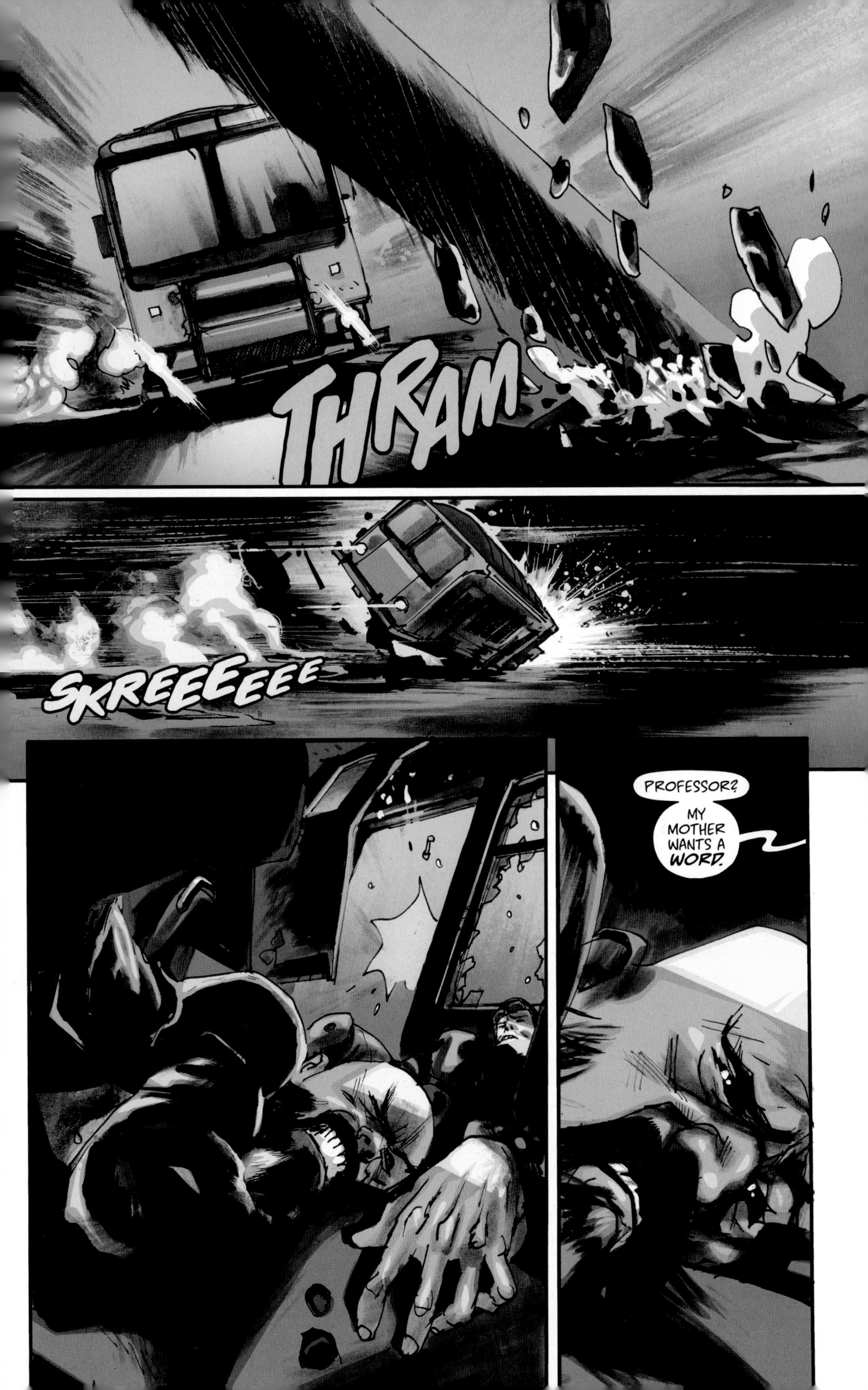
THRAM
SKREEEeeee
PROFESSOR?
MY MOTHER WANTS A WORD.

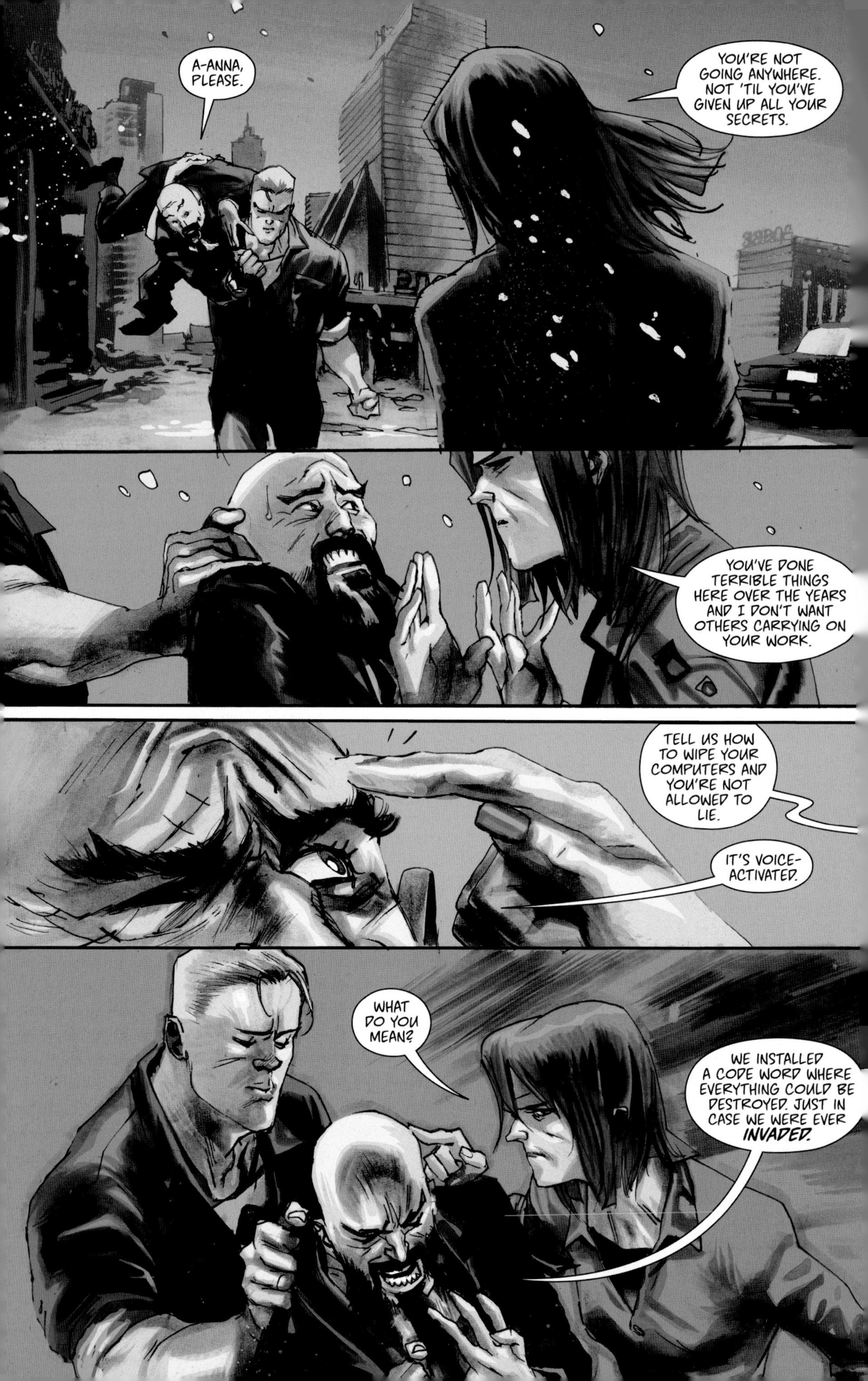
A-ANNA, PLEASE.
YOU'RE NOT GOING ANYWHERE. NOT 'TIL YOU'VE GIVEN UP ALL YOUR SECRETS.
YOU'VE DONE TERRIBLE THINGS HERE OVER THE YEARS AND I DON'T WANT OTHERS CARRYING ON YOUR WORK.
TELL US HOW TO WIPE YOUR COMPUTERS AND YOU'RE NOT ALLOWED TO LIE.
IT'S VOICE-ACTIVATED.
WHAT DO YOU MEAN?
WE INSTALLED A CODE WORD WHERE EVERYTHING COULD BE DESTROYED. JUST IN CASE WE WERE EVER ***INVADED.***

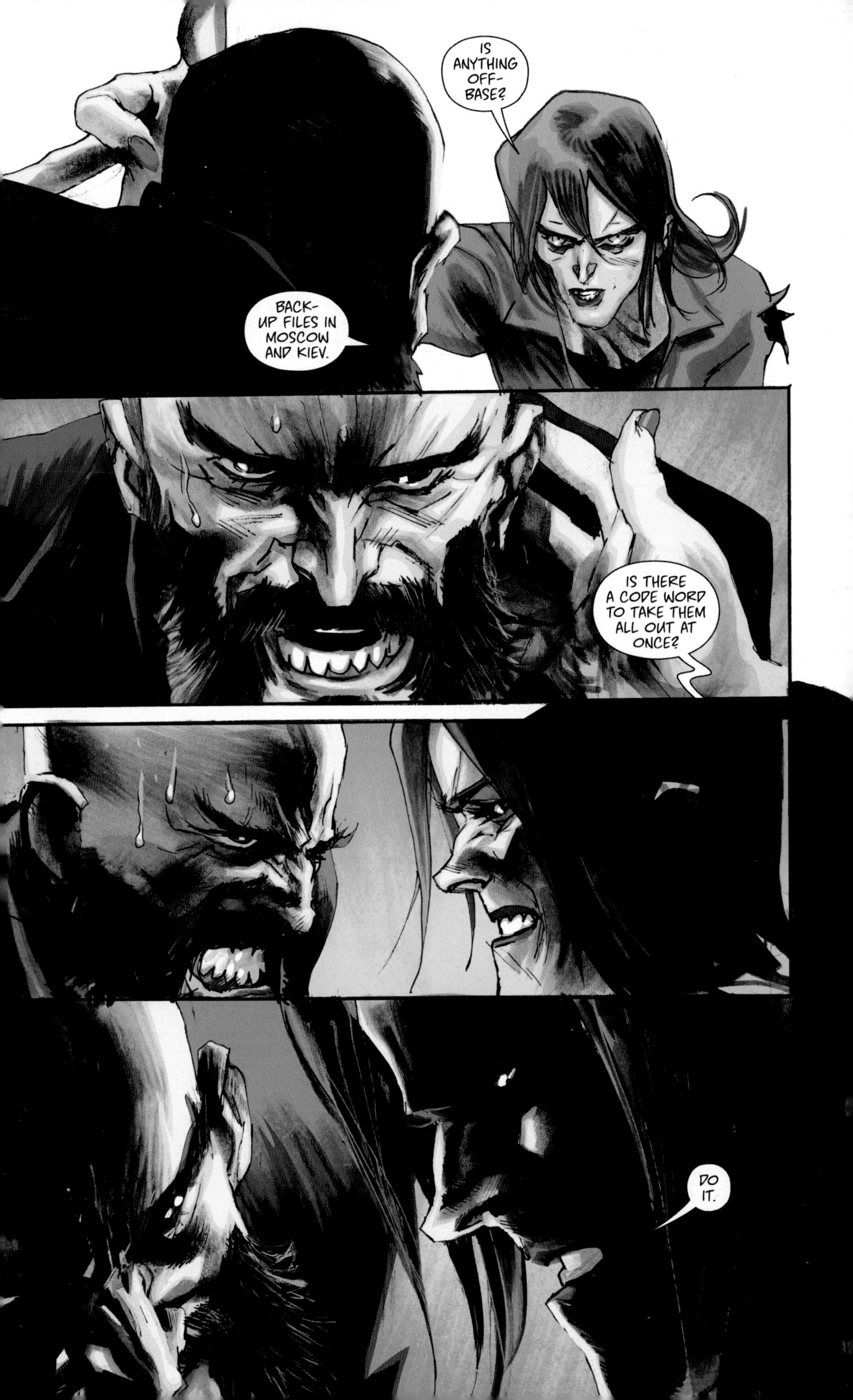
IS ANYTHING OFF-BASE?
BACK-UP FILES IN MOSCOW AND KIEV.
IS THERE A CODE WORD TO TAKE THEM ALL OUT AT ONCE?
DO IT.

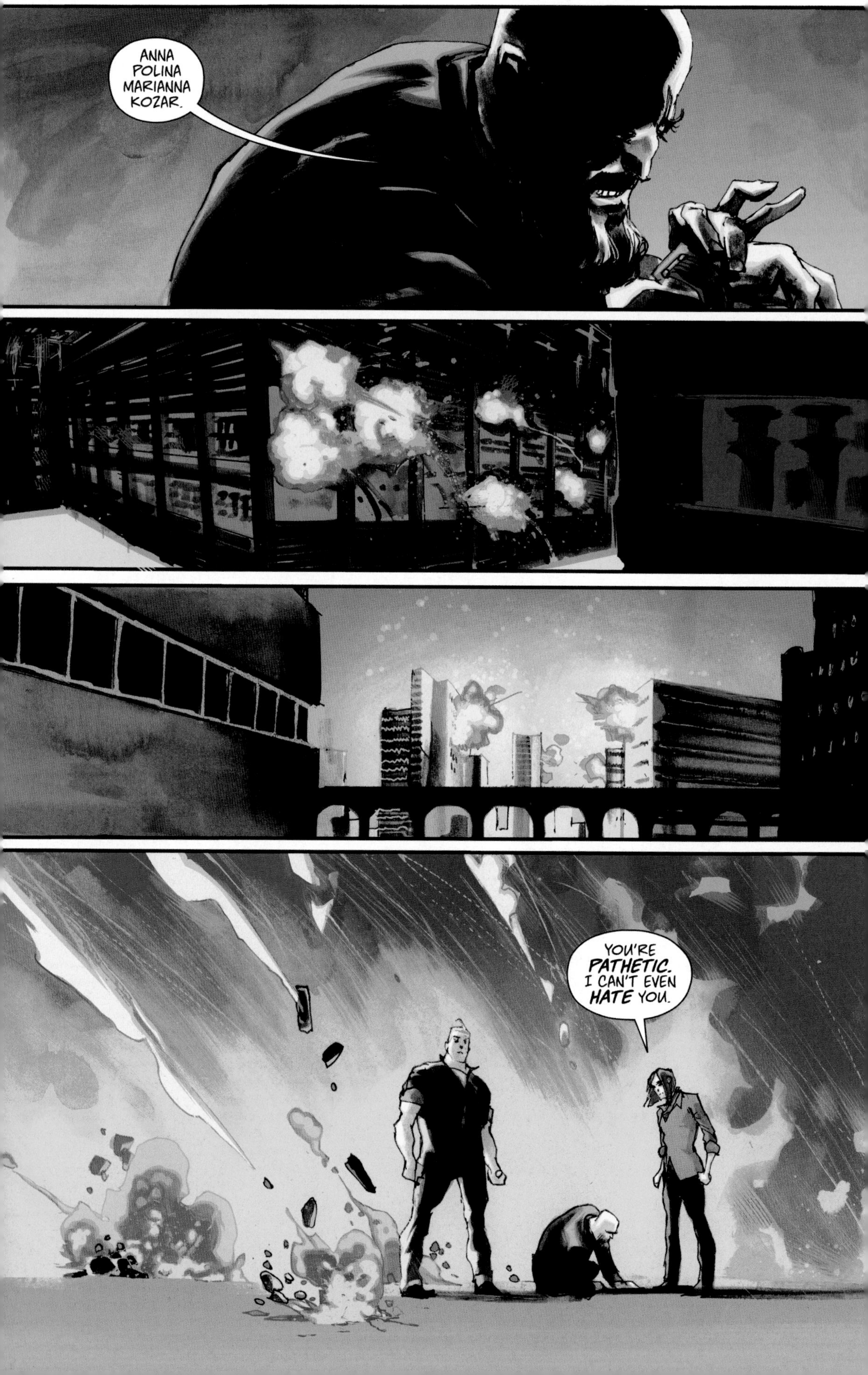
ANNA POLINA MARIANNA KOZAR.
YOU'RE PATHETIC. I CAN'T EVEN HATE YOU.

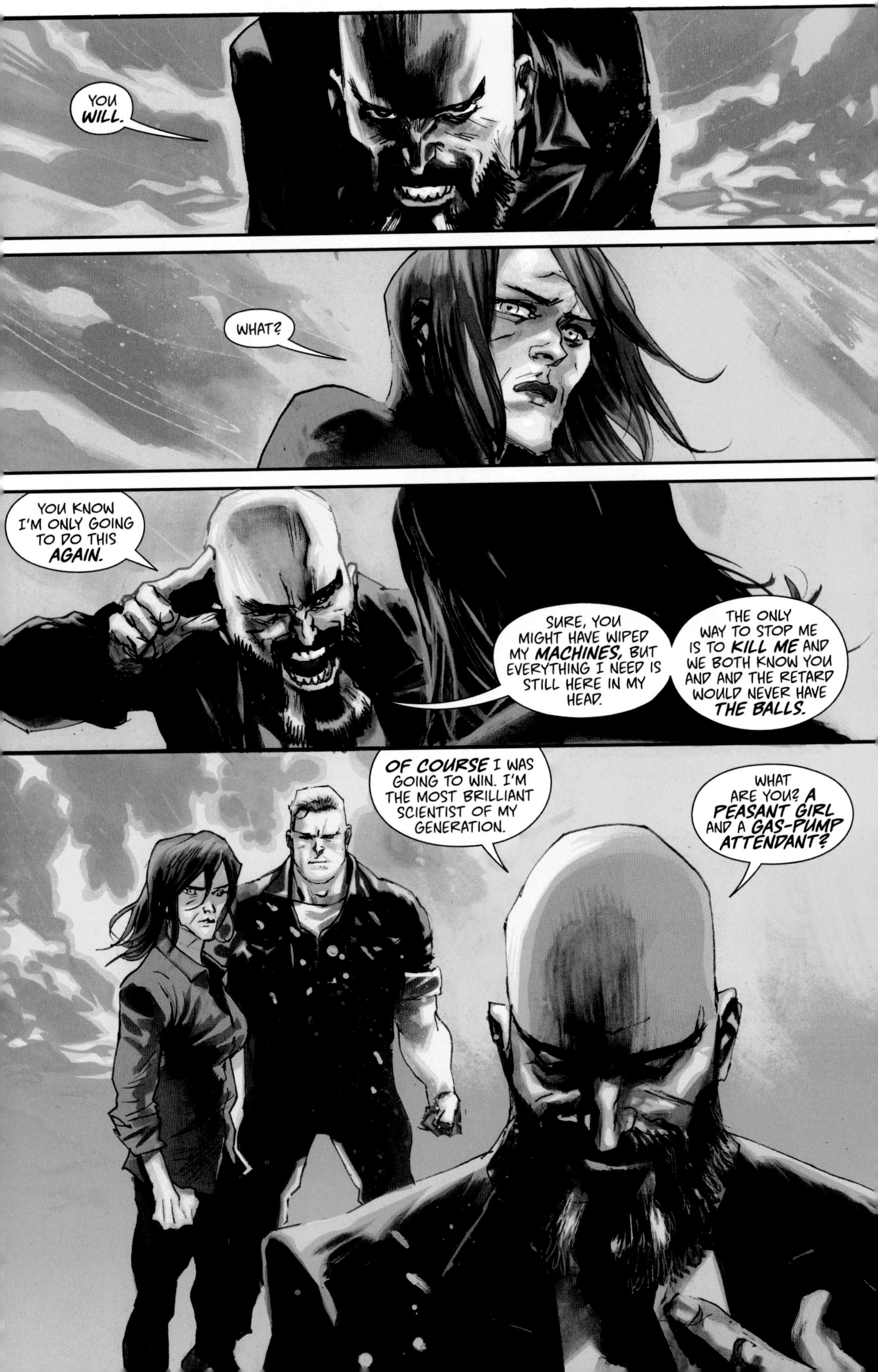
YOU WILL.
WHAT?
YOU KNOW I'M ONLY GOING TO DO THIS AGAIN.
SURE, YOU MIGHT HAVE WIPED MY MACHINES, BUT EVERYTHING I NEED IS STILL HERE IN MY HEAD.
THE ONLY WAY TO STOP ME IS TO KILL ME AND WE BOTH KNOW YOU AND AND THE RETARD WOULD NEVER HAVE THE BALLS.
OF COURSE I WAS GOING TO WIN. I'M THE MOST BRILLIANT SCIENTIST OF MY GENERATION.
WHAT ARE YOU? A PEASANT GIRL AND A GAS-PUMP ATTENDANT?

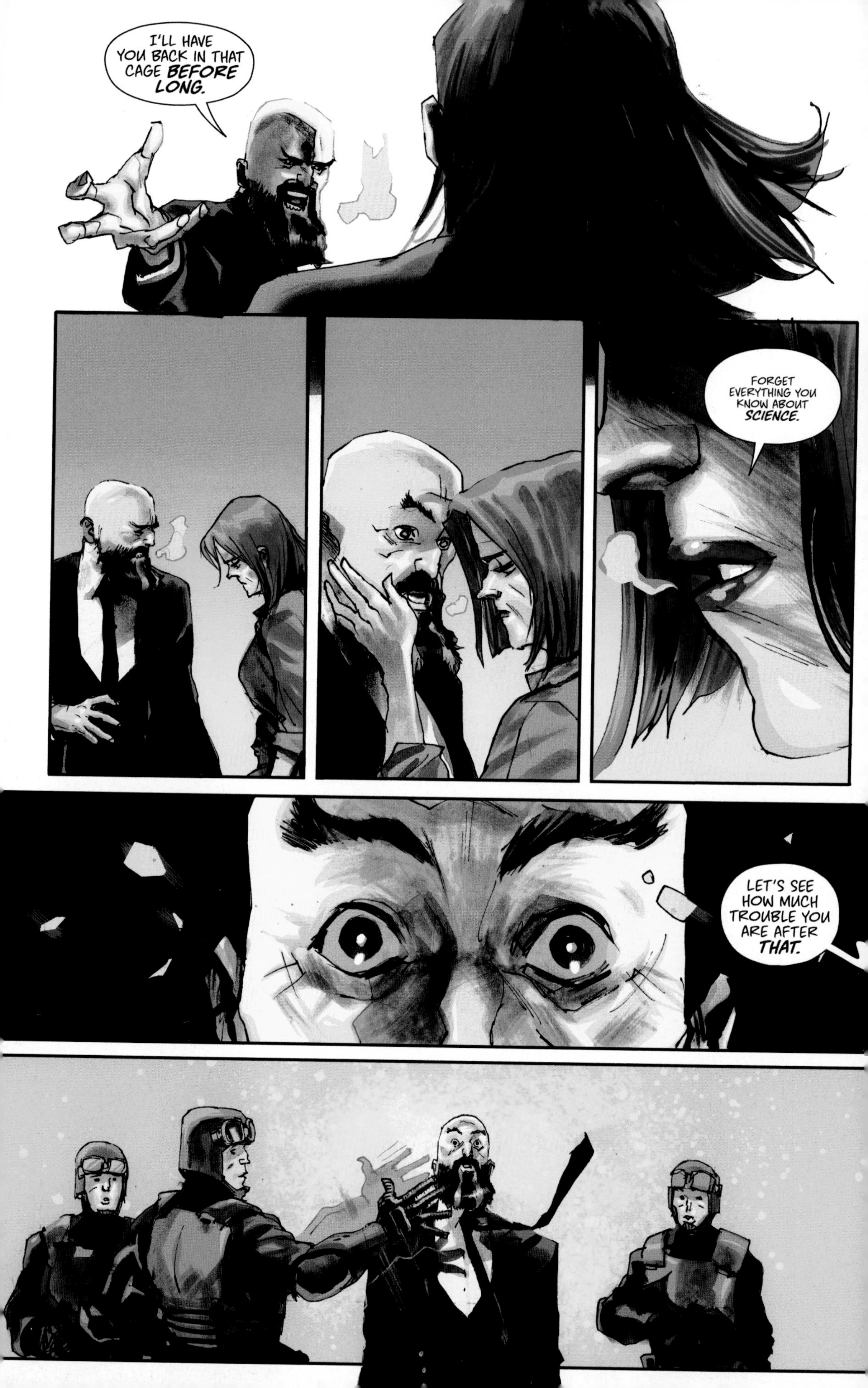
I'LL HAVE YOU BACK IN THAT CAGE BEFORE LONG.
FORGET EVERYTHING YOU KNOW ABOUT SCIENCE.
LET'S SEE HOW MUCH TROUBLE YOU ARE AFTER THAT.

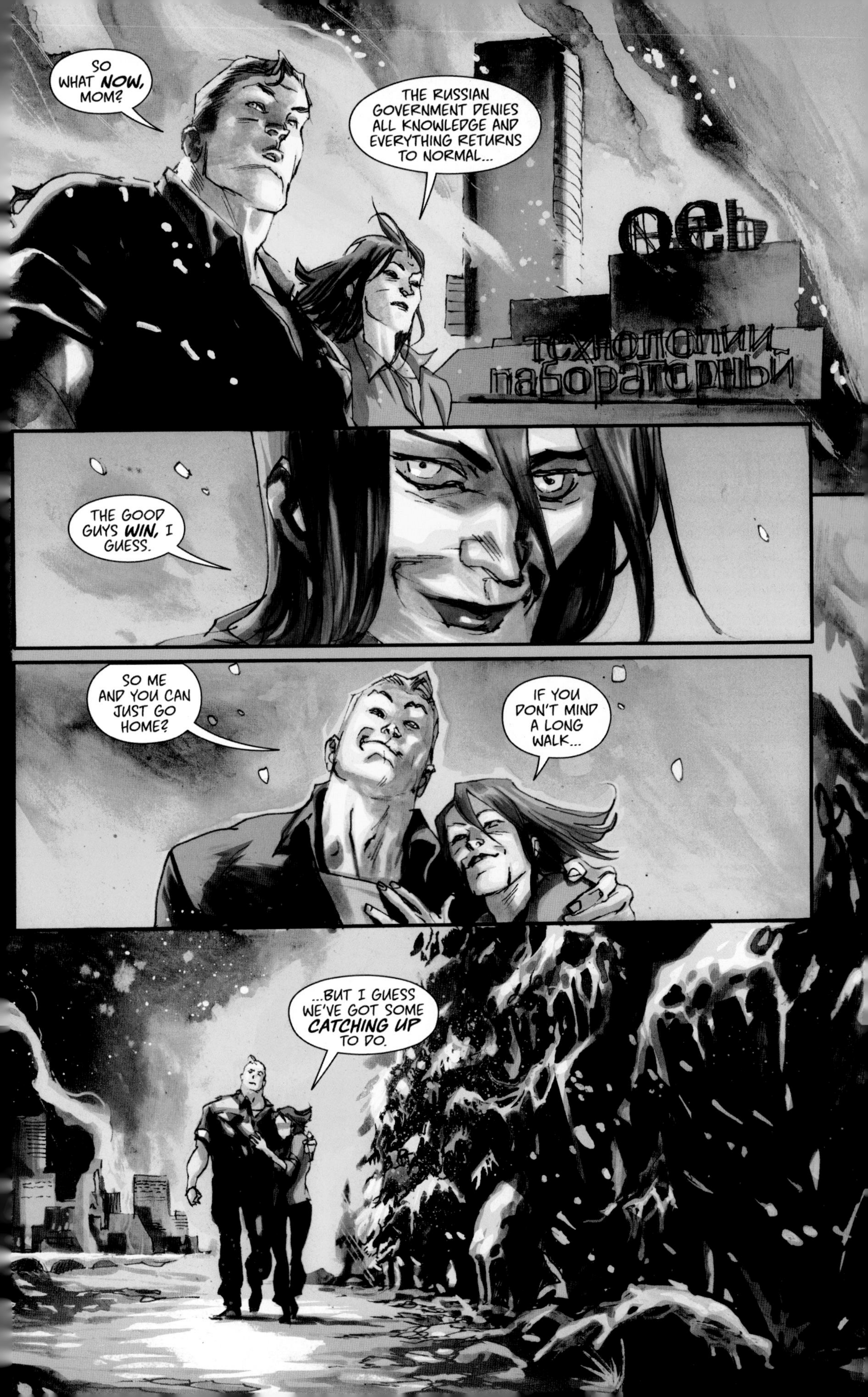
SO WHAT NOW, MOM?
THE RUSSIAN GOVERNMENT DENIES ALL KNOWLEDGE AND EVERYTHING RETURNS TO NORMAL...
THE GOOD GUYS WIN, I GUESS.
SO ME AND YOU CAN JUST GO HOME?
IF YOU DON'T MIND A LONG WALK...
...BUT I GUESS WE'VE GOT SOME CATCHING UP TO DO.

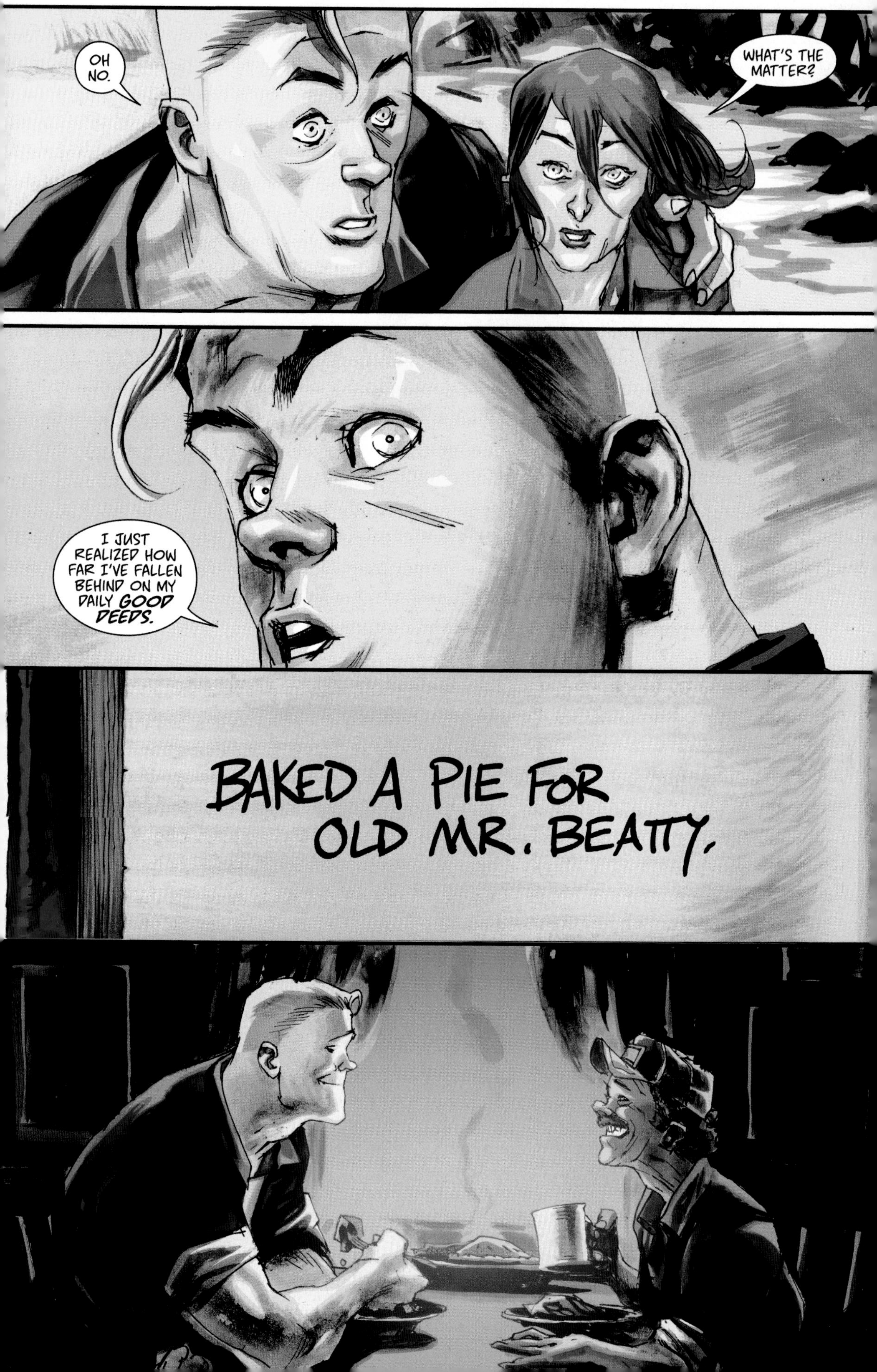
OH NO.
WHAT'S THE MATTER?
I JUST REALIZED HOW FAR I'VE FALLEN BEHIND ON MY DAILY GOOD DEEDS.
BAKED A PIE FOR OLD MR. BEATTY.

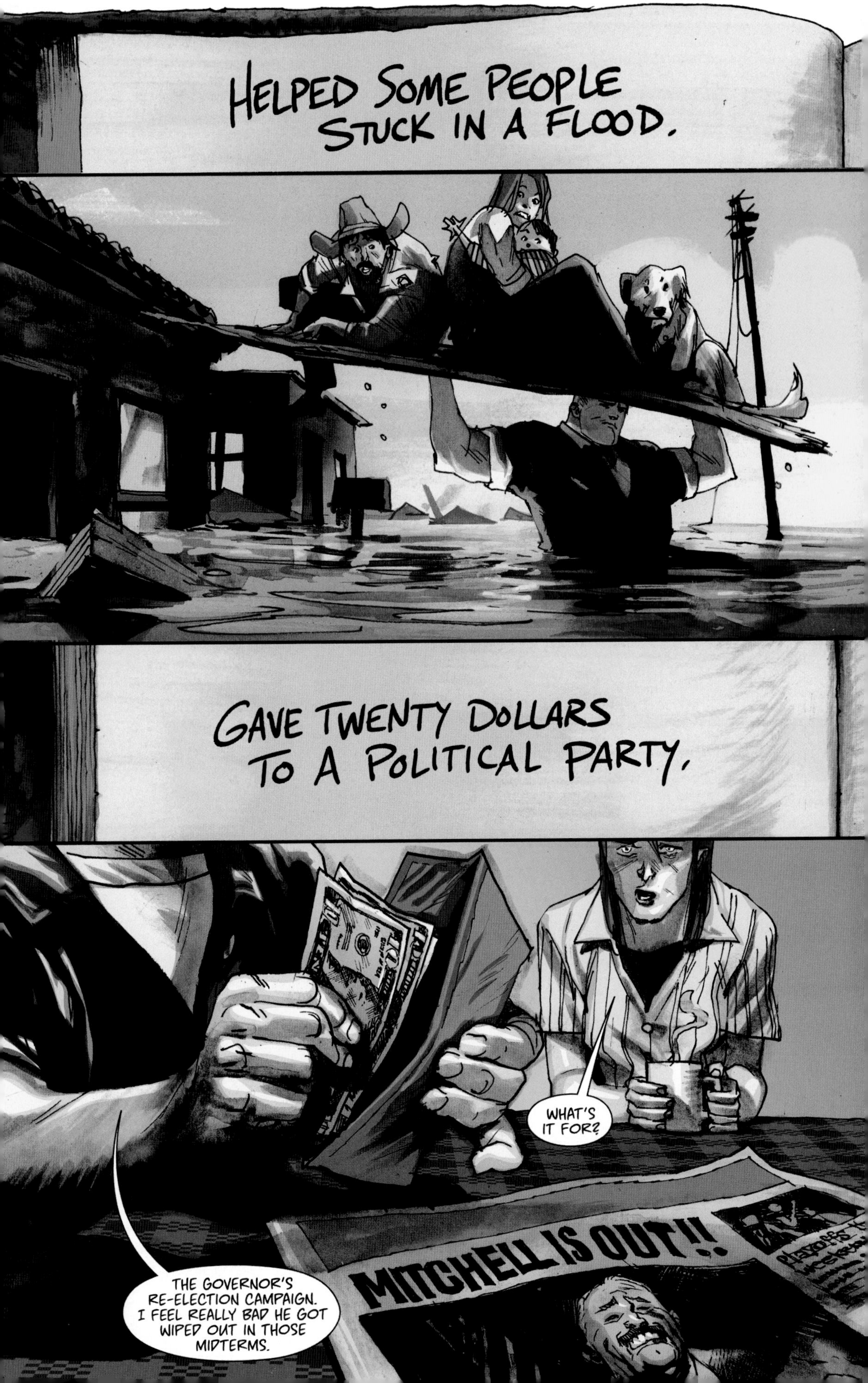
HELPED SOME PEOPLE STUCK IN A FLOOD.
GAVE TWENTY DOLLARS TO A POLITICAL PARTY.
WHAT'S IT FOR?
MITCHELL IS OUT!!
THE GOVERNOR'S RE-ELECTION CAMPAIGN. I FEEL REALLY BAD HE GOT WIPED OUT IN THOSE MIDTERMS.

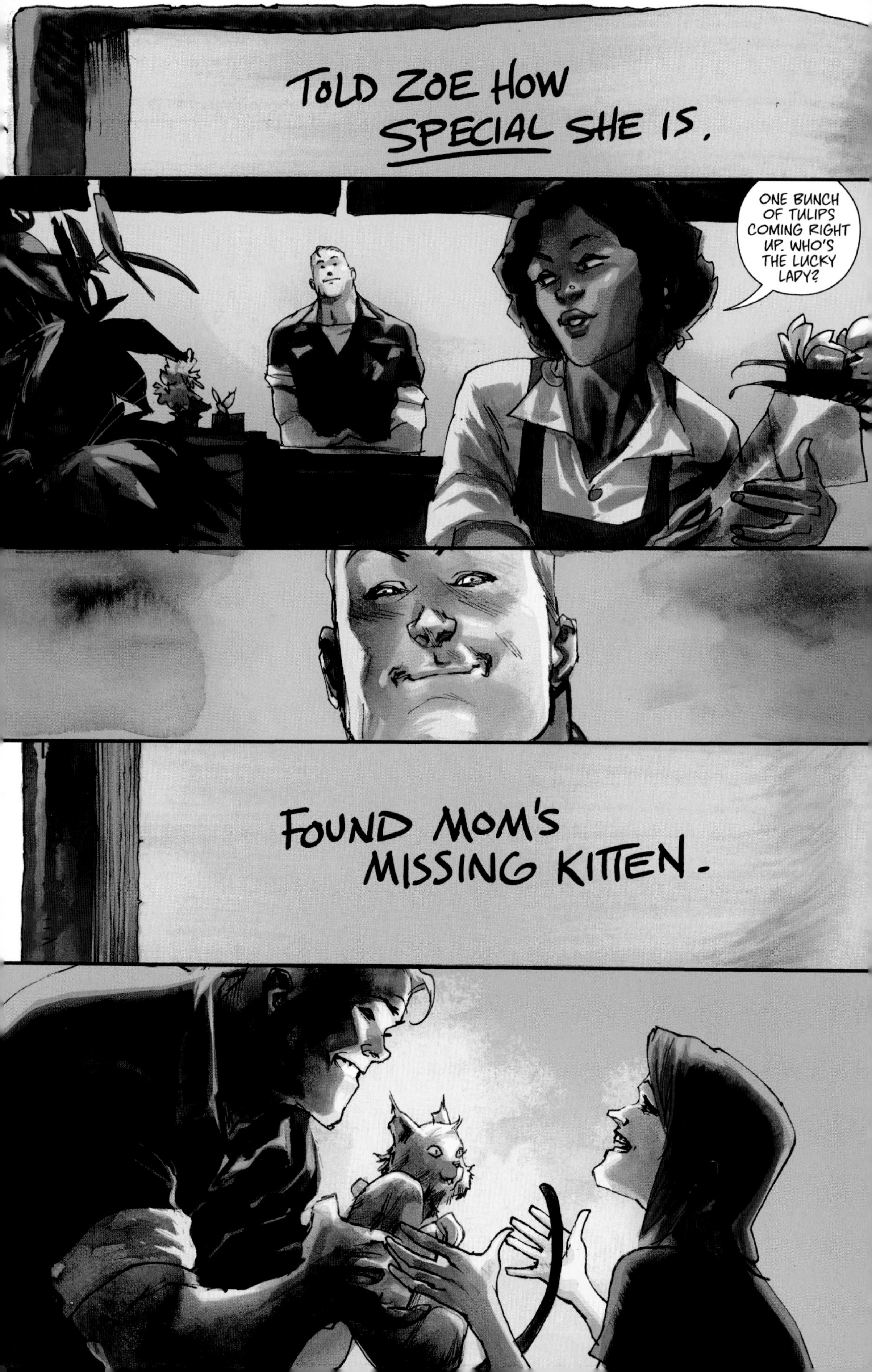
TOLD ZOE HOW SPECIAL SHE IS.
ONE BUNCH OF TULIPS COMING RIGHT UP. WHO'S THE LUCKY LADY?
FOUND MOM'S MISSING KITTEN.

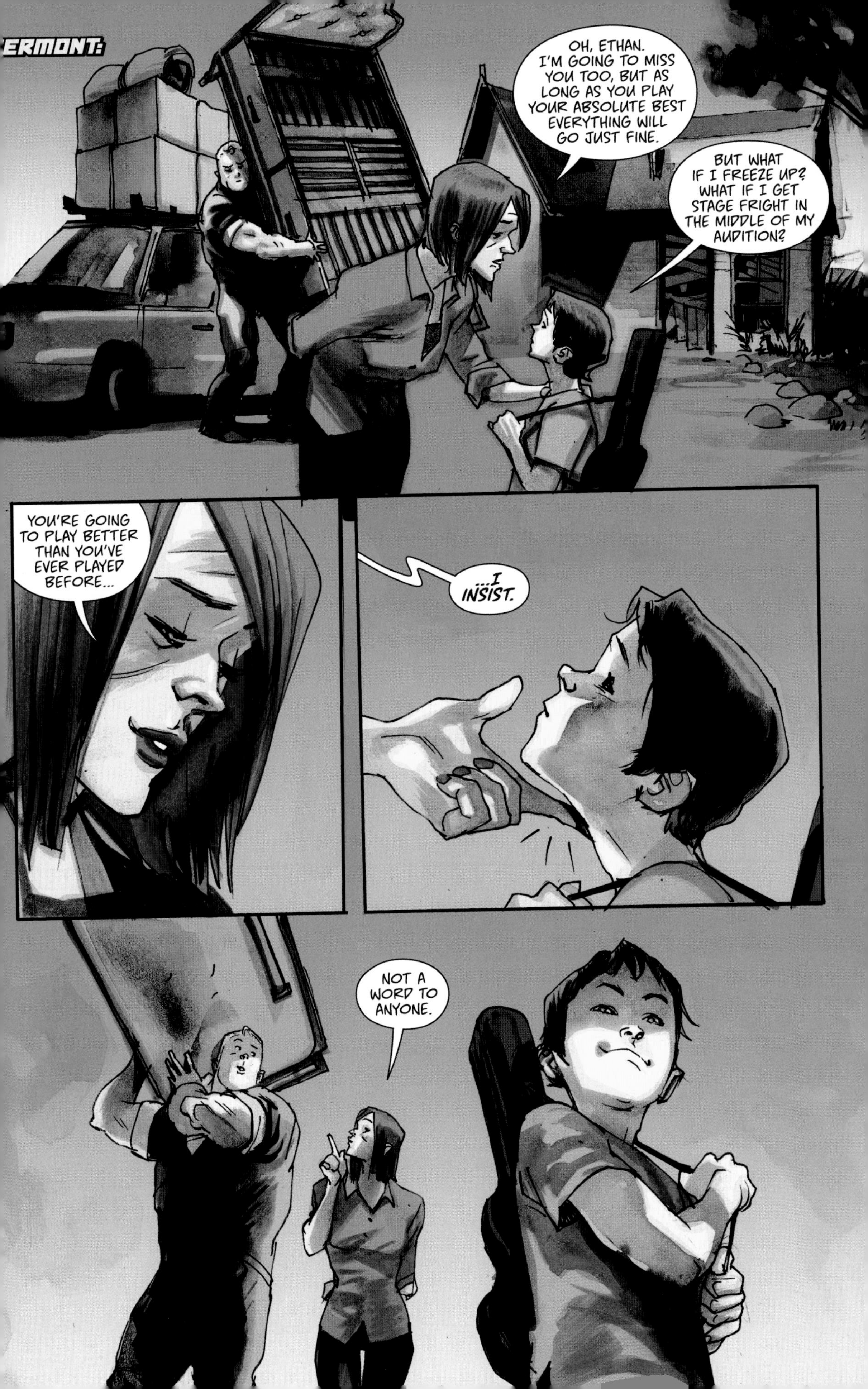
ERMONT:
OH, ETHAN. I'M GOING TO MISS YOU TOO, BUT AS LONG AS YOU PLAY YOUR ABSOLUTE BEST EVERYTHING WILL GO JUST FINE.
BUT WHAT IF I FREEZE UP? WHAT IF I GET STAGE FRIGHT IN THE MIDDLE OF MY AUDITION?
YOU'RE GOING TO PLAY BETTER THAN YOU'VE EVER PLAYED BEFORE...
...I INSIST.
NOT A WORD TO ANYONE.

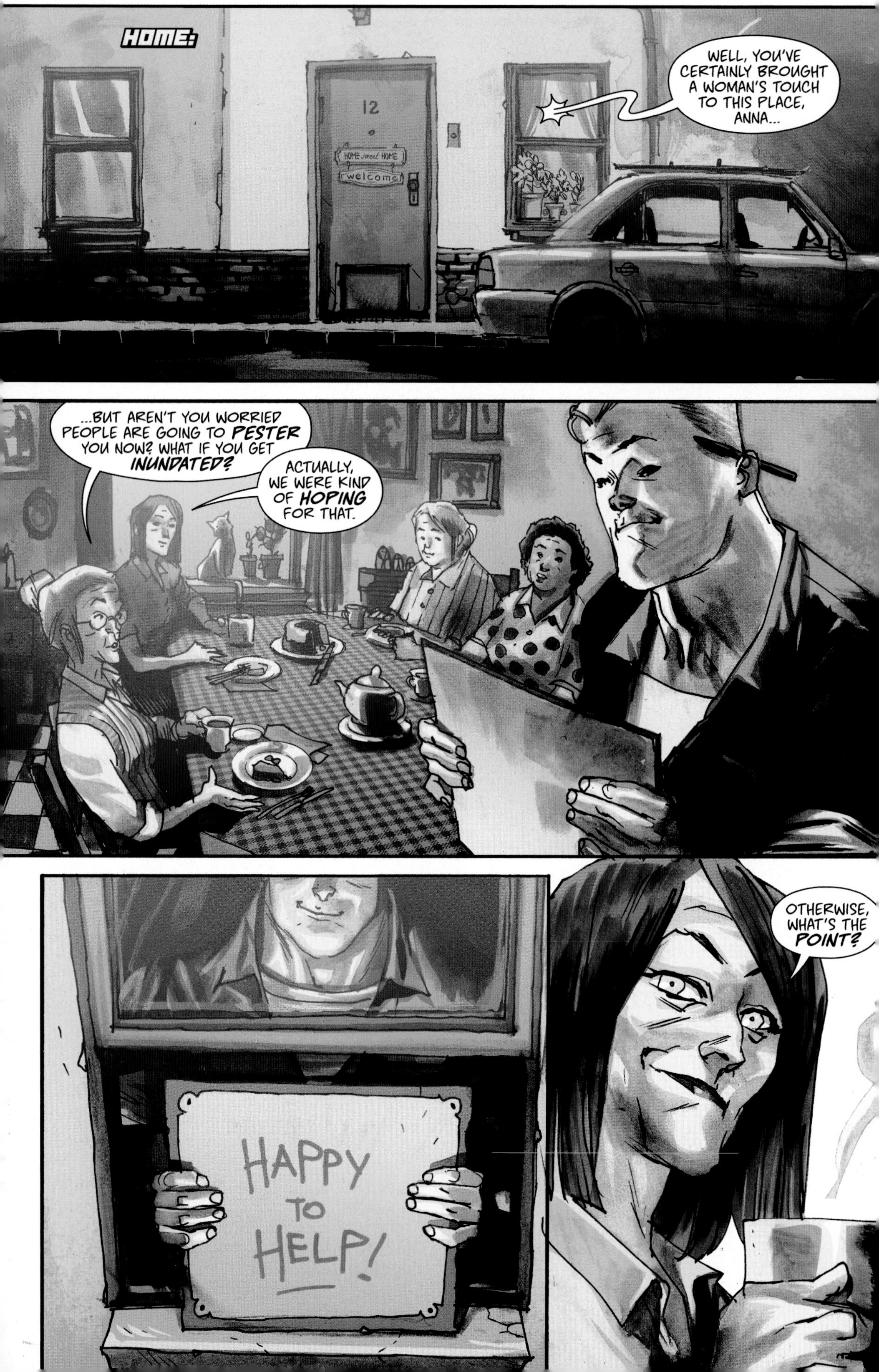
HOME:
12
HOME sweet HOME
welcome
WELL, YOU'VE CERTAINLY BROUGHT A WOMAN'S TOUCH TO THIS PLACE, ANNA...
...BUT AREN'T YOU WORRIED PEOPLE ARE GOING TO PESTER YOU NOW? WHAT IF YOU GET INUNDATED?
ACTUALLY, WE WERE KIND OF HOPING FOR THAT.
HAPPY TO HELP!
OTHERWISE, WHAT'S THE POINT?

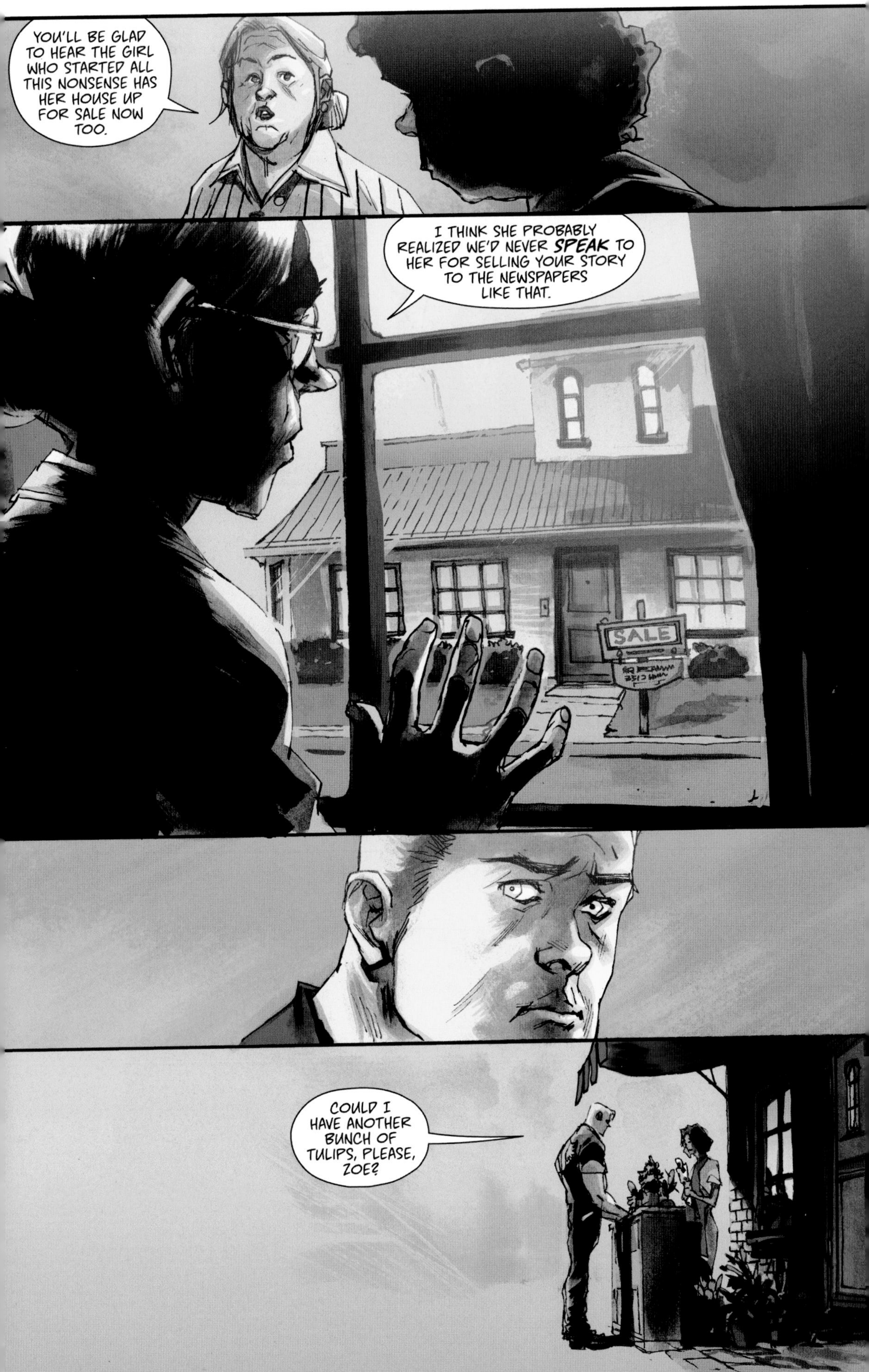
YOU'LL BE GLAD TO HEAR THE GIRL WHO STARTED ALL THIS NONSENSE HAS HER HOUSE UP FOR SALE NOW TOO.
I THINK SHE PROBABLY REALIZED WE'D NEVER **SPEAK** TO HER FOR SELLING YOUR STORY TO THE NEWSPAPERS LIKE THAT.
SALE
COULD I HAVE ANOTHER BUNCH OF TULIPS, PLEASE, ZOE?

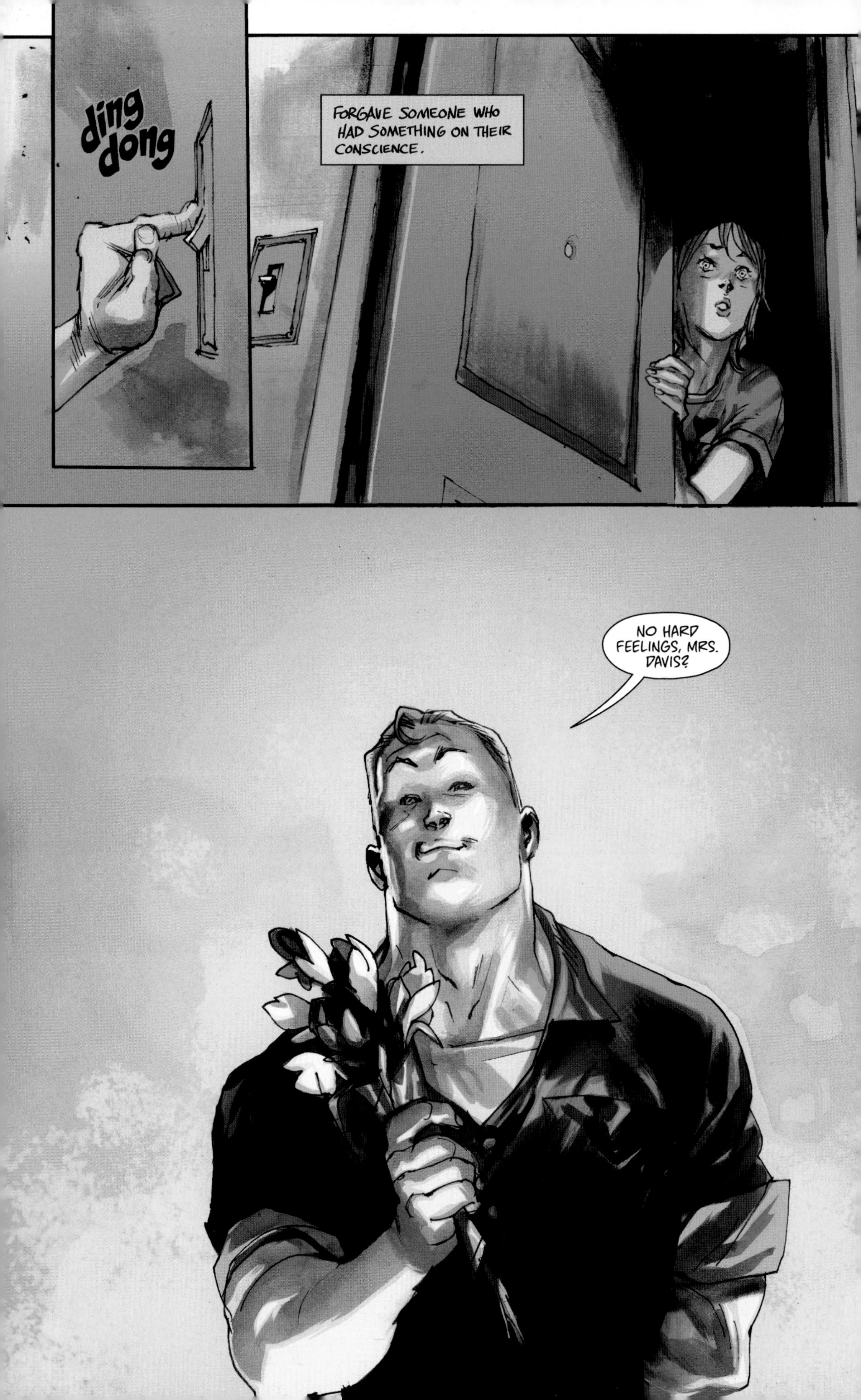
ding dong
FORGAVE SOMEONE WHO HAD SOMETHING ON THEIR CONSCIENCE.
NO HARD FEELINGS, MRS. DAVIS?

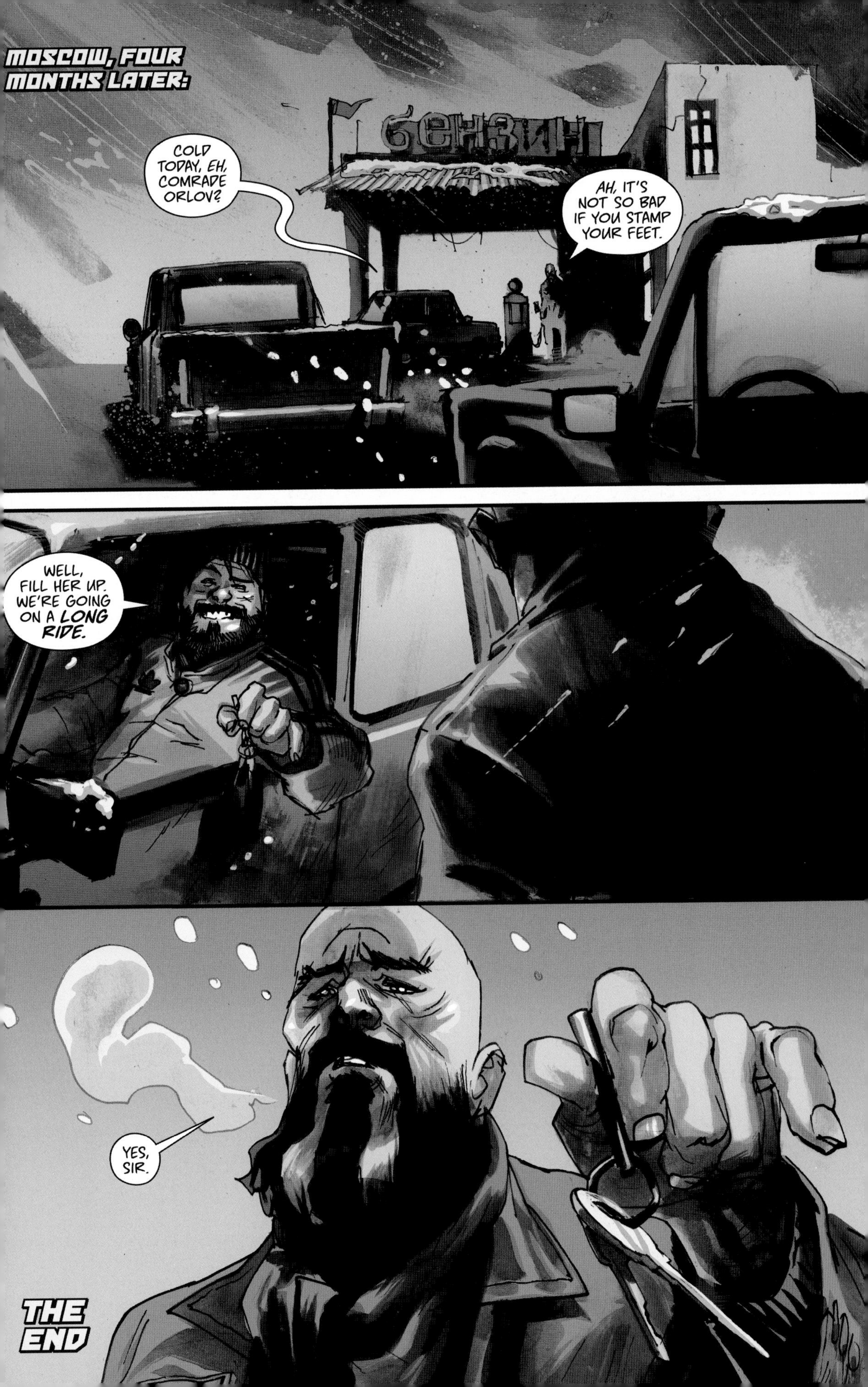
MOSCOW, FOUR MONTHS LATER:
БЕНЗИН
COLD TODAY, EH, COMRADE ORLOV?
AH, IT'S NOT SO BAD IF YOU STAMP YOUR FEET.
WELL, FILL HER UP. WE'RE GOING ON A LONG RIDE.
YES, SIR.
THE END

MEET THE CREATORS OF *HUCK*

MARK MILLAR

Mark Millar is the *New York Times* best-selling writer of *Kick-Ass*, *Wanted*, *The Secret Service*, *Jupiter's Legacy*, *Nemesis*, *Superior*, *Super Crooks*, *American Jesus*, *MPH*, *Starlight*, and *Chrononauts*. *Wanted*, *Kick-Ass*, *Kick-Ass 2*, and *The Secret Service* (as *Kingsman: The Secret Service*) have been adapted into feature films, and *Nemesis*, *Superior*, *Starlight*, *Huck*, *War Heroes*, *Jupiter's Legacy* and *Chrononauts* are all in development at major studios.

His DC Comics work includes the seminal *Superman: Red Son*, and at Marvel Comics he created *The Ultimates*, described by screenwriter Zak Penn as his major inspiration for *The Avengers* movie and selected by *Time* magazine as the comic book of the decade; *Wolverine: Old Man Logan*, and *Civil War*, one of the biggest selling comic books of this generation and the basis of the *Captain America: Civil War* movie.

Mark has been an Executive Producer on all his movie adaptations and is currently creative consultant to Fox Studios on their Marvel slate of movies. His new series *Empress* has just launched with *Star Wars* artist Stuart Immonen and he is currently working on a brand new Millarworld project with *Batman* superstar Greg Capullo. Mark's much-anticipated autobiography, *Reflections of a Golden Soul*, will be published next year.

RAFAEL ALBUQUERQUE

Rafael Albuquerque is the Eisner and Harvey Award winning co-creator of the *New York Times* bestseller *American Vampire* (DC Comics/Vertigo) written by Scott Snyder and Stephen King, and *Ei8ht*, from Dark Horse Comics.

Having been in the comics industry since 2003, Rafael has worked with all major publishers in the business, illustrating popular books such as *Batman*, *Wolverine*, *Animal Man*, and currently *Batgirl*, for DC Comics.

Rafael lives in Porto Alegre, in the south of Brazil.

DAVE McCAIG

Dave McCaig is an Inkpot and Emmy award winning colorist for comics and animation. He's known for coloring *Superman: Birthright, Nextwave, American Vampire, Avengers, X-Men, Northlanders*, and the animated series *The Batman*, amongst other things. He lives in New York with his two humans and two cats.

NATE PIEKOS

Nate Piekos graduated with a Bachelor of Arts degree in graphic design from Rhode Island College in 1998. Since founding Blambot.com, he has created some of the industry's most popular typefaces and has used them to letter comic books for Marvel Comics, DC Comics, Dark Horse Comics, and Image Comics, as well as dozens of independent publishers. Nate's design work has not only been utilized in comics, but in product packaging, video games, on television, and in feature films.

NICOLE BOOSE

Nicole Boose began her comics career at Harris Comics' *Vampirella*, before joining the editorial staff at Marvel Comics. There, she edited titles including *Cable & Deadpool, Iron Man*, and Stephen King's adapted novels. She also oversaw Marvel's line of custom comics, developing projects for corporate and nonprofit clients. Since 2008, Nicole has been a freelance editor and consultant in the comics industry, working regularly with Mark Millar, and serving on the staff of the educational company, Comics Experience.

RACHAEL FULTON

Rachael Fulton joins the Huck team as Associate Editor. She is an award-winning features writer, specializing in magazines and online journalism. Rachael was formerly a television producer, presenter and reporter for Scottish Television but now finds herself happily embedded in the Millarverse of superheroes, space operas and explosive plot lines. Rachael is based in Glasgow and can be found on the Millarworld forum or on Twitter @Rachael_Fulton.

CHARACTER DESIGNS BY RAFAEL ALBUQUERQUE

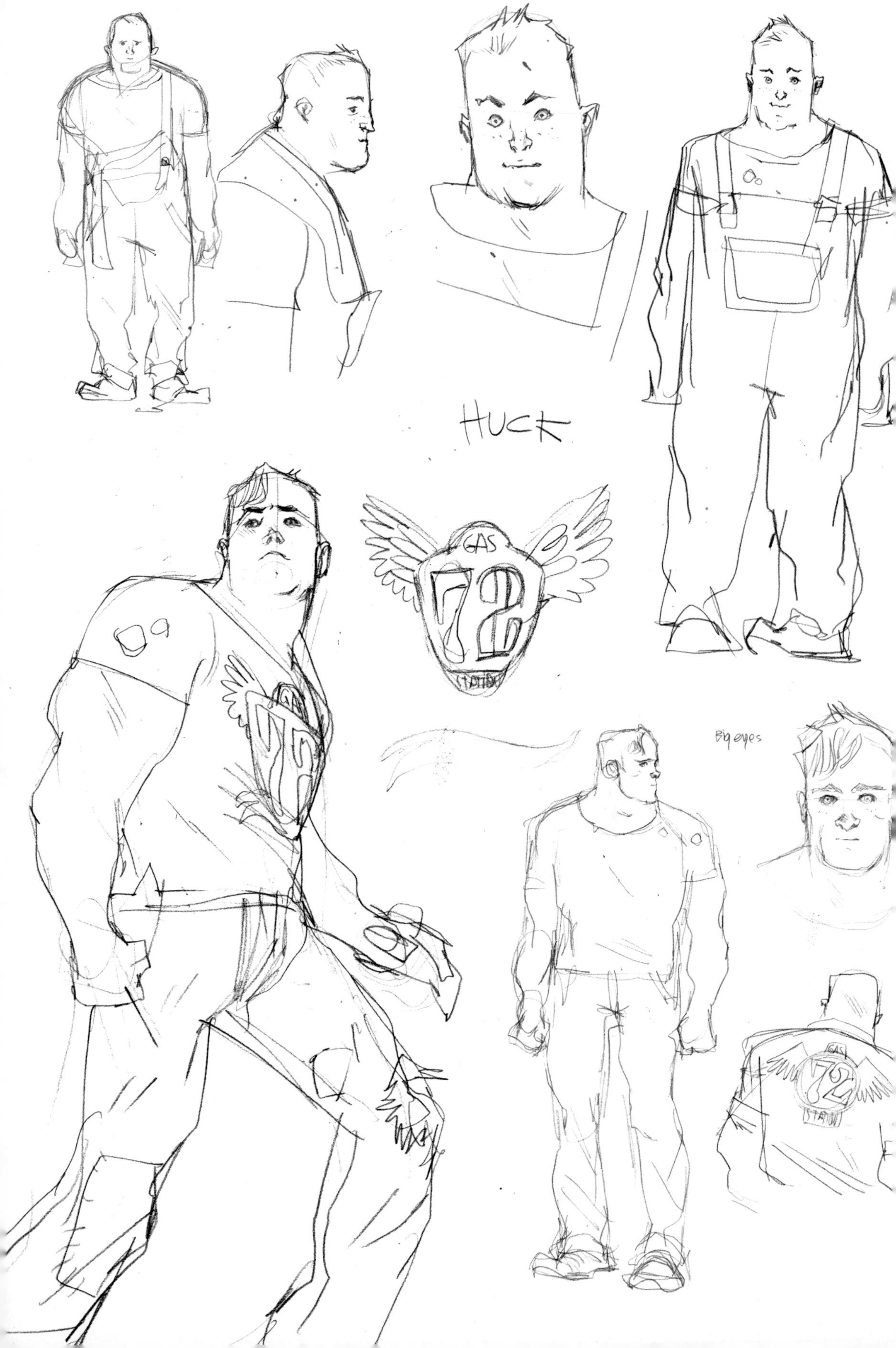
HUCK
GAS
72
STATION
Big eyes

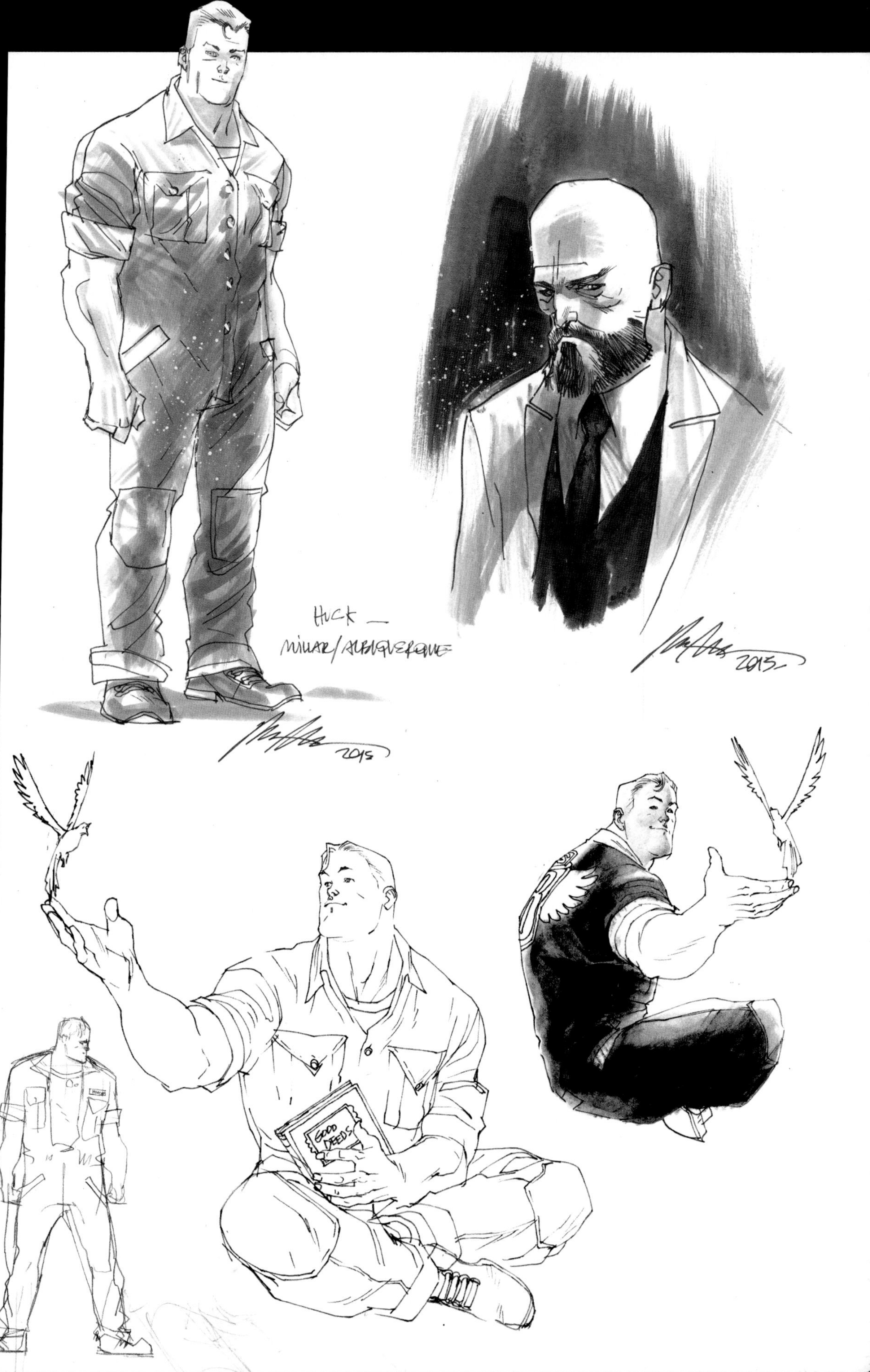
HUCK —
MILLAR/ALBUQUERQUE
2015
2015
GOOD DEEDS

LAYOUTS & INKS BY RAFAEL ALBUQUERQUE

ISSUE 2, PAGE 12

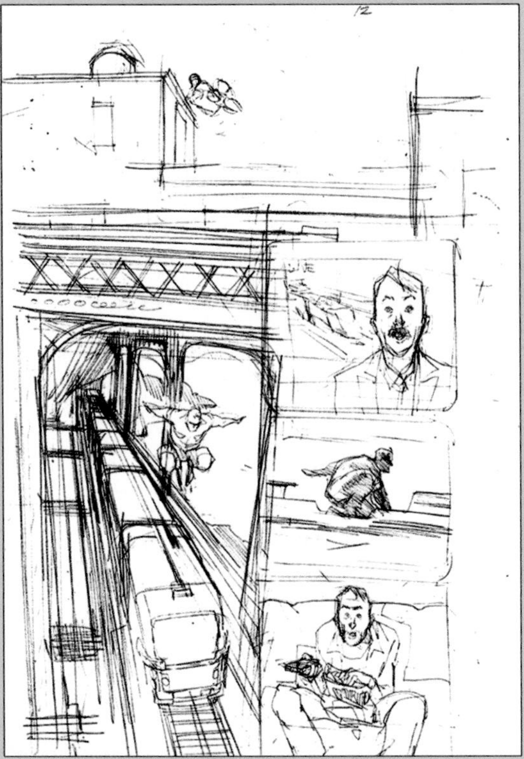
12

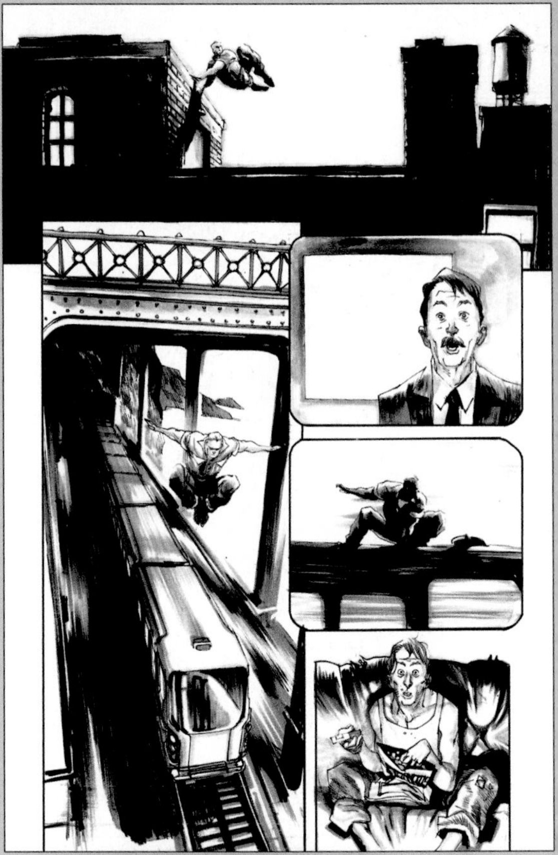

ISSUE 3, PAGE 7

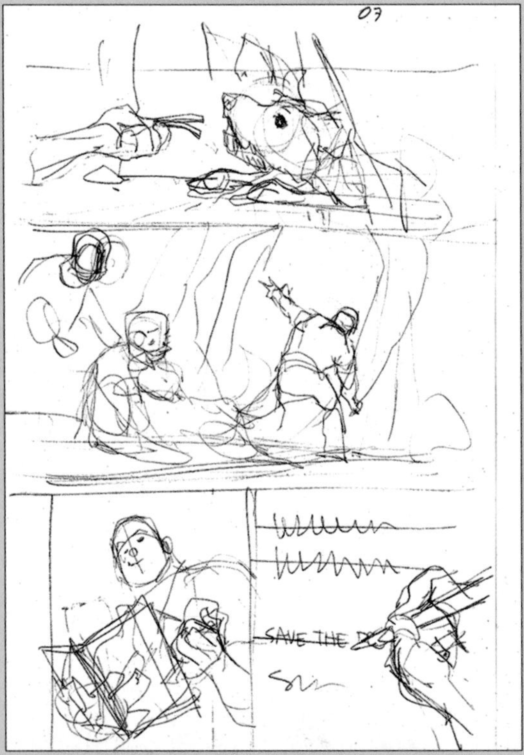
07

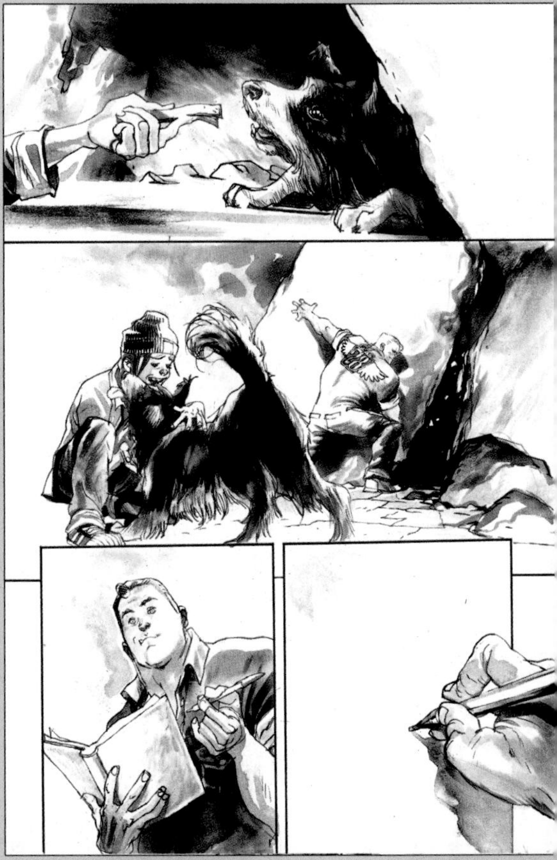

ISSUE 5, PAGES 2 & 3

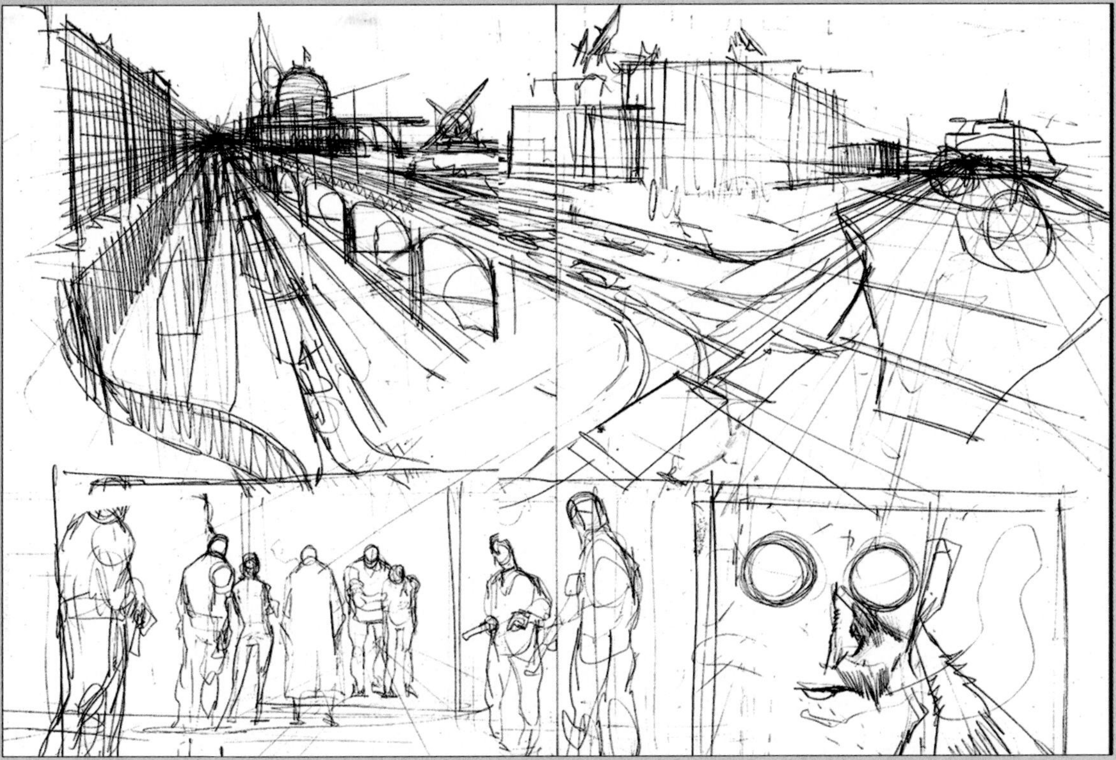

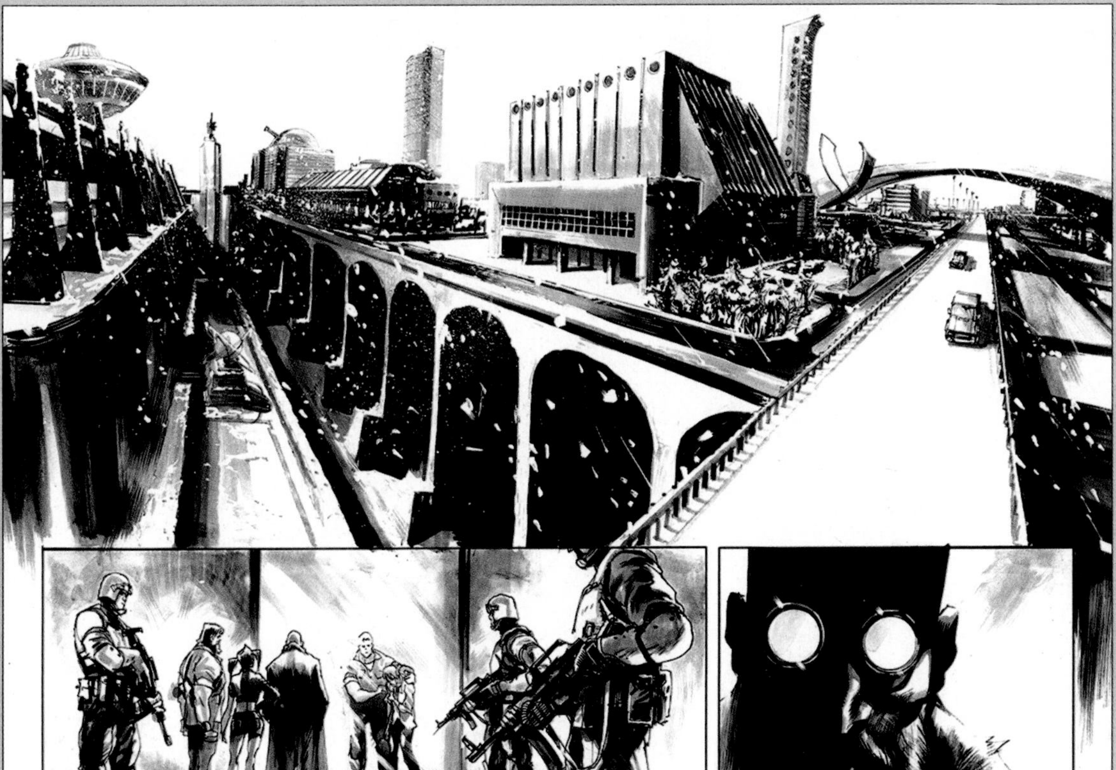

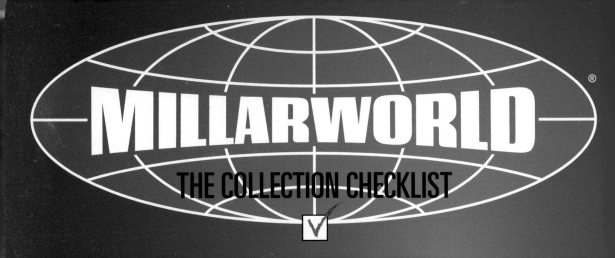

MILLARWORLD®

THE COLLECTION CHECKLIST

KICK ASS
MARK MILLAR
JOHN ROMITA JR.

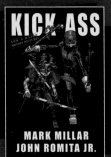

KICK-ASS 1-3
Art by John Romita Jr.

KICK-ASS 2 PRELUDE:
HIT-GIRL
MARK MILLAR
JOHN ROMITA JR.
TOM PALMER and DEAN WHITE

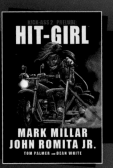

HIT-GIRL
Art by John Romita Jr.

EMPRESS
MARK MILLAR
STUART IMMONEN

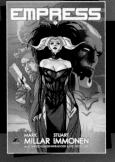

EMPRESS
Art by Stuart Immonen

MILLAR • ALBUQUERQUE
Huck
"The Feel-Good Book of the Year"

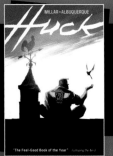

HUCK
Art by Rafael Albuquerque

MILLAR MURPHY
CHRONONAUTS
#1
$3.50

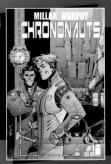

CHRONONAUTS
Art by Sean Gordon Murphy

MARK MILLAR DUNCAN FEGREDO
MPH

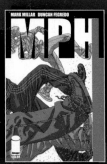

MPH
Art by Duncan Fegredo

MARK MILLAR • GORAN PARLOV
STARLIGHT

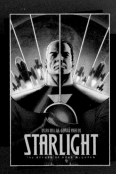

STARLIGHT
Art by Goran Parlov

MARK MILLAR DAVE GIBBONS MATTHEW VAUGHN
KINGSMAN
THE SECRET SERVICE

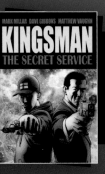

KINGSMAN: THE SECRET SERVICE
Art by Dave Gibbons

MILLAR • TORRES • GIANFELICE
JUPITER'S CIRCLE
BOOK ONE

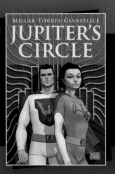

JUPITER'S CIRCLE 1 & 2
Art by Wilfredo Torres

MARK MILLAR • FRANK QUITELY
JUPITER'S LEGACY
BOOK ONE

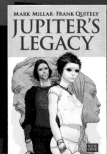

JUPITER'S LEGACY
Art by Frank Quitely

MARK MILLAR LEINIL YU
SUPER CROOKS
THE HEIST

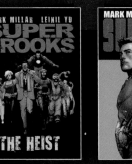

SUPER CROOKS
Art by Leinil Yu

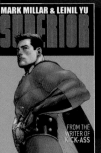

MARK MILLAR & LEINIL YU
SUPERIOR
FROM THE WRITER OF KICK-ASS

SUPER
Art by Le

MILLAR & McNIVEN'S
NEMESIS

WANTED
MARK MILLAR • JG JONES • PAUL MOUNTS
UNIVERSAL PICTURES

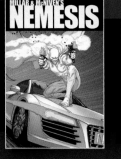

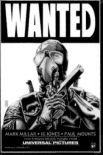

WANTED
by JG Jones

AMERICAN JESUS
BOOK ONE : CHOSEN
MARK MILLAR • PETER GROSS

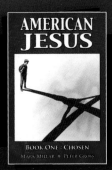

AMERICAN JESUS
Art by Peter Gross